BRUTALITY AND BENEVOLENCE

Recent Titles in
Contributions in Latin American Studies

Modernization and Stagnation:
Latin American Agriculture into the 1990's
Michael J. Twomey and Ann Helwege, editors

State Formation in Central America: The Struggle
for Autonomy, Development, and Democracy
Howard H. Lentner

Cuba and the Future
Donald E. Schulz, editor

Ambivalent Anti-Colonialism: The United States
and the Genesis of West Indian Independence, 1940–1964
Cary Fraser

Mexico Faces the 21st Century
Donald E. Schulz and Edward J. Williams, editors

Authoritarianism in Latin America Since Independence
Will Fowler, editor

Colombia's Military and Brazil's Monarchy: Undermining the
Republican Foundations of South American Independence
Thomas Millington

BRUTALITY AND BENEVOLENCE

Human Ethology,
Culture,
and the Birth of Mexico

ABEL A. ALVES

Contributions in Latin American Studies,
Number 8

GREENWOOD PRESS
Westport, Connecticut • London

Library of Congress Cataloging-in-Publication Data

Alves, Abel A.
    Brutality and benevolence : human ethology, culture, and the birth
of Mexico / Abel A. Alves.
        p. cm.—(Contributions in Latin American studies, ISSN
1054–6790 ; no. 8)
    Includes bibliographical references and index.
    ISBN 0–313–29982–X (alk. paper)
        1. Mexico—History—Conquest, 1519–1540. 2. Mexico—History—
Spanish colony, 1540–1810. 3. Indians of Mexico—First contact
with Europeans. 4. Indians, Treatment of—Mexico. 5. Sociobiology.
6. Human behavior. 7. History—Methodology. I. Title.
II. Series.
F1230.A49   1996
972′.01—dc20   95–51382

British Library Cataloguing in Publication Data is available.

Library of Congress Catalog Card Number: 95–51382
ISBN: 0–313–29982–X
ISSN: 1054–6790

First published in 1996

Greenwood Press, 88 Post Road West, Westport, CT 06881
An imprint of Greenwood Publishing Group, Inc.

Printed in the United States of America

The paper used in this book complies with the
Permanent Paper Standard issued by the National
Information Standards Organization (Z39.48–1984).

10 9 8 7 6 5 4 3 2 1

Copyright Acknowledgments

Contents

Preface

While writing this book I have been fortunate enough to have benefited from the analytical probity and editorial skills of Carol Blakney. If this book has anything to say, it is because of her excellent questions and suggestions. I would also like to thank Robert A. Potash and Jeffrey A. Cole for having introduced me to the complexities of Latin American reality, and Miriam Usher Chrisman for her unwavering support.

Extended excerpts from the *Florentine Codex* of Bernardino de Sahagún were made possible by the School of American Research in Santa Fe and the University of Utah Press, who own rights to the translation of that work by Arthur J. O. Anderson and Charles E. Dibble (1950-1982). Excerpts from J. M. Cohen's translation of *The Conquest of New Spain* (1963) were made possible by Penguin Books UK, while Yale University Press allowed usage of excerpts from Anthony Pagden's edition of *Hernán Cortés: Letters from Mexico* (1986). The publishing house of Aldine de Gruyter supplied permission to cite extracts from Irenäus Eibl-Eibesfeldt's *Human Ethology* (1989). In Mexico City, the staff of the Archivo General de la Nación proved patient and efficient, and the University of Texas's Benson Latin American Collection has provided aid above and beyond the call of duty. In various citations and references from Mexico's colonial period archaic spellings have been maintained.

Finally, I would like to thank Richard Blakney of the Redhouse Press (PK 142 Sirkeci 34432 Istanbul, Turkey) for providing camera-ready copy.

1

Introduction

In the necessary struggle to abandon the purely Eurocentric, history and the other social sciences have frequently lost touch with reality in recent years. This has contributed to the creation of a multiplicity of tribalisms, including numerous interpretations that favor the conquered and oppressed in ways similar to earlier, unreflective allegiance given the conquerors. From an epic tradition delineated by David Quint as glorifying the conquerors and their "justice," historical studies, in an attempt to represent the "losers" adequately, have sometimes waxed romantic in recent years, mourning the passage of all-too-human cultures as repeated expulsions from the Garden of Eden.[1] Thus, even though José Rabasa, in his thought-provoking *Inventing America*, admires Bernardino de Sahagún for inscribing Aztec "ethnicity in spite of (and as a result of) a tension that arises from the need to use European discourse to express ideas foreign to it" and writes that *Inventing America* has no intention to "reduce subalternity to some kind of privileged perspective on power and oppositional consciousness," he still ends his study by attacking the Jesuit ethnographer Joseph de Acosta (ca. 1539-1600). Rabasa argues that despite its religious language, Acosta's evolutionary model of development for the Americas

in substance still informs nineteenth- and twentieth-century anthropologies and theories of development. Indeed, the "let's save brown women and little folk from abusive brown men" syndrome can still be heard among theorists of development who have only recently come to postulate patriarchy as a specifically noncapitalist social formation; now it is not missionaries who come to rescue but multinational corporations.[2]

For better or worse, Rabasa still selects a privileged position within contemporary twentieth-century struggles for power, and his defense of "brown men" is indicative of the persistence of traps that would make reason serve political, economic, and religious prejudices. While the author of this study understands the difficulty inherent in trying to divorce reason from emotive states and desires, this study does aim at attempting to reach Jürgen Habermas's "ideal speech situation," in which one tries to gain awareness of one's proclivities and prejudices in order to minimize their effect: to argue and investigate as though there were no cultural and personal emotive influences. Although many would see this as culturally influenced "Western" science, this is science—an investigatory pursuit that tries to abandon dogmas, though scientists, as human beings, are often plagued by comforting paradigms that are treated as dogmas. Still, science aims at knowledge arrived at through a preponderance of testable and verifiable evidence. It may be used to gain and hold power, but it boldly tries to go beyond power relationships to create a common ground for all people—a place where all may speak, or an "ideal speech situation." It aims at what observation, experience, and reason decree to be a common reality, and not at substantiating particular warring faiths in religion and politics.[3]

Such a supposedly nineteenth-century position is currently not fashionable in academia, nor is it fashionable to religious and political groups with their own agendas. In the pursuit of grants and acceptance, academics form self-protective tribes, while in the pursuit of votes and salvation, political factions and religious groups do likewise. In the midst of the posturing adopted by warring tribes, the fundamental structures of human reality have been lost, and Michel Foucault has even argued that humanity is "a recent invention" and "a kind of rift in the order of things."[4] On very much the same level, all sorts of religious fundamentalists attribute special status to humanity as a "kind of rift in the order of things," arguing from belief and revelation rather than rational proof, which would include taking all the evidence and counterarguments into account. If nothing can be arrived at as real and universal, humanity is left with so-called Christian, gay, and Moslem cultures vying for power in the midst of chaos— each claiming that its own particular interpretation of reality is the one true way. This study, like those enacted by Kung Fuzi and Aristotle so long ago, will seek after the generalizations that may be made on the basis of accumulated observations. For better or worse, this is the method by which humans have presented experiential knowledge in an intelligible form.

Long ago Aristotle observed that humans are speaking and social animals, and that we can divide labor, living together in peace because of our ability to communicate feelings and ideas in order to mutually arrive at some common ground in the midst of diversity. Although it might be argued that this position was culturally constructed from the perspective of the Greek *polis*, it is interesting to note that Kung Fuzi (Confucius, ca. 551-479 BCE) arrived at similar conclusions in China. Like Aristotle, Kung Fuzi accumulated observations, and he concluded that social harmony was to be built under the direction of rational gentlemen, with diverse estates and ranks working in unison toward the common good. Kung Fuzi did not teach as though he arrived at his positions through special revelation, admitting that he, on one occasion, could not answer the query of an uneducated man: "I merely discussed the two sides of the question and was at my wit's end."[5] This is science's willingness to admit ignorance, while continuing to ask questions and seek out data in order to draw general conclusions. Kung Fuzi was no Westerner, but he, like Aristotle, in the midst of limitations and cultural traditions, sought answers about an animal particularly given to social interaction.

The ideas of Aristotle and Kung Fuzi, showing their similarities and differences, could be translated into each other's languages, just as Spanish priests in the sixteenth century tried to translate Amerindian concepts and customs into their own European language. Although it is true that some words translate without exact precision, it would be difficult to deny the reality that humans do interact across linguistic differences. Even the words of Jacques Derrida and Michel Foucault have been translated, though Derrida would stress that "speech and the consciousness of speech—that is to say consciousness simply as self-presence—are the phenomenon of an auto-affection lived as suppression of differance."[6] That humans cannot "really" understand each other because of linguistic and cultural differences is a metaphysical assumption that must bear the burden of proof vis-à-vis all the instances of functional translation at airports and the United Nations. Translation of languages and cultures may not be easy, but they are real, and far more fruitful than the invention of arcane discourses that argue the impossibility of real translation. After all, Gayatri Chakravorty Spivak does venture to translate Derrida's work from French into English.

Still, the cautions of the deconstructionists and postmodernists are not entirely without foundation. As a result of cultural bias esconced in the English language, "God" will be written throughout this work with a capital G, whereas the "gods" of the Mesoamericans are subordinated still with a lower-case g. This is culural bias and linguistic impact still at work, but even this does not belie nature and commonly experienced physical reality.

At the very heart of real translation lies the fact that all humans experience a physical body that demands food, clothing, and shelter. Likewise, we react to our fundamental desires and needs with a whole series of cross-cultural emotions and facial expressions. All humans, despite racial and cutural differences, share the same fundamental DNA code—one that is a little over 1 percent different from that of a chimpanzee (*Pan troglodytes*). In the words of the structuralist thinker Jean Piaget:

If man, as Michel Foucault puts it, is only "a kind of rupture in the order of things" . . . it is nevertheless worth remembering that this rupture and this wrinkle are the product of a great upheaval—but a well-organized one—which is constituted by life as a whole.[7]

Humans are biological. In light of this fact, *Brutality and Benevolence: Human Ethology, Culture, and the Birth of Mexico* will attempt to return history to the path of the sciences. This study proposes more of a working hypothesis than a theory, but it is a hypothesis that draws its general conclusions from historical evidence as compared to observations found in evolutionary anthropology and comparative ethology.

In recent years the field of evolutionary anthropology has experienced the sort of fruitful and controversial debate so central to the scientific method. Discussion centers on two opposing hypotheses regarding human evolution. One is known as the multiregional model, and the other is called the Mitochondrial Eve, or Noah's Ark, hypothesis. The first argues that in different regions of the globe *Homo erectus* independently developed into more modern hominids some 500,000 years ago. As a corollary to this model, it is often stated that cultural developments in hunting, gathering, food-sharing, and fire usage aided and abetted intellectual development among the early hominids in their diverse environments. In short, culture developed by humanity continued to shape and form humanity in a type of "positive feedback loop." In opposition to this, the Mitochondrial Eve hypothesis argues that all present-day humans are the descendants of what was originally a small fragment of the human population living in Africa some 100,000 to 150,000 years ago. By studying over four thousand DNA samples of modern humans, Allan Wilson and a team of Berkeley geneticists have proposed that these Africans spread throughout the "Old World," replacing extant hominid populations wherever they went without any significant genetic interbreeding. This is argued because the overall extent of genetic variation in modern populations around the world is extremely small, implying relatively recent origins. Since *Homo erectus* lived from 1.6 million to 500,000 years ago, there was more than adequate time in one million years (as opposed to *Homo sapiens'* much shorter time on earth) to develop enough mutations in mitochondrial DNA for ancient Asian *Homo erectus* traits to be detected in Asian populations in such a way as to make them noticeably distinct from African populations. Thus, the DNA taken from an energy source for the cell called the mitochondria—one inherited solely from the mother (hence the term "Mitochondrial Eve")—demonstrates that a band of *Homo erectus* mutations made their way around the world, building earth's first world empire, as it were, out of Africa.[8]

The author of this study does not pretend to be knowledgeable enough to select either one of the hypotheses, although it is interesting to note that fossils between 500,000 and 150,000 years ago "appear to be neither one thing nor the other, neither *Homo erectus* nor *Homo sapiens sapiens*, but to combine elements of both."[9] However, either variation on the theme of human origins provides useful information for the development of historical hypotheses, and human tendencies toward territorial expansion, akin to the conquests of Mitochondrial Eve's children, do repeatedly appear in highly suggestive ways. The Aztecs and Spaniards themselves stand as evidence to conflict and territoriality in this regard. On the other hand, the multiregional model clearly calls to historians' attention the importance of culture in the formation of modern humans. It is argued that through food-sharing at base camps, hominids developed social bonds that went beyond the bond between mother and offspring so common in the animal kingdom.[10] If anything, functioning under the influence of such cultural constructionists as the anthropologist Clifford Geertz, historians and many other social scientists do not have to be convinced of the importance of human culture in shaping humanity.[11] Thus, human populations exhibit differences in the maintenance of hierarchy, eating rituals, dress, and adornment. Among other things, such differences are used to maintain separate tribes, and by means of their own academic tribal affiliations, modern social scientists speak of cultural construction and customary differences to the point of creating separate alien populations who cannot truly understand each other. As a result, James Lockhart has written about how Spaniards and central Mexican Amerindians called Nahuas "misinterpreted" each other in a case of "Double Mistaken Identity"—arguing that from his privileged twentieth-century position, he can only see real dissimilarities in such things as urban organization, whereas Spaniards and Amerindians incorrectly assumed basic similarities. By addressing the issue of customary differences, many contemporary social scientists have abandoned the vital search for human universals.[12] Although the process of abandoning Eurocentric paeans has been extremely necessary in the development of social science, its replacement with such emotional attacks on Europe as David Stannard's *American Holocaust* serves only to encourage academics to rally around a new tribal totem.[13] Much more useful is Richard Leakey's assessment of "the nearly universal social and political dominance of men over women:"

If an aspect of behavior is universal or nearly so in human societies, we should at least allow ourselves to suspect some kind of genetic basis for that behavior. On the other hand, there is a great deal of flexibility in the relation between men and women in differing societies—emphasizing the importance of other factors in orchestrating those relations.[14]

In short, what is learned and adapted through culture is not inscribed on a brain functioning as a *tabula rasa*. Many among the evolutionary anthropologists can detect universal trends that link humans across cultures and across time. Thus, the items buried with a Neanderthal, and the careful burial of bodies in planned positions, imply some belief in an afterlife, given the preponderance of such linkages since the dawn of recorded history. Likewise, male dominance over women has been linked to a division of labor still prevalent among modern hunters and gatherers: namely, that women, with their children, gather, whereas men wander and hunt. Since evidence points to early man having been omniverous, meat brought to a base camp, perhaps constituting 30 percent of the diet, would have been a valued source of protein. Efficient hunters *and* foodsharers would have thereby been valued members of the troop, acquiring hierarchical rank and power as a result. Therefore, biological factors combined with cultural development in the birth of patriarchy. While males generally possess greater upper-body strength than human females, it is also the case that crying infants and nursing mothers would not make for a successful hunt. There were real biological factors involved in the male-female division of labor, it seems. However, those factors did not necessarily have to create such a valued and powerful place for the hunter, supplier of protein. The tendencies toward this development were there, but learning by means of culture around the campfire exaggerated matters.[15] Culture has provided humans with an ability to manipulate and interpret the world in such a way that nuances may be created, but culture builds from a common human material and biological reality.

Arriving at the underlying human universals is not an easy task, nor is it one that should be taken lightly, but it is a task vital to the development of a social science of mutual human understanding—one that is not constructed on the basis of cultural, political, or religious prejudices. Rather than the vying of competing discourses that assume no absolute truth, or the attempt of one culturally determined discourse to call itself the absolute truth, the quest for human universals must function as the identification of common processes and tendencies beneath the accumulation of custom. In its earliest stages, it must also be willing to present hypotheses rather than dogmas. But it must be built on the useful reality that is the scientific method as a means of acquiring knowledge.

Comparison, in very simple terms, must inform this method of arriving at human universals, and this comparison must go beyond the human itself. For while human metaphysical systems may vary wildly, all humans are observed as requiring food and protection from the elements. All humans have bodies that play a role in the development of culture, and hominid bodies are not all that different from those of our closest living animal relatives, the chimpanzees. If one wishes to emphasize hominids' dependence on bipedal locomotion, fully developed vocal language, and a fully developed precision grip, one may see vast differences between *Homo sapiens sapiens* and *Pan troglodytes*. However, there is also great room for observing similarities. At less than 2 percent, the difference in DNA between humans and chimpanzees is smaller than that between horses and zebras. Richard Leakey and Roger Lewin have written:

The degree of genetic difference between humans and the African apes is of the magnitude that geneticists usually associate with closely associated, or sister, species. For instance, horses and zebras are placed in the same genus, *Equus*. Yet anthropologists have traditionally placed humans and apes in separate biological families, which implies a big difference indeed. No wonder Morris Goodman wanted to change things in 1962, when he said that humans and apes should be classified within the same biological family.[16]

While the evidence points to a separation of the pongid-chimpanzee line and the hominid line around 7.5 million years ago, similarities go well beyond shared DNA. In fact, under tightly controlled scientific procedure, Nick Toth and Kathy Schick have tested the cognitive power of a pygmy chimpanzee, or bonobo (*Pan paniscus*), named Kanzi. By the age of ten in 1991, Kanzi had a vocabulary of some two hundred words, which he communicated by use of a board covered in some 256 geometric shapes. Kanzi is also capable of removing flakes from stone and then using the flakes to do such things as cut a cord binding a box containing bananas, grapes, or candy. This in itself is most interesting, since bonobos in their natural state are not observed to use any tools, let alone one as sophisticated, by general animal standards, as a flint-cutting implement. In terms of language usage, Kanzi is joined by such famed chimpanzees (*Pan troglodytes*) as Washoe and Sarah, who using sign language methods were able to string together more than 150 words in various sentences.[17] In addition, Washoe was the first chimpanzee to proclaim that she recognized herself in a mirror. Since then, Gordon Gallup and others have been able to demonstrate that other chimpanzees are aware of themselves as individuals.

Outside laboratories and in the wild, Jane Goodall has pioneered the study of chimpanzee behavior in a natural setting, thereby discovering that chimpanzees possess the rudiments of material culture among other things. Encouraged by Richard Leakey's father, Louis Leakey, to study chimpanzee behavior in order to hypothesize about the behavior of early hominids, Jane Goodall helped to develop modern ethology, with its emphasis on studying animal behavior in its natural setting. It is primarily the methods of comparative ethology that currently prove most fruitful in identifying the human universals in the midst of cultural differences.

Since the early 1960s Jane Goodall has been observing and describing the behavior of the chimpanzees of Gombe on Lake Tanganyika in Tanzania. In the course of her studies, she has discovered that chimpanzee bands construct methods of social interaction and articles of material culture once thought to be the exclusive domain of another primate, *Homo sapiens sapiens*. In actuality, chimpanzees construct solid arboreal nests to provide safe sleeping arrangements, and they consciously learn to make tools out of moistened blades of grass in order to extract protein-rich termites from their hills. Upon learning of the latter activity, the paleoanthropologist Louis Leakey noted that henceforth the exclusionist definition of humans as "tool-making animals" would have to be revised or abandoned, since other living primates also make tools. Sharing over 98 percent of its DNA code with humans, the chimpanzee is far from a distant cousin, and the fields of comparative ethology and sociobiology readily accept the chimpanzee as both reflective mirror of our own behavior and shadow of long-deceased ancestors.

Contrary to the stereotypes held by so many, sociobiology is not resuscitated Social Darwinism or simplistic genetic determinism. It is an attempt to understand the extent to which genotype and experience of the environment both contribute to behavior. Despite leftist and rightist political agendas that would silence it, sociobiology is taking the first faltering steps toward trying to understand the extent to which the genetic code determines behavior. Among other things, patterns of aggression and altruism are studied throughout the animal kingdom in order to understand inherent tendencies and the delicate balance between nature and nurture in the expression of such tendencies. Thus, throughout the animal kingdom, biological studies support the notion of an inherent male propensity toward ranking, competition, and aggression—a propensity possibly related to, though not necessarily caused by, levels of the hormone testosterone among other things.[18] This does not mean that every single male will be overly aggressive within a given species, nor does it mean that aggression is enough for species or individual survival. In turn, aggression may be promoted or suppressed through a system of environmental rewards and punishments. To see comparative ethology and sociobiology as merely the reduction of human behavior to biology does not take into account the fact that biologists do not argue for the creation of a particular culture with all its details as something encoded in DNA. Rather, they argue that a propensity for culture-creation is encoded, and that it follows *general* biologically determined factors in interaction with environmental factors.

Although avoiding the label "sociobiologist" and all the problems and prejudices attached to totemic clan affiliation, Jane Goodall readily cites E. O. Wilson's *Sociobiology: The New Synthesis* to support her studies at Gombe.[19] Although many, including the non-biblically inspired, would still like to see humanity as especially unique, the object of a type of special creation, this vanity is challenged by Goodall's observations and descriptive analysis. Not only are chimpanzees found to have goal-directed behavior; they teach and learn, abstract and generalize, while also retaining very real notions of selfhood and group affiliation. Only continued adherence to the intellectual fantasies of René Descartes could maintain belief that these primates are little more than machines. Like their human cousins, chimpanzees demonstrate aggression that is sometimes manifested in the warring of bands, and they also demonstrate food-sharing, compassion, and altruism. They are not uniformly benevolent or villainous. One thing, however, is quite clear. Males, who exclusively war with other bands over territory, are more violent and aggressive than females.

In 1976 and 1978 individual males and females were studied to delineate both a great range among individuals and an average preponderance of male aggression. In summation, the attack rate for males ranged from one fight per 27 hours to one per 207 hours, with an overall average of one per 62 hours. The female range ran from one fight per 47 hours to none in 230 hours, with the average being one fight per 106 hours.[20] Males are more violent. While Goodall argues for the existence of very real hierarchies among female chimpanzees, just as there are hierarchies among the males, she also stresses that ranks cannot be clearly delineated within a female hierarchy.[21] Some females associate only rarely, lessening the opportunity for antagonism, and by nature females seem to pair off in dyads whose relative status is determined "by the presence or absence of particular others—principally family members." Although not in total agreement with his observations, Goodall cites Frans de Waal, the author of *Chimpanzee Politics*, to note that female hierarchy is more stable than male ranking and more based on "'respect from below rather than intimidation and show of strength from above.'"[22]

Despite the obvious aggression in chimpanzee society, Goodall is just as quick to avoid prejudices that would portray chimpanzee society as brutish as she is to avoid the prejudice of seeing only sweetness and light. Altruism and reciprocity are also parts of the complex society of Gombe. Interestingly enough, in the discussion of "friendly behavior," she notes that mothers are usually extremely patient with their young, exposing them to their first experiences of social play and the sharing of food.[23] Adults play and share bananas and meat on the basis of behavior patterns first brought to the fore by mothers. In fact, food sharing is commonly reported among the members of captive groups. Kohler (in 1925) describes how an individual, in response to begging, "may suddenly gather some fruit together and hold it out to the other or take the banana which he was just going to put in his mouth, break it in half and hand one piece to the other."[24]

True altruism, or the risking of self to assist another, has also been demonstrated at Gombe. Mothers especially will intervene to protect infants from aggressive males, and reciprocally, often male and female adults will assist their mothers if they are nearby.[25] On one occasion, the male Goblin even ran 200 meters when he heard the screams of his mother, who was being attacked by another female. Capable of gradations of kindness and aggression, of learning and tool-using, of living in societies and going to war, chimpanzees are like us. However, Goodall is careful to point out that though we are not different from the apes in kind, we do differ in degree.[26]

In a collection of recent observations entitled *Chimpanzee Cultures*, Jane Goodall and other leading primatologists explicitly argue that very real variations among the observed chimpanzee bands of Africa point to the importance of cultural learning as well as biological determinism in the shaping of the chimpanzee. Social scientists generally define culture as a uniquely human trait, though "every chimpanzee population studied to date has proved to have its own unique combination of tools and techniques."[27] Although chimpanzee behavioral differences across Africa might be explained away by the existence of different chimpanzee subspecies (*Pan troglodytes verus* of western Africa; *P. t. troglodytes* and *P. t. schweinfurthii* of western and central Africa), learned adaptation to the environment plays a very real role. Chimpanzees have been divided into the nut crackers of far west Africa, who use a hammer-and-anvil method to obtain protein from the oil palm nut, and groups in east and central west Africa that add protein to their diets through termite fishing and digging rather than nut consumption.[28] It has been argued that this difference is mechanistically determined by what is present in the environment.

However, recent evidence from Lopé in Gabon suggests that arguments of ecological determinism will *not* explain the absence of nut cracking there. The nut-bearing species are abundant in Lopé, as are raw materials for wooden and stone hammers and for stone and root anvils. By exclusion, a more likely explanation for why Lopé chimpanzees do not crack nuts is ignorance, that is, they do not consider these nuts to be edible. Such findings, along with findings on differences in the tool kits of neighboring communities within a region, suggest that culture is involved.[29]

In short, even though some continue to deny culture to the chimpanzee, denying the chimpanzee's cognitive ability to learn by means of observation, photographic evidence of chimpanzees' observing each others' methods of termite fishing or nut cracking in the wild would suggest otherwise.[30] Chimpanzees possess both common genetic determinants and diverse cultural traditions. Therefore, a human-chimpanzee comparison proves useful on a number of levels, providing perspective to studies that might otherwise become sterile in their isolation. Richard Wrangham, W. C. McGrew, Frans de Waal, and Jane Goodall all readily use the term "culture" after observing chimpanzees for years. In Jane Goodall's words:

Given the different environmental challenges faced by chimpanzees in different habitats across Africa, given the innovative performances that have been observed in many individuals, and given the fact that chimpanzees can learn by observing and imitating adult behavior, it would be strange indeed if these close relatives of ours with their complex brains did *not* show cultural diversity.[31]

For all their cultural diversity, however, they remain chimpanzees. Likewise, we remain human beings despite our own cultural diversity. Similarities between humans and chimpanzees should not be exaggerated, and culture, as developed by human beings, is not to be found in its entirety and complexity among other animals.[32] But historians, cultural anthropologists, and sociologists often enough fail to broach the subject of human animal behavior at all. This is especially amazing when one takes into account that all of human history reflects a constant dialectic of aggression and mutual aid. Whereas the anthropologist Marshall Sahlins fears that sociobiology and the broader application of biological determinism are new totemisms attempting to stress the "differences between human groups,"[33] most researchers working in the biological fields see their studies as conducive to understanding the common biological propensities in the human species and our broader relationship to the animal kingdom and the earth. In reality, religious fundamentalisms and "politically correct multiculturalism" seem far more conducive than contemporary biological studies (correctly interpreted!) to the totemisms present in places like Northern Ireland, Bosnia, and the United States.

Historically, there is a great deal of evidence regarding "man's brutality to man," but in the midst of violence and aggression there may be found compassion, reciprocity, and even altruism. These are all tendencies found throughout the human species, although they may be expressed by means of particular customs and practices. Cultural differences do not create separate species, and despite the best efforts of many social scientists and political leaders, numerous human beings have sought out commonalities. At the turn of the twenty-first century, the quest for universality is often enough read as the most insidious method used by Western European imperialism, but it must be stressed that Western Europeans are not the only ones who seek out commonalities, nor are they the only members of the species simultaneously capable of brutality and charity.

This study will focus on Spaniards and the Spanish conquest of Mexico, an act of imperialistic violence replete with multiple incidents of brutality. However, in the midst of that brutality, acts of kindness and cross-cultural bonding will be brought to the fore. Although Nahua culture was devastatingly altered by the conquest of central Mexico and literally millions died (primarily from diseases to which they had no immunity), Nahuas did survive, and they actively salvaged aspects of their own culture of aggression and kindness as they interacted with Spaniards. While a good portion of this study will descriptively explore the quiet aspects of material culture that allowed for human interaction and expressions of kindness, the brutality inherent in the Aztec and Spanish Empires will not be ignored. In fact, it will be directly related to the construction of patriarchal regimes and male hierarchies. Still, in the midst of imperial aggression, the quiet tasks of women will be referred to as a potential origin of kindness, altruism, and cross-cultural communication.

This study will be different in its attempt to seek out the animal universals underlying the nuances of human culture and custom. As did Aristotle, it will approach humans as social animals, not as special ruptures in the fabric of reality. In turn, the spirit of this interpretive method will be found among the survivors of the Spanish conquest, for the Nahuas of central Mexico were themselves embedded in a developed recognition of humanity's animal nature. Not only did the finest warriors of the Nahua Aztec Empire adopt the jaguar and the eagle as totems; Nahua men and women who healed were seen as tapping into the forces of animal nature. They were seen as having totemic *nahualtin*—what one seventeenth-century Spanish priest referred to as animal familiars. Male and female Nahua healers could possess their *nahualtin* and be possessed by them. As a *nahualli*, one of the healer's three souls, the *ihiyotl* (the spiritual force of passion) left its body to claim the power of an animal spirit guide that would aid in the healing of a patient.[34] Through the language of religion and ritual, humans were seen as part of nature's order—as having to learn from other animals as well as from other humans. On one level, this study hopes to revive the best of that tradition, while establishing a new way to approach world history.

In the midst of this quest for animal universals, the importance of culture as educator and modifier will not be forgotten. For better or worse, culture brought form to animal raw material. Given their cultural assumptions and prejudices, sixteenth-century Spaniards proposed to reconstruct an ideal New Europe at the most basic levels of material culture and social interaction.[35] Well before an Amerindian was understood in his indigenous tongue or had learned Spanish, before he spoke of Christian beliefs or heresy, he was seen as a body to be fed properly, clothed, disciplined, and exploited for his labor power. Certainly, Spanish cultural truth was linked intrinsically to faith in the teachings of Roman Christianity and to a belief in the divine election of the Spanish Crown and people to lead a crusade against heresy and infidelity, but that truth was also revealed through a series of ordinary, everyday activities. It was revealed in the preparation of meals, the wearing of clothes, and the hierarchical and reciprocal relations of individuals. In short, Spanish culture not only was to be found in the mental realm of ideas and beliefs; it reacted to universal physical needs and biological reality.

Culture functioned as a series of material and mental patterns by which a sense of belonging was communicated to human adherents, but it was determined by its reliance on the natural physical environment and bodies as reference points. Common terms of agreement—or communication by means of language, literature, dress, ritual, institutions, and the arts—were consistently used by Spanish conquerors to set themselves apart from the mass of conquered Amerindians; to allow access to Amerindians whom they deemed acceptable; and to eliminate aspects of the indigenous cultures they found the most reprehensible. It was in the face of alien cultures and physical environments that the Spaniards became most aware of themselves. By observing practices different from their own, they became much more capable of defining the unique and vital qualities of their own culture. This also allowed the Spaniards to identify practices similar and acceptable to their own, opening the door to the recognition of human universals that transcend the sixteenth century. Still, Spain's confrontation with difference and otherness served primarily to justify conquest: The Spaniards were upholding culturally based interpretations as "Universal Truth." They readily practiced cultural imperialism, identifying self as supreme in defense of rank and territory. In the words of William S. Maltby, "The development of national stereotypes implies a standard of comparison with one's own nation."[36] In that sense, the Spaniards not only created the mental category "Indian," falsely identifying Nahua, Maya, and Otomí ethnic groups as entirely the same; the Aztecs, Tlaxcalans and all of Mexico created Spaniards from Andalusians, Old Castilians, and Extremadurans.

As a result of their centuries-long Reconquest of the Iberian Peninsula, Spaniards were more than equal to the practice of cultural chauvinism and cultural syncretism. Author of the first Castilian grammar, the humanist Antonio de Nebrija argued that a common language, or means of communication, truly binds realms, and twentieth-century theoreticians have made much of the Spanish use of discourse as a weapon in the conquest of the Americas.[37] On a less-exalted plane, Spanish conquistadores like Hernán Cortés and Bernal Díaz del Castillo defined culture in terms of its material aspects—the eating practices, clothing, and bodily needs—which were more familiar to them than were the arts and letters. In turn, those who debated whether the Amerindians were natural slaves or fully rational human beings referred to both material aspects and mental interpretations of culture, the 1550 Valladolid debate between Bartolomé de las Casas and Juan Ginés de Sepúlveda being the prime example.

At its heart, the Valladolid debate of 1550 was an attempt to define rationally good and bad customs, appropriate social organization, and human culture itself. Valladolid asked whether Amerindian cultures were intrinsically corrupt because of customs and practices that flew in the face of Christian and Greco-Roman morality. Las Casas determined that they were not, while Sepúlveda reasoned the opposite. Eurocentric to the core, Sepúlveda could find nothing good among the diverse Amerindian cultures of the New World, whereas las Casas spent his time carefully distinguishing what he considered good from what he deemed bad. Not wanting New World foods to be considered inferior to those of the Old World, he argued for the nutritional value of the peanut, describing it as more delicious than any Spanish nut or dried fruit.[38] Not wanting the "evil" custom of human sacrifice to be used against the Amerindians, he compared this practice to those of Greco-Roman paganism.[39] Reason was employed by both parties to justify positions that were arrived at through emotional and volitional inclination. This Humean appreciation of reason as the tool of emotional choice may also be applied to Spaniards in the Americas.

Very few Spaniards consciously wrote of cultural values (as did Nebrija, las Casas, and Sepúlveda), but casual reference to those values was common in the discourse of the day. Royal edicts and questionnaires, petitions to the Crown, letters, popular sermons, tax lists, wills, inventories, court records, and novels placed these debates and differences of opinion within the limitations of commonly accepted terms of discourse. Sepúlveda and las Casas vehemently disagreed on the legitimacy of Amerindian lords and on the appropriate method of introducing the Amerindians to Christianity, but they agreed on the legitimacy of the principles of lordship, hierarchy, and estates, and on the ultimate value and truth of Christianity. In the New World, the first conquistadores and pobladores were uniformly shocked by cannibalism and human sacrifice. Indigenous nudity could not be accepted as an element of particular cultures but was interpreted as a sign of depravity or of innocence comparable to that of Adam and Eve before the Fall. Bread made of manioc flour or maize was eaten, and even occasionally enjoyed, but the farming of wheat and consumption of wheaten bread was clearly linked with Spanishness and civilization. Conquerors and settlers competed to prove their value to the Crown by emphasizing their introduction of European cattle, horses, and sheep into the Americas. Recognizing the value of saving their Amerindian laborers from the devastation wrought by European diseases, New World Spaniards also competed in performing acts of Christian charity. Wills zealously listed the construction of hospitals and the distribution of alms. Works performed in the material plane reflected spiritual values and a natural adherence to the agent's Spanish culture. Spaniards consistently recast elements of their culture in the Americas.

In sixteenth-century Mexico (called "New Spain" by the Spaniards), Spaniards encountered a culture they deemed civilized yet brutal, enchanting yet horrifying, similar yet alien. They desperately sought themselves in the midst of the alien, for the alien challenged their very existence and their interpretation of their culture as the only true way. The Spanish fear of the alien was reflected by Miguel de Cervantes in his recitation of certain Castilian proverbs. He had Don Quixote's niece ask, "Would it not be better to remain peacefully here at home and not go roaming through the world in search of better bread than is made from wheat, without taking into consideration that many who go for wool come back shorn?"[40] Conquistadores and pobladores certainly roamed the world, but they did so in search of gold and land to provide themselves with sheep, Spanish titles, and wheaten bread in abundance. Although many did come home shorn, they had not been searching for "better bread than is made of wheat." They were searching, paradoxically, for a better place or estate within a Spanish social system that prejudicially viewed itself as perfectly fixed and enduring. In fact, what were fixed and enduring were the human animal tendencies toward hierarchy, reciprocity, aggression, xenophobia, territoriality, display, culture-creation, and even altruism. In the midst of cultural biases and preferences, some very real universal structures may be observed in the sixteenth-century conquest of Mexico. It is these structures that will be sought out in the following chapters.

NOTES

1. David Quint, *Epic and Empire: Politics and Generic from Virgil to Milton* (Princeton, NJ: Princeton University Press, 1993).

2. José Rabasa, *Inventing America: Spanish Historiography and the Formation of Eurocentrism* (Norman and London: University of Oklahoma Press, 1993), 211. Also 11-12.

3. For an overview of how the ideas of Jürgen Habermas and Thomas Kuhn inform this discussion of the "ideal speech situation" and scientific paradigms, see the excellent articles on their thought by Anthony Giddens and Barry Barnes respectively in *The Return of Grand Theory in the Human Sciences*, ed. Quentin Skinner (Cambridge: Cambridge University Press, 1985), 123-39 and 85-100.

4. Michel Foucault, "Preface," in *The Order of Things: An Archaeology of the Human Sciences* (New York: Vintage Books, 1973), xxiii.

5. *The Aphorisms of Confucius*, trans. Lin Yutang, in *The Wisdom of China and India*, ed. Lin Yutang (New York: Random House, 1942), 816. For Aristotle's notion of the common good and the body politic, see *Politics* 1253ᵃ, in *The Basic Writings of Aristotle*, ed. Richard McKeon (New York: Random House, 1941).

6. Jacques Derrida, *Of Grammatology*, trans. Gayatri Chakravorty Spivak (Baltimore: Johns Hopkins University Press, 1974), 166.

7. Jean Piaget, *Structuralism*, trans. Chaninah Maschler (New York: Basic Books, 1970), 51.

8. For a summary of the debate, see Richard Leakey and Roger Lewin, *Origins Reconsidered: In Search of What Makes Us Human* (New York: Doubleday, 1992), 203-36.

9. Ibid., 209.

10. Glynn Isaac, "The Food-Sharing Behavior of Protohuman Hominids," reprinted in *Human Ancestors: Readings from Scientific American*, intro. by Glynn Isaac and Richard E. F. Leakey (San Francisco: W. H. Freeman, 1979), 110-23.

11. Here, Clifford Geertz's *The Interpretation of Cultures: Selected Essays* (New York: Basic Books, 1973) has been particularly influential, as has been his method of "thick description" of a cultural custom or event—a description that takes into account as many broad ramifications and relationships as possible.

12. For culture and rituals as methods of separation, see Richard E. Leakey and Roger Lewin, *Origins* (New York: E. P. Dutton, 1977), 103.

Of "Double Mistaken Identity," James Lockhart writes:

Each side takes it that a given form or concept is essentially one already known to it, operating in much the same manner as in its own tradition, and hardly takes cognizance of the other side's interpretation. Each could view Indian town government, the monastery complexes, mural painting, land tenure, and many other phenomena of the postconquest Nahua world as falling within its own frame of reference. Under the unwitting truce thus created, Nahua patterns could continue indefinitely in a superficially Hispanic guise that was sometimes no more than a label.

See James Lockhart, *The Nahuas after the Conquest: A Social and Cultural History of the Indians of Central Mexico, Sixteenth through Eighteenth Centuries* (Stanford, CA: Stanford University Press, 1992), 445-46.

Of the above passage from Lockhart, it must be asked to what extent Spaniards and Amerindians chose to emphasize similarities rather than the differences that divide. Must it be assumed that they were not essentially the same? *Brutality and Benevolence* predicates a human essence. For a recent study of the existence of "human universals," see Donald E. Brown, *Human Universals* (Philadelphia: Temple University Press, 1991).

13. Thus Stannard, a professor of American studies at the University of Hawaii, writes, "The only thing demonstrably true in this litany of Christian hate was that the Indians often were understandably reluctant to give up the truths of their forefathers and adopt the foreign religious beliefs of the people who had come to kill and torture and enslave them." David E. Stannard, *American Holocaust: The Conquest of the New World* (New York and Oxford: Oxford University Press, 1992), 217-18.

14. Leakey and Lewin, *Origins*, 230.

15. Ibid., 230-37.

16. Leakey and Lewin, *Origins Reconsidered*, 93.

17. Ibid., 243-44; Leakey and Lewin, *Origins*, 200; Donald Johanson, Lenora Johanson, and Blake Edgar, *Ancestors: In Search of Human Origins* (New York: Villard Books, 1994), 126-28; Jane Goodall, *The Chimpanzees of Gombe: Patterns of Behavior* (Cambridge, MA, and London: Belknap Press of Harvard University Press, 1986), 35.

18. The plasma testosterone levels of rhesus monkeys increase when males attain or defend dominance, whereas levels drop when rank is lost. Likewise, plasma testosterone levels increase when human male tennis players win a match and are pleased with their performance. Victors dissatisfied with their performance demonstrate no increase. Recent graduates of medical school also demonstrate elation and an increase in plasma testosterone levels. Irenäus Eibl-Eibesfeldt, *Human Ethology* (New York: Aldine de Gruyter, 1989), 300-301.

19. Thus she builds on Wilson's notions of territoriality to argue for this trait among the chimpanzees of Gombe. Goodall, *Chimpanzees of Gombe*, 525-28.

20. Ibid., 341.

21. Ibid., 437.

22. Ibid.

23. Ibid., 368, 369, 372.

24. Ibid., 374.

25. Ibid., 376.

26. Ibid., 592.

27. Richard W. Wrangham, Frans B. M. de Waal, and W. C. McGrew, "The Challenge of Behavioral Diversity," in *Chimpanzee Cultures*, ed. Richard W. Wrangham, W. C. McGrew, Frans B. M. de Waal, and Paul G. Heltne (Cambridge, MA, and London: Harvard University Press, 1994), 1-2.

28. Ibid., 6. W. C. McGrew, "Tools Compared: The Material of Culture," in *Chimpanzee Cultures*, 33, 36.

29. McGrew, "Tools Compared," in *Chimpanzee Cultures*, 35.

30. Ibid., p. 32, fig. 2, and p. 34, fig. 4.

31. Jane Goodall, "Foreword," in *Chimpanzee Cultures*, xix.

32. Wrangham, de Waal, and McGrew, "Behavioral Diversity," in *Chimpanzee Cultures*, 1.

33. Marshall Sahlins, *The Use and Abuse of Biology: An Anthropological Critique of Sociobiology* (Ann Arbor: University of Michigan Press, 1976), 106.

34. Alfonso López Austin, *Cuerpo humano e ideología: las concepciones de los antiguos nahuas* (Mexico City: Universidad Nacional Autónoma de México, 1980), 1:416-30; Kevin Gosner, *Soldiers of the Virgin: The Moral Economy of a Colonial Maya Rebellion* (Tucson and London: University of Arizona Press, 1992), 110-11; Hernando Ruiz de Alarcón, *Tratado de las supersticiones y costumbres gentilicas que oy viuen entre los indios naturales desta Nueua España*, in *Tratado de las idolatrias, supersticiones, dioses, ritos, hechicerías y otras costumbres gentilicas de las razas aborigenes de México*, ed. Francisco del Paso y Troncoso (Mexico City: Ediciones Fuente Cultural, 1953), 23-28.

35. Colin M. MacLachlan, *Spain's Empire in the New World: The Role of Ideas in Institutional and Social Change* (Berkeley, Los Angeles, London: University of California Press, 1988), ix-xiv.

36. William S. Maltby, *The Black Legend in England: The Development of Anti-Spanish Sentiment, 1558-1660* (Durham, NC: Duke University Press, 1971), 135.

37. Tzvetan Todorov, *The Conquest of America: The Question of the Other*, trans. Richard Howard (New York: Harper & Row, 1984), 123; Stephen Greenblatt, *Marvelous Possessions: The Wonder of the New World* (Chicago: University of Chicago Press, 1991), 52-57; René Jara and Nicholas Spadaccini, "Introduction: Allegorizing the New World," in *1492-1992: Re/Discovering Colonial Writing*, ed. René Jara and Nicholas Spadaccini(Minneapolis: Prisma Institute, 1989), 11-12; Antonio Gómez-Moriana, "Narration and Argumentation in the Chronicles of the New World," in *1492-1992*, trans. Jane E. Gregg and James V. Romano, 98.

38. Lewis Hanke, *All Mankind Is One: A Study of the Disputation between Bartolomé de las Casas and Juan Ginés de Sepúlveda on the Religious and Intellectual Capacity of the American Indians* (De Kalb: Northern Illinois University Press, 1974), 39.

39. Ibid., 99.

40. Miguel de Cervantes Saavedra, *Don Quixote*, trans. Samuel Putnam (New York: Viking Press, 1949), Pt. 1, chap. 7, p. 60.

2

Spanish Culture

When the Spaniards arrived in the Americas they brought with them their own definitive, dogmatic concepts of social order and the means of maintaining it. Like so many others, including Christopher Columbus, Hernán Cortés used European Spain and its cultural hierarchy as a standard by which to feel dominant in the Americas:

I will say only that these people live almost like those in Spain, and in as much harmony and order as there, and considering that they are barbarous and so far from the knowledge of God and cut off from all civilized nations, it is truly remarkable to see what they have achieved in all things.[1]

By conquering lands with different people, cultures, flora, fauna, and climates, the Spaniards were forced to determine which elements of their culture they considered absolutely essential to the maintenance of their "Spanishness." Individual Spaniards differed on the vital particulars of Spanish culture, but few among them suggested abandoning Spanish ways and going native.[2] When confronted with alien ways, be they Jewish, Moorish, Protestant, or Amerindian, Spaniards re-entrenched in defense of their own basic culture.

Whereas the drive to defend one's culture and customs is a human trait laden with overtones of biologically innate terrritoriality, the culture to be defended is a human creation. Very much a set of ideals and aspirations, as well as material adaptations, culture is never truly static. In *Sociobiology: The New Synthesis*, Edward O. Wilson interprets culture as "a hierarchical system of environmental tracking devices"—as adaptive in the Darwinian sense so as to enhance group survival.[3] Irenäus Eibl-Eibesfeldt, in turn, argues that there are cultural universals that are the result of the same human animal adapting to similar demands, but cultures also evolve and demonstrate differences over time and space.[4] After

1492 a number of Spaniards were confronted by issues of constancy and change where cultures are concerned. Exposed to Amerindian and other cultural traditions, Spaniards usually responded by perceiving their own Spanish cultural tradition, developed within a set of very particular environmental circumstances, as a universal human norm. While ethology seeks out human universals in such tendencies as aggression and altruism, sixteenth-century Spaniards defined the religion and ritual of their particular culture in such a way that it was interpreted as the one true universal, or catholic, church. Among other things, Spanish Christianity helped to bind a number of disparate trends in Spanish culture, but it was obviously not the one faith for all humanity, although all human cultures demonstrate the development of ritual and even religion as a means of bonding. The creation of modern Spain was a process of creating common customs and, therefore, a common family. Christianity was a powerful tool in creating those common customs, both in Spain and in the Americas.

Until the marriage in 1469 of Isabella of Castile and Ferdinand of Aragon—known as *los reyes católicos* after 1494—their two separate kingdoms were as politically distinct as Spain and Portugal today. In fact, they continued to be recognized as distinct legal entities until the eighteenth century, although they were placed under the rule of one monarch with the ascension of Charles V (1519-1556), the grandson of Ferdinand and Isabella. Still, throughout the sixteenth century, Aragon and Catalonia maintained privileges, tax structures, and legislative assemblies different from those of Castile. Language and customs differed as well. It is therefore quite legitimate to ask if one Spanish culture existed around 1492. It was in that very year that the last Moslem realm, the Kingdom of Granada, finally fell in the south.

Despite these very real divisions, Américo Castro observed that as early as the fifteenth century Castilians felt the right to speak for all the Spains.[5] In the conquest of the Americas, Castilians found ample opportunity to create a "New Spain" in the image of Castile even before the Iberian Peninsula had been itself recast in that image. Between 1493 and 1600, Andalusia, Extremadura, New Castile, Old Castile, and Leon accounted for 88.8 percent of the total registered emigrants to the Americas. Among the early-sixteenth-century encomenderos of New Spain, a total of 69.5 percent originated in the same five regions, 17.2 percent of the encomenderos are of unknown origin, and only 13.3 percent came from other known regions.[6] By Castilian decree, the New World was a Castilian venture, and any Catalans or Basques who made their way to the Americas found themselves submerged in a sea of Castilians. The Castilians themselves experienced regional differences, and Andalusians, accounting for 36.9 percent of the registered emigrants and 25.3 percent of New Spain's early encomenderos, had much to do with the cultural definition of Spaniards in the Americas, introducing their plows and fishing nets throughout the Western Hemisphere.[7] However, all Castilians shared a Reconquista and a sense of the alien that bound them together in the midst of a New World. Castilians would speak for Spain in the Western Hemisphere, but even as they did so they claimed to be the true representatives of broader European cultural traditions.

If anything, the Castilian rationalization of cultural and political imperialism was developed from centuries of fighting Moslems for territory on the
Iberian Peninsula. Although Christians also readily fought Christians for land
and livestock throughout the Middle Ages, a common Christianity served as a
totemic means of affiliation and coalition construction in the midst of constant
warfare. In the pursuit of wealth and terrritory, coalitions could be broadened
quickly by rallying around Saint James, the patron of the Christian reconquest.
A virtual warrior deity, Santiago Matamoros (Saint James, Killer of Moors)
was spoken about as appearing on horseback in battles between Christians and
Moslem Moors. This search for otherworldy support in the midst of battle is no
doubt older than its literary portrayal in Homer's *Iliad*, and Spanish conquistadores in the Americas would bring this Reconquista tradition with them. In
Mexico, Bernal Díaz, himself one of the conquerors, constantly makes reference to "Santiago" as a battlecry, although he records his doubts concerning a
legend that the saint had actually made an appearance to lead the Spaniards to
victory.[8] Though a myth, Santiago was, in a sense, incarnated through the
beliefs and actions of early modern Spaniards themselves.

A common Catholic faith was used as a learned cultural means of maintaining unity in the midst of diversity. Late in the sixteenth century, *licenciado*
Nicolás de Abila summarized the binding force of the Catholic faith in his
Exposición del segundo mandamiento del decalogo (1596). He argued, among
other things, that the Lord's name could never be taken in vain, since all
manners of perjury could then be committed. By binding people to their oaths
and contracts, the appropriate Christian words magically created community:

The surest foundation of human *policía* [i.e., law and order; civilization] is faith, and
constancy, which one must maintain in decrees, and in contracts among men: especially when oath-taking intervenes. . . . [W]ithout the blessed bonds of oath-taking, the
entire foundation of the republic is destroyed. For if we cannot put our faith in the
oaths of Christians, in what should we confide? And therefore it is clear that perjury
perverts the republic and human *policía*.[9]

Many written sources of the time discuss the hierarchy, reciprocity, and
compromise of Christian corporatism in the abstract, yet the activities of early
modern players demonstrate the failures and successes of the paradigm. When
both Ferdinand and Charles V suffered through a series of Italian alliances
against the French monarchy, they truly believed that they did so on behalf of
Christendom, for they identified their own interests with the best interests of
Christendom.[10] Crusading zeal lived in Spain, and Spaniards expected to be
rewarded by God with gold and glory. The selfish blended with the selfless,
and monarchs like Charles and Philip II (1556-1598) were quite ready to bleed
their patrimonies financially dry in order to maintain and extend less tangible
aspects of their own lordship and of divine sovereignty as they defined it. The
indebtedness of the Spanish Crown for the sake of its crusades against Protes-
tantism and Islam reveals that the monarchy could consider its wealth and

patrimony safe only in a social milieu consecrated by Catholic ritual. Common truths and oaths allowed society to function as a unit, and justice was to be defined exclusively in Catholic moral terms. Economic interests took a back seat to the defense of the society's fundamental "intangibles," for they were not seen as intangibles but as the language that created community out of a common mode of communication. In his political testament, Charles admitted that extraordinary military expenditures left him in financial need and forced him to tolerate the usurpation of some taxing powers of the royal patrimony, but he still left Philip a crusading mission that became the Spanish Crown's justification for existence: "And watch over the liberties of Churches and ecclesiastical personages . . . and be zealous and carefully observe the veneration of God; and with all your heart love Justice."[11]

In Spain, men and kingdoms still wanted to be rich and powerful, but the magical ritualism of the Catholic faith was the structural paradigm by which their disintegrative tendencies were controlled. Writing about religion in general terms, Edward O. Wilson differentiates it from a shaman's magic by observing that religion is more tribally oriented in scope, creating bonds that reinforce "tribal good behavior" by means of sacrifice and priestly intercession: "In more complex societies, polity and religion have always blended naturally. Power belonged to kings by divine right, but high priests often ruled over kings by virtue of the higher rank of the gods."[12]

It should be no surprise, then, that Ferdinand and Isabella were granted the title *los reyes católicos* by the Spanish pope Alexander VI in 1494. The language of Catholicism helped to stabilize the natural construction of social hierarchy. Royal justice and law were, in effect, supported by beliefs and mythologies concerning divine equity and justice. If Charles V, who was Austrian and Burgundian, as well as Castilian and Aragonese, could be accepted as King in Spain, it was because he was the scion of a divinely ordained family. Castile and Aragon were family territories, and it was believed that they were held by divine favor. The benevolence that can be expressed and enjoyed in leadership was reinforced by religious tradition. Thus, Ferdinand and Isabella's royal secretary Fernando Alvárez de Toledo could write, "The Saints have said that the Monarch is put on earth to execute Justice in God's place."[13] And Charles V's secretary, Alfonso de Valdés, could distinguish between king and tyrant by writing:

The tyrant seeks his own profit, while the king seeks the good of the republic. If you aim all your works at the well-being of the republic you will be a king and if you do it for yourself you will be a tyrant. Try to leave your kingdom better than you find it, and this will be your true glory.[14]

The king, therefore, was meant to build his prestige on the basis of benevolence and concern for the common good. Far from being an exclusive trait of human cultures, the tempering of power by means of benevolence is a primate tendency. In her earliest studies at Gombe, Jane Goodall noted that alpha males often reassure subordinate victims of their aggression after an attack and display of dominance. When Mike was alpha male at the Gombe stream in the late 1960s, he was an enthusiastic groomer of others and was found to distribute meat generously, especially with a suspected sibling.[15] However, he was quite capable of attacks and aggression. On one occasion early in his reign, Mike savagely beat the female Flo because she had presumed to take some fruit while he was gathering bananas in the same area.

And Flo, after Mike's vicious attack, and even while her hand dripped blood where she had scraped it against a rock, had hurried after Mike, screaming in her hoarse voice until he had turned. As she approached him and crouched low in apprehension, he had patted her several times on her head and then, as she calmed, had given her a final reassurance by leaning forward to press his lips to her brow.[16]

Although the chimpanzee male is quick to attack, he is also equally quick to calm and reassure his victim. Chimpanzees show great hostility and violence, but peaceful exchanges do occur more frequently than violent ones. Writing in 1990, Goodall can now generalize that embraces, kisses, and pats are employed by dominant apes to console subordinates after aggression.[17] However, aggression and dominance displays exist as means by which an alpha male retains position in the flux that is chimpanzee social structure. Not only are there always younger males waiting to topple him; there are subordinates who squabble among themselves in the pursuit of status. In this fashion, chimpanzee society is not far removed from the realities of social conditions in early-sixteenth-century Spain.

Still officially the separate Crowns of Castile and Aragon, sixteenth-century Spain was also divided along class lines in both realms. In Castile, real tension existed between the interests of leading noble houses that dominated the sheep-herders' guild, or Mesta, and urban textile producers, among others. These tensions exploded in the Comunero Revolt of 1520-1521. Vying for a more powerful position in the social hierarchy, the artisans, merchants, and lesser nobles who rebelled demanded an immediate meeting of the traditional representative assembly of Castile, the Cortes. This would have provided them with representation and leverage within a system that, under Ferdinand and Isabella, had increasingly come to be centralized through royal appointed officials called *corregidores*, who supervised and controlled the actions of local town councils, or *cabildos*. Local elites felt a lessening of power, and the Comunero Revolt was a blatant test of the new "alpha male." The new monarch, Charles, had just turned twenty, and at that time he was by all accounts culturally more Flemish and Burgundian than Castilian and Spanish. His power and position seemed eminently contestable.

The comuneros' Valladolid Articles reveal a strong desire to "Castilianize" young Charles and the Flemish retainers he then favored. Charles was called specifically to dismiss his foreign advisors and to marry Princess Isabel of Portugal. Although not a Castilian herself, Isabel was described through the

prism of Castilian identification with all the Spains: "'She is a firm friend of
our nation and of all Castilians and she speaks Castilian as we do.'"[18] In
addition to this, the Valladolid Articles reveal a marked respect for the reciprocal linkages between the monarchy and the people of Castile. The royal high
courts of appeal, the Audiencias, were to be reformed, not dismissed, and the
residencia system of judicial review and audit was to be broadened to cover
royal officials other than *corregidores*. The Crown was seen as necessarily
responsible to its subjects, but it still was seen as the supreme authority in the
land. All in all, this reflects the extent to which leadership among humans and
chimpanzees includes elements of cooperation and compromise with subordinates. After a hunt, an alpha male will sometimes share his protein with a
supplicant. Likewise, alpha status may be challenged by younger males, and
even when attained, alpha status does not guarantee absolute authority. Goodall
observes that being the highest-ranking male does not guarantee control of all
situations, but it does provide a certain level of protection from the intimidation of other males, including coalitions.[19] It is interesting to note that even
though the comuneros challenged Charles, they did not fully challenge the
institution of monarchy—the official position of leadership in their society.
Rather, the need for economic recovery was stressed in declarations by the
comuneros' Junta—economic revitalization being seen as a sure sign of the
Crown's commitment to the prosperity of the realm.[20]

Royal commitment to the common good had come under the scrutiny of the
comuneros for a number of pertinent reasons. Local farmlands were being
consumed by the latifundia and sheep *cañadas* of the grandees and their Mesta,
while local textile producers could not compete with the prices for raw wool
offered the grandee-dominated sheepherders' guild, or Mesta, by the cities of
Flanders. Queen Isabella had issued a series of edicts, or *cédulas*, extending
the terrain of the Mesta's *cañadas* or sheepwalks. Together with deforestation
to extend human habitation and agriculture, the Mesta's activities furthered
soil erosion in Spain. Sheep literally consumed the Castilian countryside by its
very roots as the *cañadas* enveloped more and more of the Spanish heartland,
and Isabella's *cédulas* sacrificed agricultural interests and common lands to the
needs of the Mesta corporation.[21] The comuneros wanted a representative but
oligarchic Cortes to limit a royal authority that seemed arbitrary in its grants of
offices and sinecures, and the interests of local urban oligarchs were defined as
the popular will and the source of royal sovereignty. The Cortes of Castile was
meant to be their instrument for the representation of their interests, but the
power of the potentially rebellious grandees worked to destroy the comuneros'
dreams. The Crown's need for some secure power base forced it to turn again
and again to the grandees' political, military, and economic might. They were
males of greater potency than the comuneros within Castile's hierarchy, and as
a result they received greater responsiveness from the Crown. Ultimately, the
Crown crushed the comuneros at the Battle of Villalar with the assistance of
the grandees, but the Crown then found itself in a position to use the defeated
comuneros to check some of the power of the great noble houses.[22]

Politically, the young king and his advisors could not afford a recurrence of the rebelliousness of the Castilian grandees under Henry IV (1454-1474), but the great ones were still needed. Militarily, grandee support helped to further such ventures as the taking of Granada and the French and Italian wars of the sixteenth century. Economically, the grandees' dominance in the sheepherding Mesta meant that they held the controlling interest in Spain's most profitable economic activity. Thus, the first steps to using the comuneros as a counterbalance involved mercy akin to the reassuring pats of a dominant male chimpanzee after a particularly violent display. When the Comunero Revolt failed, general pardons were issued to the rebel towns involved, and only a muted example was to be made of the comunero leadership. The historian Stephen Haliczer has noted that a modest 293 persons were excluded from Charles V's pardon of 1522, and that only 23 were actually executed while 20 died in prison. Unsurprisingly, familial influence and patronage played a role in saving many.[23] Far from being outsiders, leaders of the Comunero Revolt included powerful local personages. Still, examples had to be set, and one of the twenty-three executed was Pedro de Sotomayor, *procurador* of the comuneros of Madrid. He was not only executed at Medina del Campo on October 13, 1522; he was shamed. Taken to the public pillary, bound hand and foot, and mounted on a lowly ass, Pedro de Sotomayor was to provide a beheading that would set an example for those who were there to watch—the exemplary function explicitly being mentioned in his sentence dated August 12.[24] No doubt the public authorities thought of his being mounted on an ass, rather than the horse to which he would have been accustomed, as a warning to those who might consider a challenge to royal authority. When all was said and done, Charles, as a primate leader, balanced aggressive display with reassurance. He needed local oligarchs to persist as a thorn in the side of the great noble houses and the Mesta, or else he would have to stand alone against the wealth and might of his most powerful subordinates—subordinates who were, at the moment, loyal, but who had demonstrated their capacity for disloyalty in the fifteenth century.

This intrinsic need for compromise was both the strength and the weakness of Spanish society in the sixteenth century. The Mesta was enriched, but its wealth was tapped for the common defense of Christendom through a series of sales taxes, subsidies, and forced loans.[25] Through this revenue the Crown and grandees hoped to maintain the unity and defense of Christendom against the internal threat of heresy and the external threat of the Turks.[26] In turn, by the 1580s an informal alliance of noble *latifundistas* and towns was able to check Mesta pasturage demands more effectively. Throughout the sixteenth century, the Mesta lost more and more of its legal battles, and the Crown tried to promote regional commerce and manufacture among the towns and cities of Spain.[27] The poor, for their part, received relief in congested urban areas while a maximum price on grain, or *tasa*, ineffectively tried to combat inflation in matters of subsistence. Unsurprisingly, this enraged peasants who sold grain and had to turn to blackmarket methods to maximize profit.[28]

Rather than being a static and unchanging society, sixteenth-century Spain was characterized by constant conflict and flux. Primates are not social insects, and primate leadership seemingly succeeds when it learns to manipulate alliances and coalitions formed by subordinates. In the course of doing that, some degree of responsiveness, reassurance, and benevolence must, in fact, be shown subordinates. However, there are always those subordinates who wish to improve their lot in the hierarchy—be they comuneros or conquistadores. Centuries of Reconquista had identified success with battlefield victory and the taking of territory. Young Spanish males hoping to climb the social ladder could fight in the Italian wars, in the Germanies, or in the Americas. Gold and glory were much-desired tangible rewards, and the totemic, tribal vision of the need to defeat and convert infidels helped to reassure in the midst of the doubts that necessarily arise when "brothers-in-arms" fall mutilated or dead. Christianity became a rationalization for violence in the pursuit of status and dominance. It was already that on the Iberian Peninsula before it was ever exported by Spanish conquerors. Just as U.S. workers and millionaires of the Cold War era united against a common Soviet threat, Spaniards of diverse estates and classes united behind the banner of the faith against the outsider. In early modern Spain, when necessary, the integrity of the "ingroup," of its hierarchy and reciprocity, was to be sustained by hierarchical display and actual brutality. The enemy within, as well as the enemy without, faced dehumanization and demonization.[29] This, above all else, was the social task of the Spanish Inquisition.

On January 21, 1590, and May 21, 1595, Córdoba's tribunal of the Holy Office of the Spanish Inquisition burned two women, each thought to be approximately seventy years of age. Such brutality was not uncommon in Spain or in the entirety of early modern Euorpe, where perceived threats to the integrity of totemic belief were concerned. Religion was meant to keep cultures moral, communitarian, and intact. Individuals who challenged the "one true" religious definition of the cosmos were thereby not only expendable but abhorrent as well. All this served as the learned rationalization for the horrible deaths of La Hardona and Isabel Alvarez. It also served to rationalize the deaths of 826 men and women burned at the stake in Castile and Aragon between 1540 and 1700—at least according to the estimates given by Jaime Contreras and Gustav Henningsen.[30] Set up to deal with *conversos*, or converted Jews, who continued to maintain at least some of their Jewish customs or beliefs, the Inquisition did most of its bloody work in its very first decades from 1483 to 1540. Henry Kamen has written that "in rounded terms, it is likely that over three-quarters of all those who perished under the Inquisition in the three centuries of its existence, did so in the first twenty years."[31] It is estimated that in Valencia alone 754 persons were relaxed to the secular arm and burned in person between 1484 and 1530. For an interesting contrast, Toledo saw about 250 people burned between 1485 and 1501, but only 11 between 1575 and 1610, and 8 between 1648 and 1794. Once the perceived threat had been neutralized by the clerical and secular arms of the body politic, the horrid work of the Inquisition did slow in Spain, but this could have been no consolation to La Hardona and Isabel Alvarez.

The cases of these two women serve as excellent examples of the Inquisition's social control function and of the use of ritualized and displayed brutality to maintain both a human hierarchy and a sense of communal bonding. As has been noted by numerous ethologists, evolutionary psychologists, and even postmodern theorists, the sense of "Us" is often enough created in relation to the existence of the enemy "Them." In *Sociobiology: The New Synthesis*, Edward O. Wilson noted that cooperative behavior among social animals reaches a peak when the members of a particular group are repelling an outsider. Experiments have been done demonstrating this trend among such diverse creatures as Canadian geese, barnyard chickens, and rhesus monkeys. However,

human behavior provides some of the best exemplification of the xenophobia priniciple. Outsiders are almost always a source of tension. If they pose a physical threat, especially to territorial integrity, they loom in our vision as an evil, monolithic force. Efforts are then made to reduce them to subhuman status, so that they can be treated without conscience. They are the gooks, the wogs, the krauts, the commies—not like us, another subspecies surely, a force remorselessly dedicated to our destruction who must be met with equal ruthlessness if we are to survive. Even the gentle Bushmen distinguish themselves as the !Kung—the human beings.[32]

It is this innate tendency to fear the unknown and the outsider that aids a human infant in its initial survival and creates all the horrors of prejudice. La Hardona and Isabel Alvarez were burned because of such a tendency exacerbated by culture—a sixteenth-century Spanish Christian culture that emphasized the differences between Old and New Christians, thus making New Christians (i.e., converted Jews and Moslems) the subjects of brutal social and cultural displays. There is no doubt that early modern Spanish society was capable of real reciprocity and charity as methods of community-building, but it was also quite capable of using brutality and violence to that end in both Old World Spain and New Spain. Exploring Spanish brutality as a culturally elaborated human phenomenon should make the cultural elaboration and innate human tendencies in Aztec human sacrifice all the more understandable. The drive to brutalize the outsider is unfortunately very human, but even more tragically, it can be magnified by means of brutal customs, mores, and values.

On January 21, 1590, at a public *auto de fe*, Angela Hernández, also known as Isabel Jiménez and La Hardona, was burned at the stake for teaching Islam and for observing Ramadan and other Moslem practices. A total of twelve witnesses, including at least eight other *moriscos*, appeared to bear witness against her. In actuality, at least seven of the *moriscos* were imprisoned at the time they presented this testimony, and they may have been thinking of easing their own fates by accusing others. Certainly, La Hardona faced the full brutality of the Inquisition in that she was tortured in the attempt to extract a confession from her, but she never did confess. Never confessing, and never begging for mercy, she was decreed guilty and incorrigible. As a result, this woman, who had been born in the Alpujarras of Granada and appeared to be older than seventy, "was relaxed to justice and the secular arm," her worldly possessions confiscated. That very same day she was burned alive at Córdoba with another native of Granada also accused of being a secret Moslem. Unlike La Hardona, sixty-year-old Isabel de Mendoza begged for mercy and confessed to some Moslem practices, but her confession was deemed to be insincere by the Córdoba tribunal of the Inquisition, and she too was relaxed and burned along with the statue of a dead fourteen-year-old *morisca* named Lucia.[33]

Five years later, on May 21, 1595, seventy-year-old Isabel Alvarez of neighboring Ecija was burned for "keeping the law of Moses." She had been accused by two formal witnesses, and by another using hearsay. Fourteen others appeared in the course of her trial, but she defended herself, denying the charges against her. The result of her efforts was the confiscation of her worldly possessions and her death by burning. She died with three other *conversas* accused of practicing Judaism in secret. Of higher social standing than she, they were Doña Leonor Gutiérrez, the forty-year-old wife of Licenciado Aguilar, a physician; Doña Francisca de Aguilar, twenty-five and the daughter of Gutiérrez and Aguilar; and Doña Isabel de Avila, fifty years of age. All the women involved came from Ecija.[34]

In both these cases, as with all *autos de fe*, the actual burning of human victims was the culmination of an entire process that included the burning in effigy of the dead and escaped, as well as the forgiveness of many others who were assigned penance while they continued to live. Thus, the public *auto de fe* included not only the cruel burning of those deemed heretics but also the procession of those assigned penances for blasphemy, fornication, bigamy, false testimony, witchcraft, and the like. Thus, at the 1590 *auto de fe*, the twenty-year-old *morisco* slave Juan de Montoya was given two hundred lashes for trying to escape and for confessing to having denied belief in God and the Virgin Mary. At the 1595 *auto de fe*, the twenty-six-year-old widow of a silversmith, Juana de Almagro, appeared as a penitent for having blasphemed against the virginity of Mary and invoked demons to foretell the future. She was to wear the insignia of a witch at the *auto*, and she was sentenced to receive one hundred lashes and a two-year exile from Córdoba.[35]

As observed by Maureen Flynn in "Mimesis of the Last Judgment: The Spanish *Auto de fe*," spectators at the procession of penitents and public burning were called to reflect upon God's final judgment of their sins.[36] Both the Holy Office of the Spanish Inquisition and its public *auto de fe* were well-planned expressions of social brutality, public control, and hierarchical reinforcement. The evidence also demonstrates that they were both a source of fear and comfort to a human culture trying to reinforce its tendencies toward ordered hierarchy and exclusivist binding values.

Established in 1483, the Holy Office of the Spanish Inquisition was a synthetic and complex organ of hierarchical and popular brutality. Although appointments to the highest official ranks of Grand Inquisitor and regional tribunals were made by the Crown, the papacy and clerical hierarchy never fully abandoned their say where religious trials and clerics were concerned. Likewise, while the Iberian kingdoms of Castile and Aragon were unified at first only by means of the marriage of Isabella of Castile and Ferdinand of Aragon, the Spanish Inquisition was an institution that had the same hierarchical structure and Grand Inquisitor for both kingdoms. The kingdoms maintained separate laws and cortes, or parliaments, that were appealed to against the interests of the Inquisition on many occasions, but Aragon and Castile experienced the first tastes of real unification through the Inquisition.

In local tribunals, found in major cities like Córdoba, Toledo, Barcelona, and Valencia, various cases were tried, ranging from blasphemy, fornication, and bigamy to witchcraft and heresy. In areas such as witchcraft, local civil jurisdiction was often more severe than that of the Inquisition, so that it immediately becomes apparent that tribunals of the Inquisition possessed some very real standards for judgment and procedure. It is well known that testimony could be given by secret witnesses who were kept from cross-examination by the accused, but the accused was permitted to draw up a list of personal enemies who might wish to see him or her hurt. If the secret witness had been identified independently as an enemy, then the testimony was to be discounted. In fact, witnesses were kept secret to protect them from retribution from the accused's family—a very real possibility in the early modern period.

All this concern for detail does not mean that the detail was not, in turn, linked to a very real brutality. Although evidence had to be gathered to pronounce anyone guilty, personal confession by the accused was always deemed the most important demonstration of guilt. Torture was thereby used to extract confessions for major crimes such as heresy. Even though the torture was limited by the health of the accused, as certified by an attending physician, the attention to procedure only magnifies the cruelty involved in the entire process. Methods used included the stretching of limbs and the simulation of drowning. They were the same means used by secular courts and were far more tightly controlled than in many secular jurisdictions, but they still had the propensity of eliciting confessions of guilt from the innocent as well as the guilty. The Inquisition realized this. As a result, an official, signed confession had to be agreed to by the accused twenty-four hours after the actual torture. However, if the accused retracted at that time, he or she could look forward only to more torture, if deemed fit. Many were, of course, broken, as in the famous recorded details regarding the torturing of Elvira del Campo in 1568. Accused of secret Judaism in Toledo, Elvira's pathetic fate on the rack was first published by Henry Lea in his classic *History of the Inquisition of Spain* and has since been reprinted by Henry Kamen in *Inquisition and Society in Spain*. After the torture had commenced, Elvira's recorded words are quite telling indeed:

She said, "Take me from here and tell me what I have to say—they hurt me—Oh my arms, my arms!" which she repeated many times and went on "I don't remember—tell me what I have to say—Oh wretched me!. . . ." She was told to tell in detail truly what she did. . . . More turns were ordered and as they were given she cried "Oh! Oh! loosen me for I don't know what I have to say—if I did I would tell it."[37]

Finally, after being told to confess to what witnesses had said, namely, that she refused to eat pork and always put out clean linen on Saturdays, Elvira said that she did not eat pork because she did not want it. After a second torture session four days later, she confessed fully.[38] In their pursuit of "truth," and in their attempt to maintain "the one true faith," the inquisitors and their servitors readily lost propensities toward mercy.

It became the task of the Inquisition's *auto de fe* to remind a general Spanish audience of its humanity and mortality and of its place in the social and cosmic hierarchy. Imitating the Last Judgment, "The *auto de fe* was the ceremony at which the Inquisition judged and punished prisoners for violations against the Catholic faith."[39] Texts that described the Last Judgment were emphasized at the public *auto*, and the very cosmic order itself was meant to be illustrated by means of procession and ceremony. Early in the morning, public and inquisitorial officials led a procession with men at arms. They were then followed by sinners to the seat of the local tribunal—some of those sinners to be reconciled and penanced, others to be relaxed. The general public was ordered to attend as an "act of faith" and to see the "mercy and justice" of the Church in action. A sermon was always preached, and then the sentences of all the victims were read. The reconciled kissed the cross and were once again made part of the fold, although they might easily have to wear the mark of their past error as a *sanbenito*, an outer garment that described in writing and symbols the faults of the accused, and that would generally be hung in a local church after the victim's death. Finally, those condemned to death were marched to the *quemadero*, the place of burning, at the end of the day. Huge crowds attended such "pitiful spectacles," and there the central message of the Inquisition was taught using the spectacle of brutality. In a 1625 account of a Córdoban *auto*, Juan Páez de Valenzuela made special note of a condemned Portuguese *converso* named Manuel López. López admitted to being a secret Jew, and then he refused to abandon his beliefs. As a result, he was burned alive, without first being strangled. Páez de Valenzuela explicitly wrote that he thereby became a martyr for Satan, condemned to the eternal flames of hell.[40] Manuel López, through his terrible suffering, was meant to represent the sad fate awaiting all those who could not be reconciled to an all-embracing cosmic and social order.

In the last analysis, the Inquisition and its *auto de fe* were meant to reinforce the hierarchy, taking advantage of a xenophobic society's fear of outsiders. The Inquisition itself was feared by many common people and failed to receive the utmost cooperation in many regions where it experienced difficulty recruiting clerical and lay assistants called *comisarios* and familiars respectively. However, it also reinforced prejudices that were there long before its arrival. Before its very founding in 1483, rumors concerning the ritual murder of a

Christian child by Jews occured at Sepúlveda in 1468, and after its founding, the myth of ritual murder was again revised with the tale of the death of the Niño de La Guardia at the hands of *conversos* and Jews in 1491—an event that prepared popular sentiment for the expulsion of the Jews in 1492 and that actually reflected the real desire of many Old Christians to see that expulsion.[41] Given war, famine, plague, and death, life was far from easy in the early modern period. Living in constant fear, common and not-so-common folk often turned to outsiders, to those who were somehow deemed strange, to find scapegoats. In much of Spain, *conversos* and *moriscos* served this function. It is interesting that in Catalonia, on the French-Spanish border, poor French outsiders held a special place: "In the auto of July 1563, out of forty-five penitents thirty-six were French, and in the great auto of February 1564 put on specially for Philip II in the Born, out of thirty-eight penitents thirty-two were French; in that of August 1565, out of forty-seven penitents only nine were Spanish and all the five 'relaxed' were French."[42] The Inquisition used popular prejudice and xenophobia. It was a brutal means to maintaining religious and cultural "purity," and it taught that brutality was an acceptable means to this. As children exposed to violence are more likely to play in an aggressive and violent fashion, sixteenth-century Spaniards saw their paternalistic Church and Crown use violence in an attempt to maintain a confining social order.[43]

Rather than inhibiting violence among early modern adults, recent psychological studies of contemporary humans indicate that observed brutality "often engenders *emotional arousal* in the observer, and considerable empirical evidence exists that arousal facilitates the occurrence of aggressive behavior, especially in persons for whom such a response is well-practiced and readily available in their behavioral repertoires."[44] Although the "social learning theory" of aggression does not deny genetic human aggressive potential, it does stress that three types of models can exacerbate the expression of violence in any culture: (1) familial violence, which can create a cycle of abuse in which the abused child does often go on to be an abuser when parenting in turn; (2) subcultural modeling and reinforcement, as when an adolescent succumbs to peer pressure or a soldier learns military discipline; and (3) symbolic modeling, as found in television and movies. In all cases, "the aggressive model, be it parent, peer, or television character, is very often reinforced for behaving aggressively."[45] What may have been intended as exemplary discipline by a royal parent may actually have become a legitimization of brutality as a means of problem solving. Given the contemporary evidence regarding the lack of deterrence found in capital punishment, such a possibility of the inculcation of violence remains. It is true that human children are, on the whole, most susceptible to learning to express violence more readily, but adult soldiers are trained to abandon revulsion to killing a fellow human. An innate disposition among males to use violence may, however, be worsened by example. It can be ritualized in such a way that "maleness" itself is linked to acts of domination and violence. The Crown's very potency, therefore, was predicated on its ability to use violence. Hierarchy necessarily understands brutality.

Thus, Eibl-Eibesfeldt has noted that "people in the most varied cultures carve figures that display *a threatening face and an erect penis*."[46] When feeding, vervet monkeys are guarded by males who keep watch and display their erect penises if an unknown member of the group approaches. Likewise, in July 1962, the victorious Algerians assaulted the French Consul sexually; the initiation rituals of French youth gangs include the leader's having anal sex with the initiates; and U.S. college fraternities hold hazing rituals that frequently involve the exposure of the initiate's bare buttocks to the established members of the group.[47] In *The Labyrinth of Solitude*, Octavio Paz has written that in Mexico, "masculine homosexuality is tolerated, then, on the condition that it consists in violating a passive agent."[48] The Córdoban Inquisition's brutal slayings of La Hardona and Isabel Alvarez for their resistance to male authority, as well as the execution of Pedro de Sotomayor for treason, amounted to a ritualized male display of potency by means of brutality. Since numerous Spanish judicial officials received a *vara*, or staff of office signifying their rank and potency, the linkage between the penis and the threat is apparent.

In *Books of the Brave*, published in 1949, Irving Leonard convincingly argued, using ship inventories and the stock on hand at the shops of booksellers and printers who supplied Mexico City, that the early Spanish conquerors and settlers in Mexico read chivalric romance. Above all others, they read *Amadís de Gaula*.[49] Today's evolutionary psychologists might note that in so doing they were receiving an education in the idealization of violence. In "Honour and Shame: A Historical Account of Several Conflicts," that is just what Julio Caro Baroja argues, without the benefit of ethological terminology. He identifies the morality of the chivalric romances as that of a ruling class or Nietzschean superman. Value and honor are related to deeds replete with violence, and they were literally imitated by men like the South American rebel Lopé de Aguirre, who, in a letter explaining his rebellion to Philip II, wrote that he had originally come to Peru in order to gain prestige with his lance.[50] In fact, the influence of chivalric romances led to the very naming of California, originally an island in chivalric fantasy; the pursuit of a fountain of youth; and the reported existence of Amazon warriors in South America. In the conquest of Mexico, Bernal Díaz del Castillo not only battled Aztec "demons" and "wizards" but also compared the beauty of Tenochtitlan to what he had read in chivalric romance, describing the stone buildings and temples rising from Lake Texcoco as the enchanted sites of *Amadís de Gaula* made real.[51]

Díaz and other Spaniards in the Americas who had read the "Amadís" would have been exposed to countless romanticized versions of violence rewarded. The entire tale itself is nothing but the accumulation of violent achievements by the hero Amadís in order to have his honor recognized so that he can wed his love Oriana. The violence itself is indeed quite detailed and graphic. When Amadís, disguised as the Child of the Sea does battle with King Abies of Ireland in Book I, "their swords made the armor of little avail, so that for the most part they cut into their flesh, for there remained nothing of their shields with which they could cover or protect themselves, and so much blood flowed from them that it was a wonder that they were able to hold themselves up; but so great was the courage that they brought with them that they were not aware of this."[52] When Amadís, this time disguised as the Knight of the Green Sword, does battle with the monstrous Endriago on the island of the Devil, the gore is even more explicitly displayed. First, he crushes one of the monster's eyes, and then he impales the monster through the tongue and gills. Then, with the help of God, Amadís pierces the Endriago's brain.

But the Endriago, when it saw him so close, embraced him with his very strong and sharp claws and tore all the armor from his back and the flesh and bones as far as the vital organs. And as the monster was suffocated by the large amount of blood that it was imbibing and on account of the sword thrust that had penetrated to its brain—and especially the sentence that had been given it by God and which could not be revoked—being unable to sustain itself any longer, it opened its arms and fell senseless to one side as if dead. The knight, when he saw it thus, drew his sword and thrust it through its mouth as far as he could so many times that he finished killing it.[53]

From this passage it is apparent that Amadís not only achieved earthly acclaim through his brutal violence, but was also doing God's work by slaying a demon. In fact, God is portrayed as the ultimate cause of the demon's death, although Amadís is the instrument because of the strength of his faith—a faith that allows for all sorts of slaughter in its defense. That the conquistadores, readers of these romances, could slaughter thousands in the defense of their faith is therefore not surprising, especially when the sacred books of that faith include God's approval of forced labor for conquered peoples (Deuteronomy 20:10-12) and the "holy" slaughter of the Midianites (Numbers 31:1-24). Within Christianity, as within the Aztec warrior-noble dichotomy, there lies a real tension between sacred brutality and loving care. Reciprocity and sharing are never forgotten, but they are often enough lost behind a desire to destroy the demonized enemy and to thereby accumulate acclaim and honor.

Rather than completely eliminating basic primate behavior, human culture and learning have exaggerated certain basic trends and tendencies. Other primates readily form coalitions that display reciprocity within the ranks and agonistic behavior outside of the coalition's ranks, but to the best of our knowledge, they fail to form coalitions around shared religious beliefs. Motivation is usually more direct and related to a nepotism still quite prevalent in the behavior of Aztecs and conquistadores alike. Where sixteenth-century Spaniards are concerned, Ida Altman has noted that "people already in America . . . often returned to collect family members themselves or sent friends or agents to do so." After approximately twenty-five years without them, a merchant named Alvaro Rodríguez Chacón finally brought his three sons, his married daughter, her husband, four children, and her brother-in-law's family from Spain to Mexico.[54] Even though there were those who abandoned families in Spain, many planned to build their own personal empires on kinship affiliation, a trend we obviously share with our primate cousins. Among Japanese macaques, for example, females will groom unrelated, higher-ranking females, perhaps to gain protection in the future; but a study by Takeshi Furuichi demonstrates that close spatial proximity is more highly tolerated by related females than by the unrelated. Among six young captive chimpanzees, Joan Silk noted, "the success of food solicitations . . . varies with the degree of relatedness between the immature and the target of the appeal, with appeals to nonrelatives less successful than those to relatives." Where violence is expressed by coalitions of primates, relatedness once again proves to be a key factor, whether it be by pigtail macaques, a Cayo Santiago troop of rhesus monkeys studied by Jay Kaplan, or by Goblin, one of the alpha males made famous at Jane Goodall's Gombe site.[55] Apes and monkeys are much more likely to aid relatives in violent struggles than nonrelatives, just as they are more likely to share food with kin. Among humans, biological relationship remains crucial to understanding coalitions, but humans have also abstracted the notion of kinship to the level of tribes with mythical common ancestors or "brotherhood in Christ." Those left out of the coalition may become targets of violence, thereby strengthening coalition ties by means of a common threat.

Centuries of warfare against the Moors during the Reconquista had already helped to breed a violent culture in the Medieval Spains. In *Social and Cultural Dynamics*, Pitirim Sorokin noted that for eleven European countries studied over periods of 275 to 1,025 years, they were found to be engaged in warfare on average at least 47 percent of the years studied, though not necessarily for the full year. Spain far exceeded the average by being engaged in some type of warfare at least 67 percent of some 450 years studied after the marriage of Ferdinand and Isabella in 1469.[56] When Spaniards came to the Americas, they brought with them a primate tendency toward violence that had been honed by environmental experience and education. In turn, the religious means they used to bind culturally also bore this legacy. In central Mexico they would meet their spiritual and cultural brethren.

NOTES

1. Hernán Cortés, "Second Letter," in *Hernán Cortés: Letters from Mexico*, trans. Anthony Pagden (New Haven, CT: Yale University Press, 1986), 108. For perspectives of a similar nature, see Antonello Gerbi, *Nature in the New World: From Christopher Columbus to Gonzalo Fernández de Oviedo*, trans. Jeremy Moyle (Pittsburgh: University of Pittsburgh Press, 1985), 6, 18-19, 95-99; Fray Toribio de Benavente o Motolinía, *Memoriales o libro de las cosas de la Nueva España y de los naturales de ella*, ed. Edmundo O'Gorman (Mexico City: Universidad Nacional Autónoma de México, 1971), 240-44; Valerie I. J. Flint, *The Imaginative Landscape of Christopher Columbus* (Princeton, NJ: Princeton University Press, 1992), xiii.

2. One of the few Spaniards to go native was Gonzalo Guerrero, a castaway who made a life for himself among the Maya. He eventually died fighting the Spaniards in 1534 or 1535. More typical was the fear experienced by Cabeza de Vaca when he traveled among the alien cultures of present-day Texas and northern Mexico. See Inga

Clendinnen, *Ambivalent Conquests: Maya and Spaniard in Yucatan, 1517-1570* (Cambridge: Cambridge University Press, 1987), 17-18, 21-22; Rolena Adorno, "The Negotiation of Fear in Cabeza de Vaca's *Naufragios*," *Representations* 33 (winter 1991): 163-99.

3. Edward O. Wilson, *Sociobiology: The New Synthesis* (Cambridge, MA: Belknap Press of Harvard University Press, 1975), 560.

4. Irenäus Eibl-Eibesfeldt, *Human Ethology* (New York: Aldine de Gruyter, 1989), 148, 16.

5. Américo Castro, *The Structure of Spanish History*, trans. Edmund L. King (Princeton, NJ: Princton University Press, 1954), 11.

6. Peter Boyd-Bowman, "Patterns of Spanish Emigration to the Indies until 1600," *Hispanic American Historical Review* 56:4 (November 1976): 585; Robert Himmerich y Valencia, *The Encomenderos of New Spain, 1521-1555* (Austin: University of Texas Press, 1991), 21-26, 93.

7. George M. Foster, *Culture and Conquest: America's Spanish Heritage* (Chicago: Quadrangle Books, 1960), 67-68, 230-31.

8. Bernal Díaz del Castillo, *Historia verdadera de la conquista de la Nueva España*, ed. Joaquín Ramírez Cabañas, 3 vols. (Mexico City: Editorial Pedro Robredo, 1944), 1:138, 146-47. For "The Belief in Saint James of Galicia," see Castro, 130-70, 181-201.

9. Nicolás de Abila, *Exposición del segundo mandamiento del decalogo, y ley de Dios, e inuectiua contra el abuso del jurar, y remedio efficacissimo para desterrar del pueblo Christiano el tal abuso* (Alcalá de Henares: Iuan Gracian, 1596), chap. 4, 58.

10. "El Rey, a su embajador en Londres," March 1514, in *El Testamento político de Fernando el católico*, ed. José M. Doussinague (Madrid: Consejo Superior de Investigaciones Cientificas, n.d.), 287. For this ideological defense as found in the work of one of Charles V's bureaucrats, see Alfonso de Valdés, *Dialogue of Mercury and Charon*, trans. Joseph V. Ricapito (Bloomington: Indiana University Press, 1986), 22-35.

11. "Testamento de Carlos V," Brussels, June 6, 1554, in the *Corpus documental de Carlos V*, ed. Manuel Fernández Alvarez, 5 vols. (Salamanca: Consejo Superior de Investigaciones Científicas, 1973-1981), 4:75.

12. Wilson, 560.

13. "Confirmación de privilegios. 23 de abril de 1497," *Colección de documentos inéditos relativos al descubrimiento, conquista y organización de las antiguas posesiones españolas de América y Oceanía, sacados de los archivos del reino, y muy especialmente del de Indias*, ed. Joaquín F. Pacheco, Francisco de Cárdenas, and Luis Torres de Mendoza, 42 vols. (Madrid: Manuel G. Hernández, 1864-1884), 10:381. Henceforth referred to as *CDIR*.

14. Valdés, 130.

15. Jane Goodall, *The Chimpanzees of Gombe: Patterns of Behavior* (Cambridge, MA, and London: Belknap Press of Harvard University Press, 1986), 75.

16. Jane van Lawick-Goodall, *In the Shadow of Man* (Boston: Houghton Mifflin, 1971), 122.

17. Jane Goodall, *Through a Window: My Thirty Years with the Chimpanzees of Gombe* (Boston: Houghton Mifflin, 1990), 210.

18. Stephen Haliczer, *The Comuneros of Castile: The Forging of a Revolution, 1475-1521* (Madison: University of Wisconsin Press, 1981), 178.

19. Goodall, *Chimpanzees of Gombe*, 424; Wilson, 545-46.

20. Haliczer, 172-79.

21. A 1480 *cédula* ordered the evacuation of enclosures set up by farmers under Henry IV, while nine years later an ordinance called the "Defense of the Cañadas" redrew sheepwalk boundaries to expel squatting farmers. In 1491 an edict banned agricultural enclosures in Granada. See Jaime Vincens Vives, *An Economic History of Spain*, trans. Frances M. López-Morillas (Princeton, NJ: Princeton University Press, 1969), 302-4.

22. Haliczer, 211-23.

23. Ibid., 211-12.

24. "Sentencia contra Pedro de Sotomayor . . . y su ejecución en Medina del Campo á 13 de octubre de 1522," *Colección de documentos inéditos para la historia de España*, ed. M. F. Navarrete et al., 112 vols. (Madrid: Imprenta de la viuda de Calero, 1842-1895), 11:459.

25. In addition, after 1550 the Mesta experienced economic decline as the rise in Castilian prices and overall inflation in the maintenance and husbanding of sheep joined royal revenue demands to make the price of Castilian wool prohibitory abroad. From 1556 to 1561 the Mesta lost 15 percent of its animals. Vincens Vives, 349-50.

26. This is reflected by the number of times Charles V directly linked his revenue demands to the Turkish and Protestant threats. See the following letters found in the *Corpus Documental de Carlos V*: "Carlos V a D. Pedro de la Cueva," Augsburg, October 30, 1530, 1:242-46; "Carlos V a Clemente VII," Augsburg, October 30, 1530, 1:247-50; "Carlos V a Isabel," Spyre, December 6, 1530, 1:256-59; "Carlos V a Alvaro de Lugo," Ratisbon, April 6, 1532, 1:345-46; and "Carlos V a Isabel," Ratisbon, April 6, 1532, 1:349-52.

27. Haliczer, 211-23. For a case study that demonstrates a modicum of regional economic success until the full effects of onerous taxation and military expenditure became evident in the early seventeenth century, see Carla Rahn Phillips, *Ciudad Real, 1500-1750: Growth, Crisis, and Readjustment in the Spanish Economy* (Cambridge: Harvard University Press, 1979), 49, 53-55, 94, 113-16.

28. David E. Vassberg, *Land and Society in Golden Age Castile* (Cambridge: Cambridge University Press, 1984), 18, 191-94; Linda Martz, *Poverty and Welfare in Habsburg Spain: The Example of Toledo* (Cambridge: Cambridge University Press, 1983), 81, 85.

29. Wilson, 565.

30. Jaime Contreras and Gustav Henningsen, "Forty-four Thousand Cases of the Spanish Inquisition (1540-1700): Analysis of a Historical Data Bank," trans. Anne Born, in *The Inquisition in Early Modern Europe*, ed. Gustav Henningsen and John Tedeschi with Charles Amiel (DeKalb: Northern Illinois University Press, 1986), 114.

31. Henry Kamen, *Inquisition and Society in Spain in the Sixteenth and Seventeenth Centuries* (Bloomington: Indiana University Press, 1985), 42.

32. Wilson, 286-87.

33. "Relación de las causas que se han despachado en el Auto Público de Fe (Córdoba, 21 enero 1590)," in *Autos de fe y causas de la inquisición de Córdoba*, ed. Rafael Gracia Boix (Córdoba: Colección de textos para la historia de Córdoba, Publicaciones de la excma. diputación provincial, 1983), 245-47.

34. "Relación de las causas que se han despachado en el Auto de la Fe . . . en la Plaza de la Corredera . . . domingo de la Santisima Trinidad veinte y uno de mayo de mil quinientos y noventa y cinco años," Ibid., 308-10.

35. "Relación (1590)," 224, and "Relación (1595)," 287, in *Autos de fe*, ed. Gracia Boix.

36. Maureen Flynn, "Mimesis of the Last Judgment: The Spanish *Auto de fe*," *The Sixteenth Century Journal* 22:2 (summer 1991): 281-97.

37. Henry Charles Lea, *A History of the Inquisition of Spain*, 4 vols., reprint (New York: American Scholar Publications, 1966), 3: 24-25; Kamen, *Inquisition and Society*, 176.

38. Lea, 26.

39. Flynn, 281.

40. "Relación del Auto General de la Fe que se celebró en la ciudad de Córdoba a dos días del mes de Diciembre deste presente año de 1625," *Autos de fe*, ed. Gracia Boix, 393-94.

41. Kamen, *Inquisition and Society*, 15.

42. Henry Kamen, *The Phoenix and the Flame: Catalonia and the Counter Reformation* (New Haven, CT, and London: Yale University Press, 1993), 231.

43. Here the classic work was done by Bandura and Walters in 1963. After being exposed to an adult mishandling a rubber doll, and after being frustrated with some task, different groups of children all handled a procured doll more aggressively than children who had not been exposed to an aggressive model. Other studies, such as one done by D. J. Hicks in 1965, have demonstrated that the effects are long-lasting. Eibl-Eibesfeldt, *Human Ethology*, 366.

It is important to note that only adults were required to attend an *auto de fe*, but adults exposed to aggression also act aggressively and thereby become models for children. In a state of fear adults may very well act aggressively so as to influence actions then taken by children, who will be predisposed to act aggressively as adults in stressful situations. Likewise, the mere fact that children were not required to attend does not mean that they never saw such a deliberately public spectacle as an *auto de fe*.

44. Arnold P. Goldstein, "United States: Causes, Controls, and Alternatives to Aggression," in *Aggression in Global Perspective*, ed. Arnold P. Goldstein and Marshall H. Segall (New York: Pergamon Press, 1983), 449.

45. Ibid.

46. Irenäus Eibl-Eibesfeldt, *Love and Hate: The Natural History of Behavior Patterns*, trans. Geoffrey Strachan (New York, Chicago, San Francisco: Holt, Rinehart & Winston, 1972), 30.

47. Ibid., 29.

48. Octavio Paz, *The Labyrinth of Solitude: Life and Thought in Mexico*, trans. Lysander Kemp (New York: Grove Press, 1961), 40.

49. Irving A. Leonard, *Books of the Brave: Being an Account of Books and of Men in the Spanish Conquest of the Sixteenth-Century New World* (Berkeley, Los Angeles, Oxford: University of California Press, 1992), 16-19, 42-43, 94-98, 160-62. The first monopolist of the Mexico City book trade, Jacob Cromberger of Seville, left behind a posthumous inventory in 1529 that included 398 "Amadises" valued at 44,376 maravedís and 80 other "Amadises" at 12,000 maravedís. Leonard speculated that the latter group of eighty probably represents another title in an ongoing series of sequels to the original *Amadís de Gaula* in four books. The numbers represented are substantial for the period, and they are repeated in other inventories. *Amadís* was printed and reprinted again and again.

50. Julio Caro Baroja, "Honour and Shame: A Historical Account of Several Conflicts," trans. R. Johnson, in *Honour and Shame: The Values of Mediterranean Society*, ed. J. G. Peristiany (Chicago: University of Chicago Press, 1966), 94-95.

51. Bernal Díaz, *Historia verdadera*, 1:330.

52. *Amadís of Gaul. Books I and II. A Novel of Chivalry of the 14th Century Presumably First Written in Spanish. Revised and Reworked by Garcí Rodríguez de Montalvo prior to 1505*, trans. Edwin B. Place and Herbert C. Behm, 2 vols. (Lexington: University Press of Kentucky, 1974), 1:101.

53. Ibid., 2:173.

54. Ida Altman, "A New World in the Old: Local Society and Spanish Emigration to the Indies," in *"To Make America": European Emigration in the Early Modern Period*, ed. Ida Altman and James Horn (Berkeley, Los Angeles, Oxford: University of California Press, 1991), 38.

55. J. Patrick Gray, *Primate Sociobiology* (New Haven, CT: HRAF Press, 1985), 90-93.

56. Pitirim A. Sorokin, *Social and Cultural Dynamics*, Volume III: *Fluctuation of Social Relationships, War, and Revolution* (New York: American Book Company, 1937), 326-29, 352, 606-11. Also cited in Wilson, 572-73.

3

Aztec Culture

In the early to mid-1450s the Valley of Mexico suffered from the deprivations caused by three to five years of famine. During such a period of trial, awareness of the body and its needs became preeminent in human consciousness. Humanity's fragility and interrelationship with the broader material environment became crystal clear. In Europe, periodic famines and plagues bred special holy rites and penances as Christians tried to make amends for their sins before divine and natural law. In pre-Columbian Mexico similar patterns seemingly existed.[1]

Accounts vary on the specific causes of the Valley of Mexico's Great Famine, but they all indicate immediate causes in nature. The *Anales de Tlatelolco* report five years of crop failure, originating in diseases affecting the lacustrine fauna of Lake Texcoco (an important source of Aztec protein) and followed by early and late frosts that decimated the valley's maize plants. All this culminated in serious drought.[2] The Franciscan friar Diego Durán, for his part, ascribed the food shortage to a lack of rain, and his *Historia* went on to describe epidemics among the Aztec people resulting from their weakened condition and consumption of inedible plants. At the start of the famine, Moctezuma I provided relief to his people from the storage granaries he maintained. Then, when they gave out, he provided one last feast and commended his people to seek their own salvation. According to Durán, many sold their own children into bondage, and others fell dead on the roadside while trying to escape the parched lands of Tenochtitlan. Only the precipitous return of the rains at this point saved the Aztecs from disintegrating as a people. Those who had fled Tenochtitlan returned, and many who had sold their children to other Amerindian groups were able to ransom them back.[3] Ironically, these tragic events followed the glorious successes of Moctezuma I in battle and conquest —successes that still could not hinder the deleterious astrological forces of the Year One Rabbit, the year of the famine's start.[4]

The immediate causes of the famine were acts of nature, but physical nature was, in itself, controlled by the gods. The physical was interpreted in reciprocal relationship with the spiritual, and in this way the Aztecs were very much like the Spaniards. Based on the accounts of his Indian informants, Diego Durán wrote that while the Mexica of Tenochtitlan were still a migratory people, some time before 1193 they settled temporarily, sowed and reaped according to the will of the gods: "If their god decreed a good harvest, then they reaped; if he determined otherwise, they abandoned the fields."[5] When they became a sedentary people in the Valley of Mexico, they believed that the divine will could be read in the stars, an opinion also held by the many Spaniards who accepted astrology.[6] The astrological forces of the Year One Rabbit had brought famine, and the Aztecs believed that they played a role in its manifestation. Hence, the Year One Rabbit brought drought and famine in symmetrical relation to their own corruption as a people.

The macrocosm mirrored the microcosm.[7] Inappropriate acts brought castigation and pestilence upon the community and the individual. Thus, inappropriate sexual behavior might bring disaster, and legal deterrents guarded against adultery and homosexuality. In the language of the Aztec Empire, the Nahuatl word "*cocoxqui*" draws a connection between physical illness and sexual lapses in that it means withered and sick as well as homosexual and effeminate. The sexually corrupt emitted *ihiyotl* (breath and sustenance), which caused *tlazolmiquiliztli*, or "filth death," among children and other weak entities. The cosmos recoiled at aberrant behavior.[8] In the land of corruption, "poverty, misery, uselessness prevail. Destitute are they whose tatters hang from their necks, their hips. . . . Verily they go skin and bones, like a skeleton."[9] The Aztecs believed they were brought low for aberration and corruption, but also for presumption and pride.[10]

In any given social rank, or estate, the ideal type always demonstrated consideration for the good of others, whereas the evil representative of the estate was concerned only with self. Arrogance and corruption were to be eschewed at all costs. Thus, "the good merchant [is] a follower of the routes, a traveller [with merchandise; he is] one who sets correct prices, who gives equal value. He shows respect for things; he venerates people. The bad merchant [is] stingy, avaricious, greedy."[11] "The physician [is] a curer of people, a restorer, a provider of health. . . . The bad physician [is] a fraud . . . a killer with his medicines."[12] Likewise, an evil and stupid craftsman is "a mocker, a petty thief, a pilferer. He acts without consideration; he deceives, he steals."[13] At the very pinnacle of the hierarchy is the good noble, described as he who "loves others, benefits others:" and "The good ruler [is] a protector; one who carries [his subjects] in his arms, who unites them, who brings them together."[14]

Just as Aztec men had their diverse roles to play in the maintenance of their social hierarchy and community, so too women had their specific functions. Across class lines, women were identified as those who made clothing and those who prepared food and chocolate.[15] Again and again, the good noblewoman is described as a protector, one "who guards people." She is called contrite and tender, whereas her evil counterpart is called lewd, drunken, impetuous, foolish, and selfish. The good noblewoman followed the admonitions of her father to do her duty in the face of hardship and suffering.[16] According to the *Florentine Codex*, rulers told their daughters not to forget their domestic roles as women:

Look well to the drink, to the food: how it is prepared, how it is made, how it is improved; the art of good drink, the art of good food, which is called one's birthright. This is the property of—it belongeth to—the lords, the rulers. . . . Look with diligence . . . and thus thou wilt be loved. . . .

Pay good attention to the spindle whorl, the weaving stick, the drink, the food.[17]

Admonished so as not to covet carnal pleasures, the young noblewoman was told to esteem herself as "a precious person," "a precious green stone"—"this, even though thou art a woman."[18] When serving as an administrator or governor, the good noblewoman is "a provider of good conditions, a corrector, a punisher, a chastiser, a reprimander. She is heeded, obeyed; she creates order; she establishes rules."[19] In short, she was expected to be the sustainer of hierarchy, like any noble male, when cast in a public, hierarchical function. She fulfilled a role with which Queen Isabella of Castile was familiar: Bravery itself is not to be denied the good noblewoman.[20] Other respectable women were not expected to have such a public, political function.

Her commoner counterpart was told not to be gaudy in dress and not to be haughty in manner. A chaste helpmate to her husband, she was to avoid cosmetics and drink, to travel the road in tranquility when in public, since "[haste] meaneth restlessness," and cosmetics, drunkenness, and restlessness all indicated the harlot.[21] The *Florentine Codex* does describe the good mature woman as "brave, like a man," but she also "goes in humility." To be a bad female commoner was to be impetuous, given to vice, lazy, impatient, chagrined, and fitful.[22] When taken to the extreme, the worst possible woman, totally lacking in humility, was the public woman, the harlot, who "goes about pushing": "She pushes; she insults; she goes about insulting; she goes about constantly merry, ever on the move, wandering here and there, never coming to repose, unquiet, restless, flighty."[23] Traveling the canals and "disgracing the streets," the harlot nearly became "a part of the marketplace." Rather than being humble, she went about "haughtily, shamelessly." To the Nahua men who were Sahagún's interlocutors in the composition of the *Florentine Codex*, the harlot was much too "pushy" and proud. She was too aggressive to fulfill the gender role assigned women by Aztec society. Submission was meant to be the female role, despite different tendencies within individual women. Only the noblewoman was allowed to surpass the submissive role because of her birth. However, men and noblemen, though taught the ways of aggression, were also taught submission so as to play their appropriate role within the hierarchy. If anything, the Aztecs recognized that innate human traits may be emphasized or subdued by means of education and training. Most women were indoctrinated so as to bring out the tendencies toward submission, whereas men had to balance submission and aggression on the battlefield as a warrior.

Although nobles commanded, they also set an example of humility for others to learn and follow. Alonso de Zorita, an *oidor*, or judge, of the second Audiencia of New Spain (established in 1530), wrote that the Aztecs were long-suffering, obedient, and teachable: "If you blame or scold them for some negligence or vice, they display great humility and attention, and their only reply is, 'I have sinned.' The more noble they are, the more humility they display."[24] Zorita was quick to point out that this was not a function of their conversion to Christianity, for the *tlatoani* (the ruler of the Aztecs) did severe penance upon his election. The Aztecs looked to humility and social reciprocity as a cure, but they also looked to ritual cleansing before the gods. For as long as a year or two, the *tlatoani* served as the scapegoat for Aztec society, bearing the collective guilt of his people, burning incense and being pricked with maguey thorns.[25]

Like the sixteenth-century Spaniard who might make restitution for his sins by performing self-flagellation, the *tlatoani* and other Aztec priests and nobles performed grueling autosacrifices, lacerating ears, tongues, and genitals. Louise Burkhart and other students of Nahuatl have recently made much of how Spanish missionaries had difficulty finding an exact linguistic cognate for "*pecado*," or "sin," yet the actions attached to restitution for inappropriate behavior were quite similar in both cultures. It was understood that "wrong" behavior brought undesirable consequences—that disorderly conduct and perversion were to be punished. In Nahuatl, the word was *tlahuelilocayotl*, from the root *tlahuelli*, meaning anger, frenzy, and a disorderly state of emotion.[26] Evil Nahuas suffered the "madness of Heracles," and it must be remembered that in that state Heracles did evil and killed his family. While Christian theologians might abstract the notion of sin to emphasize the personal responsibility involved, the Christian notion of sin still involves attonement by means of penance for actions deemed inappropriate in the eyes of the Christian deity. It must be noted that although the gods of the Nahuas included the standard tricksters, harlots, and drunkards, the god of the Bible is not above deception (the story of Abraham and Isaac), punishment of the innocent (Job), and genocide (the Israelites' conquest of Canaan). Louise Burkhart assumes a great deal in writing, "The indigenous deities did not, as a group, represent moral authority. . . . The same being could incite immoral behavior and then afflict the wrongdoer."[27] Especially in the earliest written books of the Bible, the biblical god also is more interested in having his will done than in consistent standards of good and evil. No doubt this could justify any amount of evil done by the Spanish Inquisition, just as it might demand the flagellation and other penances of the Inquisition for such an omission as failing to eat pork "like a good Old Christian." Both Aztec and Spanish notions of evil ultimately descended from a need to do right in the sight of power, the divine being the ultimate power. Serving as abstracted dominance, the gods demand appropriate behavior as dominant chimpanzees do within a troop. When disputes arise at Gombe, they often enough come under the scrutiny of other apes intent on stopping hostility within the same band. Thus, "in the conflicts shown at Gombe . . . the impartial intervenors were dominant to both protagonists in 36 out of 39 conflicts, with a top male or alpha male accounting for 23 interventions, all successful."[28]

As has often been noted in the social sciences, the deities do serve as a great cosmic police force. On earth, this role is assumed by the dominant, and among primates it appears that subordinates demand a certain degree of suffering, dedication, and sacrifice on the part of those recognized as elites. At Mahale, Toshisada Nishida noted that the alpha male Kalunde was chased by his friend and ally Musa when he prevented Musa from taking a female's colobus meat. Although Kalunde could have easily intimidated his friend, he climbed a tree and submitted to Musa's display—only mounting a rival named Nsaba in response. For breaking the bonds of friendship in order to defend the female, Kalunde submitted to punishment and penance.[29] Likewise, Aztec elites underwent penance on behalf of peace and order—in this case, cosmic peace and order.

Before Panquetzaliztli, the high festival honoring Huitzilopochtli, the Aztec priests fasted on behalf of their society, asking forgiveness of the god for any affronts to his veneration. The fasting lasted forty days and included a number of ceremonial penances.[30] Fasting was followed by feasting, as the symbolic value of food played a primary role in the communal bonding of the Aztec people. The propitiary sacrifice of captives taken in battle released the priests and the captives' captors from purgative fasting, and musical instruments signaled that the feasting, dancing, and singing could commence.[31] Social hierarchy was reaffirmed through Huitzilopochtli's precedence to the priests and honored warriors. The mortal elite ate only after the god quenched his thirst for blood. In this way the mortal elite demonstrated to the commoners their subordination to divine precepts, but the elite also showed its dedication to the commoners by addressing them with honorifics attached to their names. Polite inversion in speech not only demonstrated social reciprocity; it also protected nobles and priests from being struck down by the gods because of undue magnificence.[32] Therefore, it is not truly surprising that the Nahuas were impressed by the poverty and humility of the first fifteen Franciscans who arrived as missionaries in 1523-1524. Fray Toribio de Benavente even came to be known by a Nahuatl-based nickname, Motolinía, meaning the poor and afflicted one. Through symbolic inversion, these Franciscans gained respect and power, even as the pope still calls himself "the servant of the servants of God." Louise Burkhart writes:

Because they contrast so strikingly with the colonists in their concern for the Indians, the friars have an undeniable appeal to the modern humanist and the Church historian alike. . . . Yet in their own seemingly gentle way they were as ruthless as any conquistador. They supported conquest and colonization in theory; they merely objected to its abuses.[33]

In effect, they did this by reflecting the Nahua vision of the truly noble, just as the friars were impressed by reflections of the "Christian" humility they saw in Nahua behavior. According to the *Florentine Codex*, good noblemen were expected to show humility to those of lesser rank, to the old and the poor, and the *tlatoani*, or "he who possesses speech," was expected to be a loving father to his people. On the day of his coronation, priests prayed that the gods would

open his eyes, open his ears, advise him, set him upon the road. . . . Verily, now, inspire him, for thou makest him thy seat, for he is thy flute. Make him thy replacement, thy image. Let him not there on the reed mat, the reed seat become proud; let him not be quarrelsome. May he in peace and calm go accompanying, leading the common folk. May he not make sport of the common folk. May he not disunite the people; may he not destroy them in vain.[34]

Thus, the *tlatoani*, like the Spanish monarch, was to unite society and promote the common good, maintaining both hierarchy and reciprocity within the Aztec nation. In his *Historia*, Diego Durán, like the friar Sahagún and his informants in the *Florentine Codex*, portrayed the *tlatoani*'s role as that of loving father, a shelter for widows and orphans. A speech he ascribed to an Aztec elder upon the death of the *tlatoani* Acamapichtli, circa 1404, is a paraphrase of the *Florentine Codex*'s priestly prayer.[35] The *tlatoani*, according to Tlacaelel's funeral oration upon the death of Moctezuma I, "was like one who carries a load upon his back for a time . . . like a slave subjected to his master/ Sheltering and defending this republic."[36] In Alonso de Zorita's *Brief and Summary Relation of the Lords of New Spain*, the *tlatoani* was described once again in these terms. Drawing on Aztec informants, Zorita wrote that upon his coronation the high priest admonished the *tlatoani* to consider the honor done him by his vassals and to protect them like his children.[37] Lesser lords approached the *tlatoani* by beseeching him to remember his upright forefathers and to emulate them in protecting his subjects. In touch with the sacred and set apart from the rest of society by means of special status and sacrifice, the *tlatoani* was seen as the arbiter of justice and above particular interests. According to Zorita, the *tlatoani* was an instrument of divine justice, sent to protect the weak and punish the guilty.[38] It was his task to lead Aztec society in ritual cleansing before the gods and to provide for those in need. Communal food-sharing became a method of communal bonding, and during the feast of Uey tecuilhuitl, humble Mexica laborers and the poor gathered to receive freely distributed food.[39] On a daily basis, simple acts of charity served as signs of the reciprocal relations among the ranks:

If any poor vassal, who made bold to hail the ruler, greeted him pleasingly, then [the ruler] commanded the majordomo to give him a cape, a breech clout, and a place for him to sleep, and that which he might drink and eat.[40]

{Reprinted, by permission, from the *Florentine Codex: General History of the Things of New Spain* by Fray Bernardino de Sahagún. Book 8: Kings and Lords, p. 59. Translated by Arthur J. O. Anderson and Charles E. Dibble. Copyright 1954 by the School of American Research, Santa Fe.}

For the Aztecs, the reaffirmation of cosmic harmony was manifested in numerous feasts where food and alms were distributed and where prisoners of war were sacrificed as gifts and food for the gods. On some days as many as two thousand to eight thousand men may have been sacrificed.[41] Wars were initiated to accumulate tribute for the gods: both in the form of human sacrifices to appease the bloodlust of gods like Huitzilopochtli and Tlaloc, and in the form of special tributary items indispensable for the lavish rites and giftgiving surrounding the veneration of Huitzilopochtli and other gods.[42] Like that of their Spanish conquerors, the Aztec cosmic vision was a web of intricate interrelations. According to Durán, when their husbands went off to battle, Aztec women prayed that Huitzilopochtli would remember "his servant," since he had gone off to "offer blood in that sacrifice which is war."[43] As with the Spaniards, warfare was viewed as a holy act and a support to both religion and empire. The warrior, as in so many other cultures, was sacrificing himself to a cause deemed greater than himself, and women were asked to approve of this blood sacrifice.

At birth, the midwife greeted a male infant with war cries, and with the hope that he would meet the "flowery death" of the warrior in battle or as a sacrifice to the Sun. Most Aztec males were part-time warriors, also serving society as merchants, artisans, and even priests, but professional warriors were also present in Tenochtitlan: They were the nobles and the famed and honored Jaguar and Eagle warriors. On the battlefields, warriors were easily distinguished from each other on the basis of display. The more captives taken in battle, the more elaborate was one's attire as a warrior. Until finally one might perhaps become a formidable Eagle or Jaguar warrior, garbed in cotton-padded feathers and pelts, and fighting in the shadow of totemic animals. The element of awe-inspiring display in all this should not be minimized. Although the historian Inga Clendinnen fails to make use of sociobiology or primatology, she is quick to point out that "'Fortune' came through battle," providing tributary material rewards, sexual rewards, and "a desirable Mexica girl for marriage." Most importantly perhaps, a warrior, like a dominant rhesus, received "prestige, honor, fame."[44] Nahua warriors fought as individuals for these things, and "intervention to aid a companion who was being worsted was liable to be interpreted as an attempt to pirate his captive, and to be accordingly resented."[45] In turn, if one was captured alive, the goal of much battlefield activity, one faced the final act of brutality and aggressive display: human sacrifice.

The Crucifixion, and its reenactment in the Holy Eucharist, is a blood sacrifice; its major distinction from Aztec blood sacrifice is that the deity involved sacrifices himself to himself in order to end any human need to sacrifice the creatures of this world. Still, in its interpretation by Christians, Jesus's sacrifice remains a purging of "sin and evil" (that peculiar inappropriateness inherent in the Judaeo-Christian-Islamic tradition), and participation in communion is, on one level, a symbol of the Christian community's purified union before God. Besides sacrificing victims to Huitzilopochtli, the Aztecs also partook of the symbolic consumption of their chief deity on his feast day, Panquetzaliztli. An image of Huitzilopochtli made out of amaranth seed dough was broken and consumed:

His heart was apportioned to Moctezuma. And as for the rest of his members, which were made, as it were, to be his bones, they were distributed and divided up among all. Two parts were given the Tlatelulca. . . . And as much was given to the Tenochca. And afterwards it was divided up among them, to each in his order. . . . And [of] this which they ate, it was said: "The god is eaten." And of those who ate it, it was said: "They guard the god."[46]

{Reprinted, by permission, from the *Florentine Codex: General History of the Things of New Spain* by Fray Bernardino de Sahagún. Book 3: The Origin of the Gods, p. 6. Translated by Arthur J. O. Anderson and Charles E. Dibble. Copyright 1978 by the School of American Research, Santa Fe.}

Of course, the noblemen and leading merchants also partook of the flesh of human sacrifices at the various Aztec feasts, and both the symbolic consumption of Huitzilopochtli and ritual cannibalism were perceived by the Spanish clerical chroniclers as demon-inspired perversions of communion. In their own separate ways both communion and the Aztec rituals served as means to mystical union with the divine and with other members of society.

In lands beset by periodic hunger, food and eating were layered with a multiplicity of meanings. Periodically themselves the victims of famine and food shortages throughout the fifteenth and sixteenth centuries, some Spaniards, like the Aztecs, also ascribed their suffering to divine retribution for society's wrongdoing. Their response to plagues and famines included votive masses and public spectacles of penance and flagellation.[47] The needs of body and spirit were inextricably linked, just as the individual and society were bound, and nature and society paralleled and reflected each other. To sixteenth-century Spaniards, acts of nature were acts of God, or of Satan. If the mass could stop famine and plague, comets and the birth of deformed "monsters" were portents of famine, pestilence, war, and death. The evil befalling a Christian European king could be foretold in nature, just as the Aztecs foresaw the coming of Cortés and the Spaniards in a series of evil omens.[48] In pre-Columbian Nahua thought, life was never portrayed as one endless idyll.

Four previous suns and their universes had died, and the earth's fifth sun was doomed to extinction at the end of one of the Aztecs' fifty-two-year-calendar cycles. Flux permeated the cosmos, and the struggle to prevent the sun's extinction required the offering of human blood. Just as maize was watered by Tlaloc, providing food for humanity, so too the liquid blood provided sustenance for the gods. It was a fertilizing resource, and when it was deliberately shed, it served as "'most precious water.'"[49] Thus were the matrices of cosmic hierarchy and reciprocity defined in brutality.

Aside from the all too common human displays of aggression found on the battlefields of history and the parade grounds of military preparedness, humans sometimes take aggression and display to the level of terror-invoking art form. The Holy Office of the Spanish Inquisition, as well as the punishments prescribed by other Spanish courts of law, must clearly be seen in this light. Likewise, unless the Nahuas of central Mexico were a different species of humanity, the act of human sacrifice must be seen as a type of terrorism used to maintain power and reputation.

Evidence of human sacrifice in Mesoamerica dates back thousands of years to the hunter-gatherers of the Tehuacan Valley. In central Mexico's Classic period (200-800 AD), there are artistic protrayals of military orders, the major participants in human sacrifice in Aztec times. At the Classic site of Tula and at other sites there are skull racks, which were used by the Aztecs to display the heads of sacrificial victims and chacmools, or reclining stone figures with cavities in their stomachs. The chacmools were used in Aztec times to receive the hearts of sacrificial victims. By the time the Mexica Aztecs arrived in central Mexico, human sacrifice was an important part of the display of power.[50]

What history commonly refers to as the Aztec Empire was actually a political alliance of three city-states: Tenochtitlan-Tlatelolco, Texcoco, and Tlacopan (also called Tacuba). Centered at Lake Texcoco, the leading city in the alliance appears to have originally been Texcoco, but around the 1440s Tenochtitlan appears to have gained ascendancy in the alliance. The inhabitants of all these cities were Nahuas, speakers of the Amerindian language Nahuatl, and those of Tenochtitlan-Tlatelolco were also called Mexica, originally a small group of wandering nomads from the north who seem to have entered the central valley sometime in the thirteenth century. First serving as hired mercenaries to the Tepanecs of Azcapotzalco, the Mexica rose to power with their allies around 1428, defeating the previously dominant Tepanecs. The Aztec Empire they created in turn was quite different from standard European notions of imperialism. Territories defeated in battle were cowed more than they were conquered.[51] Tribute was collected and annual payment schedules were established, but rebellion against Aztec dominance was constant. Moreover, it was desired, since rebellion created opportunity for battle and the acquisition of human sacrifices to sustain the Sun, Tonatiuh, and the other gods. If humans required Tlaloc's rain, Cihuacoatl's fertility, and Tonatiuh's light for their food, the deities also required sustenance in the form of human hearts and blood. This became the theological explanation for the constant warfare, tribute collection, and aggressive display pursued by Aztec warriors, by the groups they subordinated, and by recalcitrant enemies like the Nahuatl-speaking inhabitants of Tlaxcala, who would prove vital allies to the Spaniards.

Anthropologists like Geoffrey Conrad and Arthur Demarest are quick to point out that human sacrifice was a well-integrated part of the Nahua worldview, and of the Aztec justification of tribute collection and the growth of a tributary "empire." Aztec individuals and the alliance collectively were seen as deserving rewards for the valiant service they did, promoting the sun's health and preventing its passing away like four suns before it. They served the source of human sustenance and thereby served greater humanity by extension. Aztec warriors also knew that they might see their lives end on a sacrificial altar belonging to enemies like the Tlaxcalans, for aggressive display permeated all of central Mexico. It is estimated that a minimum of perhaps fifteen thousand persons were sacrificed each year in central Mexico.[52] The most-honored victims were the warriors.

In 1487 the Mexica chief speaker, or *tlatoani*, Ahuizotl and the leaders of Tenochtitlan's two allied cities sacrificed a minimum of ten thousand captives in a massive bloodfest that lasted four days.[53] Whether warrior captives, Mexica children, slaves, or social deviants, sacrifices were people deemed different from the dominant warriors, as Inga Clendinnen points out.[54] Although a brave enemy might first be honored with special care, sexual partners, and a special role in the ritual impersonation of a god, the fate was always the same.

In the words of the sixteenth-century *Florentine Codex*, compiled by Nahuas under the direction of the Franciscan friar Bernardino de Sahagún, warriors who had captured prisoners held an all-night vigil for their captives. Then on the day of sacrifice, in this case in the month of Tlaxcaipeualiztli, the prisoners were taken by their captors to the priests at the temple of the Mexica totemic deity Huitzilopochtli, a deity who was also associated with Tonatiuh, the Sun:

Those who slew them were the priests. Those who had taken them captive did not kill them; they only brought them as tribute, only delivered them as offerings; [the priests] went laying hold of their heads, and seizing [the hair of] their heads. Thus they went leading them up to the top of the temple.

And when some captive faltered, fainted, or went throwing himself upon the ground, they dragged him.

And when one showed himself strong, not acting like a woman, he went with a man's fortitude; he bore himself like a man; he went speaking in a manly fashion; he went exerting himself; he went strong of heart and shouting, not without courage nor stumbling, but honoring and praising his city.[55]

{Reprinted, by permission, from the *Florentine Codex: General History of the Things of New Spain* by Fray Bernardino de Sahagún. Book 2: The Ceremonies, pp. 46-47. Translated by Arthur J. O. Anderson and Charles E. Dibble. Copyright 1981 by the School of American Research, Santa Fe.}

Despite such bravery, or perhaps because of it, the "manly victim" met the same fate as the "womanly" coward. Six priests threw him on the sacrificial stone and proceeded to cut open his breast to remove his heart.

Amazingly, analyses of human sacrifice often focus on the "manly victim" and even on the "care and pride" with which captors nurtured their captives before the sacrifice. Inga Clendinnen is no exception. She does stress the way a captor addressed his victim as "beloved son," and she does argue that the captor shed tears for his own potential fate as a sacrificial victim, not for the captive's immediate fate. However, she speculates that victims "were often enough teased into anger and so to high performance"; that "most" warriors tethered to a stone to fight with blunted and useless weapons "seem to have performed adequately"; and if the victim died well, "his name would be remembered and his praises sung in the warrior houses of his home city."[56] Unlike Clendinnen, Tzvetan Todorov states that the sacrifice must not be too alien—that captor and captive must be understood as "neither identical nor totally different." Thus, Todorov emphasizes identity, whereas Clendinnen stresses the other side of the coin. Todorov also identifies sacrifice as a "religious murder" that "testifies to the power of the social fabric, to its mastery over the individual." For Todorov, human sacrifice is to be contrasted with Spanish atrocities or massacres, which show social decay in the group committing the massacre. With massacres, the group's moral coherence is called into question, and the violence committed should be performed in remote places where the alien nature of the victim is not in question. Massacres occur where European imperialism occurs, and Todorov points out how Spaniards committed their atrocities in the Americas and in Italy, some distance from Spain.[57] Likewise, David E. Stannard, in his *American Holocaust*, first presents las Casas's argument that Spaniards were wont to exaggerate human sacrifice in order to justify their own abuses, and he then argues that "modern scholars have begun to support the view that the magnitude of sacrifice was indeed greatly exaggerated." He goes on to write, "Even if the annual figure of 20,000 were correct, however, in the siege of Tenochtitlán the invading Spaniards killed twice that many people in a single day—including (unlike Aztec sacrifice) enormous numbers of innocent women, children, and the aged."[58]

That the Spaniards committed brutalities and atrocities is unquestionable. However, to imply a lack of infant sacrifice among the Nahuas is unconscionable, especially after claiming that there is no gain in countering "the anti-Indian propaganda that dominates our textbooks with pro-Indian propaganda of equally dubious veracity."[59] Although 20,000 were probably not killed under the direction of Ahuizotl during four days in 1487, anthropologists like Geoffrey Conrad and Arthur Demarest estimate the most conservative number possible to have been somewhere around 10,000.[60] It is also significant to note that the postconquest Nahua source Ixtlilxochitl estimated 80,400. Conrad and Demarest see this number as "Mexica propaganda aggrandizing the event." The sacrifice was to dedicate the Great Temple of Huitzilopochtli, and the dedication iconography at the spot refers to some 20,000.[61] If anything, these figures compare with those of many other human cultures, including the Spaniards. Humans are capable of brutal displays, and Conrad and Demarest write: "Faced with such gruesome rituals and alien concepts [as human sacrifice], not only the Spanish friars but many modern ethnohistorians have had great difficulty in trying to analyze Aztec warfare and sacrifice objectively."[62]

They then go on to state that human sacrifice was a "rational phenomenon" that supported Aztec self-imagining and, through tribute, "the specific political and economic interests of the people and the state." While the elaborate nature of the human sacrifice display included numerous aspects of learned culture, its fundmental basis, like that of the Spanish Inquisition, was a far more primal urge to display potency. Rationality and rationalization only served thereby as super-structures and elaborations on a core aggression accepted by so many biologists and rejected by so many social scientists. It is in fact surprising that so little is made of the honorable captive's "manly behavior." As demonstrated in the above citation from the *Florentine Codex*, the victim's "fortitude," "strength," and "manly fashion" are contrasted to unseemly behavior that is referred to as "womanly."[63] In the twentieth century, scholars will never know how many sacrifices truly acted so "bravely," just as it will never truly be known to what extent *copal* and other drugs given to many victims induced a certain level of docility. However, given the findings of ethology, it can be argued that human sacrifice displayed the victors' reputation and power for all to see, while also giving the "most manly" among the vanquished a last chance to display. Many levels of human behavior and cosmological meaning met at the nexus that was the Aztec Templo Mayor. In the words of Eduardo Matos Moctezuma:

In summary, the four themes addressed here show that the Templo Mayor is a physical manifestation of the birth and triumph of Huitzilopochtli and the need for human sacrifice to reenact this mythological event. The temple expresses the agricultural requirements of the Mexica for water and sun, and it reflects clearly the economic and political power Tenochtitlan exercised over other people; it is a place of glory for the Mexica and of disgrace for those who were subjugated.[64]

Unlike so many other animals, however, human aggressive display may actually result in killing to dramatize the point of dominance. In wild chimpan-zees, as demonstrated by both Goodall and de Waal, display minimizes actual fights, violence, and deaths.[65] In the human case study at hand, display also serves as a threat and a statement of reputation, but it involves actual death. Could this be because human learning allows us to imprint in far greater detail where causal sequences are concerned? Recent comparative studies between human infants and chimpanzees suggest this.

In a study that requires the subjects to flip a rake in order to appropriate a piece of fruit, a human infant and a chimpanzee are both shown that the rake must first be turned over to entrap and drag the fruit. The human infant assimilates this information and succeeds at the task, whereas the chimpanzee must learn by his own trial and error.[66] While chimpanzees may not recognize that charging and brandishing displays normally do not lead to any actual injury, humans may actually learn to discount constant threats without conse-quences. Actual killing in support of one's territory and reputation may thereby be more required of human beings than of other primates. Indeed, in recent U.S. history, President Bill Clinton was actually called to task for delaying the implementation of real violence in Bosnia-Hersegovina, for relying only on threats not taken seriously by the Bosnian Serbs. Given the immense ability of humans to learn, and through learning to develop cultures far more complex than those of the chimpanzees, one is forced to hypothesize that human displays and human aggressive behavior might exaggerate themselves on occasion in order to command the desired attention. This may have been the case for Aztec human sacrifice, and it may also have been the case for the Holy Office of the Spanish Inquisition.

It must also be recognized that both Mesoamerican human sacrifice and the purging of heretics are clearly instances of instrumental brutality and aggression. As classified by psychologists, instrumental aggression assumes that the aggressor is trying to maximize benefits and minimize costs—that the sort of cost-benefit analysis so often assumed by sociobiology is actually operative. Thus, the Spanish Inquisition maintained "true religion," but Mexica human sacrifice maintained the cosmos. Both were premeditated so as to maximize perceived benefits. They were not instances of emotional or hostile aggression, which are characterized by relatively involuntary outbursts.[67] Although hostility was no doubt present and aimed at the victims of brutality, hostility itself easily blends with other behaviors. In the words of Jerome Kagan:

Although physical assault, verbal criticism and dominance are popular outcomes of anger and hostility, less frequently, sexual behavior, mastery, seeking of recognition and accumulation of wealth and signs of status are used to gratify hostility motives. Indeed, any time a person believes he can hurt another by gaining a particular resource that the resented one values, the basis for an instrumental aggressive action is created. But many of these aggressive behaviors can also be the product of other motives— affiliation or sexuality, for example. Hence many responses that appear to gratify hostility do not always do so, and most of these psycho-dynamically complex behaviors are ambiguous with respect to their primary motivational origin.[68]

If anything, humans are overdetermined creatures, with the full complexities of our genetic encoding still to be mapped. Aggression and brutality are often enough the expressions of mixed motivation, therefore explaining the causal debates that often enough arise in the confused literature of the social sciences. Still, it is quite apparent that learning and culture are immense influences on human self-expression. Therefore, the routinizing and romanticizing of violence and brutality have their impact, and without a doubt both the Spaniards and Mexica were guilty of such cultural constructs, exacerbating the aggressive tendency within humanity.

If Sahagún's *Florentine Codex* is any indication, the Mexica readily and openly recognized the brutality and aggression inherent in a warrior's life. Thus: "The good, the true brave man [is] one who stands as a man, who is firm of heart, who charges, who strikes out at [the foe]. He stands as a man, he rallies, he takes courage; he charges, he strikes out at the foe. He fears no one, none can meet his gaze."[69] And: "The good valiant warrior [is] a sentinel, a strategist, a tracker, a seeker of roads [to the foe], a skirmisher, a taker of captives. He commands respect; he spreads—implants—fear; he terrorizes; he takes captives; he is reckless."[70]

A number of characteristics stand out in both these statements. The brave warrior "stands as a man," striking terror in the hearts of the enemy. His main objective is the destruction of the foe. In this respect, his role is similar to that of any charging male lion in hot pursuit of the hyenas that would disrupt the life of the pride; and through their recognition of humanity's place in nature, the Mexica were even explicit about this. The bravest warriors attained the status of Eagle or Jaguar warriors, who could not retreat in battle, and who were characterized as "scarred, painted, courageous, brave, resolute."[71] In turn, this much-praised animal ferocity in defense of the Mexica people, and of their expansionist interests, was reinforced by a warrior's self-discipline. The good commander is described as "a holder of vigil," and a Mexica warrior's vigil bore both similarities and differences to the European cult of chivalry's idealized nights of fasting and prayer. Mexica men in vigil were known to cut their ears, pierce their bodies with maguey thorns, and cut their flesh with obsidian so as to pull straws through the wounds.[72] The warrior was "glorified" through his own personal scars and pain, as well as through the pain he inflicted, and although some doubt the veracity of the Codex Mendoza's portrayal of the disciplining of children, it may very well have been that warriors were brutalized since childhood. According to the Codex Mendoza, children were punished by being held bound over a fire of chilis; by being pierced with maguey thorns; and by being thrown naked into icy puddles. Inga Clendinnen accepts the veracity of all this, arguing, "It was a dour world for which the children were being prepared, where discipline, especially for males, would be tough, physical and immediate."[73] Famines, disease, and war plagued the peoples of Mesoamerica, and it may have actually been some comfort to revel in their very harsh human condition. Again, in Clendinnen's words, "we have that extraordinary Mexica determination to transcend painful emotion not by suppression, but by its acknowledgment."[74]

Interestingly enough, and reflective upon the fact that any Mexica male could fight in battle, the good warrior is sharply distinguished from the good noble. Although nobles received superior training and armament and were expected to fight, their prime characteristics as nobles were not related to aggression or brutality. As nobles, they were expected to be the purveyors of reciprocity, just as dominant male chimpanzees engage in food-sharing and the settlement of disputes. The good noble is described as one who is "withdrawn," living in quiet and peace. He speaks calmly; "is a shelter"; and he is explicitly a provider for the people in need: "The good one of noble lineage [is] an attendant upon others, a server of food, a provider of nourishment. He sustains one, he serves food, he provides comfort, he provides solace."[75]

In juxtaposition, a method used throughout the Florentine Codex in describing the good and the bad, the bad noble "eats to excess" and is "stingy." In a land that could be beset by famine and physical human suffering, the ability to withstand trials was balanced with a call to provide solace to one's people. The good noble was to set an example and thereby receive honor and praise. Reciprocity and sharing within the ranks were meant to bind the wounds caused by brutality and violence. Likewise, other male primates are known to balance aggression and assurance in acts of reconciliation within their bands. Although chimpanzees can kill in interband conflicts, within a healthy band attempts are made by the dominant to maintain unity. Early in her ground-breaking studies, Jane Goodall noticed this, asking why an attacked individual will interact with the attacker soon after the act of brutality: "The secret perhaps lies in the fact that, although a male chimpanzee is quick to threaten or attack a subordinate, he is usually equally quick to calm his victim with a touch, a pat on the back, an embrace of reassurance."[76]

Like Goodall's Gombe chimpanzees, the Mexica focused on immediate natural experiences. Thus, human sacrifice provided sustenance for the gods, just as the gods provided sustenance for humanity through rain and sunlight. The cycles of nature were everywhere and immediate, and the good man as a human being was capable of both great brutality and kindness—of a wild swing of emotions and actions. Rather than being completely alien to the Spanish conquerors, Mexica behavior evoked a level of mutual understanding. Both Spaniards and the Mexica lived as human animals given to displays of aggression and kindness, and both cultures interpreted their behavior through mental prisms given to political and social theology.

On earth, hierarchy and reciprocity were defined by means of the rituals already discussed and by means of aspects of material culture like food, clothing, and shelter. Vertically, the Aztec social organism could be divided into nobles and priests, leading merchants called *pochtecah*, and commoners called *macehualtin* (the Spanish "*maceguales*"). However, social organization was more complex than this schema alone would allow. Priesthood and high-ranking warrior status could be earned, but special schools, detailed training, and the best armaments favored the children of the nobility in the attainment of status. All males were warriors, sacrificers, and sacrifices to the gods, but only a small number could attain the special status ascribed to such warriors as those of the Eagle or the Jaguar. Although the local wards and neighborhoods —*calpolli*—of various communities continued to adhere to common rituals and customs, including relief to the *calpolli*'s impoverished and preparation for war, the *tlatoani*, or chief speaker, of Tenochtitlan also maintained his systems of relief and ritual. The city or town, the *altepetl*, was little more than a loose confederation of equal constituent parts in Mesoamerican tradition, and in places like Tlaxcala, such decentralization continued unabated.[77] But in the Aztec tributary empire, local ties competed with the bonds of empire, even as they did among the Spaniards. After 1428 the Mexica *tlatoani* of Tenochtitlan had to struggle for an Aztec hegemony, even as Ferdinand and Isabella struggled to do likewise on the Iberian Peninsula.

Aztec hegemony was based on battlefield success and on the sacrifice of hearts to keep the gods appeased, but it was also based on the payment of tribute to the Mexica of Tenochtitlan. It was a discourse of exchange and commerce that literally bound the Aztec tributary empire.[78] The language of exchange, however, functioned on a multiplicity of levels, all the way from trade in ceremonial luxury items and slaves to local craftspeople and farmers who sold their wares in the marketplace. The *Florentine Codex* lists tortilla sellers, sellers of coarse maguey-fiber capes, gourd sellers, sandal sellers, clay workers and basket makers.[79] Zorita's *Brief and Summary Relation* borrowed from Cortés's second letter to the Emperor Charles V, stating that Tenochtitlan had numerous plazas open to trade: "'One of these squares is twice as large as that of Salamanca and is surrounded by arcades where there are daily more than sixty thousand souls buying and selling.'" The commodities exchanged included "'foodstuffs, jewels of gold and silver, lead, brass, copper, tin, stone, bones, shells, and feathers.'"[80]

Many of the goods of Tenochtitlan's markets originated as tribute. The one nearly universal item of tribute received by the Aztecs was textiles, and the textiles provided were of the finest quality, to be worn by nobles alone.[81] Nigel Davies writes that Aztec military ambitions focused on "preciosities" for use by the elite and for use in ceremonial ritual. Feathers, cacao, gold, jadeite, and turquoise (what we today would deem luxury items) were the items of preference in Aztec tributary lists.[82] To this list, Diego Durán's *Historia* adds "exceedingly rich mantles for the lords, differently woven and worked," high quality women's clothing, colors and dyes, building materials, cotton armor, and weapons. Foodstuffs—maize, beans, chian seeds, amaranth seeds, and chili—were provided by certain tributaries, while the less settled sent wild animals, including parrots, eagles, buzzards, ocelots, jaguars, wildcats, snakes, and even scorpions and spiders. "Provinces that lacked foodstuffs and clothes paid in maidens, girls and boys, who were divided among the lords—all slaves."[83]

While the Aztec *macehualtin* could expect some tributary foodstuffs to satisfy their dietary needs, the lords of Tenochtitlan received luxuries sought after by *pochtecah* who served as their auxiliaries in conquest and tributary domination. Some of the leading Aztec merchants even served as spies in search of preferred items of tribute. These disguised merchants took on the appearance of the local population in order to determine the wealth of the region and its general characteristics. Upon returning to Tenochtitlan, they made their report to the principal merchants, and the wheels were set in motion for conquest if the Aztec lords found the area valuable for tributary reasons. The Aztec economy rested on trade and tribute paid in fairly reasonable quantities, and the principal merchants and vanguard merchants, described as the companions of governors, were the dealers in the luxury items vital to Aztec religious ceremony.[84] As Pedro Carrasco has argued, Mesoamerica experienced no separation of economic, religious, and political institutions comparable to that present in industrial society. To divide the religious from the economic would be artificial, and much of the tribute came to be displayed at

Tenochtitlan's chief place of worship, the Templo Mayor.[85] However, on the whole, forced trade and tribute permitted the Aztecs to balance their commercial accounts with other independent Amerindian groups, and a proportion of the tributary levy provided many with labor, which actually may have benefited the conquered Amerindian peoples to some extent, providing surplus labor among them with the task of producing goods for their Aztec masters.[86] Upon defeating Tepeaca, the Aztecs were promised maize, chili, pumpkin seeds, cloth, sandals, deerskins, carriers, workmen, and sacrificial slaves in perpetuity.[87] For his part, Moctezuma I also had something to offer Tepeaca in exchange. His councilor and brother Tlacaelel announced to the lords of Tepeaca that Moctezuma wished to bring honor to their city:

The king also wishes that a great market place be built in Tepeaca so that all the merchants of the land may trade there on an appointed day. In this market there will be sold rich cloth, stones, jewels, feather work of different colors, gold, silver and other metals, the skins of animals such as jaguars and ocelots, cacao, fine loincloths and sandals.[88]

All this commercial exchange between conquerors and conquered came under the direct supervision of both Aztec nobles and leading merchants: "As were noblemen, so also were the merchants, capable and enterprising."[89] Moctezuma assigned a noble governor to Tepeaca, while Aztec merchants were provided with a marketplace in which to deal. The merchants also did their part by having incited the war with Tepeaca. The killing of Aztec merchants by the Tepeacans, as well as by other potential tributary groups, was used as a justification for conquest. Durán failed to see this, and he thought that the constant slaying of Aztec vanguard merchants was an unfortunate accident that led to wars the Aztecs did not want.[90] Zorita, on the other hand, wrote that the Aztecs possessed a series of criteria that had to be met in order to declare war justly. All the elders and warriors convened as the *tlatoani* proposed his reasons for waging war. Trivial reasons were rejected, but the murders of merchants or royal messengers, among other things, were grounds for just war.[91] Nigel Davies and other contemporary scholars have since demonstrated that other Indian groups viewed the Aztec vanguard merchants as precursors to invasion. Often the slayings were anticipated by both sides involved.

The leading merchants were compensated for their efforts by being assigned a rank of distinction within the Aztec hierarchy. They formed a distinct order, with social responsibilities ascribed them that would be familiar to late medieval and early modern Spanish merchants:

And thus was it that the work of the principal merchants became precisely that they cared for the market place. They sponsored the common folk, so that none might suffer, might be deceived, tricked, mistreated. These same pronounced judgment upon him who deceived others in the market place, who cheated them in buying and selling.

Or they punished the thief. And they regulated well everything: all in the market place
which was sold; what the price would be.[92]

Aside from price regulation and quality control in the marketplace of
Tenochtitlan, the leading merchants also possessed the privilege of trying and
punishing any of their own number. They could even assign the death penalty
if they saw fit. In a number of ways their self-regulatory powers resembled
those of a Spanish merchant guild, or *consulado*, which normally possessed
fueros, or privileges, in the areas of justice, quality control, and price regulation.[93] Of course, it could well be argued, as it has been by Américo Castro and
others, that the Castilian mentality would never identify merchants as being
honorable like noblemen. This can be debated, however, since Ruth Pike and
others have demonstrated that Castilian nobles were not adverse to entering
into large-scale trading ventures.[94] Sevillian nobles were intensely involved in
New World shipping, and the mighty Mesta itself was a monopolistic, privileged guild of producers. The fact of the matter is that Sahagún's Indian
interlocutors may have been presenting a view entirely alien to the Spaniards
when they presented noblemen and merchants as being equally "capable and
enterprising." But it is more likely that they held the same complex attitudes
that the Spaniards held, both derrogating and taking an active interest in trade.
In other passages of the *Florentine Codex* it can be determined that the capa-
bilities of merchants and nobles were valued at different levels. Noble warriors
alone could consume the flesh of captives taken in battle. Merchants who had
not participated in combat themselves ate the flesh of purchased slaves sacrificed during the feast of Panquetzaliztli.[95]

The intimate relationship of the nobility and the principal merchants, or
pochtecah, was reflected by the fact that the *pochtecah* dealt in clothing marked
by the insignias of the Aztec nobility and warrior estates:

The good principal merchant . . . seeks out . . . the fresh, the new, the good, the strong,
the designed—designed capes, capes to be worn; those of a weave not compressed;
those of a ball-court eagle design, those with a sun design on them- provided with
suns; ocelot capes—the ocelot, the eagle stand thereon; those with a design of scattered
feathers, a design of stone discs, a scattered flower design.[96]

Clothing of great value marked the Aztec nobility as a group set apart from
the rest of the populace, and value was ascribed to this clothing because it was
the chosen apparel of the Aztec nobility. For example, feathers received in
tribute were used in warrior costumes, and featherworkers were equated with
the leading merchants. They lived side by side with those merchants, occasionally worked at the palace itself, and were permitted to sacrifice purchased
slaves. These craftspeople were so highly valued because of their indispens-
ability, feathers being the necessary mark of distinction in any Aztec noble's
vestments. When Moctezuma's messengers wished to honor Cortés as the god
Quetzalcoatl, they dressed him in a "turquoise mosaic serpent mask; with it

went the quetzal feather head fan. . . . And they gave him, and placed upon his arm, the shield . . . on whose [lower] rim went spread quetzal feathers and a quetzal feather flag."⁹⁷ No Aztec commoner was permitted feathers, articles of distinction worn in the public space of the temple grounds and battlefields.

In his *Historia*, Diego Durán wrote that in accordance with the laws issued under Moctezuma I and his brother Tlacaelel, only the *tlatoani* and Tlacaelel could be shod in the palace. Only the *tlatoani* could wear a gold diadem in Tenochtitlan, and he alone could wear cotton mantles with threads of different colors and featherwork. The common *maceguales* were not allowed to wear cotton clothing under pain of death, and they were also forbidden self-adornment with gold jewelry. Clothing of maguey fiber was their lot. House construction and embellishment also was restricted so that only nobles were permitted a second storey and gables. At the royal palace itself, commoners were allowed to enter only to perform menial tasks, according to Durán, and different rooms and halls were maintained to receive the different ranks of the nobility.⁹⁸ Fray Durán approvingly wrote that all this was done to maintain a sense of hierarchy appropriate to a social organism: "These laws . . . were issued for the health of the entire land. They were like medicine which, given in its time and season, will profit the human body and be the cause of its welfare."⁹⁹

Hierarchy and reciprocity were ever present in Aztec society—with items like cloth and cacao often serving as symbols of vertical division and as media of exchange. The demand for goods fostered an increased desire for such goods acquired inexpensively by means of tribute. Thus, already extant commerce and tributary relations aided the establishment of Spanish and Indian tributary relations immediately after the conquest. In theory, Aztec commoners, or *maceguales*, were *calpolli* members who cultivated inalienable common lands. In practice, they were also "renters" who worked for the noble lord of the administrative *calpolli*. This lord, the *pilli*, was set apart as the receiver of rents.¹⁰⁰ The *maceguales* paid tribute in kind and personal service, whereas merchants and artisans paid solely in kind, except during time of war.¹⁰¹ The *pipiltin*, according to Zorita, constituted "a class of Hidalgos and caballeros" and were free from tributary demands. On the eve of the conquest, the Aztecs of the Valley of Mexico were ready for encomienda and repartimiento, but they were not ready for all aspects of Spanish evaluation.

The Aztecs themselves were amazed that Cortés and his fellow conquistadores placed value only on gold; that they burned or ignored all the precious featherwork of which they came into possession.¹⁰² Marked differences existed here between what the Aztecs and the Spaniards considered valuable. Still, the Spaniards were primarily able to re-create the Aztec tributary language of exchange at its most fundamental levels: the demands placed by Aztec nobles on the production of food and clothing. The conquistadores were new and exotic *pipiltin*, but they were *pipiltin* nonetheless. The Aztecs may have marveled at their range of strange customs and values, but they, like the Spaniards, also learned to identify similarities. Sahagún's interlocutors noted the shock experienced by Moctezuma II (reigned 1502-1520) and his emissaries when it became evident that the Spaniards, apparently for a brief time presumed by some to be deities, were nauseated by food soaked in human blood.[103] Durán's *Historia* reports that Cortés prevented human sacrifice to be offered him—something incomprehensible if the Spaniards were gods.[104] Just as the Spaniards marveled at the manner in which Moctezuma II ate and the food he consumed, so too Moctezuma "marveled" at the Spanish food:

And their food was like lords' food [also translated "like people's food"]—very large, and white; not heavy like [tortillas, but] like the stalks of maize plants—as if of ground maize stalks; it tasted a little sweet, a little honeyed—it tasted honeyed, it tasted sweet.[105]

Initially astounded by the fact that Quetzalcoatl and his minions did not consume human hearts and blood, the Aztec emissaries sent to Cortés's coastal encampment were forced to use simile in order to describe the Spaniards and their practices. As with the Spaniards, new demands were being placed upon their categories of understanding and their worldview.

The Aztecs, like their Iberian conquerors, defined civilization, at its most basic level, in terms of a people's material culture. Food, clothing, and shelter entered into their assessment of the Chichimecas when they described their lack of fixed abode, grass huts, wild meats, and skin vestments. When a word of praise was granted the Chichimecas, it was done by describing them as noble savages, living a simpler, healthier, and purer existence than that of the Aztecs. They were not viewed in their fullness, but as ideals. They were free of adultery, and they were strong and lean as a result of their "limited food and clothing."[106] The Otomí, on the other hand, "had a civilized way of life," but they were given to decadence, the curse of a "civilized" existence—a curse the Aztecs feared.[107] They were vain and gaudy dressers, who were stupid, lazy, and shiftless by Aztec assessment. They possessed maize bins and highly developed agriculture, but they swiftly used up their harvests. Their cloth was of poor quality, and their liberality so self-destructive that an Aztec maxim stated, "Thou destroyest thyself just like an Otomí."[108] It appears that the Aztecs hoped for a middle course between the Chichimecas and the Otomí.

Diego Durán's *Historia* relates a legendary account of how Moctezuma I (reigned 1440-1468) sent a group of magicians to discover the land of the seven caves from which the Aztec people originally traveled. Upon arriving in the land of the seven caves, the magicians found the Aztecs who had remained and saw that they were the very same individuals who had been left behind by their ancestors. It was explained to the wizards why their people grew old and died:

You have become old, you have become tired because of the chocolate you drink and because of the foods you eat. They have harmed and weakened you. You have been spoiled by those mantles, feathers and riches that you wear and that you have brought here. All of that has ruined you.[109]

To be overly enamored with the the luxuries of civilization was to flirt with self-destruction through decadence. Thus, both the Aztecs and the Spaniards could sometimes express an ambivalence where civilization was concerned. Both cultures had their Edens. When Cortés was among the Aztecs, he deemed the inhabitants of Tenochtitlan a people of *policía* (i.e., civilized), but he also pointed to certain habits he compared to those of the sultans' "opulent courts." Thus, for both Aztecs and Spaniards, cultural embellishment could quickly become mere vanity and decadence—their own values being the standards of judgment.

Still, despite the numerous calls to humility in Aztec and Nahua culture, Tenochtitlan, as a public space, was deliberately built to be a microcosm of supernatural order. Noble houses were spacious, with gardens and courtyards, while the Templo Mayor and its plaza were to serve as the *axis mundi* of the empire: "the main center in the political, economic, and religious sense."[110] It received tribute, and it was the place where heaven, earth, and the underworld met. A symbol of elite conceptions of hierarchy, power, and empire, it was also the place where order was maintained in a fluctuating cosmos through cosmic reciprocity—human blood for the sunlight and Tlaloc's rain. In this last capacity, monumental architecture reflected idealized social organization built on principles of hierarchy and reciprocity. As fellow humans given to the same primate tendencies, to some extent the Spaniards could read and understand all this.[111] Their self-appointed task became the preservation of what they deemed good and like their own culture and the elimination of what they perceived as evil. In the words of Bernardino de Sahagún:

The doctor cannot correctly apply medicine to the sick without first knowing from what disposition and cause the sickness proceeds . . . and preachers and confessors, being doctors of the soul, should be experienced in the medicine and illnesses of the spirit in order to cure the spiritual ills; the preacher should know the vices of the republic in order to direct his teaching against them . . . [for] among this people... the sins of idolatry, idolatrous rites and beliefs, omens, superstitions and idolatrous ceremonies have not yet totally disappeared.[112]

Recently, in *The Nahuas after the Conquest*, James Lockhart has written that "sixteenth-century Spaniards found in central Mexico a society remarkably like their own."[113] In confrontation with the differences and similarities of Mesoamerican rituals and material realities, we can see the manner in which sixteenth-century Spaniards defined themselves. The Aztecs and the Spaniards were eminently aware of their common humanity, individual and social, but this awareness was informed by a belief that physical entities were the partners of things spiritual—that the material and spiritual spheres shared reciprocal and hierarchical interaction. On the necessity and inseparability of their dualisms, at least, the Spaniards and Mexican Indians could agree. On this basis they could communicate and interact.

In their capacities as male warriors, both the Europeans and the Native Americans were agonistic, or expressive of aggression, an expressiveness that among primate males is often enough linked to issues surrounding sexuality. Although it is true that chimpanzees do not maintain closely watched harems like hamadryas baboons, humans have been known to maintain harems, and many Aztec and Spanish males expressed their virility by collecting sexual experiences with different partners. More importantly, given the weight of cultural learning done through human language, to be cowardly in either culture was often enough expressed as being womanly. When complimenting Malintzin—Cortés's Nahuatl translator, also known as La Malinche and Doña Marina—Bernal Díaz del Castillo felt compelled to mention that she was brave and resolute, "although a native woman."[114] More importantly, in something not entirely clear to Díaz del Castillo, man of violence and reader of *Amadís de Gaula*, Doña Marina was the very first translator between two alien languages and cultures. She knew Nahuatl, the language of the Aztec Empire, and she learned Castilian Spanish. Even though many still persist in seeing her as the betrayer of her people, she was a young Mexica woman who had been sold to the Maya as a slave. Cortés's mistress and translator, she was seen by the male warriors around her as one of the spoils of conquest, but far from being passive, she first presented the opportunity for cross-cultural exchange in the midst of violence. She taught reciprocal exchange among bands through her translation and through the birth of a son whom Cortés recognized as his. Later, her daughters, the indigenous women of Mesoamerica, would be far more successful at salvaging aspects of their culture than were their male counterparts. The metate would continue to produce the tortilla, despite the introduction of wheat, and the backstrap loom would continue to produce clothing despite the introduction of the European loom. In the countryside, *curanderas* would continue indigenous healing practices and healing prayer, despite the opposition of Spanish priests, their competitors in more ways than one.

Although the Basque founder of the Jesuits, Ignatius of Loyola (1491-1556), read chivalric romances at one time, he, like the Nahua interlocutors of the *Florentine Codex*, tried to distinguish between the noble and the fighter. The struggle against Satan might be described in the battlefield imagery of Ignatius's *Spiritual Exercises*, but it was not to be fought literally with swords.[115] It was to be fought by teaching, preaching, caring for poor lepers, feeding the hungry, and clothing the naked. Nobility was to be defined by actions more akin to altruism than aggressiveness. Although the division was never maintained in utmost purity, so too the Aztec noble, the male caretaker, was also expected to be an aggressive battlefield warrior. Spanish priests were males who sometimes resorted to the lash to inculcate religious discipline in their Amerindian charges—they even burned some Amerindians at the stake before this was forbidden in the late sixteenth century—but they were also those who defended their charges against the worst brutalities of the conquistadores, from Bartolomé de las Casas and Vasco de Quiroga to the Jesuits, upon their arrival in the Americas. Priests committed abuses, but many tried to prevent what they saw as abuse in an attempt to emphasize reciprocal interaction, "brotherhood in

Christ," over and above the alien nature of many Amerindian customs. Some Spanish clerics allowed for a certain amount of indigenous survival, perhaps best represented in the Virgin of Guadalupe, who, despite her Spanish name, is represented as an Amerindian lady bearing a marked resemblance to the Nahua goddesses of motherhood, nature, and fertility. Once again, it is the female aspect of Mesoamerican culture that shows great staying power. Known in Nahuatl as Tonantzin, "Our Honored Mother," the Virgin of Guadalupe came to be honored by Spaniards, Amerindians, and mestizos alike. Like La Malinche, she mediates the differences, while male warriors would emphasize them to the point of killing each other and brutalizing the other "tribe." In Tonantzin, the sustaining mission of an Amerindian woman's daily life activities met the charitable mission of those priests not completely given to inquisitorial brutalization, for both Aztec and Spanish cultures reflected the human tendencies toward mutual aid and violent reinforcement of rank and territory. Although the earliest written sources of the Bible speak of a chosen people slaughtering their way into Canaan, there is also the nurturing imagery surrounding the Psalms' shepherding deity; the recognition of blessed and righteous gentiles like Cyrus the Persian emperor; and Jesus, who defied preconceived notions of masculinity by denouncing violent retribution, and of kinship and masculinity by having the small children of strangers surround him. Some Spaniards, especially among the clerics, learned from this religious tradition to love, rather than hate, the newly conquered Amerindians. The tragedy lay in that part of that love always involved the annihilation of the spirit, if not every last detail, of Amerindian cultures. This would often enough set the priests at odds with women who also stressed healing rather than destruction—with many among the *curanderas*.

Despite unfortunate lapses into Freudian terminology, as early as the 1950s, Octavio Paz recognized the destructive tendencies of machismo in Mexico, writing that it represented aggressive performance for other males, a performance that often enough involves using women as objects of conquest: "He comes from far away: he is always far away. He is the Stranger. It is impossible not to notice the resemblance between the figure of the macho and that of the Spanish conquistador."[116] Although that conqueror destroyed the reign of Huitzilopochtli and the brutality of his human sacrifices, only to install the brutalities of European church discipline, the Nahua fertility goddesses survived:

The Indian goddesses were goddesses of fecundity, linked to the cosmic rhythms, the vegetative processes and agrarian rites. The Catholic Virgin is also the Mother (some Indian pilgrims still call her Guadalupe-Tonantzin), but her principal attribute is not to watch over the fertility of the earth but to provide refuge for the unfortunate. . . . The Virgin is the consolation of the poor, the shield of the weak, the help of the oppressed . . . . In addition, the Virgin—the universal Mother—is also the intermediary, the messenger, between disinherited man and the unknown, inscrutable power: the Strange.[117]

As shall be demonstrated in chapter 9, women alleviated the brutalities of male aggression in the conquest of Mexico. They are the missing link in this tale of cultural evolution.

NOTES

1. Historians and anthropologists disagree about the prevalence of famine conditions in pre-Columbian central Mexico. In 1978 G. W. Cox argued for more famines in the Old World than the New, but final judgment has yet to be passed. In any event, there was a famine of immense proportions after 1450, and given the Aztec propensity to reinterpret and amend past events, there is no reason to believe that other famines did not occur and are simply not recorded. Bernard R. Ortiz de Montellano, *Aztec Medicine, Health, and Nutrition* (New Brunswick, NJ, and London: Rutgers University Press, 1990), 72-84. On the Aztec propensity to revise and use history to confirm social order, see Susan D. Gillespie, *The Aztec Kings: The Construction of Rulership in Mexican History* (Tucson: University of Arizona Press, 1989), 208-30.

2. Nigel Davies, *The Aztec Empire: The Toltec Resurgence* (Norman and London: University of Oklahoma Press, 1987), 58-59.

3. Diego Durán, *Historia de las Indias de Nueva España e islas de la tierra firme*, ed. Angel María Garibay K., 2 vols. (Mexico City: Editorial Porrúa, 1967), 2:241-44.

4. Bernardino de Sahagún, *Florentine Codex: General History of the Things of New Spain*, trans. Arthur J. O. Anderson and Charles E. Dibble, 13 vols. (Santa Fe and Salt Lake City: Monographs of the School of American Research/University of Utah Press, 1950-1982), Bk. 8, chap. 1, pp. 1-2.

5. Durán, 2:29.

6. See "The Occult Sciences: The Crown's Support and Controls," in David C. Goodman, *Power and Penury: Government, Technology and Science in Philip II's Spain* (Cambridge: Cambridge University Press, 1988), especially 1-19.

Although Aztecs and Spaniards both believed in astrology, there were some particular differences in their beliefs: "In Aztec astrology, the equilibrium of the universe affected the human body. . . . Cosmic influence for the Aztecs was much more general, and organs of the human body were not associated with individual heavenly bodies or day names in the calendar." In European astrology, "the planets could cause diseases, and particular planets affected particular organs." Ortiz de Montellano, 134-35.

7. Louise M. Burkhart, *The Slippery Earth: Nahua-Christian Moral Dialogue in Sixteenth-Century Mexico* (Tucson: University of Arizona Press, 1989), 132.

8. Ortiz de Montellano, 15ᴼ ⁻2, 224-25.

9. *Florentine Codex*, Bk. 6, chap. 2, p. 7.

10. Ibid., pp. 8-9.

11. Ibid., Bk.10, chap. 12, p. 43.

12. Ibid., chap. 8, p. 30.

13. Ibid., chap. 7, p. 25.

14. Ibid., chap 4, p. 15.

15. Ibid., Bk. 8, chap. 16, p. 49.

16. Ibid., Bk. 6, chap. 18, p. 93.

17. Ibid., pp. 95-96.

18. Ibid., pp. 97, 94.

19. Ibid., Bk. 10, chap. 13, p. 46.

20. Ibid., p. 50.

21. Ibid., Bk. 6, chap. 19, pp. 99-103.

22. Ibid., Bk. 10, chap. 14, p. 51.

23. Ibid., chap. 15, p. 56.

24. Alonso de Zorita, *Life and Labor in Ancient Mexico: The Brief and Summary Relation of the Lords of New Spain*, trans. Benjamin Keen (New Brunswick, NJ: Rutgers University Press, 1963), 94-95.

25. Ibid. Burkhart, 87, 97, 130, 143. The reciprocal nature of the relationship with the gods and the purgations used to make amends in case of a breakdown are discussed by Frances Karttunen in "After the Conquest: The Survival of Indigenous Patterns of Life and Belief," *Journal of World History* 3:2 (fall 1992): 249.

26. Burkhart, 38-39.

27. Ibid., 39.

28. Christopher Boehm, "Pacifying Interventions at Arnhem Zoo and Gombe," in *Chimpanzee Cultures*, ed. Richard W. Wrangham, W. C. McGrew, Frans B. M. de Waal, and Paul Heltne (Cambridge, MA, and London: Harvard University Press, 1994), 216.

29. Toshisada Nishida, "Review of Recent Findings on Mahale Chimpanzees: Implications and Future Research Directions," in *Chimpanzee Cultures*, 391.

30. *Florentine Codex*, Bk. 2, chap. 15, p. 27. After the conquest, Motolinía noted how willing the Mexican Indians were to punish themselves physically for their sins. Old men whipped themselves at night, while many, during Lent, went from church to church as flagellants. Alms also were given to the poor. Fray Toribio de Benavente o Motolinía, *Memoriales o libro de las cosas de la Nueva España y de los naturales de ella*, ed. Edmundo O'Gorman (Mexico City: Universidad Nacional Autónoma de México, 1971), 103, 133-34.

31. *Florentine Codex*, Bk. 2, chap. 15, p. 28.

32. Karttunen, 250-52; James Lockhart, *The Nahuas after the Conquest: A Social and Cultural History of the Indians of Central Mexico, Sixteenth through Eighteenth Centuries* (Stanford, CA: Stanford University Press, 1992), 89.

33. Burkhart, 17.

34. *Florentine Codex*, Bk. 6, chap. 4, p. 19.

35. Durán, 2:61.

36. Ibid., 249. For the English translation, see Diego Durán, *The Aztecs: The History of the Indies of New Spain*, trans. Doris Heyden and Fernando Horcasitas (New York: Orion Press, 1964), 151.

37. Zorita, 93.

38. Ibid., 98.

39. *Florentine Codex*, Bk. 2, chap. 27, p. 91. Yet resources were scarce, and this was demonstrated through the exclusion of the last of the poor to arrive at the festivities. Ibid., 92-93.

40. Ibid., Bk. 8, chap. 17, p. 59.

41. Durán, 2:415.

42. Davies, 65.

43. Durán, 2:359.

44. Inga Clendinnen, *Aztecs: An Interpretation* (Cambridge: Cambridge University Press, 1991), 113, 120.

45. Ibid., 116.

46. *Florentine Codex*, Bk. 3, chap. 1, p. 6.

47. See especially the work of William A. Christian, Jr., *Local Religion in Six-*

teenth-Century Spain (Princeton, NJ: Princeton University Press, 1981), and *Apparitions in Late Medieval and Renaissance Spain* (Princeton, NJ: Princeton University Press, 1981).

48. *Florentine Codex*, Bk. 8, chap. 6, p. 17.

49. Clendinnen, *Aztecs*, 183.

50. Geoffrey W. Conrad and Arthur A. Demarest, *Religion and Empire: The Dynamics of Aztec and Inca Expansionism* (Cambridge: Cambridge University Press, 1984), 19-20.

51. Ibid., 53.

52. Ibid., 47.

53. Ibid.

54. Clendinnen, *Aztecs*, 110.

55. *Florentine Codex*, Bk. 2, chap. 21, pp. 46-47.

56. Clendinnen, *Aztecs*, 95-97.

57. Tzvetan Todorov, *The Conquest of America: The Question of the Other*, trans. Richard Howard (New York: Harper & Row, 1985), 144.

58. David E. Stannard, *American Holocaust: The Conquest of the New World* (New York and Oxford: Oxford University Press, 1992), 80.

59. Ibid., 51.

60. Conrad and Demarest, 47.

61. Ibid., p. 78 n. 128-29.

62. Ibid., 47.

63. *Florentine Codex*, Bk. 2, chap. 21, pp. 46-47.

64. Eduardo Matos Moctezuma, "The Templo Mayor of Tenochtitlan: Economics and Ideology," in *Ritual Human Sacrifice in Mesoamerica: A Conference at Dumbarton Oaks, October 13th and 14th, 1979*, ed. Elizabeth H. Boone (Washington, DC: Dumbarton Oaks Research Library and Collection, 1984), 162.

65. Jane Goodall, *The Chimpanzees of Gombe: Patterns of Behavior* (Cambridge, MA, and London: Belknap Press of Harvard University Press, 1986), 314ff.; Frans de Waal, *Chimpanzee Politics: Power and Sex among Apes* (New York: Harper & Row, 1982), 189.

66. Michael Tomasello, Sue Savage-Rumbaugh, and Ann Cale Kruger, "Imitative Learning of Actions on Objects by Children, Chimpanzees, and Enculturated Chimpanzees," *Child Development* 64 (1993): 1688-1703.

67. Leonard Berkowitz, "On the Escalation of Aggression," in *The Dynamics of Aggression: Biological and Social Processes in Dyads and Groups*, ed. Michael Potegal and John F. Knutson (Hillsdale, NJ, and Hove, UK: Lawrence Erlbaum Associates, 1994), 34-35; Seymour Feshbach, "The Bases and Development of Individual Aggression," in *Aggression and War: Their Biological and Social Bases*, ed. Jo Groebel and Robert A. Hinde (Cambridge: Cambridge University Press, 1989), 78-81.

68. Jerome Kagan, "Developmental and Methodological Considerations in the Study of Aggression," in *Determinants and Origins of Aggressive Behavior*, ed. Jan de Wit and Willard W. Hartup (The Hague and Paris: Mouton & Company, 1974), 108.

69. *Florentine Codex*, Bk. 10, chap. 6, p. 23.

70. Ibid., p. 24.

71. Ibid., p. 23. In Nahuatl, an *ocelotl* is a jaguar, and the smaller ocelot is the *tlalocelotl*.

72. Ibid., p. 24. Also Bk. 2, appendix, pp. 184-85.

73. Clendinnen, *Aztecs*, 192.

74. Ibid.

75. *Florentine Codex*, Bk. 10, chap. 5, p. 21. Also see p. 20.

76. Jane van Lawick-Goodall, *In the Shadow of Man* (Boston: Houghton Mifflin, 1971), 122.

77. James Lockhart, "Complex Municipalities: Tlaxcala and Tulancingo in the Sixteenth Century," in *Nahuas and Spaniards: Postconquest Central Mexican History and Philology* (Stanford, CA: Stanford University Press and the UCLA Latin American Center, 1991), 23-38.

78. Ross Hassig, *Trade, Tribute, and Transportation: The Sixteenth-Century Political Economy of the Valley of Mexico* (Norman: University of Oklahoma Press, 1985), 85, 92-93, 103-20.

79. *Florentine Codex*, Bk. 10, chaps. 19-23, pp. 69-83.

80. Zorita, 157.

81. Davies, 144-45.

82. Ibid., 135.

83. Durán, 2:205-10. The English citation may be found on p. 131 of the Heyden and Horcasitas translation of Durán.

84. *Florentine Codex*, Bk. 9, chaps. 2-4, pp. 3-18; Davies, 152-58.

85. Pedro Carrasco, "La Economía del México prehispánico," in *Economía política e ideología en el México Prehispánico*, ed. Pedro Carrasco and Johanna Broda (Mexico: Nueva Imagen—CIS-INAH, 1978), 13-74. Also Johanna Broda, "Templo Mayor as Ritual Space," in *The Great Temple of Tenochtitlan: Center and Periphery in the Aztec World*, ed. Johanna Broda, Davíd Carrasco, and Eduardo Matos Moctezuma (Berkeley: University of California Press, 1987), 67-69, 84-85.

86. Davies, 158.

87. Durán, 2:158.

88. Ibid., 2:162.

89. *Florentine Codex*, Bk. 9, chap. 4, p. 19. Alonso de Zorita wrote that the leading merchants were "rich and prosperous, and cherished by the rulers." See Zorita, 188.

90. Durán, 2:155-56, 163, 357, 383.

91. Zorita, 134.

92. *Florentine Codex*, Bk. 9, chap. 5, p. 24.

93. Robert Sidney Smith, *The Spanish Guild Merchant: A History of the Consulado, 1250-1700* (New York: Octagon Books, 1972).

94. Ruth Pike, *Aristocrats and Traders: Sevillian Society in the Sixteenth Century* (Ithaca, NY, and London: Cornell University Press, 1972), 22-26.

95. *Florentine Codex*, Bk. 9, chaps. 10-14, pp. 45-67.

96. Ibid., Bk. 10, chap. 17, pp. 63-64.

97. Ibid., Bk. 12, chap. 5, p. 15.

98. Durán, 2:194-95, 211-14.

99. Ibid., 214.

100. Davies, 112, 122.

101. Zorita, 181, 184.

102. *Florentine Codex*, Bk. 12, chap. 40, p. 118. Also chaps. 17-18, pp. 45-48.

103. Ibid., chap. 8, p. 21.

104. Durán, 2:521.

105. *Florentine Codex*, Bk. 12, chap. 7, p. 19.

106. Ibid., Bk. 10, chap. 29, pp. 172, 174.

107. Ibid., p. 176.

108. Ibid., pp. 176-80; Burkhart, 60.

109. Durán, 2:222.

110. Johanna Broda, Davíd Carrasco, and Eduardo Matos Moctezuma, "Introduction," in *The Great Temple of Tenochtitlan*, 5; Davíd Carrasco, *Quetzalcoatl and the Irony of Empire: Myths and Prophecies in the Aztec Tradition* (Chicago and London: University of Chicago Press, 1982), 149-50, 160-70, 182-87.

111. Eduardo Matos Moctezuma, "The Templo Mayor of Tenochtitlan: History and Interpretation," in *The Great Temple of Tenochtitlan*, 26-27, 38.

112. Bernardino de Sahagún, *Historia general de las cosas de Nueva España*, ed. Angel María Garibay K., 4 vols. (Mexico City: Editorial Porrúa, 1969), 1:27. Translation by John G. Copeland, cited in Matos Moctezuma, "The Templo Mayor of Tenochtitlan," in *The Great Temple of Tenochtitlan*, 17.

113. James Lockhart, *Nahuas after the Conquest: A Social and Cultural History of the Indians of Central Mexico, Sixteenth through Eighteenth Centuries* (Stanford, CA: Stanford University Press, 1992), 94. For the differences, see his discussion of the *altepetl* and *calpolli* in the same book. Ibid., 20-40.

114. Bernal Díaz del Castillo, *The Conquest of New Spain*, trans. J. M. Cohen (Harmondsworth: Penguin Books, 1963), 153.

115. Ignatius of Loyola, *The Spiritual Exercises of St. Ignatius*, trans. Anthony Mottola (Garden City, NY: Image Books, 1964), Second Week, Fourth Day, "A Meditation on Two Standards," 75-77.

116. Octavio Paz, *The Labyrinth of Solitude: Life and Thought in Mexico*, trans. Lysander Kemp (New York: Grove Press, 1961), 82.

117. Ibid., 85.

4

Coalitions: An Ethological Account of a Coup

It is the greatest of historical inaccuracies to claim that Cortés and his Spanish conquistadores were alone responsible for the collapse of the Aztec Empire. Ross Hassig has written, "The war was more of a coup or, at most, a rebellion, than a conquest."[1] He has, in fact, described what has traditionally been called "the conquest of Mexico" as more of "an Indian victory over Indians" than a Spanish victory. The Spaniards merely provided new technologies, strategies, diseases, and a general impetus to action that incited long-simmering tensions in central Mexico.[2] The Spaniards, then, were used by their Amerindian allies; but Hassig is also quick to point out that the conquistadores were quite capable of using their allies so as to construct a sort of European conquest over the next century.[3] In general terms, this entire tale of alliance and eventual European dominance easily falls within modern ethology's categories of investigation. Among primates, it is common to witness the formation and disintegration of coalitions with specific goals. Dominance changes hands. Wars or protowars are fought. And males engage in a series of ritualized displays in order to limit the potential for violence as they vie for hierarchical status and power. Contemporary science demonstrates a great deal in human nature that is inherently natural and biological. However, it is equally as clear that culture intervenes to refine or inhibit certain natural tendencies. The coup or rebellion that occurred in central Mexico from 1519 to 1521 exhibits all these qualities.

The details of the Mexican case study are extremely well known, but it is worthy to analyze them from the perspective of ethology, and from the perspective of a preexisting Mexican situation into which the Spaniards wandered as an unanticipated variable. For centuries, central Mexico, from the desert north of present-day Mexico City to the Isthmus of Tehuantepec, provided for the expansion of a number of city-states, much like old world Mesopotamia. Fertile soils and food-producing lakes provided richer resources than could be found in more desert-like regions to the north. Ecologically diverse, given the interplay of tropical lowlands and more temperate mountain valleys, the region also provided a diversity of potential trading goods and products. This benefited a trading empire like Teotihuacan, which held sway over the Valley of Mexico proper from 100 to 600 AD. Teotihuacan's merchants became active in regions as far afield as Veracruz and Guatemala, but their influence was always that of trade and tribute collection. The direct acquisition of conquered lands was not to be the set pattern for Mesoamerican powers, and this cultural trend may very well have contributed to the volatility of the region. Internal difficulties and conflicts joined with invasion from the more arid north to bring about the collapse of Teotihuacan's hegemony between 650 and 750 AD. By 900, however, the warlike nomads and remnants of the earlier population had blended to create what has come to be called the Toltec Empire.

Dominating the Valley of Mexico from 950 to 1200, the Toltecs seemingly maintained the type of tributary empire that would be replicated by the Mexica and their Aztec Empire. Given the existence of no written records, archaeology and legends maintained until the time of the Spanish arrival can provide us only with the general outlines of the Toltec tradition. Still, archaeologists have been able to discern that Toltec governance probably consisted of a loose military coalition of nomadic Chichimeca, northern agriculturalists from outside central Mexico, and central Mexican survivors of Teotihuacan's disintegration.[4] Centered at Tula, Toltec power exacted tribute from other city-states, while failing to consolidate a permanent presence in regions defeated in war. Rather than replacing local elites with Toltec governors, the locals were allowed to continue to rule themselves and their lands autonomously as long as the tribute was paid. As with Teotihuacan before it, such loose central organization led to a centrifugal breakdown. Warfare was frequent, and cults of human sacrifice seemingly expanded in their activities when compared to the Teotihuacan era.[5] Like Teotihuacan before it, Toltec hegemony broke down around 1200. According to Geoffrey Conrad and Arthur Demarest, "In the thirteenth and fourteenth centuries the Valley of Mexico had been balkanized into competing city-states and fragile alliances, each battling militarily and ideologically for the claim to be the Toltec heir."[6]

By 1300 two loose confederations had formed. One, the Tepanec alliance, was centered at Azcapotzalco, while a more heterogeneous group called the Alcohua eventually came to center themselves at Texcoco. Conrad and Demarest have gone as far as to call this landscape "Darwinian" in its violence and competition.[7] Although very little is actually known about their origins, it is known that a small group of northern barbarians wandered into this situation. They called themselves the Mexica. Claiming some Toltec ancestry to enhance their reputation, they built island cities called Tenochtitlan and Tlatelolco in the marshes of Lake Texcoco. They then became mercenaries in the valley's conflicts. For a time they served Azcapotzalco, but in 1428 they joined in a successful alliance with Texcoco and Tacuba, defeating dominant Azcapotzalco.[8]

At first Texcoco appears to have been the dominant city within this Triple Alliance, but around 1450 dominance seems to have shifted to Tenochtitlan. By the time of the Spanish arrival, there is no doubt that Tenochtitlan was the dominant city in central Mexico.

The Spaniards found a tributary empire that stretched from the Valley of Mexico around Lake Texcoco to certain regions in present-day Guatemala. Trade was also maintained along these lines by merchants called *pochtecah*. However, there was no significant centralizing bureaucracy, nor were there many garrisons. "Subjugation did not mean incorporation."[9] In fact, constant attempts to overthrow the tributary yoke aided the Mexica in maintaining a steady stream of sacrifices, providing the life-sustaining gods and life-sustaining nature with a source of sustenance, and providing the constant wars of central Mexico with a spiritual justification.

Originally organized socially on the basis of extended families or clans called *calpoltin*, the Mexica increasingly developed a priestly and noble hierarchy that demanded ever-increasing levels of tribute. Simultaneously, it was argued that the gods increasingly needed the blood of valiant warriors to prevent the passing of this era of the fifth sun. Four suns had died previously, and without appropriate sustenance the fifth sun could follow suit: "The initial unity of the ideological and economic rationale for Mexica imperialism presupposed the existence of a world of limitless conquests, innumerable victims, and endless resources. Unfortunately, by the end of the fifteenth century such a boundless environment was no longer available to the armies of Huitzilopochtli."[10]

In 1503 the Mexica *tlatoani* Moctezuma II inherited an untenable situation. His predecessor, the great conqueror Ahuitzotl, had extended Aztec campaigns as never before. As a result, lines of supply and other logistics had become overextended, and Moctezuma II dedicated a great deal of time and effort to reconquering the conquests of Ahuitzotl.[11] Since his army could move only at a rate of 1.5 miles per hour, distances were not covered with great alacrity, giving the farthest removed tributaries adequate opportunity to prepare and sustain a revolt. Supplying an Aztec army on the march was a major difficulty. It is estimated that with no Mesoamerican draft animals to be had, attendant porters could carry only up to eight days of food. The Aztec system of tributary demands was modified so that one of Moctezuma's armies on the march could demand support from tributary towns, but there was no guarantee that they would maintain their loyalty once one of their number had already rebelled.[12] Given the cost of long marches to put down far-flung rebellions, the Aztec Triple Alliance was experiencing a case of diminishing returns on the eve of the Spanish arrival. The power of Tenochtitlan, Texcoco, and Tacuba (also called Tlacopan) was still preeminent in central Mexico, but it was constantly being harrassed by the assaults of disgruntled tributaries. Both Moctezuma II and Ahuitzotl before him fought costly wars to maintain tributary control over the Zapotecs of Oaxaca and to maintain a thin line of outposts en route to Guatemalan tributary enclaves and their cacao.[13] This situation would not last indefinitely.

In 1517 and 1518 the Spanish governor of Cuba, Diego Velásquez de Cuellar, launched two exploratory missions to the Mesoamerican coast under the command of Francisco Hernández de Córdoba and Juan de Grijalva respectively. Following in the wake of Caribbean trading tales of great wealth and magnificent civilizations to the west, these expeditions returned with confirmation where marvels and wealth were concerned. Traveling with the expedition of Francisco Hernández, Bernal Díaz del Castillo reported that the Amerindians they encountered wore cotton shirts and loin cloths, and that artisanal work and items of gold and copper could be found. As a result, these Amerindians were considered more civilized than the Cubans, who, except for the women among them, wore nothing resembling clothing.[14] Still, their civilization was seen as tainted by "evil-looking gods" and blood-stained altars in the midst of prayer-houses of "fine masonry."[15] From the very start learned Spanish customs and cultural biases would inform the European documentation regarding the conquest of Mexico. However, the same can easily be said of the remaining Amerindian record.

In and of itself, the Nahuatl record of the conquest of the Mexica tributary empire is tainted by its lack of proximity to the events described. It is now known that the first stages of the protoethnographic interviews that would lead to the composition of the *Florentine Codex* took place no earlier than the late 1550s. The Franciscan Bernardino de Sahagún then went on from these interviews to compile completed manuscripts in Nahuatl and Spanish in the 1570s.[16] The account given by Fernando de Alva Ixtlilxochitl, noble of Texcoco, is even later, dating to the early seventeenth century, while the *Anales de Tlatelolco* are marked by their brevity. To the present day, with surviving sixteenth-century painted codices like the *lienzo de Tlaxcala*, these remain the classic Amerindian perspectives on the conquest. Although intervening years may have altered perspectives and interpretations among Sahagún's Nahua interlocutors and the oral tradition accounts and interpretations of painted codices upon which Ixtlilxochitl depended, it must equally be noted that Cortés possessed numerous ulterior motives while writing his letters to Charles V during the actual conquest. Likewise, the conquistador Bernal Díaz did not compose his account until he was over seventy in Guatemala. All accounts of the conquest, like all historical documents, are tainted by the interpretative strategies of their authors from the very start. The *Florentine Codex* at least provides us with a painted version of the conquest that builds on pre-Columbian traditions of record-keeping, while Ixtlilxochitl clearly drew on Nahua documents in his possession and the traditions of his Nahua community. From an Amerindian perspective, the importance of the Amerindian role in toppling the Mexica tributary empire becomes clear. Likewise, it must be noted that although often enough downplayed, the importance of the Amerindian allies is not completely ignored by the Spanish accounts. There is clear corroboration, then, from two distinct sets of sources, and that corroboration clearly points to mutually understood coalition behavior built on a deep understanding of male display, acts of aggression, and reciprocal needs. Although cultural differences did lead to misunderstanding and tension, the events that transpired in Mexico between 1519 and 1521 were not merely the tale of "double mistaken identity." Beneath the cultural differences, human commonalities were found. Before actual battles were fought, Spaniards and Amerindians encouraged themselves and tested each other through a series of displays, and like other animals, they were quite capable of understanding as well as using display behavior.

Bernal Díaz, conquistador and chronicler, first introduces Cortés as a man who established hierarchy by means of show. In an early modern Spanish world that identified one's rank by such articles of material culture as clothing, Cortés immediately went into debt to identify himself as a "great captain" while plotting the voyage to Mexico on the island of Cuba. According to Díaz del Castillo, Cortés had a good encomienda and gold for his services in the conquest of Cuba under Governor Velásquez, but he spent it all on finery for his wife, on entertaining guests, and on himself. While preparing his expedition to Mesoamerica, "he began to adorn himself and to take much more care of his appearance than before. He wore a plume of feathers, with a medallion and a gold chain, and a velvet cloak trimmed with loops of gold. In fact he looked like a bold and gallant Captain."[17]

Just as the Aztec *tlatoani* and *pipiltin*, or nobility, would wear clothing to establish rank and distance and would feed dependents as well, so too Cortés displayed authority before embarking with his eleven ships and 450 conquistadores. Such a display was far from superfluous.

While Governor Velásquez of Cuba was commissioning Cortés to engage in yet another reconaissance mission along the Mesoamerican coast, Cortés seemed to be planning much more from the very start. Velásquez grew wary of Cortés's behavior, and at the very end of it all Cortés sailed February 10, 1519, without the governor's permission and against a final effort to stop him. In displaying so proudly, Cortés was simultaneously challenging his superior's rank and trying to build confidence in his subordinates, who saw a "gallant Captain." Ethology has noted that clothing serves communicative functions in diverse human societies—most obviously in the display of gender, rank, and class. Sometimes these functions even cross cultures, as in the case of men's shoulders being emphasized with special adornments. When a male chimpanzee displays aggressively, his fur stands on end, including his shoulder tufts:

If we analyze the hair growth patterns on a man we find that tufts of hair would develop on the shoulders if hair growth were increased to a significant length. We can assume that males had more hair in earlier times than they do today and that the hair growth patterns served to enlarge the body outline of our upright ancestors.[18]

Thus the shoulder feather ornaments of the Yanomami, the vests of Japanese samurai, European military epaulets, and suits with padded shoulders all bear traces of inherent hominid memory—a memory that crosses both time and cultures. Cortés's displays, starting on Cuba, were eminently meaningful. Many of the events transpiring between 1519 and 1521 would be peppered with cross-cultural display, some of it badly misunderstood, but much of it eventually, if not immediately, understood.

For the most part, however, contemporary historians, in their flight from biography, have failed to analyze the character of Cortés in any detail. From merely observing his behavior and actions, the portrait of a willful and egomaniacal individual is cast. Above all else, Cortés sought status in his own Spanish culture—to be recognized by his cohorts through his displays and actions. As a result of this he was willing to challenge his immediate superior, but he would always be on his best behavior with the distant king. Thus, at the end of his first letter to Charles V, he attacks Velásquez as an arbitrary tyrant, while demonstrating his own loyalty to the Crown by sending articles of Mesoamerican wealth and art as tribute. At the end of his second letter to Charles, he begs royal pardon for the poverty of his writing style and "kisses the Very Royal feet and hands," using appropriate language of submission before the Crown.[19] It is also in the second letter, dated June 16, 1519, that Cortés further ingratiates himself by making the extension of Spanish sovereignty eminently apparent in his chosen name for Mesoamerica:

From all I have seen and understood touching the similarity between this land and that of Spain, in its fertility and great size and the cold and many other things, it seemed to me that the most suitable name for it was New Spain of the Ocean Sea, and so in Your Majesty's name I called it that. I humbly entreat Your Highness to look favorably on this and order it to be so called.[20]

In itself, this serves as an excellent example of Cortés's skill at simultaneously ingratiating himself and imposing his will. "New Spain" would be the Spanish name for colonial Mexico. What Cortés failed to mention in his letter is that a conquest had not been achieved. In fact, in his single-mindedness to acquire Spanish status, Cortés was quite oblivious to the dangers that surrounded him. Soon after dispatching a ship with his first two letters and tribute to the Crown, Cortés sank the remaining ten ships, eliminating a route of escape for men who were increasingly challenging his authority. Single-mindedly bent on becoming a governor rather than a pirate, Cortés tried to rally his worried men with comparisons to the ancient Romans. One of those men, Bernal Díaz, also reports that he bribed some supporters of Velásquez "with gold, the great peacemaker!"[21] From the very start Cortés was bent on ascending above Velásquez, whom he despised, according to Díaz, for not giving him the Cuban encomienda he felt he deserved.[22] This made him an immense risk taker, and a man who would spend his first gold acquisitions to invest in greater prestige in the future. He would stop taking risks only at the point at which he might lose the Crown, for his achievements and displays meant nothing to him unless they could be viewed by other men of his own culture. Although later accused of killing his first wife so as to make a better match for himself, Cortés was never prosecuted formally and married a woman of high noble lineage after his arrival in Spain in 1528. By all standards, he was a master at attaining his own ends by skirting the limits of propriety in his own culture, and he was so concerned with signs of his prestige that soon after the fall of the Aztec tributary empire he tried to preserve some temples and idols as a type of memorial. Tzvetan Todorov, in *The Conquest of America*, writes that Cortés admired artifacts of Aztec culture, but not the whole cultural achievement.[23] Of course, artifacts might be possessed by a Spaniard wishing to impress his own culture, but an entire alien culture and its own worldview could not be accepted. Cortés had come to aggrandize himself at all costs—including the lives of his men. His classical references are well taken, for he was Odysseus revisited, and his journey was also full of circumstances beyond his immediate control and the rhetoric of hero creation.

After some brief exploratory escapades in the Yucatan, Cortés and his men disembarked near present-day San Juan de Ulúa. There they would have their first prolonged encounters with Mesoamericans, after some brief encounters with the Maya to the south. Before the Spaniards' actual disembarcation, two large canoes approached Cortés's flagship—all this on the very day of arrival, Holy Thursday, April 21, 1519. Far from being confused, Bernal Díaz del Castillo reports that the Amerindians knew immediately which ship was the flagship from its size and standards on display. Since Mesoamericans used banners and flags themselves, their knowledge was quite understandable.[24] Messengers boarded the ship, where they politely greeted Cortés with Nahuatl honorifics and said that they had been sent by Moctezuma to learn what manner of men these were. Cortés responded that they should think of the arrival of the Spaniards "as fortunate rather than troublesome," and he then gave them food, wine, and blue beads.[25]

The first encounter with representatives of Moctezuma was a cordial conversation enhanced and aided by the presence of two translators in the retinue of Cortés. At Cozumel in the Yucatan Cortés had ransomed the Spaniard Jerónimo de Aguilar. Shipwrecked while on the way to Santo Domingo from Darien, Aguilar had spent years among the Maya as a bondsman and servant. He therefore could translate from coastal Maya dialects into Spanish. However, he knew no Nahuatl. This problem was solved when, near Tabasco, Cortés met Malintzin—better known historically as La Malinche or Doña Marina.

Since the voyages of Hernández and Grijalva to the Yucatan, Spaniards had replenished their supplies as they saw fit, readily committing theft where Amerindian property was concerned. In the meantime, the Maya had been informed of the potential danger of Spanish conquest by a Spaniard castaway named Gonzalo Guerrero, a sailor and former companion of Aguilar who had taken a native wife and become Maya. Unsurprisingly, Cortés and his men were attacked as they traveled through the Yucatan and near Tabasco. After some battlefield successes by the Spaniards, forty Maya nobles came to negotiate tribute payments. Gold ornaments, cloaks, and twenty women were given the Spaniards as a result. Among the twenty was Malintzin, described by Bernal Díaz as "a most excellent person."[26] A young Nahua woman who had been sold into slavery by her people, Malintzin would rapidly become Cortés's main interpreter. Originally she spoke Nahuatl and Maya. While living in the Spanish camp, she quickly learned Castilian, making her invaluable as a knowledgeable interpreter of cultural mores. In fact, Bernal Díaz points out that later, at Tlaxcala, the Tlaxcalans called Cortés "Malinche" because "Doña Marina was always with him. . . . So they gave Cortés the name of 'Marina's Captain,' which was shortened to Malinche."[27] Likewise, Nahua painted accounts of the conquest show Doña Marina at Cortés's side in nearly every situation, including battle.

Aside from providing Cortés with his future translator, the coastal excursion provided him with some important precedent. He learned some of the Mesoamerican rules of engagement, and of the propensity to pay tribute when defeated. Even though he wishfully misinterpreted this as the establishment of a permanent vassalage along European lines, he was exposed to spoken, as well as military, encounters with Mesoamericans. More importantly perhaps, he learned the effectiveness of certain types of Spanish aggressive display. After noting the effectiveness of their horses in battle and how the Amerindians were frightened by these alien beasts, Cortés decided to test his hypothesis: "'Let us bring Juan Sedeno's mare, which foaled the other day aboard ship, and tie her up here, where I am standing. Ortiz the Musician's stallion is very randy, and we can let him get a sniff of her.'"[28] This was done. Then, when Cortés was discussing terms with the nobles who had come to offer tribute—the tribute which would include Doña Marina—he had the lusty stallion brought forth.

At that moment they brought the horse that had scented the mare, and tied him near the place where Cortes [sic] was talking to the *Caciques*. And as the mare had been tethered at that actual spot, the horse began to paw the ground and neigh and create an uproar, looking all the time towards the Indians and the place from which the scent of the mare came. But the *Caciques* thought he was roaring at them and were terrified once more. When Cortes observed their terror he rose from the seat, went over to the horse, and told two orderlies to lead him away. He then informed the Indians that he had told the beast not to be angry, since they were friendly and had come to make peace.[29]

Whereas he would need translators to understand the particular words of Mesoamerican languages, Cortés could readily understand human terror. Although human facial musculature does vary among the races,

much of the behavioral repertoire by which emotional states and intentions to act are communicated has a long phylogenetic history. Most of our facial expressions are therefore found as universals. Basic facial expressions develop even in children who are born deaf and blind and thus deprived of the opportunity to imitate social models. For a number of expressive patterns such as the relaxed open mouth-display (play face), homologous counterparts are found in other primates. The cross-cultural similarity of some of the expressive patterns is sometimes astounding (for example, "eye-brow-flash").[30]

Some behaviors, like winking to show complicity, are limited to particular cultures and learned, but they are extremely rare.[31] It is far more common to find the slow eyebrow raising across the cultures as a sign of indignation and disapproval. Cortés, like any human, could understand other humans, despite cultural and linguistic differences. And where those differences raised questions, Cortés was not the only one to run tests.

Moctezuma II had been running an ongoing investigation where the Spaniards were concerned. Written some thirty years after the events described, and after the devastations of disease and tribute collection had been introduced, Sahagún's *Florentine Codex* was quite dependent on Nahua interlocutors who would have been too young to have been privy to Moctezuma's innermost counsel. As a result, it is unsurprising that Moctezuma should be portrayed as a frightened fool who consistently thought of Cortés as a god.[32] Mexica legend spoke of the return of Quetzalcoatl, it is true—that this god who once ruled in legendary Tula would one day return to reclaim his kingdom. However, the *Florentine Codex* itself shows that Moctezuma was not merely willing to accept this tale of his culture as soon as creatures of marvels appeared on the coast. He tested it again and again, whereas some more adaptive individuals within the Aztec milieu seem to have seen the Spaniards as humans from the very start.

All in all, the Aztecs exhibited a very understandable human curiosity upon hearing of strangers that were beyond the range of their everyday experience. Although humans do demonstrate proclivity to xenophobia, we also exhibit curiosity as a behavioral trait:

Indeed, we seek novelty even into our old age. We read newspaper accounts of events that do not concern us at all, learn about foreign countries and research findings, visit museums or travel as tourists to find new sights and experiences. Entire areas of our economies are based on our curiosity, and one of the most severe punishments that can be meted out consists of removing or restricting those possibilities for satisfying our curiosity, e.g., by imprisonment.[33]

Just as Cortés was awed by Aztec creations, Amerindians wondered at the cannons and the "deer" that the Spaniards rode.[34] Given the constant struggles for possession of territory in central Mexico, it would also have been reasonable to assume that a Spanish alliance might prove beneficial. Moctezuma lived in a society of skull racks, his own self-mutilation, and the constant display of terror. That he should be "filled with a great dread, as if he were swooning," as reported by the *Florentine Codex*, is a possibility, but it is more likely the creation of hindsight and the disasters that would follow the Spanish arrival.[35] The Spaniards were a new variable in the Mesoamerica equation, and Cortés may have not been the only risk taker.

When Cortés met Moctezuma's representatives for the first time at San Juan de Ulúa, he had his linguistic and cultural translators, as the Maya had the Spaniard Gonzalo Guerrero, but Moctezuma had some accumulation of experience. The two high-ranking representatives sent to meet with Cortés were

Tentlil (*Span.* Tendile), the Aztec regional representative, and Cuitlalpitoc (*Span.* Pitalpitoque), an ambassador who had met with Grijalva.[36] Thus, Cortés met with one individual who had prior experience with Spaniards, and Moctezuma had been gathering information on these mysterious coastal appearances for some time.

Bringing with them fine gifts deliberately chosen to honor Quetzalcoatl, the Aztec ambassadors also brought with them "some of those skilled painters they have in Mexico":

Tendile . . . gave them instructions to make realistic full-length portraits of Cortes [sic] and all his captains and soldiers, also to draw the ships, sails, and horses, Doña Marina and Aguilar, and even the two greyhounds. The cannon and cannon-balls, and indeed the whole of our army, were faithfully portrayed, and the drawings were taken to Moctezuma.[37]

It is clear that the Aztec officials were ordered to be polite and assess the situation. They were bureaucrats sent to report. It is true that they brought presents that Cortés may have misconstrued throughout as mere signs of subordination and vassalage—at least he represented them as such to Charles V, whose support he clearly sought in the five letters addressed to him. We will never truly know if Doña Marina interpreted them as polite gifts that were also meant to display the power and wealth of Moctezuma and the Mexica, much like potlatch or Cortés's feasts in Cuba. To assume, as Inga Clendinnen does, that Cortés did not understand this is quite a leap of logic, however, especially when the words in his letters were quite deliberately selected to impress his king.[38]

Given Spanish and Amerindian ability to read "nonverbal messages" on many other occasions, and given human universals that do cross cultures, contemporary cultural constructionists should be less than certain that culture and language serve as insurmountable barriers. On this occasion, as on so many others, twentieth-century readers will never know just how much Cortés wished to reveal to Charles V. Far better that Charles think that Moctezuma's emissaries came to inform Cortés that Moctezuma "wished to be Your Highness's vassal and ally" than otherwise.[39] Cortés had burnt his bridges by disobeying Governor Velásquez in Cuba. He would literally destroy his ships to prevent his men's turning back. If he had any hope of ever gaining re-cognition in his Spanish culture, he needed the support of Charles V. This could encourage deliberate omissions on many occasions in his letters. Among other things, he was very reluctant to give Doña Marina credit, referring to her only as "my interpreter, who is an Indian woman," although he would later recognize their child.[40] Cortés readily presented or repressed information according to the degree it would benefit his general display. Clendinnen should be less than certain that he entirely misunderstood the ambassadors of Moctezuma.

After all, he understood human behavior well enough to display the potential for violence that the Spaniards represented. While entertaining the *pipiltin*

Tendile and Pitalpitoque on the Veracruz coast, he mounted what Bernal Díaz himself recognized as a significant show of force. Cortés's chief lieutenant, Pedro de Alvarado, was told to gallop with all his horsemen directly in front of the Aztec representatives. The horsemen wore little bells attached to their breastplates in order to make an impressive noise, and they were led by Alvarado's mare, "a great runner and very quick on the rein." Then the Spaniards' cannons were loaded with an extra charge of powder to make the greatest noise possible when fired. Bernal Díaz recorded that when the cannons were fired, they "resounded with a great din" and "the two governors and the rest of the Indians were frightened by this strange happening." He also noted that the *pipiltin* ordered the experts in Nahua pictographs to set about recording the information immediately—obviously the Nahua bureaucrats were not entirely bereft of their senses or cowed.[41] They were on an exploratory mission, and they intended to report. Written after the conquest, the *Florentine Codex* reported that the *pipiltin* "lost their senses and fainted away" when the cannons were fired; that a stench like that of "rotten mud" penetrated their brains; and that the Spanish "deer" (i.e., horses) were as tall as the roof of a house and carried the Spaniards on their backs wherever the Spaniards wanted to go.[42] Still, the Spanish force was small, and more had to be learned regarding the Spaniards' real status and purpose. Ross Hassig has speculated that given that most of the Aztec army was made up of commoners who were just then busying themselves with sowing crops, Moctezuma was in no position to launch a full assault against this alien force—at least not without fostering resentment and possible crop failure among the masses who supported his empire.[43] There were multiple considerations at work on both sides of the encounter, but the display behavior of the Spaniards clearly had its desired effect in making great Amerindian lords at least temporarily act like submissive subordinates, and in no doubt boosting Spanish morale.

In his original rise to power in Holland's Arnhem Zoo, before the formation of a coalition with the younger Nikkie, the wily old chimpanzee Yeroen impressed other chimpanzees into submission by rhythmically stamping and pounding on large, hollow metal drums. The noise created by these "drumming concerts" seemingly cowed the other chimpanzees into submission while minimizing actual violence.[44] Likewise, at Gombe in the 1960s, Jane Goodall studied Mike, a male chimpanzee who used the pounding and clanging noises made by empty kerosene cans to rocket to the top of the male hierarchy.[45] Not only do these displays indicate a type of cross-cultural chimpanzee behavior, they demonstrate the extent to which display is used aggressively by primate males in attempts to gain preeminence within a hierarchy. To the present day we still speak of the rattling of sabers. Cortés knew what he was doing.

Among other things, Cortés used male display to build coalitions, another goal inherent in much of primate behavior. This became particularly apparent after the Mexica ambassadors departed on May 12, 1519. At first the Spaniards feared attack with the departure of the fact-finding mission. Instead, they were visited by Totonac representatives, tributaries of the Mexica who had feared approaching the Spaniards while Tendile and Pitalpitoque were there. Uncomfortable with their vassalage to an ethnic group different from themselves, the Totonacs willingly alluded to the possibility of an anti-Aztec alliance with the Spaniards. The Amerindian rebellion against Aztec dominance was commencing, and Cortés proceeded to the Totonac city of Cempohuallan (Cempoala).[46]

In Cempohuallan, Cortés met a ruler whom Bernal Díaz refers to as "the fat cacique." The exchange between them was an obvious jockeying for position in the formation of an alliance against the Mexica. When Cortés started on a standardized description of his faith and political system, the fat cacique responded with "a deep sigh" and "bitter complaints" against the Mexica, who "had taken away all his golden jewellery" and "grievously oppressed him and his people."[47] Going to a neighboring Totonac town of Quiahuitzlan, Cortés heard a similar tale of woe from their ruler: "Every year many of their sons and daughters were demanded of them for sacrifices, and others for service in the houses and plantations of their conquerors."[48] Cortés once again reiterated his version of the *requerimiento*—his description of his own submission to his faith and to Charles V, thus explaining his culture to the Amerindians and justifying his own actions to himself. At this point, according to Bernal Díaz del Castillo, he made only vague promises concerning aid, but such promises gained the use of Amerindian porters provided by the fat cacique.

Quite clearly, the Spaniards and the Totonacs were in the process of negotiating a coalition. Primatologists have readily recognized for some time that the higher apes and monkeys seldom function on the basis of brute force and simple hierarchies alone. Rather, the experts speak of social nexuses and the recognition of multiple, shifting, and intertwining social relationships among all the participants in a particular band.[49] Alliances are more important to the formation of dominant status than any personal strength, and by marching through central Mexico with Amerindian allies in addition to his own Spanish force, Cortés was displaying dominance and success.[50] Where chimpanzees are concerned, both Jane Goodall and Frans de Waal have noticed the importance of this behavior. In her early days at Gombe, Goodall noted the close and comforting relationship maintained by the alpha male Goliath and the high-ranking David Greybeard. They reinforced each other's status, and Goliath most clearly started to lose status to Mike, the chimpanzee of the kerosene cans, when David Greybeard joined three other males in grooming Mike after he had displayed against Goliath. Indicating a willingness to submit to Mike, David Greybeard had reassessed the viable alliance system within his community, even though he continued to groom and comfort the fallen Goliath until his disappearance during the pneumonia epidemic of 1968.[51] Likewise, the alpha male Goblin built on his close alliance with Figan, the alpha male before him. Figan consistently supported his heir in struggles with other males until Goblin ranked second in the troop. In 1979 Goblin began challenging Figan, and a struggle laden with temporary victories and reversals ensued until Goblin achieved undisputed alpha status in 1985.[52] At de Waal's Arnhem Zoo, after suffering defeat at the hands of the younger Luit, old Yeroen formed a successful ruling coalition with Nikkie, a coalition that temporarily developed into a tripartite male division of power. Karl Grammer has noted that among human children, high-ranking children support others more frequently and receive support more frequently than low-ranking children; that friends are more often supported; that repeated victory leads to status gain; and that children map out strategies "to establish reciprocal supporting relationships."[53] Cortés and the fat cacique were playing a game inherent to some extent in all primates—a game they could mutually understand. Obviously, misunderstandings arose where learned cultural nuances intervened, but the most significant factor that differentiated the behavior of Cortés and the fat cacique from that of other primates was their taking the formation of a coalition to the next level. Rather than merely building an alliance within a particular troop, they built one between two troops, two cultures, and they did this by recognizing universal human goals and desires that cultural constructionists would now downplay in the conquest of Mexico and other human activities.

Just as the settling of rank among chimpanzees requires time and a series of displays, charges, and scuffles, the alliance between the Spaniards and the Totonacs was not built overnight. Cortés initiated a strategy of using divisive tactics where the Amerindians were concerned, first encouraging the Totonacs to seize Mexica tribute collectors who had arrived at Cempohuallan, and then surreptitiously saving the five Nahuas before the Totonacs could sacrifice them. He sent the tribute collectors back to Moctezuma, telling them that he had saved them out of friendship for the Mexica *tlatoani*.[54] Then he immediately, and duplicitously, reinforced his alliance with the fat cacique by marching with some four hundred Spaniards, four thousand Totonac warriors, and one hundred porters to take an Aztec garrison at Tizapantzinco. The garrison had already departed, and Cortés merely had to disarm local Amerindians. Obviously Moctezuma II did not trust Cortés enough to keep his garrison within striking distance of the Spaniards. Likewise, it was the fat cacique who requested this action. No doubt suspicious of the disappearing Mexica tribute collectors, he wished to run his own series of tests where the Spaniards were concerned. As has been readily pointed out by the anthropologist Ross Hassig and others in recent decades, the Amerindians were full-fledged actors in their own right, and the coalition forming would make the events in Mexico between 1519 and 1521 simultaneously a conquest, civil war, rebellion, and coup.[55]

Given the Spanish willingness to march against an Aztec garrison, it was now the Totonacs' turn to reciprocate. The Totonacs now offered the Spaniards food and eight women upon their return. In his own biased way, Bernal Díaz recognized a type of shared humanity in all this: "For although they were Indians, they saw that justice is good and sacred, and that Cortés's statement that we had come to right wrongs and abolish tyrannies was proved true by the events of that expedition."[56] The Spaniards, in turn, seem to have quickly understood the gift of the eight women. Being given daughters of the Totonacs by which to have children identified the Totonacs as kinship allies. Seven of the women were intended for Cortés's captains, while the fat cacique's own niece was to be Cortés's.

The exchange of women in marriage and concubinage had a long-standing history in Mesoamerica. Likewise, it is significant to note that among chimpanzees, females visit neighboring communities and actually relocate. At Gombe, Jane Goodall has detected peripheral females who "continue to move back and forth between communities," as well as permanent and temporary transfers.[57] Not only does territoriality seem far more significant to many male primates than it does to female primates; females (through patrilineage in many human cultures) are expected to relocate with males from groups other than their natal one. In Mesoamerica intermarriage among allied rulers was common, since polygamy allowed for its multiple usage in Mesoamerica as it did in the ancient Near East. Given the Spanish practice of official monogamy, Spaniards would commonly treat the women they received as concubines and nothing else, but this does not mean that they did not understand the significance of the practice.[58] In fact, perhaps through the gift of hindsight, and writing as an old man, Bernal Díaz stated that the fat cacique wanted this transaction to make the Spaniards and Totonacs brothers and that Cortés said, "Before we could accept the ladies and become their brothers, they would have to abandon their idols . . . and sacrifice no more souls to them."[59] Interestingly enough, Cortés may have so recognized the significance of this action that he failed to mention it in his letters to Charles V and refers only to women given the Spaniards to grind maize for them. Spanish men were far from monogamous, in many instances maintaining illicit mistresses if they could, but the legal and religious adherence to monogamy was not to be challenged openly. Just because the Spaniards, in most instances, recognized these women as concubines rather than wives does not prove that they misunderstood the Amerindian intentions. It simply means that there was a real cultural difference. Likewise, just because the Mesoamericans recognized polygamy does not mean that women were not treated as sexual property to be enjoyed by men. This "gift" of women means that women were given to demonstrate the formation of an alliance between males. Quite explicitly, in Mesoamerica such a gift could also signify subordination and submission of a temporary or more permanent nature. When Cortés's forces had defeated Maya warriors in the Yucatan, Maya nobles brought tribute in the form of food, gold, clothing, and twenty women, including La Malinche.[60] The great irony is that although the women were treated as chattel by men, throughout the conquest period Amerindian women expressed their agency. This fact is muted by male filters in all the surviving documentation, but as future chapters will demonstrate, if any aspects of Nahua cultural traditions survived the conquest, it was to a large extent through the quiet persistence of women, who made food and clothing, maintained shelters, and even fought with some men to maintain old religious traditions and beliefs. As shall be demonstrated, women were the "missing link" in this tale of cultural evolution, and it starts with the vital role played by Malintzin. Although Cortés himself downplayed her role, Amerindian sources and Bernal Díaz recognized the extraordinary nature of a woman publicly serving as the means of communication between two cultural traditions. Aztec women, like Spanish women, were not meant to be major political actors. However, La Malinche was, and this is reflected in her power as a symbol to the present day in Mexico. She was not only Cortés's translator and source for Aztec cultural information but also the mistress by whom he had Don Martín Cortés "el indio," a natural son Cortés recognized as his, and a mestizo who would die fighting the Moors of North Africa. The Amerindian women of the conquest worked within the limitations of expression ascribed to them, and despite these limitations they managed to maintain some control of the syncretic culture that would be shaped in New Spain.

When Cortés accepted the eight noblewomen given to the Spanish leadership, it was on the condition that the Totonacs should abandon human sacrifice, the worship of their gods, and sodomy. The Totonac dignitaries readily agreed to abandon sodomy, but they balked at the idea of abandoning their religion. Cortés and Doña Marina forced the issue, according to Díaz del Castillo. The Spaniards threatened to destroy the Totonac idols themselves if the Indians did not comply:

When the Indians heard these threats—and Doña Marina was not only quite capable of explaining them in their language, but also threatened them with the power of Montezuma, who might fall on them any day—they replied in fear that they were unworthy to approach their gods, and that if we were to overthrow them it would not be with their consent, but that we could overthrow them or do whatever else we liked.[61]

As once before, after defeating the Maya of Tabasco, Cortés forced the destruction of indigenous statues and the erection of a Spanish altar. This was significant on two counts. Firstly, it couched his actions in the language of a Reconquista crusade, thus justifying them from a Spanish perspective. Secondly, it was a clear display of dominance in the newly formed Totonac alliance. It was one the Totonacs could understand, since upon taking a recalcitrant city, Mesoamerican conquerors destroyed temples and the gods of those they had just defeated. The Totonacs had little choice but to accept this "marking" because as Doña Marina quite correctly observed, they had resisted the Aztecs, and the Aztecs would take their revenge. The Totonacs were no match for the Aztec warrior elite and their cadres. Cortés had become their only option, and they submitted.[62]

Deciding to march to Tenochtitlan in order to "meet" with Moctezuma II, Cortés and the Spaniards would take some forty to fifty Totonac warriors and some two hundred porters with them. The Totonac alliance provided the Spaniards a coastal sanctuary of sorts, but it was apparent that the Totonacs wished to use the strangers against the Aztecs. They themselves were submissive and cautious allies, reinforcing a Spanish chivalric fantasy that they had come to Mexico to do good and avenge robberies.[63] Leaving Cempohuallan, the Spaniards could think of themselves as dominant lions, but they still needed staunch allies. The next stage in Cortés's alliance-building activities would prove crucial and even more intricate and dangerous. It involved Tlaxcala.

Estimates of Tlaxcala vary. Whereas Ross Hassig argues that it was only a matter of time before the Tlaxcalans were subdued in a war of attrition with the Aztecs, Conrad and Demarest state that the Tlaxcalans were a serious opponent who deflected the Aztecs from the even more threatening Tarascans. Inga Clendinnen, in turn, sees the Aztecs and Tlaxcalans trapped in a bloody symbiosis in which each opponent perpetually needed the other to provide the most honored and valuable sacrifices at their festivals mimicking the cycles of life and death.[64] Tlaxcala was encircled by regions owing tribute to the Mexica, although they themselves remained a region free of tributary obligations. However, Tlaxcala was in the process of losing allies and tributaries (among them, the inhabitants of Cholula or Churultecal). The Tlaxcalans also suffered from the potential internal weakness of being made up of four equally dominant *altepemeh*, or cities, each with its own lord or *tlatoani*. Still, according to Conrad and Demarest, "the Tlaxcalans, surrounded and besieged, fought on fanatically, inspired by their state cult of the god Camaxtli, a cult that through time functioned more and more like the Mexicas' worship of Huitzilopochtli."[65] They, like the Mexica, fought to preserve the cosmic order, as well as their own survival in a highly volatile situation. Whether their days were numbered or not is a matter of speculation. What is certain is that they took advantage of the arrival of the Spanish strangers.

According to Cortés in his second letter to Charles V, it was the Totonacs of Cempohuallan who recommended that he march to Tenochtitlan by way of Tlaxcala if he truly intended to proceed to the Mexica *altepetl* and meet personally with Moctezuma II. The Totonacs made up Cortés's mind for him, saying that the Tlaxcalans were their friends and the hated enemies of Moctezuma.[66] In a sense, the Totonacs were constructing an alliance to defeat the Aztecs from behind the scenes, just as subordinates in any primate band will use the dominant individuals to keep the peace and settle disputes. The dominant never truly rule alone, and subordinates seldom recognize dominance without receiving some benefits from the arrangement. The Totonacs were willing to submit to the Spaniards, if they and the Tlaxcalans defeated Tenochtitlan for them. First, however, the Tlaxcalans clearly wished to test the Spanish mettle.

Upon entering Tlaxcalan territory, Cortés and his men were first attacked by the Otomí tributaries who guarded the Tlaxcalan perimeter, and then by a well-disciplined force of Tlaxcalans under the command of Xicotencatl, who bore the same name as his father, one of the four lords of Tlaxcala. The Tlaxcalans numbered in the thousands. Díaz del Castillo readily admitted, "It was all we could do to hold our own and save ourselves from defeat, for we were in great danger."[67] Cortés wrote Charles V that God was certainly with him, since casualties among the Spaniards and their allies were light.[68] Writing to win his sovereign's support, Cortés failed to admit that his "light casualties" meant forty-five men slain since leaving the coast, several horses killed, the remaining ten wounded, and approximately a dozen men seriously ill. If the Tlaxcalans chose to press their advantage, the Spanish expedition could have been defeated then and there, but against the wishes of the warlord Xicotencatl, the four lords of the Tlaxcalan alliance decided to accept Cortés as an ally.

Rather than a strange reversal of policy, this shift made eminently good sense given the Mesoamerican situation. The Spaniards had fought well enough to resist the initial assaults of a massive Tlaxcalan force sent to test them. From the Tlaxcalan perspective, this meant that they would make worthwhile allies in their ongoing struggle with the cities of Tenochtitlan, Texcoco, and Tlacopan. In the light of Mesoamerican precedent, the Tlaxcalans no doubt assumed that they could use the Spaniards as allies and that after victories and tribute had been won, the Spaniards would go home, which was no doubt far away. Nahua cultural traditions had taught the Tlaxcalans that victors leave their tributaries in possession of their lands and local autonomy. They did not conceive of what European experience had taught the Spaniards—or at least the most influential leaders could not conceive of this. It is interesting to note that the younger Xicotencatl remained suspicious until his early death. He even sent spies into the Spanish camp (the unfortunates were summarily brutalized by Cortés and returned to Tlaxcala without hands or thumbs). It is always dangerous for the historian to claim that learned culture so determines the individual that he or she cannot see beyond its confines. Some individuals learn and relearn quickly.

When the Tlaxcalan lords decided to form an alliance with the Spaniards, there remained some question as to who, if anyone, would become the dominant partner. It is true that like the Totonacs before them, the Tlaxcalans gave the Spaniards women and other "gifts," and that Cortés refers them to Charles V as "vassals of your Sacred Majesty."[69] Yet, when Cortés erected an altar and began to preach Christianity, he was told in no uncertain terms that the Tlaxcalan gods and priests were not to be touched. At this point, he quickly abandoned his efforts as a missionary—most likely because he was not attracting the favorable attention he so desired in this particular display. Cortés was made to fall in line with Tlaxcalan desires, and the first action taken by this coalition was definitely to the benefit of the Tlaxcalans. As Cortés was preparing to continue his march to Tenochtitlan, he insisted on going by way of Cholula (Cholollan; Churultecal). Bernal Díaz del Castillo reports:

But when the Tlascalan chiefs heard that we intended to follow the way the Mexicans recommended they grew very gloomy and said once more that at all costs we ought to go by Huexotzinco, where the people were their relations and our friends, rather than by way of Cholula, where Montezuma always kept concealed ambushes.[70]

Once allied to Tlaxcala, the Cholulans had recently gone over to the Aztecs. According to Bernal Díaz, Cortés arrived peacefully and only massacred Cholula's elite under false pretext of peaceful assembly after Malintzin had learned of their plot to slaughter the Spaniards. That Cortés should ever have gone to Cholula after hearing Tlaxcalan warnings is a bit of a mystery. Since Cholula was a central location on the route between the Totonac coast and Tenochtitlan, and since the Tlaxcalan alliance had weakened Cortés's need to be openly friendly to Moctezuma II, Ross Hassig has speculated that

his decision to go to Cholollan can best be understood as political, to secure his rear and his lines of resupply, and chastise his friends' enemies. Cortés's actions cannot be seen exclusively in terms of his own interests. . . . [T]he attack may have been orchestrated by the Tlaxcaltecs as a litmus test of Spanish loyalty. If they attacked the Chololtecs, they would prove themselves by undermining a now-despised enemy. But this would also be an assault on an Aztec ally, so it would put the Spaniards in opposition to Moteuczoma [sic], a position from which they could not easily withdraw. This forced the Spaniards to demonstrate their loyalty at a point when the Tlaxcaltecs had risked nothing.[71]

In any event, when Cortés finally left Cholula around October 25, 1519, he was on the final leg of his journey to Tenochtitlan and his much-desired meeting with Moctezuma. Whereas the Totonacs had only provided Cortés with some fifty to sixty warriors, the Tlaxacalans had given him approximately two thousand.[72] With forces thus augmented by Tlaxcala, the Spaniards looked more than ever like some kind of threat to Mexica tributary hegemony. Two eminently logical questions therefore arise at this point: Why did Moctezuma fail to stop the march to Tenochtitlan? And what were Cortés's exact intentions in any event—to conquer an Aztec alliance numbering in the millions with less than three thousand men?

Perhaps playing his own duplicitous game, Moctezuma may have been drawing the Spaniards into his web like the proverbial spider. He had to await the upcoming harvest in order to field commoners as well as noble warriors, and he no doubt had no wishes to send a truncated force of his warrior elite into enemy territory. Likewise, as the veritable high priest of his religion, he was inculcated with the tales of Quetzalcoatl of Tula and his promised return from the waters. Given the Aztecs' dependence on their gods to justify their imperial expansion and human sacrifice, the deities were as real and central as the Christian god was to many Spaniards. Moctezuma had to assess the alien nature of the Spaniards before he made a grievous mistake. By this time, a great deal of evidence was accumulating toward proving the humanity of Spaniards who did die in battle, but according to Amerindian sources written after the conquest, Moctezuma paid heed to portents foretelling the imminent destruction of Tenochtitlan. Passages to this effect may very well have been written with the gift of hindsight, but it is well known that the Mexica were quite given to omens and mystical interpretations. Moctezuma may have been affected by bad signs, or he may have been the scapegoat for a devious strategy gone awry. In actuality, the *Florentine Codex* shows Moctezuma hedging his bets. As the Tlaxcalans and their Spanish allies were among the volcanoes that rim the Valley of Mexico, Moctezuma sent envoys with gold and gifts, possibly to divert the threat. As the Byzantine Empire often bribed Germanic barbarians with gold, requesting that they proceed to the west after their payment, Moctezuma may have been trying to bribe a potential threat, or he may still have been trying to win a potential ally. He sent a nobleman to play the part of Moctezuma, in any event, but this subterfuge was uncovered by the Tlaxcalans present. Hastening back to Tenochtitlan, the ambassadors were quickly followed by sorcerors and priests who tried to blind and harm the assembled allies with spells of enchantment. Needless to say, they failed. Far from greeting the Tlaxcalans and Spaniards ingenuously, however, Moctezuma was taking the appropriate steps toward war—at least according to Mesoamerican protocol. Among other things, he even sent a force to the coast to attack Cempohuallan and the rebellious Totonacs. This strategy shows some foresight in that the Totonacs were rather weak and subordinate allies to the Spaniards—allies who might be swayed back into the Aztec tributary fold with relative ease, thus blocking a coastal escape route for the Spaniards and simultaneously displaying against a rather presumptuous group of subordinates.[73] Of course, by this time Cortés had sunk all his ships except for one sent on to Spain via Cuba. The coastal escape route was not really a Spanish option.

Cortés and the Spaniards had crossed their Rubicon. Inga Clendinnen suggests that Cortés may have been attempting a vast confidence scheme, trying to exact as much wealth as he could from the Amerindians by means of the Spaniards' mysterious appearance and magical methods of warfare. This does not ring entirely true once the sinking of the ships in late July—well before the Tlaxcalan alliance—is taken into account. As mentioned previously, one ship was sent to Spain with all the gifts and tribute collected up to that point, and with Cortés's own written words in an attempt to win over Charles V and gain forgiveness for Cortés's disobedience to Governor Velásquez. That one ship was also meant to stop quickly and quietly at Cuba in order to recruit more men for the Mesoamerican endeavor. In the meantime, the sinking of the ships meant that any men with Cortés who were still loyal to Velásquez's original reconaissance plans had no remaining escape route. They either lived or died with Cortés in what was quickly becoming a potential suicide mission.

Although he did not immediately force crosses and altars against overwhelming numbers, Cortés did do this where he thought he had the upper hand. Even Hassig admits that a prejudicial sense of superiority cannot be discounted where the Spaniards are concerned. Having seen the successful Reconquista against the powerful Moors, some Spaniards may have truly felt that God was on their side, and Bernal Díaz even reports that a number of Spaniards claimed to see Santiago Matamoros (y *Mataindios*) during their battles in Mexico. Aside from suffering from a superiority complex that is discussed throughout this work by means of accumulated cultural evidence, Cortés no doubt thought that Tenochtitlan was much smaller than its 200,000 to 500,000 inhabitants. The largest European cities, all outside Spain, had in the vicinity of only 100,000 inhabitants circa 1500, and the cities Cortés and

his Spaniards had been to in Mesoamerica so far approached only 30,000.[74] On
a number of fronts Cortés probably did have an overinflated sense of his own
worth and that of his Spanish forces. He was also a relatively young risk taker,
and at some thirty-four years of age, this was his big opportunity.

Writing about his first meeting with Moctezuma in Tenochtitlan on November 8, 1519, Cortés revealed to Charles V that he planned to capture and use
Moctezuma from the very moment he detected ambivalence in his actions.
Although Cortés's letter has Moctezuma literally submitting to Charles as a
vassal, something quite difficult to believe, it does also portray a friendly
greeting, something upon which all sources agree.[75] Ultimately, Cortés did
move against Moctezuma, imprisoning him in one of his own palace chambers
on November 14. He used Moctezuma's duplicity in attacking the Totonacs and
killing some Spaniards who remained with them as an excuse for his own
duplicitous actions. The game of power was proceeding from the level of
display to that of outright war, and at this point the events become increasingly
well known, although they are often ascribed multiple and conflicting interpretations.

Having seized the *tlatoani* of Tenochtitlan, Cortés's display was agonistic in
the least. Yet, it seems that he hoped to rule through a compliant Moctezuma.
In his second letter to Charles V, Cortés claimed that he had done all he could
to please Moctezuma, even announcing publicly that it was the European
emperor's will that the Mexica should continue to obey their *tlatoani*. Of
course, one must wonder whether he actually made such an announcement,
and whether it would have been received with any favor by the heretofore
dominant Aztecs. Compliant or not, Moctezuma had created the opportunity
for his own imprisonment.[76]

To the present day, historians are no more certain of Moctezuma's motivation than they were in past eras. Moctezuma had insisted that the enemy
Tlaxcalan warriors not be allowed into the city proper. They were thus en-
camped on the shore of Lake Texcoco, on the outskirts of the island city of
Tenochtitlan. Thus, Moctezuma had not abandoned all caution. He let just a
small group of Spaniards with a few Amerindian allies as attendants into a city
of 200,000 to 500,000. He seems to have been engaged in a continuing act of
assessment, for it certainly must have been difficult to believe that a small
group of Spaniards could be much of a threat. Writing in the early seventeenth
century from Nahua sources, the Texcocan noble Don Fernando de Alva
Ixtlilxochitl argued that Moctezuma could not conceive of defeat at the hands
of mortal Spaniards. By this time there was ample evidence that although
strange, the Spaniards could die. What threat could they therefore be to the
"greatest throne" the Mexica had ever known: "So with the great power which
he had, Moctezuma did not believe he could be subject to any prince, although
he were the greatest in the world."[77]

Certainty will probably never be attained, but a radical hypothesis might
serve to stimulate useful debate. Inga Clendinnen readily admits that few
would have had access to Moctezuma's thoughts and assessments "in the

closed politics of traditional Tenochtitlan," that the tale given Sahagún by his Amerindian informants in the 1550s is far too similar to the "'official' Spanish accounts." Moctezuma in both is the docile, compliant, and religious vacilator of legend. Her final conclusion is that "much of Moctezuma's conduct must remain enigmatic." We do not know the degree of physical coercion used on him, given differences in the Cortés and Bernal Díaz accounts, and we do not know whether he cooperated with the Spaniards "to save his empire, his city, his position, or merely his own skin." The most telling suggestion made by Clendinnen is that "we know neither the nature and extent of Moctezuma's authority within and beyond Tenochtitlan."[78] Likewise, Ross Hassig has alluded to Moctezuma II as potentially cooperating out of weakness and fear for his own political future.[79] Unfortunately, both authors do not explore this very real insight in any depth, yet the accumulation of evidence is highly suggestive of a politically insecure Moctezuma who wished to use the Spaniards as much as they wished to use him.

Before the arrival of the Spaniards the Aztecs had reached the physical limits of their tributary empire. Incessant long-distance wars were waged merely to maintain tribute collection from the mountain valleys of Oaxaca—all in an attempt to keep open the routes to the profitable tribute of coastal Guatemala, to quetzal feathers, cacao, and jaguar pelts. In turn, the lowland Maya of the Yucatan promised little in terms of finished manufactured products taken as tribute; Tarascan armies prevented expansion to the west; and even though the Aztec hegemony was able to reach the Pacific coast through what is now the state of Guerrero, the mountain tribes constantly revolted and required reconquest like those of Oaxaca. Moctezuma's so-called conquests referred to in the *Anales de Tlatelolco* and other sources were really reconquests or attempts at the consolidation of control.[80] He especially targeted pockets of resistance within the Aztec hegemony, and as Geoffrey Conrad and Arthur Demarest have noted, this policy failed to correspond with traditional Mexica warfare, in which short campaigns fulfilled the desire for rich booty and sacrificial victims. Moctezuma and his people were not truly prepared to fight wars of attrition in the mountains against people who refused to yield.[81]

Moctezuma presented the Mexica with "pyrrhic victories" and even some real defeats. His so-called conquests were numerous only because rebellions were numerous. He did not contribute to the extension and growth of a tribute-based economy, and as a result he had to face very real dissatisfaction among very real Mexica classes at home. By all accounts, he limited his advisors to the most highly born, and he warned the *pochtecah* merchants that they were not to use their wealth to live above their station.[82] In short, his choice in trying times was to consolidate social hierarchy and ranks in a society that, through the *calpolli*, still had strong tendencies toward reciprocal clan behavior. One is forced to speculate how many families among the *macehualtin* questioned Moctezuma's wars of diminishing returns. Their status was not being improved, and the *tlatoani* was emphasizing hierarchical differences. Could *macehualtin* families have continued to see the loss of a son to war as an honor when so little was thereby gained through it? Did families in the United States do so during the Vietnam War?

Finally, it must be noted that tensions existed within the Triple Alliance of Tenochtitlan, Texcoco, and Tlacopan. Texcoco could remember its glory days at the head of the Triple Alliance and its cultural achievements under the poet, legalist, and *tlatoani* Nezahualcoyotl; yet in 1515 Moctezuma placed his own man on the throne as *tlatoani*. This was a clear indication that one of Moctezuma's consolidating efforts was to be the full-scale subordination of the former dominant ally.[83] In the early seventeenth century the Amerindian historian Don Fernando de Alva Ixtlilxochitl readily noted that Moctezuma "controlled all of what formerly belonged to Texcoco and its kingdoms and provinces, since King Cacama was his nephew and was placed on the throne by his hand, and the King of Tacuba was his father-in-law and a very old man who no longer had the strength to govern."[84] As Fernando de Alva Ixtlilxochitl was quick to point out, this was not favored by all Texcocan factions. His ancestor, also named Ixtlilxochitl, proved to be a constant malcontent. At twelve he had terrorized the city with a veritable "street gang" of youths. After being pardoned from a death sentence for his activities, this grandson of Nezahualcoyotl became a respected warrior captain at seventeen. He hotly contested the rulership of Texcoco when Moctezuma II chose as *tlatoani* his half-brother, and Moctezuma's nephew, Cacama. Ixtlilxochitl was waiting in the wings when the Spaniards arrived, and Moctezuma no doubt worried about his popularity in Texcoco.[85]

After superbly outlining the weaknesses inherent in the Aztec Empire at the time of the Spanish arrival, Geoffrey Conrad and Arthur Demarest, the source of much of the above information and analysis, fail to hypothesize where Moctezuma's apparent capitulation to the Spaniards is concerned. They readily write that "Moctezuma II was the first *tlatoani* to realize the true nature of the Aztec dilemma and to attempt a policy of consolidation and stabilization."[86] They also readily state that "The Mexica were a people divided against themselves; many had come to resent their *tlatoani*, Moctezuma II."[87] However, they fail to mention that Moctezuma may have seen the Spaniards as the sort of wild variable that he might use to make a rather insecure throne more stable. Although other analyses cannot be completely eliminated as possibilities, given a lack of direct evidence, it is not far-fetched to assume that Moctezuma may have viewed the Spaniards as other Amerindian players in the Mesoamerican game did: as an intriguing new variable that might be used and manipulated by means of a coalition in order to gain more power. Moctezuma's gifts and willingness to demonstrate at least some signs of submissiveness may have been an attempt to woo these strangers to his side. Through the prism of his egotism, Cortés may have actually seen a willing vassal of Charles V, yet it is interesting that he writes of his attempts to please him after the very easy capture—specifically claiming to have announced publicly that Charles V wished Moctezuma to remain in power.[88] In his attempt to "please" Moctezuma, Cortés may have been providing him with a legitimation of his troubled rule that

might be interpreted as the will of the gods or of the original ancestors of the
Mexica, still living in Aztlan, their fabled home. In fact, this latter possibility
is what Moctezuma is reported as having suggested in Cortés's second letter to
Charles V: that the Mexica had come from far away and that Charles in his
Castile was to be identified with the original sovereign lords they had left
behind them.[89] Given that late medieval Venice found security and independence in acknowledging the distant and weak overlordship of the Byzantine
emperor—a sovereignty that the emperor could never truly enforce—is it so
far-fetched to assume that Moctezuma saw a few hundred avaricious strangers
from far away as valuable arguments for his authority and subject to manipula-
tion? Moctezuma may have been playing a very dangerous game, given the
danger inherent in his situation. After all, as noted by Conrad and Demarest, he
was bright enough to recognize the untenable nature of the Mexica situation
circa 1519. No human can currently predict the outcome of a risk taken.
Neither could Moctezuma in 1519. Given that he continued to be recognized
as *tlatoani* for months after his capture by Cortés, or the formation of a
coalition with Cortés, it is apparent that factions within the Triple Alliance
were biding their time to assess the situation.

Cacama of Texcoco actually did much more than that. This nephew of
Moctezuma actually started to plot an attack on the Spaniards. News of the plot
reached the Mexica *tlatoani*, and he told Cortés, who had Cacama captured by
six *pipiltin* loyal to Moctezuma. At this point, Moctezuma's son Cocozca was
named *tlatoani* of Texcoco by Moctezuma and Cortés.[90] Offering assistance like
this, it is unlikely that Moctezuma had lured the Spaniards into Tenochtitlan in a
self-sacrificing act so that they could then be slaughtered by the full Mexica
army after the harvest in the fall. That attack never came. Rather, the Spaniards
and Moctezuma ruled as a sort of symbiotic entity until trouble arose in May
1520.

While Moctezuma remained a prisoner, an ally, or both, Cortés departed to
the coast to deal with the arrival of a Spanish force sent by Governor Velásquez
of Cuba to arrest Cortés and stop his rebellious campaign. Eighteen ships
carried Pánfilo de Narváez and some one thousand men. Under the ruse of
engaging in negotiations, with only 266 men, Cortés launched a surprise night
attack on the Narváez encampment, capturing the commander and convincing
the band to join his enterprise. All this was achieved in May 1520, and Cortés
was seemingly in a stronger position than ever before.

In Tenochtitlan, however, Cortés's lieutenant, Pedro de Alvarado, was simultaneously weakening that position with a massacre reminiscent of Cholula.
During the festival of Toxcatl, while leading Aztec nobles and priests were
gathered at the Templo Mayor, Alvarado ordered his men to block the four
entrances to the great temple and initiate a slaughter of the unarmed Aztec
leadership. Writing long after these events, Diego Durán estimated that the
slaughter easily numbered in the thousands.

Like so many other things, Alvarado's exact motivation is never explicitly
proven in any of the sources. He may have wished to impress Cortés with a

striking blow similar to Cortés's at Cholula, while his greed for the nobles' finery may have provided further incentive. It is true that Bernal Díaz cited Alvarado's capacity for theft. Upon first arriving in the Yucatan, he took forty indigenous fowl and was reprimanded by Cortés, who told Alvarado that pacification would never be achieved by means of robbery.[91] However, as the early-seventeenth-century Texcocan source Don Fernando de Alva Ixtlilxochitl suggests, he may have been convinced by the small number of Tlaxcalans with him that the Aztecs were planning an attack. Likewise, it may be significant to note that Alvarado had been given one of the daughters of the *tlatoani* Xicotencatl at Tlaxcala. In this particular case, the binding alliance created through women given as "gifts" seems to have been taken quite seriously. Alvarado did not seek a Spanish wife until his Amerindian princess, Doña Luisa Tecuilhuatzin died, and even after that he was constantly accompanied by their daughter, Doña Leonor, who would eventually marry Don Francisco de la Cueva, nephew of the powerful duke of Alburquerque. Into the seventeenth century, mestizo descendants of Alvarado and Doña Luisa would seek and receive privileges, including encomienda rights in certain Guatemalan towns. Alvarado's ties to the Tlaxcalans perhaps ran deeper than those of other conquistadores. They even named him "Tonatiuh," the sun, because he was fair of hair and skin and martial in bearing.[92] That the Tlaxcalans could have influenced him to slaughter members of the hated Mexica nobility is highly likely and has even been taken as likely by such analysts as R. C. Padden in *The Hummingbird and the Hawk*.[93]

However, Pedro de Alvarado also maintained significant ties with Moctezuma, who seemingly enjoyed his company.[94] It is reported in *La Historia de Tlatelolco* that both Moctezuma and Tonatiuh gave permission for the celebration of Toxcatl, a celebration dedicated to the planting or harvest. If Moctezuma had any reason to fear assassination or rebellion from ambitious members of the Mexica *pipiltin*, Alvarado's massacre at the Templo Mayor promptly eliminated many a potential enemy. In all fairness, however, it is important to note that upon seeing the unarmed and "naked" *pipiltin* being slaughtered, Moctezuma cried out, " 'My lords, stop. What are you doing? The people suffer.' " But he is recorded as saying this only after three hours of "assassination."[95] Likewise, the *Florentine Codex* reports that Alvarado encouraged Moctezuma to have the feast observed, since he wished "to marvel at and see how and in what manner it was done."[96] According to Díaz del Castillo, upon his return Cortés found it suspicious that Alvarado had permitted such a gathering of premier Mexica warriors when he feared attack. When confronted by Cortés, Alvarado stated that it was a ploy to launch his attack first. Cortés remained enraged, calling the massacre "a great mistake."[97] Not only a mistake, the massacre clearly upstaged Cortés's leadership and control. On one level, it was very much Alvarado's display of potency, and such an independent display by a subordinate was more than Cortés could bear.

Whether the massacre occurred with or without Moctezuma's or, more likely, the Tlaxcalans' complicity, Alvarado's bloody actions created a desperate situation. Approximately eighty Spaniards had caused "the blood of chieftains" to run "like water":

And when [all this] became known, there then was a shout: "O chieftains! O Mexicans! Hasten here! Let all prepare the devices, shields, and arrows! Come! Hasten here! Already the chieftains have died; they have been put to death, destroyed, shattered, O Mexicans, O chieftains!"[98]

The Mexica responded by forcing the Spaniards back to Moctezuma's palace:

Quickly the chieftains marshaled themselves; as if working with a will they brought the arrows and shields. Then the fray joined. They shot . . . and they loosed darts with broad, obsidian points at them. It was as if a [mass of] deep yellow reeds spread over the Spaniards.[99]

When Cortés returned from his successes on the coast, he was furious at the chaos he discovered. Allowed back into Tenochtitlan only to find himself surrounded, Cortés and his men were besieged in their quarters for twenty-three days. He unsuccessfully tried to negotiate a withdrawal on his own, and only when this failed did he bring Moctezuma to the roof of the besieged palace in order to demand that his people stop the attack. This proved to be an utter failure, and Moctezuma died as a result of the effort. Spanish sources argue that Moctezuma II died of wounds received at the hands of his own people, but Nahua accounts claim that the Spaniards, no longer having any use for the wounded *tlatoani*, killed him in the palace. Although the *Florentine Codex* places the blame for Moctezuma's death on the Spaniards, it admits to Mexica animosity where he was concerned. Leaving the roof unwounded, Moctezuma still experiences a barrage of Mexica arrows when he tries to negotiate peace. He is also called a fool and one of Cortés's men. Even when his body is discarded by the Spaniards and burned by the Mexica on a traditional funeral pyre, it is reported specifically to have "smelled foul as it burned."[100] There is no doubt that Cortés was quite capable of killing an expendable former ally, but he and Bernal Díaz both reported that a stone thrown at the *tlatoani*'s head ultimately killed him—either directly or indirectly—Díaz del Castillo reporting that he refused treatment and food after the wounding.[101] Of course, Díaz's account also claims that all Spaniards who knew him mourned him like a father "since he was so good."[102]

According to Bernal Díaz, even before he died, the surviving Mexica nobility had deposed Moctezuma as *tlatoani* and appointed his brother Cuitlahuac to his place of honor. It was Cuitlahuac, the new *tlatoani*, and representative of an early anti-Spanish faction, who led the assault that would result in La Noche Triste.

On June 30, 1520, the day after Moctezuma's death, Cortés and his forces fled Tenochtitlan. The Spaniards would later remember this night as La Noche Triste, and it is significant to note that it occurred so soon after the death of

Moctezuma. Ross Hassig has the Spaniards killing Moctezuma in order to gain a four-day respite of official mourning for the *tlatoani*, but it is important to note that the Spaniards did not use all the time that could have been allotted, and the Mexica high nobility may already have chosen a new *tlatoani*.[103] There is no doubt that in the brief life remaining to him, Cuitlahuac proved to be a successful warrior. According to Díaz, when the Mexica learned of Moctezuma's death, they cried out that they had chosen a less faint-hearted ruler than "good Moctezuma," and that he would not be deceived by false speeches as Moctezuma was.[104] With anti-Spanish sentiment in the ascent after the massacre at the Templo Mayor, this was to be Cuitlahuac's moment at the head of a far from monolithic Aztec Empire.

The Spaniards would experience heavy casualties before they reached the western causeway from the palace, only one of three leaving the island city of Tenochtitlan. Again and again, Bernal Díaz del Castillo writes that it was only by the grace of God that any Spaniards escaped with their lives.[105]

Spaniards were cut off from each other, with some remaining behind in Tenochtitlan to await their fate as human sacrifices. Important prisoners, including children of Moctezuma and Cacama, the lord of Texcoco, were killed by the Mexica warriors. By all accounts, the Spaniards' Amerindian allies did valiant service that night, and it may be most accurate to report that the Tlaxcalans, Huexotzincans, Atlixcans, Totonacs, and others saved their Spanish allies. It is known that the Tlaxcalans made a special point of guarding the translator Doña Marina and Alvarado's Tlaxcalan princess, Doña Luisa. However, after a series of fierce battles fought around Lake Texcoco, the allied forces reached Tlaxcalan territory in a shambles. They had lost all their cannons, many of their horses, over eight hundred Spanish men, the five Spanish women who had come with Narváez, and over one thousand Tlaxcalans.[106]

Unsurprisingly, when the remnants of Tlaxcalan-Spanish alliance made it back to Tlaxcala, the value of an alliance with the unsuccessful Spaniards was hotly debated. The warlord Xicotencatl, son of the *tlatoani* Xicotencatl and brother of Doña Luisa, now once again voiced his opposition to an alliance with Cortés. Others joined him, but the final decision of the four lords of Tlaxcala was to continue the coalition. After all, there could be no doubt that the Tlaxcalans seemed the dominant partner. Although the approximately 460 Spaniards and their remaining twenty horses had gained some prestige by making an extremely difficult escape from Tenochtitlan, they were a small force and in no position to claim dominance within the coalition—or so it seemed. Narváez's men had brought with them an unseen ally that Alfred Crosby has rightfully called the determining factor in European imperial expansion before the nineteenth century: European microbes. Before industrialization, European imperialism was most successful where immunities to diseases such as smallpox, typhus, and measles had not been built up. By October 1520, smallpox swept into Tenochtitlan, devastating the rest of central Mexico on the way. It is estimated that some 40 percent of the population of central Mexico was killed in this first wave of European disease. Of course, Spanish allies died like the

Mexica, but they were not about to face a prolonged siege. By early December, smallpox would claim the *tlatoani* Cuitlahuac as one of its victims.[107]

While the European disease spread, Cortés was preoccupied securing territories to the south of Tlaxcala, serving as a type of condottiere for the Tlaxcalans. Successful in his battles of this period, Cortés also saw his forces replenished by 145 new Spanish arrivals and nineteen horses.[108] He was ready to return to Tenochtitlan by late December 1520.

Here, the importance of alliance and coalition behavior among human animals once again becomes central to the tale. The Amerindian allies possessed sheer numbers, even though smallpox killed them as it did the Mexica, but siege warfare had not been perfected in Mesoamerica. Cortés and his Spanish men now gained a certain preeminence in the coalition because of their warrior culture, which taught them how to kill by means of prolonged siege. Once again, they had cannons that they mounted on small ships to patrol Lake Texcoco. They now settled on a plan to starve Tenochtitlan into submission, and the Amerindian allies were with them.

The Tlaxcalans and other Amerindian groups were with Cortés because of the internal tensions and struggles for power that existed well before the Spanish arrival in central Mexico. Now, much to Cortés's pleasure, the Spaniards were rapidly becoming the focal point of new coalitions, of new attempts to order and organize Mexican reality. All parties involved in the final defeat of the Mexica were in pursuit of a better arrangement from their perspective. Cortés and his Spaniards were the catalysts to change.

All this became eminently apparent when an alliance was formed with Texcoco. If anything sounded the deathknell of the Mexica, it was the splintering of the Aztec Triple Alliance itself. With the opening of 1521, the Tlaxcalans and Spaniards were invited into Texcoco in peace. The new *tlatoani*, Ixtlilxochitl, represented a faction that despised the subordination of his proud city to Tenochtitlan. Now, with Cacama dead, this faction came to the fore, under a young man who would eventually be portrayed by his descendant, Don Fernando de Alva Ixtlilxochitl, as a warrior of superheroic qualities at the final storming of Tenochtitlan.

That the Spaniards proved to be the focus of the new Mesoamerican alliance cannot be doubted. When old allies continued to question the growing Spanish preeminence, they were now eliminated. By May 1521, the younger Xicotencatl of Tlaxcala was hanged at Texcoco for supposedly conspiring with the Mexica and their new *tlatoani*, Cuauhtemoc. Given his past history of suspicion where the Spaniards were concerned, the reality of the charges against this prophet are not entirely unbelievable. After the death of their commander, the Tlaxcalans remained part of the alliance nonetheless, Spanish worth perhaps becoming increasingly apparent in the course of the siege.

To the bitter end the Mexica of Tenochtitlan fought to maintain their dominance, their control of resources, and their pride. In June 1521 sixty-eight Spaniards were captured alive in battle and sacrificed. Following gruesome Mesoamerican traditions of display, Spanish body parts were sent to tributary

towns as proof of continued Mexica success and Spanish mortality.[109] Bernal
Díaz writes:

They sacrificed all our men in this way, eating their legs and arms, offering their hearts
and blood to their idols as I have said. . . .

He [Cuauhtemoc] sent the hands and feet of our soldiers, and the skin of their faces,
and the heads of the horses that had been killed, to all the towns of our allies and their
relations, with the message that as more than half of us were dead and he would soon
finish off the rest, they had better break their alliance with us . . . because if they did
not desert us quickly he would come and destroy them.[110]

It is certain that the Mexica were well aware of the power of display, just as
Cortés was. By all accounts, most of the Amerindian allies departed at this
point, but Cortés and his Spaniards, together with a few hundred of the most
loyal allies, continued to hold the siege, eventually convincing the other allies
to return.[111] Water and food supplies were diminishing in Tenochtitlan, and
resistance was growing weaker. After house-to-house fighting in August, the
city finally surrendered with the capture of Cuauhtemoc on August 13, 1521.

According to the Amerindian historian Fernando de Alva Ixtlilxochitl and
other sources, "The Tlaxcalans and other nations which were not well disposed
toward the Mexicans took vengeance on them very cruelly for the past, and
they sacked everything they had."[112] Bernal Díaz reports that in the midst of
their own sacking and fighting, Alvarado and a contingent of men made their
way to the temple of Tlatelolco, where for two hours they fought priests and
warriors guarding their idols: "Nevertheless we climbed to the top, set the
shrines on fire, burnt the idols, and planted our banners there."[113] According to
the *Florentine Codex*, "Everywhere the Spaniards were seizing and robbing the
people. They sought gold; as nothing did they value the green stone, quetzal
feathers, and turquoise."[114] "Pretty women" were set apart to be raped. However, even in the midst of these brutalities, the complexity of human nature
was maintained. According to Bernal Díaz del Castillo, the Spaniards received
into their camp "many poor Indians who had nothing to eat."[115] Exhausted by
siege, Tenochtitlan fell:

When the news spread through all these distant provinces that Mexico was destroyed
their *Caciques* [sic] and lords could not believe it. However, they sent chieftains to
congratulate Cortes [sic] on his victories and yield themselves as vassals to His Majesty, and to see if the city of Mexico, which they had so dreaded, was really razed to
the ground. They all carried great presents of gold to Cortes, and even brought their
small children to show them Mexico, pointing it out to them in much the same way
that we would say: "Here stood Troy."[116]

Tenochtitlan's final days and the cultural construction of New Spain that
followed the Aztec collapse serve as an excellent illustration of the extent to

which nature and culture are operable in the most complex of human circumstances. One historian alone will never be able to unravel all the finely intertwined nuances, but for too many years historians have fallen farther and farther into a cultural constructivist abyss that is producing less and less of value the more removed it is from a reality that it often denies or multiplies. That reality is intrinsically linked to humanity's biological nature. Although Shakespeare's Shylock was a Jew, living in an age of rampant anti-Semitism, like the rest of humankind he still bled when cut. Likewise, Mesoamerican Amerindians and Spaniards both exhibited innate tendencies that run deep in our biological natures. In turn, these deep structures lead to parallels in cultural development that can be understood across cultural boundaries—boundaries that are never impervious in any event.

As demonstrated in the course of this study, chimpanzees fight over territory, display aggressively, have real hierarchies, engage in reciprocal relationships to mutual benefit, and even form what appear to be premeditated coalitions. Much of this basic behavior is also found in the interaction of human children and in what the fossil evidence tells us about early hominids. In turn, the events surrounding the Spanish intervention in Mesoamerica are replete with these fundamental patterns of animal behavior.

Starting with Jane Goodall's pioneering work, it is now commonly known that chimpanzees are capable of great violence. When seven males set themselves up as a new independent community at Gombe in Tanzania, they became subject to the scrutiny of intense patrols launched from the original Gombe community. The patrols proved to be war parties, which culminated in the killing of the seven independently minded males. The killing of full-grown adults of the same species is not common among mammals, but Goodall witnessed savage attacks that were never shorter than ten minutes and always involved gang activity on the part of the aggressors. The attacks continued until the victims were clearly incapacitated, and they involved twisting legs, tearing strips of flesh, and drinking blood as well as beating and pounding.[117] Since Goodall's initial studies, protowarfare has also been detected among other communities of chimpanzees. Likewise, evidence of ritualistic cannibalism, and all the violence that may entail, have been detected at *Homo erectus* sites.[118]

Cannibalism sometimes followed intergroup conflict at Gombe, and as Jane Goodall has written, "The bizarre behavior directed at the corpse by some adult males could well, with a little more intellectual sophistication, evolve into a ritual."[119] Not only are the precursors of human sacrifice found in chimpanzee cultural developments; the brutal reality of rape is also found among chimpanzees. When the Spaniards chose women to be raped during the taking of Tenochtitlan, they were engaging in the basest of primal male behaviors: The perpetuation of one's own genes, an expression of personal potency, with or without female approval. However, not all innate tendencies inevitably lead to competitive violence. To solely focus on these tendencies would be to revive the fallacies of the nineteenth-century Social Darwinists. Today's ethologists readily note the amount of mutual aid and reciprocity inherent in primate communities. Often aggressive display is enough to avoid outright violence, especially within a common community. The Spaniards and Amerindians actually took their display behaviors and used them in their interactions with each other, both during and after the fall of the Aztec Empire. This adaptation eliminated some necessity of outright violence, and it was only possible because the different human cultural groups involved understood enough about the underlying skeletons upon which cultural particulars are fleshed out to be able to read many actions across cultural confines. Many actions were misinterpreted, but mistakes were corrected, and neither the Amerindians nor the Spaniards were so stupid as to continuously be in error. They found parallels within their own cultures to feel more comfortable with the new, and in some instances different cultures arrived at very similar behaviors. Mesoamericans sacked each other's temple precincts upon taking a city. Likewise, during Tenochtitlan's last days, Pedro de Alvarado planted Spanish banners at the temple of Tlatelolco, after fierce resistance from Mexica priests and nobles. Like all male mammals marking their intended territories, Spaniards and Amerindians alike could recognize the significance of desecrating a temple. The action spoke a silent language of dominance and submission. War and intergroup conflict creates a horrible performance art that is all its own.

However, reciprocity and coalition behavior also play their roles, easing some of the tensions exacerbated by ongoing struggles defining dominance and submission within a hierarchy. Within primate groups, a high-ranking male will stop violence and conflict between lower-ranking individuals, adopting a type of policing function as it were: "When performing control activities, males seem to place themselves *above* the conflicting parties in the sense that their interventions are not guided by affiliative preferences. The more protective the interventions by an adult male during a given time period, the less did his interventions correspond with his affiliative relationships."[120] While an obvious benefit is thus provided submissive individuals within any troop or band, the high-ranking primate receives a type of collective support often demonstrated in frequent ritual greetings from grateful low-ranking individuals. Thus, in one primate coalition yielding a type of joint rule at Holland's Arnhem Zoo (ca. 1977), the older and physically weaker Yeroen received three times as many greetings from females and children than his stronger and younger coalition partner Nikkie.[121] Yeroen actually fought Nikkie with female support on a number of occasions to reserve the right of intervention in female conflicts.[122] Coalitions, however, can shift within primate communities, and one summer day in 1980, Nikkie turned on Yeroen with the assistance of Luit, the third male in the Arnhem community. Nikkie and Luit displaced Yeroen from a female in estrus. The old partnership was shattered, and a new triadic relationship among the three males developed, ultimately strengthening Nikkie's position as a type of first among equals. All this had been indeed foreshadowed through Nikkie's systematically isolating and beating females who supported Yeroen. In this, his behavior resembled that of Figan, an alpha male at Goodall's

Gombe site who successfully intimidated potential adversaries when they were found alone.[123] But this was not the end of the story. Yeroen and Nikkie finally joined forces again to kill Luit, tearing off both of his testicles for good measure. Frans de Waal says not only that he cannot look at Yeroen without seeing a murderer; but that he sees human political activity as part of an evolutionary heritage shared with our closest living relatives.[124] In summary, chimpanzees are quite capable of manipulating and shifting coalitions to their advantage. At the top of a chimpanzee hierarchy, different players all come to the game with their own objectives, thus leading to an outcome that must be determined by multiple variables.

In central Mexico from 1519 to 1521, multiple variables and shifting coalitions were once again the reality. Spaniards, Mexica, Texcocans, and Tlaxcalans seem to have been vying for the top position in a hierarchy to be built through coalition. This is normal where male primate behavior is concerned, and it has even been observed continuously at the level of the schoolyard and across cultures where human children are concerned.[125] Coalitions are formed and changed as animals pursue control and power, but coalitions are not built on the basis of violence and intimidation alone. Alpha male chimpanzees engage in food-sharing with their subordinates, and chimpanzees who do not share are more likely to encounter aggression when they beg for food.[126] It is thereby intriguing to note that even during the most violent days of the storming of Tenochtitlan, the Spaniards received "poor Indians," who were starving, into their camp. Likewise, Cortés and Díaz del Castillo both write of the Spaniards' mission to right wrongs and bring justice to Mesoamerica. As noted by Frans de Waal and many others before him, a feeling of noblesse oblige, and its actual manifestation, seems crucial to upholding human chieftainship.[127] For too long many historians have seen this as a mere façade behind which to hide true motivations based on greed and the lust for power. Ethology demonstrates that violence, a lust for dominance, and a willingness to keep the peace and share throughout the ranks are not mutually exclusive where male coalitions are concerned. As has already been demonstrated, these inherent tendencies were as true of the Aztec system as they were of the Spanish system. The introduction of new variables, such as the arrival of Spaniards in central Mexico, merely allows for the more disgruntled individuals and groups within a system to try to redefine the hierarchy and reciprocity of that system. It had happened where Tula and Azcapotzalco were concerned. It happened where Tenochtitlan was concerned, and in the seventeenth century it would happen on a global scale as the Dutch, French, and English began to test and supplant Spanish and Portuguese might in Europe and along the Asian trade routes. On one level, Thucydides and Machiavelli were quite right to view human history as a tale of shifting alliances and shifting power. However, that can never be the whole story, and it remains primarily a story told from the perspective of male aggression.

There are also women in human history. Where sixteenth-century Mexico is concerned, from a male perspective women were often enough seen as the chattel by which to bind coalitions and alliances, but women always remained their own agents. Quietly, at the perimeters of public space assigned them, women spoke "in a different voice," and whenever they were given the opportunity to speak up in the formation of a central coalition or in an important performance of display, they spoke loudly. Malintzin and Cortés were virtually considered the same entity by the Amerindians they encountered. Translator and cultural analyst, "as brave as any man" according to Bernal Díaz, Malintzin spoke publicly and politically before the rulers of central Mexico. By doing this, she was also a cultural innovator, since such public speech was not the norm where women were concerned in Mesoamerican Indian societies. Likewise, that Bernal Díaz had to compare her actions to those of a Spanish man demonstrates that she pushed at the boundaries of the normal where Spaniards were concerned. Whereas Malintzin speaks throughout the "conquest" of Mexico, it will never truly be known if Pedro de Alvarado's Doña Luisa of Tlaxcala and other Amerindian women provided an equally important silent influence in the events described in this chapter.

It is a fact, however, that the aspects of Ameridian cultural traditions that most readily survived after the Spanish arrival were not those associated with male games of dominance and display. As with *curanderas* of the Peruvian altiplano, Mexican *curanderas* maintained the observance of local animistic traditions and healing customs. It is true that they were joined by men in these salvage operations, but of all the pre-Columbian deities, it was Tonantzin, the honored mother of the gods and creation, who survived in the form of the Virgin of Guadalupe. Likewise, tortillas, the backstrap loom, and adobe survived with the *temazcalli* or sweathouse still used in many areas of Mexico today. On one level, these survivals helped to place Amerindians below Spaniards in the new hierarchy, but on another level they eased the transition for Amerindians. Finally, after much initial resistance, every time a maize tortilla is eaten by someone of European ancestry, a victory has been won, and a part of Mesoamerican Amerindian culture has survived in some form. The practices found among women helped to ease the brutalities committed by men, and this work will not ignore this "missing link" in the "conquest" tale.

The machinations of men ultimately led to the embittered realization by Amerindian males that they were to be subordinate partners in a new Mexico —a "New Spain"—dominated by Spaniards. This would never have happened had it not been for smallpox, the microscopic ally that finally won Mexico for the Spaniards by reducing Amerindian numbers and, according to many postconquest sources, the Amerindian will to resist. Elsewhere in the sixteenth century, Portuguese merchants often had to play diplomacy carefully at African and Asian courts. If the Aztecs had been exposed to smallpox and other Old World diseases before the Spanish arrival, the tale told in this chapter would probably have been quite different. Even if the anti-Aztec coalition had won without the assistance of smallpox (a conceivable outcome), the Tlaxcalans would have been in an excellent position to have claimed dominance. Instead, they were forced to adopt the role of proud and respected, but subordinate, allies. Their nobles received encomiendas, coats of arms, Spanish clothing, Spanish horses, and certain limited tax privileges. They helped to subdue territories in Guatemala, portions of the north, and the powerful Mixtón Revolt of the early 1540s. They bought sheep and a European clock for Tlaxcala's plaza mayor, and they continued to rule locally through their own *cabildo*. However, they did have to adopt the Spanish *cabildo* form of governance, collect tribute from their own people for the Spaniards as well as themselves, and obey the Castilian Crown's regulations as stated by the local *corregidor*. They were members of a ruling coalition that did not include the mass of Amerindian commoners, but they were not the dominant members. Biological factors, in the form of smallpox, had given that position to the fortunate Spaniards.

In fact, all of history revolves around a series of accidents and choices, building on natural realities and very real innate biological tendencies that operate through the prisms of learned cultures where hominids, chimpanzees, and perhaps some other primates are concerned. At first history appears to be nothing but a series of accidents. In actuality, it is the most complex of systems, composed of so many combinations of innate tendencies, learned responses, and individual choices that historians are faced with as daunting a task as that facing many natural scientists. This is especially so because the documents read by historians must always be recognized as subjective accounts. There are lies and errors in archives, and historians are left writing plausible and probable fictions that establish patterns of human behavior. These patterns are more easily arrived at if the historian is open to all sorts of accumulated experience rather than trying to re-create a past as "it truly was." Historians function best through metaphor and analogy. Comparative ethology and biologically based psychology serve as natural complements to understanding the tale told about the human animal. As ecologists seek environmental and scientific wisdom among the teachings of Amerindian elders, historians must broaden their outlook so as to seek knowledge and wisdom in biology, for the reality of our material existence is very difficult to deny.

NOTES

1. Ross Hassig, *Mexico and the Spanish Conquest* (London and New York: Longman, 1994), 149.

2. Ibid., 144-49, 101-2.

3. Ibid., 150-58.

4. Geoffrey W. Conrad and Arthur A. Demarest, *Religion and Empire: The Dynamics of Aztec and Inca Expansionism* (Cambridge: Cambridge University Press, 1984), 17.

5. Ibid., 19.

6. Ibid., 20.

7. Ibid.

8. Inga Clendinnen, *Aztecs: An Interpretation* (Cambridge: Cambridge University

Press, 1991), 24.

9. Ibid., 25.

10. Conrad and Demarest, 60.

11. Ibid., 61.

12. Hassig, *Mexico and the Spanish Conquest*, 24.

13. Conrad and Demarest, 62.

14. Bernal Díaz del Castillo, *The Conquest of New Spain*, trans. J. M. Cohen (Harmondsworth: Penguin Books, 1963), 18.

Whenever available, English translations will be referred to in this chapter so as to facilitate further inquiries by the non-Spanish speaking reader. This too reflects on the fact that the events related in this chapter are quite familiar to the expert in Mexican history, though not necessarily to others. In future chapters, Spanish editions will be favored.

15. Ibid., 20-21.

16. H. B. Nicholson, "Recent Sahaguntine Studies: A Review," in *The Work of Bernardino de Sahagún: Pioneer Ethnographer of Sixteenth-Century Aztec Mexico*, ed. J. Jorge Klor de Alva, H. B. Nicholson, and Eloise Quinones Keber (Albany: Institute for Mesoamerican Studies/State University of New York at Albany, 1988), 17-24.

17. Bernal Díaz, 47.

18. Irenäus Eibl-Eibesfeldt, *Human Ethology* (New York: Aldine de Gruyter, 1989), 63. Also 438.

19. Hernán Cortés, "First Letter," in *Hernán Cortés: Letters from Mexico*, trans. Anthony Pagden (New Haven, CT, and London: Yale University Press, 1986), 38-46. Also "Second Letter," 159.

20. Cortés, "Second Letter," 158.

21. Bernal Díaz, 58, 105, 126-39.

22. Ibid., 130.

23. Tzvetan Todorov, *The Conquest of America: The Question of the Other*, trans. Richard Howard (New York: Harper & Row, 1984), 109, 129.

24. Hassig, *Mexico and the Spanish Conquest*, 26.

25. Bernal Díaz, 88.

26. Ibid., 80. Also 60-66.

27. Ibid., 172.

28. Ibid., 78.

29. Ibid., 79-80.

30. Eibl-Eibesfeldt, 492.

31. Ibid., 471, 455.

32. Bernardino de Sahagún, *Florentine Codex: General History of the Things of New Spain*, trans. Arthur J. O. Anderson and Charles E. Dibble, 13 vols. (Santa Fe and Salt Lake City: Monographs of the School of American Research/University of Utah Press, 1950-1982), Bk. 12, chap. 7, p. 20, and chap. 8, p. 21; Inga Clendinnen, "Fierce and Unnatural Cruelty: Cortés and the Conquest of Mexcio," *Representations* 33 (winter 1991): 69.

33. Eibl-Eibesfeldt, 581.

34. *Florentine Codex*, Bk. 12, chap. 7, p. 19.

35. Ibid., p. 20.

36. Bernal Díaz, 89.

37. Ibid., 91.

38. Clendinnen, "Fierce and Unnatural Cruelty," 70.

39. Cortés, "Second Letter," 69.

40. Ibid., 73.

41. Bernal Díaz, 91.

42. *Broken Spears: The Aztec Account of the Conquest of Mexico*, ed. Miguel León-Portilla (Boston: Beacon Press, 1962), 26-31; Bernardino de Sahagún, *Historia general de las cosas de Nueva España*, ed. Angel María Garibay K., 4 vols. (Mexico City: Editorial Porrúa, 1969), 4:34-35.

43. Hassig, *Mexico and the Spanish Conquest*, 44-45.

44. Frans B. M. de Waal, *Chimpanzee Politics: Power and Sex among Apes* (New York: Harper & Row, 1982), 58.

45. Jane van Lawick-Goodall, *In the Shadow of Man* (Boston: Houghton Mifflin, 1971), 117-22.

46. Hassig, *Mexico and the Spanish Conquest*, 55-57.

47. Bernal Díaz, 108.

48. Ibid., 110.

49. Frans B. M. de Waal and A. H. Harcourt, "A History of Ethological Research," in *Coalitions and Alliances in Humans and Other Animals*, ed. Alexander H. Harcourt and Frans B. M. de Waal (Oxford: Oxford University Press, 1992), 14.

50. Bernard Chapais, "The Role of Alliances in Social Inheritance of Rank among Female Primates," in *Coalitions and Alliances*, 29.

51. van Lawick-Goodall, *In the Shadow of Man*, 118; Jane Goodall, *The Chimpanzees of Gombe: Patterns of Behavior* (Cambridge, MA, and London: Belknap Press of Harvard University Press, 1986), 61, 69.

52. Goodall, *Chimpanzees of Gombe*, 68.

53. Karl Grammer, "Intervention in Conflicts among Children," in *Coalitions and Alliances*, 280.

54. Bernal Díaz, 111-13; Hassig, *Mexico and the Spanish Conquest*, 57.

55. Hassig, *Mexico and the Spanish Conquest*, 60.

56. Bernal Díaz, 121.

57. Goodall, *Chimpanzees of Gombe*, 86-87.

58. In *Mexico and the Spanish Conquest*, Ross Hassig implies that the Spaniards did not understand the practice. See 31-32, 51, 60, 144.

59. Bernal Díaz, 121.

60. Hassig, *Mexico and the Spanish Conquest*, 51.

61. Bernal Díaz, 123.

62. Hassig, *Mexico and the Spanish Conquest*, 60-61.

63. Bernal Díaz, 119.

64. Hassig, *Mexico and the Spanish Conquest*, 72-73; Clendinnen, *Aztecs*, 32-33; Conrad and Demarest, 69-70.

65. Conrad and Demarest, 70.

66. Cortés, "Second Letter," 57.

67. Ibid., 58; Bernal Díaz, 145; Hassig, *Mexico and the Spanish Conquest*, 68-74.

68. Cortés, "Second Letter," 59-60.

69. Ibid., 72.

70. Bernal Díaz, 185.

71. Hassig, *Mexico and the Spanish Conquest*, 80.

72. Ibid., 92.

73. *Broken Spears*, 51-53; Hassig, *Mexico and the Spanish Conquest*, 83.

74. Hassig, *Mexico and the Spanish Conquest*, 84.

75. Cortés, "Second Letter," 85-89.

76. Ibid., 91.

77. Fernando de Alva Ixtlilxochitl, *Ally of Cortés*, trans. Douglass K. Ballentine (El Paso: Texas Western Press, 1969), 3-4.

This is an English translation of Account Thirteen of Fernando de Alva Ixtlilxochitl's *Accounts* written around the turn of the seventeenth century. For the Spanish translation of the Nahuatl, see Fernando de Alva Ixtlilxochitl, "Relación de la venida de los españoles y principio de la ley evangélica," in Bernardino de Sahagún, *Historia general de las cosas de Nueva España*, ed. Angel María Garibay K., 4 vols. (Mexico City: Editorial Porrúa, 1969), 4:189.

78. Clendinnen, "Fierce and Unnatural Cruelty," 71, 69.

79. Hassig, *Mexico and the Spanish Conquest*, 88.

80. Heinrich Berlin and Robert H. Barlow, ed. and trans., *Anales de Tlatelolco: unos anales históricos de la nación mexicana y Codice de Tlatelolco* (Mexico City: Antigua Librería Robredo, de José Porrúa e hijos, 1948), 17-18.

81. Conrad and Demarest, 64-65.

82. Ibid., 65-66.

83. Ibid., 67.

84. Fernando de Alva Ixtlilxochitl, *Ally of Cortés*, 3; "Relación de la venida de los españoles," in *Historia general*, 4:189.

85. Douglass K. Ballentine, "Foreward," in *Ally of Cortés*, xiii.

86. Conrad and Demarest, 61.

87. Ibid., 183.

88. Cortés, "Second Letter," 91.

89. Ibid., 85.

90. Hassig, *Mexico and the Spanish Conquest*, 89.

91. Bernal Díaz, 58.92. Charles Gibson, *Tlaxcala in the Sixteenth Century* (New Haven, CT: Yale University Press, 1952), 164; John Eoghan Kelley, *Pedro de Alvarado, Conquistador* (Princeton, NJ: Princeton University Press, 1932), 43.

93. R. C. Padden, *The Hummingbird and the Hawk: Conquest and Sovereignty in the Valley of Mexico, 1503-1541* (Columbus: Ohio State University Press, 1967), 194-95.

94. William H. Prescott, *History of the Conquest of Mexico*, in *History of the Conquest of Mexico and History of the Conquest of Peru* (New York: Modern Library, 1936), 354.

95. *La Historia de Tlatelolco desde los tiempos mas remotos*, in *Anales de Tlatelolco: unos anales históricos de la nación mexicana y Codice de Tlatelolco*, ed. and trans. Heinrich Berlin and Robert H. Barlow (Mexico City: José Porrúa e hijos, 1948), 63.

96. *Florentine Codex*, Bk. 12, chap. 19, p. 49.

97. Bernal Díaz, 286.

98. *Florentine Codex*, Bk. 12, chap. 20, p. 54.

99. Ibid.

100. Ibid., chap. 21, pp. 55-56; Bk. 12, chap. 23, p. 63.

101. Cortés, "Second Letter," 132. Also Pagden's note 89 on pp. 477-78.

102. Bernal Díaz, 294.

103. Hassig, *Mexico and the Spanish Conquest*, 94.

104. Bernal Díaz, 295.

105. Ibid., 299

106. Hassig, *Mexico and the Spanish Conquest*, 98.

107. Ibid., 101.

108. Ibid., 106.

109. Ibid., 135-36.

110. Bernal Díaz, 387-88.

111. Ibid., 389-91.

112. Fernando Alva de Ixtlilxochitl, *Ally of Cortés*, 51; "Relación de la venida de los españoles," in *Historia general*, 4:225.

113. Bernal Díaz, 397.

114. *Florentine Codex*, Bk. 12, chap. 40, p. 118.

115. Bernal Díaz, 400.

116. Ibid., 413.

117. Goodall, *Chimpanzees of Gombe*, 489-517, 528-34.

118. Richard E. Leakey and Roger Lewin, *Origins* (New York: E. P. Dutton, 1977), 132. It is important to note that Leakey and other paleoanthropologists are unwilling to extrapolate aggressiveness from the evidence of cannibalism, but given the agonistic display behavior of contemporary chimpanzees and the fifteenth- and sixteenth-century Nahuas, Caribs, and Tupinamba, there remains a very real possibility of a link between cannibalism and aggressive behavior.

119. Goodall, *Chimpanzees of Gombe*, 533. Also 528-34.

120. Frans B. M. de Waal, "Coalitions as Part of Reciprocal Relations in the Arnhem Chimpanzee Colony," in *Coalitions and Alliances*, 242.

121. de Waal, *Chimpanzee Politics*, 151.

122. de Waal, "Coalitions as Part of Reciprocal Relations," in *Coalitions and Alliances*, 243.

123. Ibid., 245-47.

124. Reported in Richard Leakey and Roger Lewin, *Origins Reconsidered: In Search of What Makes Us Human* (New York: Doubleday, 1992), 278-79.

125. See Karl Grammer, "Intervention in Conflicts among Children: Contexts and Consequences," in *Coalitions and Alliances*, 259-83; Eibl-Eibesfeldt, 600-602.

126. de Waal, *Chimpanzee Politics*, 200; Goodall, *Chimpanzees of Gombe*, 374; van Lawick-Goodall, *In the Shadow of Man*, 50-51; W. C. McGrew, *Chimpanzee Material Culture: Implications for Human Evolution* (Cambridge and New York: Cambridge University Press, 1992), 107; de Waal, "Coalitions as Part of Reciprocal Relations," in *Coalitions and Alliances*, 250.

127. de Waal, "Coalitions as Part of Reciprocal Relations," in *Coalitions and Alliances*, 252.

5

The Structures of Material Life: Clothing, Shelter, and Community in Sixteenth-Century Mexico

Although modern primatology does not claim that chimpanzees have human material culture, it is undeniable that they do have a form of pongid material culture. Throughout Africa numerous chimpanzee communities have been observed fishing for ants and termites. At Gombe and Assirik, two independent chimpanzee populations use twigs, vines, and grass to make slender probes that are then inserted into termite mounds to acquire the desired food, but different choices have been made by the chimpanzees at different sites:

At Assirik, 86% of such twig or vine tools were totally peeled of their bark, which was always discarded. At Gombe, *no* tool was ever peeled; instead in 21% of tools the bark was used for fishing, and the twig or vine was thrown away. Both populations knew how to peel bark, but they used the result in opposite ways. This sort of contrast looks by exclusion to be social custom, a pattern "liberated" from environmental constraints.[1]

W. C. McGrew, the author of the above citation, is careful enough to note that Gombe's woody vegetation might not peel as well as Assirik's, that environmental constraints might still play their role. The significant thing about this cautious observation is that similar debates have always arisen regarding human cultural developments, often under the rubric of debates regarding free will and determinism. Whether determinism should be expressed as Calvinist predestination, Marxist economic materialism, or genetic programming, human cultures, like chimpanzee cultures, have not always been seen as the product of choices freely made. Of course, "choice" itself is a loaded term, implying a certain amount of understanding and self-awareness in the action undertaken. The fact that chimpanzees recognize themselves in the mirror and have developed compound words in human sign language may not be enough to demonstrate humanlike consciousness to anyone predisposed to anthropocentrism, but the fact that chimpanzee infants intently observe their mothers while they dip for ants suggests a capacity for observational learning that implies culture. Observation has not revealed the presumed mechanisms of learning, but "impressive circumstantial evidence exists . . . for the transmission of patterns from older to younger individuals, especially from mothers to offspring."[2]

Whereas male chimpanzees are likely to hunt, females are likely to fish for termites and ants. In a study of 194 faecal samples from thirty identified chimpanzees, Jane Goodall noted that relative to male samples, over three times as many female samples contained termites.[3] Likewise, in W. C. McGrew's study of eleven females and thirteen males over 4.5 years of age, "the proportions of those who actively dipped to those who only watched was very different though: three-quarters of the females dipped but less than half of the males."[4] Female chimpanzees fish for termites and ants in higher numbers than males, who acquire protein by periodically hunting. And where male hunting is concerned, parallels have been drawn between the hunting of chimpanzees and that of hypothesized protohominids:

Both are done mostly by males. Both concentrate on immature prey. Both parasite other predators by piracy or scavenging. Both involve either solitary or social hunting.

One major difference between chimpanzee and early hominid hunting is in the use of tools. Archaeological data from the Plio-Pleistocene onwards clearly show early hominids using tools in the processing of large, mammalian prey. Although successful predation by chimpanzees on mammals has been seen almost 400 times at Gombe alone, only a handful of cases of tool-use have been seen.[5]

Whereas projectiles may be thrown and clubs may be brandished at prey, sophisticated and constant tool use is absent from male hunting: "If the parallels between observed ape and hypothesized protohominid data are genuine, then the evolutionary origins of tool-use are more likely to have come from solitary, female gathering and not from social, male hunting."[6] In short, while male primates have developed the hunt and war, females have quietly developed their own means of sustenance and tools, and among free chimpanzee bands, tools go far beyond the use of twigs and grass.

Chimpanzee tools do vary from community to community. At Gombe, but not at neighboring Kasoje, chimpanzees smash hard-shelled fruits against anvils of stone or wood. At Taï and Bossou, in the far west of the African continent, stones are employed as hammers and flexible vegetation is used to acquire ants, but not termites. Only at Assirik, however, do chimpanzees use stones as crushing implements and pliable vegetation as "fishing" rods for insects.[7] Not all chimpanzee communities, therefore, do exactly the same things in the wild, just as human cultures do not completely resemble each other, but these variances do not prevent primatologists from seeing the chimpanzee despite the differences. Among all chimpanzee subspecies is a marked tendency to implement portions of the material environment to make their lives easier. Leaves, for example, may be used at Kasoje as food, napkins, or sponges. They may also be used to attract the attention of females during courtship, but they are never used in this fashion in neighboring Gombe.[8]

Perhaps most importantly from the perspective of material culture, leaves and other parts of trees are used for nest building. Not exclusively an aspect of chimpanzee life, nests are made by all great apes. Usually made out of live vegetation, they are used for napping during the day and for sleeping at night. Once constructed, nests are used by chimpanzees for many events other than sleeping. Eating, grooming, copulation, birth, healing, and death may all take place in nests. In fact, nest building is eminently social, and most chimpanzees sleep in parties. The basic design of such nests remains similar across regions, but the height and openness to the sky, among other things, may vary from region to region.[9]

Chimpanzee nests clearly are not human houses, yet they are, like human buildings, constructed sites with functions that go beyond the mere provision of rest. More importantly, their construction does show variance among different chimpanzee populations, although the basic design and purpose remain the same. In short, a universal animal pursuit of shelter has found different expressions within the same species because of regional environmental variations and adaptation choices made within the different environments. Increasingly, evidence points to chimpanzee inventiveness and self-awareness, thus indicating the potential for the development of material culture. As with their human cousins, chimpanzees reflect regional cultural differences and underlying species-specific universals. In the future, primatologists, including anthropologists and historians, will spend their time well by trying to discover what is biological, what is learned, and how learning and custom may affect the genetic and biological tendencies inherent in their subjects. This is no easy task, but it will be central to understanding just what impact cultural shifts, learning, and even political and social programs may have on human individuals with their well-documented tendencies to self-preservation, sexuality, aggression, competition, reciprocity, and altruism. Chimpanzees, our closest living relatives, provide the perspective necessary to realize that not only did sixteenth-century Spaniards and Aztecs share very real human traits, despite learned cultural differences, they also shared not a few of these universal traits with other animals. To separate humanity from the rest of nature is the first step toward emphasizing cultural differences among human groups. It is the existence of chimpanzee nest building that allows us to understand that although Aztec and Spanish buildings were different, they also served similar universal purposes, including the purpose of display.

Display has been defined as an evolutionary modification producing a behavior pattern that communicates or signals information.[10] Both Spanish and Aztec construction incorporated elements of display behavior most likely absent in the nest building of the great apes. Cultural learning, across human groups, has exaggerated the extent to which shelter is used to express potency and group affiliation. Likewise, although some chimpanzees have been noted to make footwear out of leaves, clothing is alien to chimpanzee material culture. Among humans, clothing not only serves to replace the protection normally provided by fur and hair but also communicates innate tendencies toward the establishment of hierarchy and community, as well as the specifics of learned customs.

Humans paint, tattoo, and clothe themselves in artificial displays that often reflect more than one function. While clothing fulfills the biological function of protection from the elements, it also may call attention to secondary sexual characteristics or indicate group and class membership. Clothing communicates, and scholars can easily refer to the ethology of clothing according to Irenäus Eibl-Eibesfeldt.[11] This is because the cultural creation of specific clothing is often used to express an innate tendency toward display that might be expressed by some other means without clothes—but it would still be expressed. Drawing on the work of P. Leyhausen, Eibl-Eibesfeldt writes that men's shoulders are artificially enhanced by clothing in various cultures, emphasizing characteristics no longer anatomically significant, but once so.

If we analyze the hair growth patterns on a man we find that tufts of hair would develop on the shoulders if hair growth were increased to a significant length. We can assume that males had more hair in earlier times than they do today and that the hair growth patterns served to enlarge the body outline of our upright ancestors. Hair growth declined during the course of hominization, but the receptor adaptation may have remained, which resulted in a preference and thus drew particular attention to this region of the body.[12]

Nineteenth-century European military epaulets, the winglike extended shoulders of a samurai's vest, and the shoulder feathers worn by the Yanomami of Brazil all reflect the continuation of this trend.[13] No doubt among australopithecine ancestors, prominent shoulder tufts would have added the appearance of intimidating size where an upright, displaying male was concerned. In her earliest studies among the chimpanzees of Gombe, Jane Goodall noted that attaining an upright position is a common practice among males who are aggressively displaying. The brandishing of tree limbs may also be included in such an aggressive display.[14] In turn, both actions increase the appearance of size and potency, just as epaulets and shoulder feathers do. Clothing serves as a cultural method of communication, and it is one tied to animal tendencies developed over the course of evolution.

Likewise, chimpanzee nest-building behavior encompasses the construction of social bonds as well as "beds." Since chimpanzees often sleep in parties, a sense of group affiliation as well as mutual protection is often enough provided in the nest. Of greater interest perhaps is that chimpanzees weave branches, although they do not wear or weave clothing. In short, the basic steps involved in the creation of clothing are present among humanity's pongid cousins.

Although culture may exaggerate and conceal, it does not completely eliminate humanity's animal nature.

CLOTHING AND CUSTOM

Given cultural prejudices that influenced their interpretations of reality, when sixteenth-century Spaniards observed Amerindians they saw incomplete people. In the Americas, Spaniards perceived their mission as the introduction of Amerindian peoples to the proper ordering of society, human individuals, and nature. They believed that Amerindian souls required the saving message of Christianity and that Indian bodies needed proper disciplining in accordance with the moral precepts of Christian civilization. Thus, clothing and construction deemed appropriate from a Spanish Christian cultural perspective were used to demonstrate the Spaniards' desired dominance over submissive Amerindians. Churches were therefore strategically placed to represent the potency of the official Spanish cult, and indigenous men and women were made to dress in a fashion that did not offend Christian teachings on modesty, if they did not already do so. In turn, the Spaniards were careful to retain enough observable material differences between themselves and the indigenous populations, just as the Indians were loathe to abandon all aspects of their own culture. The differences defined the hierarchy in visible terms, and the introduction of Amerindians to Spanish customs always remained a function both of what the Spaniards chose to impose and what the Indians chose to accept. On a visible level, the bodily applications of Christian precepts focused on the issue of appropriate uniformity and distinction in clothing and construction.

The first Spaniards to arrive in the Americas were not humanists or intellectuals. As a result, they did not define or judge Amerindian culture on the basis of art and literature, but on the basis of clothing, shelter, and food. Clothing and shelter, the protection of bodies from the forces of nature, became an indicator of how civilized the Indians were in Spanish eyes—literally of how well they had shut themselves off from "brute nature." Civilization meant the improved protection of bodies from heat, rain, cold, and "base" animal drives. Where Indians were poorly clad, they were perceived either as representatives of humanity before the Fall or as examples of humankind at its most lewd and lascivious. In actuality, reactions to Indian nudity revealed the cultural taboos of the first Europeans to make contact with peoples who often required no clothing for protection. In the Brazilian tropics, the chronicler of Pedro Alvares Cabral's Portuguese expedition of 1500, Pero Vaz da Caminha, wrote that the innocence of the Brazilian Indians was such that Adam's could not have been greater. Still, the Portuguese attempted to clothe the Indians, especially a naked young woman who "disturbed" the sailors while they were hearing mass.[15] The Indians were ingenuous to European customs and eroticism. Spanish as well as Portuguese explorers would not leave them so.

A *relación* described the Indians of Florida as being without gold, silver, or pearls, miserable, deceitful, treacherous, and naked.[16] As late as 1583 the

Indians of the Conchas River were *"desnudos"* and sustained themselves on "roots and other things of little sustenance."[17] Clothing deemed appropriate by the Spaniards became the fastest and simplest method of discriminating against Amerindians. A lack of clothing was associated with a lack of civilization and wealth. Naked Indians required proper dress in Spanish eyes, and even las Casas, the great defender of the Indians, in his *Brevisima Relación* of 1552, made an effort to explain how Indians generally covered their genitals.[18] Sixteenth-century Spaniards defined animals as subordinate and naked consumers of roots. Humans were divinely chosen and clothed.

The conquerors of Mexico brought these prejudices and sexual taboos with them, and they were impressed to find that the Amerindians of central and southern Mexico were generally unlike those of the Caribbean islands. Bernal Díaz del Castillo, foot soldier and chronicler of Cortés's expedition, wrote:

These Indians wore cotton shirts made in the shape of jackets, and covered their private parts with narrow cloths which they called masteles. We considered them a more civilized people than the Cubans. For they went about naked, except for the women, who wore cotton cloths that came down to their thighs.[19]

This passage describes Bernal Díaz's first encounter with Indians of the Mexican mainland during his participation in the 1517 expedition of Francisco Hernández. Immediately, the indigenous population of the Mexican coast was determined to be "more civilized" than that of Cuba, and this was made clear by their homes as well as by their clothing. Bernal Díaz recorded that six miles from the coast, the Hernández expedition sighted a large town they dubbed Great Cairo, since they had never seen one as large in Cuba or Hispaniola.[20] Urban settlement and a lack of nudity were so linked to the Spanish concept of civilization that Spaniards consistently complimented Amerindian cultures by means of these two attributes. In his exaggerated description of the Pueblo "seven cities of Cibola," Fray Marcos de Niza followed the same formula as Bernal Díaz. The Indians of fabulous Cibola were identified as civilized because of their vast populations, well-ordered streets, large houses, and elaborate dress.[21] Likewise, the same pattern was also followed by Hernán Cortés.

In a letter to Charles V dated July 10, 1519, Cortés provided a relatively detailed description of the clothing worn from the cape of Yucatan to the vicinity of Villa Rica de la Vera Cruz. He mentioned the basic male vestments as a loincloth and thin mantle "decorated in a Moorish fashion," and like the men of Cabral's Brazilian expedition, he paid close attention to the dress of female Indians:

The common women wear highly colored mantles from the waist to the feet, and others which cover their breasts, leaving the rest uncovered. The women of rank wear skirts of very thin cotton, which are very loose-fitting and decorated and cut in the manner of a rochet.[22]

Bernal Díaz and Cortés were representative of the Spanish reaction to Indian clothing customs. Clothing was seen primarily not as a form of protection from the elements but as protection from illicit sexual urges. Spanish customs of dress were informed by Christian myths concerning humanity's fall from innocence and grace. Cultural taboos focused on male sexual response to the naked female body, and although men were taught to control their sexual urges, an inordinate amount of emphasis was placed on a woman's "need" to cover herself and act modestly so as not to elicit a sexual response from males. As in the myth of the Garden of Eden, women were seen as the source of sin and the tempters of men. They were taught to protect their honor by not losing their virginity, whereas men could earn honor through deeds accomplished, including deeds of sexual prowess in many instances.[23] Likewise, the Nahuas of central Mexico cursed the "shamelessness" of the harlot and taught modest women to accept their subordinate role as providers of food and clothing.[24] Women were to be quiet and covered. Ideally, they were to be submissive in both cultures, unless acting in a special noble capacity or as a mother. The Spaniards, therefore, judged the Indians of Mexico to have an "inkling of propriety" in their attitudes toward the human body, but this behavior, behavior comparable to that of the Spaniards, was mixed with a certain alien otherness that could only be labeled inappropriate by the closed Spanish mentality.

Spaniards were fascinated by both the similarities and the differences between their culture and those of the Amerindians of Mexico. In the description of male Indian attire in Cortés's letter to Charles V, the differences are first alluded to in his comparison of Amerindian dyeing to that of the Moors. The Moors were the most alien culture with which the Spaniards had long-term experience, and Cortés was quite given to using analogy to the Moors to illustrate the otherness of Amerindian custom. When he saw enough similarity, the Amerindians were readily compared to Spaniards, but their differences, comparable to the customs of the infidel Moors, justified the conquest of a heathen people by Christians.

Cortés, his secretary and biographer López de Gómara, and Bernal Díaz all were impressed by the luxury that surrounded the Mesoamerican prince Moctezuma. They mentioned that he never used the same towel or dressed in the same clothes twice, and that he was approached with complete obeissance, the Aztec nobles averting their faces in his presence.[25] This led Cortés and others to draw analogies between Moctezuma and stereotypical Oriental despots, Sahagún even reviving the ancient Persian title of "satrap" to identify Moctezuma's subordinate nobles.[26] The conquistador could easily accept noble privilege, but he could not accept the virtual deification of the prince; that was something he reserved for the Christian God. Cortés's Spanish society was continuously trying to regulate luxury through ever-failing sumptuary laws,[27] and he did not have the time or inclination to seek out similar attempts among the Aztecs. He judged excessive opulence as a weakness in the cultures of the Aztecs and the other newly conquered Indians of Mexico, just as he judged human sacrifice and cannibalism as erroneous rituals.[28] Although the Indians of

Mexico were on the "right path" in matters of dress, they were not correct in matters of ritual interpretation or the "refinements" of bodily adornment.

In describing the Amerindians of coastal Mexico, Cortés took time to mention how they "deformed" their appearance by splitting their lips to the gums and wearing obsidian and gold lip plugs.[29] As such, their splendor and conceptions of beauty were so strange that the Spaniards judged them signs of ugliness. Nowhere was this ugliness deemed more perverse than when it blended with symbolic dress that could be understood and admired by the Spaniards. The native priests of Mexico provided a case in point, and Bernal Díaz described them by linking proper and improper characteristics. These priests, whom Bernal Díaz called *papas*, "wore black cloaks like those of canons" and sometimes small hoods "like Dominicans," but they also wore hair, matted in human blood, to their feet: "Their ears were cut to pieces as a sacrifice, and they smelt of sulphur. But they also smelt of something worse: of decaying flesh."[30] Not only were they practitioners of human sacrifice; according to Bernal Díaz, they were sodomites as well. Legally banned from marriage in his account, they were portrayed as a foul parody of the Roman Catholic priesthood in their appearance and behavior. The similarities of chastity and somber black dress were noted by Cortés, but the conqueror of Mexico limited his identification of dissimilarities to the long, tangled hair of the *papas*. To him, idol worship alone was enough to make the *papas* false priests, and in general he did not often criticize the people of Mexico, although the custom of human sacrifice was mentioned sparingly to invalidate the Indians' otherwise impressive achievements in the building arts.[31] It was actually in Cortés's best interest to portray the Aztecs as eminently civilized, since doing so only increased his status and prestige as the conqueror of a people with *policía*, or law and order.

Cortés and Bernal Díaz were ready to point out that the Amerindians' most striking architectural achievements, their adorned urban centers, were also the sites of the foul human sacrifices. Mesoamerican temples were admired for their size and grandeur, but their religious functions bespoke of error and barbarism to the sixteenth-century Spanish mentality.[32] On the other hand, the private homes of the nobility posed less of a threat to the first conquistadores. Cortés readily praised the homes of the Aztec nobility for their furnishings, kitchens, corridors, and gardens. On observing the Itztapalapa homes of Moctezuma's brother, Cuitlahuac, Cortés regarded them "as good as the best in Spain; that is, in respect of size and workmanship both in their masonry and woodwork and their floors, and furnishings for every sort of household task." However, he noted that they lacked the ostentation of which Spaniards approved, namely, reliefs and works of art to which they were accustomed in the homes of the rich.[33] He likewise remarked on the beautiful homes of Moctezuma's "vassals" in Tenochtitlan, on their immense rooms and pleasant gardens.[34] Bernal Díaz, mercenary that he was, paid special attention to Tenochtitlan's royal storehouses, but he also described the temple of Huitzilopochtli in detail as a slaughterhouse where innocents were offered to demons and then eaten by the *papas*. He "always called that building Hell."[35] As with clothing, the conquistadores were once again impressed by the Mexican Indians' ability to shelter themselves with great skill and art from the brutalities of nature, but as with clothing, Amerindian buildings were interpreted as a sign of both civilized culture and inappropriate behavior. Things as seemingly innocuous as shelter and clothing became tools to justify and impose imperialism, and the friar-chroniclers of the history of sixteenth-century New Spain, for all their admiration of Indian culture, proved no exception to this rule.

The Franciscans Bernardino de Sahagún and Gerónimo de Mendieta, as well as the Jesuit Joseph de Acosta, discussed the ritual use of clothing in their chronicles. It is not surprising that as men who wore ceremonial vestments themselves, they should touch upon this aspect of human adornment. However, the tenor of their argument quickly became the perverse and inappropriate use the Indians made of such adornment, ceremonial dress being linked in these works primarily to acts of human sacrifice. The Aztecs were shown as reserving their best clothing and their greatest building achievements, their temples, for acts of idolatry. Yet certain practices struck much too close to home. In detail, Sahagún described the clothing and plumage worn by various ranks of Aztec men and women at sacrificial feasts, while both he and Acosta noted that even the statues of gods like Quetzalcoatl were dressed in shirts and headdresses—Acosta describing Quetzalcoatl's headdress as similar to a papal miter.[36] The Jesuit also took time to note that Aztec priests wore vestments similar to those of Catholic ceremony, including a short alb with an ornamental fringe.[37] Sahagún, for his part, noted the various states of dress and undress among human sacrifices themselves, remarking that the victims were exceptionally well dressed and well fed while awaiting death, but naked during an actual instance of sacrifice (the feast of the tenth month or Xocotlhuetzi): "Because they no longer had need of vestments, nor anything else, since presently they would have to die, naked they awaited death."[38]

During the act of human sacrifice, Mexican Indians shed both clothing and civilization. Thus nudity was linked in the sixteenth-century Spanish worldview not only with death but with the barbarism of natural, uncivilized states. Ironically, the Spaniards selectively failed to recognize that they themselves revered a half-clad man being tortured on a cross. In the Aztec case, the sacrifice's final nudity was linked to the perverse state of a culture that could spill so much blood, dress so well, and construct such beautiful edifices as their temples––all for the sake of idols and demons. The intricacy of the temples did not hide their prime function to Sahagún, Mendieta, and Acosta. They were seen as the places of naked savagery described by the conquistadores, and Mendieta compared the legendary attempts of Cholula (Cortés's Churultecal) to construct a temple-pyramid reaching the heavens with those of the inhabitants of Babel. Ultimately, Mendieta's "one true God" confounded both attempts.[39] Shocked by the number and methods of Aztec human sacrifices, Acosta wrote about them to show the power of Satan and of spiritual evil in the material world:

"And in order to show you the great misfortune of these people blinded by the Demon, I will refer extensively to the inhuman practice which they had in this place."[40] Using their own terms and definitions, Spaniards perceived the incongruities of barbarism and civilization existing side by side in Aztec culture. Given their own cultural limitations, they generally could not see any in their own society, nor in themselves when they massacred Aztec nobles and priests at one of Tenochtitlan's religious ceremonies—nor could they see them in the activities of the Holy Inquisition.[41] Spanish violence was just and justified by the Spaniards' own familiarity with it. In their minds, the familiar culture was fundamentally the true culture.

In his *Historia eclesiástica indiana*, the priest Mendieta argued that Amerindian material culture was taking the right turn, since the postconquest Indians of Mexico were demonstrating their new Christian faith through the sponsorship and construction of numerous churches.[42] Their former devotion to "false" gods was transferred to the "Spanish Truth," and in the 1570s, even Cholula, that former Babel, supported more than thirty friars in its monastery of San Francisco de los Angeles.[43] Churches were replacing the bloody temples as a visible sign of the triumph of Spanish culture. Still, Sahagún, Acosta, and Mendieta all firmly agreed that Indian culture did not warrant complete destruction. Acosta argued that the Indians of Mexico possessed a substantial understanding of law and order, or *policía*, and Sahagún felt that the Spaniards were called to cure a diseased social organism, not to kill it.[44] Certain aspects of Amerindian cultures were to be corrected, but the fundamentals, including those in the areas of clothing and construction, could remain the same.

As late as the early seventeenth century the Spaniards continued to demonstrate a preoccupation with the propriety of "New World" material culture. The late-sixteenth- and early-seventeenth-century *relaciones geográficas* confirm this by reiterating the importance of clothing and shelter as public concerns. Developed by Juan de Ovando, president of the Council of the Indies as of 1571, the *Ordenanzas Ovandinas* (1570-1573) called for a systematic exploration of the cultural accomplishments of New World Spaniards to determine what was needed to maintain good government and social order in the Americas.[45] The *corregidores* and *cabildos* of American towns were required to respond to a series of questions, and from 1577 to 1581 a number of *relaciones*, or reports, arrived in Madrid. In 1604 the conde de Lemus, then president of the council, revised the royal questionnaire to include 355 questions, among them questions specifically dealing with the physical layout of towns and the quality of their edifices.[46] The questionnaire also asked: "What clothing is manufactured in this town?" "How many stores of Spanish clothing [are there]?" "How many of local clothing, and of what types?" "How many textile *obrajes* and fulleries does this town have in its district?" "What quality of woolens, serges and sackcloth do they manufacture every year, and what is the quality and price of each thing?"[47] An exploration of such Spanish questions provides the investigator with insight concerning Spanish attitudes toward not only material culture but also exchange, hierarchy, dominance, reciprocity—and *policía* or civilization.

CLOTHING, CULTURE, AND EXCHANGE

Among the Aztecs, as among other Amerindian groups of central Mexico, spinning and weaving were the particular domain of women, regardless of social class. In legend their invention was attributed to the goddess Xochiquetzal, who required that Aztec women be sacrificed to her during her feast day. These women, imolated in honor of the goddess, first burnt their weaving tools, which would have included the backstrap loom found to this day in innumerable Mexican towns and villages. Stretching warp threads between two horizontal bars, the weaver has one bar attached to her body, while the other is tied to a tree or post. The width of the cloth is determined by the weaver's armspan, while lengths can be quite long. Increase in width, in turn, may be achieved by seaming separate pieces of cloth together. Seemingly dating back to the second millenium BC in Mesoamerica, the production of cloth—out of maguey fiber, bark, or cotton—was not identified as one of the male "guild" crafts among the Aztecs. Whereas men functioned as goldsmiths, lapidaries, and featherworkers, women of the nobility and commoners were expected to dress themselves and their families.[48] Collected as tribute by the Aztec Empire, cloth became a woman's standard contribution to the pre-Columbian market-place and elite. Soon after the birth of any baby girl, a spindle and weaving stick were placed in her hand, foretelling her destiny in the sexual division of labor, and young noble girls received special training in schools attached to the temples. Clearly an aspect of women's subculture, weaving, using the pre-Columbian backstrap loom, has survived as such, while many other aspects of pre-Columbian cultures have not.

If anything, there is a relationship here to Aztec weaving's existence as part of the female domestic sphere. Whereas European men could readily be found in the early modern textile trades, Nahua men were not. Textile production was not bound to male prestige and hierarchy in Mesoamerica, and it was not thereby an immediate target of the conquering Spanish male's display of domi-nance. The prime target of such displays remained Aztec males, although Aztec women, of course, could be victimized by Spaniards as well. As long as the backstrap loom did not challenge a Spanish male's public authority or produce clothing deemed "indecent" by a Spanish male's public sensibility, the backstrap loom was not considered important enough for destruction. Ironi-cally, the very survival of the backstrap loom meant the survival of a portion of pre-Columbian cultures, a portion quietly maintained by women. Whereas the very public and political displays that were temples were to be eliminated, weaving, like basic home design for the poor and powerless, remained a place where Amerindians could salvage aspects of their cultures. The domestic sphere, women's sphere, became a primary expressive locus of Amerindian agency and independence. The private manufacture of cloth could remain Amerindian.

Nonetheless Spaniards made their demands where the very public accumulation of wealth in cloth and the public wearing of clothing were concerned. On a very basic level of publicly expressed and displayed material culture, that of trade and exchange, the Spanish chroniclers noted that the Indians of Mexico were prepared for the infiltration of Spanish ways. Moreover, where clothing was concerned, the adoption of certain Amerindian practices actually proved beneficial to the Spaniards. A hybridization of cultures occurred where cotton was concerned. Although much given to arguing the inferiority of New World plants, Joseph de Acosta could not fail to praise cotton as "one of the greatest benefits the Indies have."[49] Given to flourishing in hot climates, cotton thread could be woven fine or coarse, thus serving the needs of both rich and poor where wool and flax failed to flourish.[50] Recognized by individuals like Fray Motolinía as a variety of tribute payment in pre-Columbian times, cotton cloth in the form of *mantas* persisted as a type of tribute payment after the conquest of Mexico.[51] Spaniards immediately grasped that the demands of tributary imperialism could be understood easily by the Indians of Mexico. The sixteenth-century chroniclers noted that, in pre-Columbian times, clothing was traded and exchanged, thus presenting evidence for the existence of economic order and *policía*.[52] Despite their failure in matters of ritual adornment, the Aztecs and other peoples of Mexico were judged somewhat civilized, since they possessed clothes and understood trade and tributary exchange.[53]

In an attempt to regulate prices and prevent hoarding, Mexico City's *cabildo*, as the local defender of the body politic's common good, issued a May 16, 1533 ordinance that required all commercial purchasers of tributary items to declare the exact amount and condition of the items purchased for resale.[54] These goods could be either perishable or imperishable, food or articles of clothing and items for household use. If the latter, the *vecinos* of the capital were to be provided with six days in which to purchase the goods to the exclusion of all other customers. If the former, they were to be provided with three days. Since this was a standard corporate privilege of the time for an elite in good standing, the Audiencia of New Spain approved this legislation and provided future historians with a source of information regarding clothing sales.[55]

On June 1, 1535, in concordance with the *cabildo*'s ordinance, Gregorio Ruiz, *regidor* of Mexico City, recorded the arrival of tributary goods purchased from Hernán Cortés by a merchant named Juan Marín. The tribute came from the Indian townships of Cuernavaca, Yautepeque, Guastepeque, Tepustlan, and Acapistla, and foremost among the items of tribute were articles of clothing in great demand in Mexico City. The capital's *vecinos* had replaced Moctezuma and his fellow Aztec lords as the recipients of tributary clothes, with Spanish merchants replacing the merchants who once sold cloth in the marketplaces of Tenochtitlan. According to the testimony of 1535, Marín's business revolved around the resale of shirts (*camisas*), shifts (*naguas*), half-cloaks (*mantas*), and coverlets (*colchas*). The quantities involved were substantial, Cortés's tribute being as much as 234 *cargas* of *mantas* from Cuernavaca and 96 *cargas* of *mantas* from Guastepeque. Finished shirts and shifts were received in much smaller quantities—only five *cargas* total from Cuernavaca, Guastepeque, and Yautepeque combined. Still, the value of shirts and shifts made up for the lack of quantity. Rodrigo de Baeza reported that Marín paid twenty-five gold pesos for each *carga* of shirts and shifts, but only four and a half gold pesos for each *carga* of *ropa de mantas*. A number of witnesses reported that he resold the *mantas* at approximately six and a half gold pesos for each *carga*.[56] With the primary producers providing the articles of resale at no cost, a substantial profit could be turned by all Spaniards involved. The Crown, through its Audiencia in this case, approved of the profit-making economic exchange of manufactured products. An organic system of hierarchy, exchange, and reciprocity was thus administered by the Crown and its officials in the New World, as it had been in the Old.

In places as far removed as the Yucatan, Indian *mantas* came to be collected as a standard form of tribute. There, the tributary records for 1549-1551 reveal that anywhere from 60 to 1,200 *mantas* were collected annually as the produce of encomienda labor. Each *manta* was valued at two *tomines*, and individual encomenderos like Cisneros, a *vecino* of San Francisco de Campeche, could expect 120 *mantas* from the Indians of Axaba and 250 *mantas* from Ixpona.[57] Only the Crown and individuals of reputation could hope to rival the number of *mantas* collected by Cortés for resale in Mexico City. In the Yucatan, His Majesty was due annual amounts of 1,030 *mantas* from Telchiqui, 470 from Quibil, 400 from Taxan, 250 from Çabanal, 120 from Nolo, and as little as 60 from Yaxcocul.[58] A crucial qualification to all these collections, however, was that the *mantas* delivered by the Indians be "of those they are accustomed to give." Thus, the Mexican Indians' custom of tributary payment in cloth and textiles provided the Spaniards with a means of easily introducing the commercial exchange of manufactured goods from the very start. To the benefit of Spanish and Amerindian elites alike, the language of exchange was understood by all parties involved in Mexico, including the Amerindian commoners. In fact, after the plague of 1545-1548, "many Indians took up occupations as traders, frequently claiming to be descendants of pochtecah," the leading Aztec merchants of pre-Columbian times.[59] In 1553 the noble-dominated *cabildo* of Amerindian Tlaxcala complained that peasant upstarts were spending far too much time on cultivating the dye-producing cochineal cactus for profit and far too little time on subsistence agriculture: "And he who belonged to someone no longer respects whoever was his lord and master, because he is seen to have gold and cacao."[60]

Interestingly enough, by contrast, Alonso de Zorita, *oidor* of the Audiencia of New Spain, strongly argued that tributary payments in cloth provided only hardship for the Indian commoners. Each piece of tribute cloth was worth far more in time and labor than other tribute demanded from the Indians, and the poor and women who manufactured the cloth spoiled many pieces because of the great pressure under which they worked. Zorita stated:

It is no argument to say, as some do, that there will be a shortage of cloth if this tribute is not paid; it is better that there be a shortage of cloth than a shortage of people. Besides, there is always cloth available in those areas where the Indians are accustomed to make cloth; they make it for themselves and also take it to sell in places where it is not made. There are many cloth merchants, both Indians and Spaniards.[61]

Rather than supporting a forced exchange based on tributary relations, Zorita's argument contained the seeds of a free market in the cloth trade. As such, he was presenting a position anathema to a cosmology that emphasized hierarchical control from above. Rather than being "free," exchange was meant to reflect and support the society's established ranks and privileges. Free trade would have provided a means of leveling estates that simply could not be allowed. If the higher ranks were meant to provide order and equitable justice, the lower ranks were meant to provide sustenance. In this manner, Spaniards and Amerindians understood each other's economic values, for Aztec tributary lists and regulatory demands had long preceded Spanish ones. "Preciosities" such as feathers, cacao, gold, jadeite, and turquoise were the items of preference in Aztec tributary lists.[62] To this list, Diego Durán's *Historia* adds intricately worked mantles for the nobility, high-quality women's clothing, colors and dyes, building materials, cotton armor, and weapons.[63]

This mutual economic understanding was true to such an extent that the Indian beneficiaries of the Spanish system, the caciques or noble "chieftains," were often accused of greater exploitation of their fellow Indians than the Spaniards themselves.[64] Tribute and trade created a sort of modus vivendi for conquerors and conquered—one that focused on the economic values and ideas surrounding cloth. In Europe, issues surrounding the manufacture and sale of textiles already had been a determining factor in such events as the Hundred Years' War and the Spanish Comunero Revolt. In describing the marketplace of Tenochtitlan, Bernal Díaz could write:

Let us begin with the dealers in gold, silver, and precious stones, feathers, cloaks, and embroidered goods. . . . Next there were those who sold coarser cloth, and cotton goods and fabrics made of twisted thread. In this way you could see every kind of merchandise to be found anywhere in New Spain, laid out in the same way as goods are laid out in my own district of Medina del Campo, a centre for fairs, where each line of stalls has its own particular sort. So it was in this great market.[65]

The exchange of finished products on a massively organized scale pointed to a culture that was developing beyond subsistence agrarian activities and developing more and more specialization in labor and service. That not everyone was producing their own clothing was a sure sign of such "advanced development" in the sixteenth-century Spanish mentality of conquest. By seeing something of themselves in the Aztecs, the Spaniards recognized what they deemed civilization and culture, law and order: in one word, *policía*. Tenochtitlan was like the Castilian trading center of Medina del Campo.

On the other hand, the production of cloth in Mexico was often used to create uniforms of dominance and submission. Cotton cloth was used by Spaniards, but many among them desired the familiar feel of woolen textiles. Thus, when the experimental city of Puebla de los Angeles was founded in 1532, some of the new Spanish settlers established *obrajes*, or textile manufacturies, to produce coarse and fine woolen cloth. Although Amerindians accounted for some consumption at the early stages of wool-market development, the non-Indian population, estimated by Woodrow Borah and Sherburne Cook at 90,000 around 1580, accounted for much of the growth in demand. Until the eighteenth-century Bourbon reforms, the *obrajes* produced the woolen cloth desired by Spanish colonists in New Spain, as well as producing goods for contraband trade with the Spaniards of Peru.[66] By 1580, a Mexican Mesta produced 300,000 pounds of wool annually, and Puebla had as many as forty *obrajes*, while the cities of Querétaro, Valladolid (today Morelia), Texcoco, and Tlaxcala also boasted their own textile industries.[67] Initially encomienda and *repartimiento* Indians were used as a tributary labor force in the *obrajes*, but when the Crown outlawed personal service as a form of tribute in 1549, more and more encomenderos demanded tributary payment in cloth, as Cortés already did in the 1530s. Other Spaniards set up *obrajes* employing African and Asian slaves, as well as a paid labor force consisting of mulatos, mestizos, and free Amerindians. Still, hunger and shackles were often enough the rule, and as late as the 1600s, the average earnings of wage labor did not reach two *reales* per day.[68] The monarchy continued to issue *cédulas* that stated, "In no way are Indians permitted to work in textile *obrajes*," but Spanish demand made the *obraje* a fixture of the sixteenth century, and many Indian towns set up their own *obrajes de comunidad* to satisfy Spanish tributary demands in kind.[69] At the same time, a few Indians also began to use the heavier woolens preferred by Europeans.[70] The work persisted since, on one level, Spanish superiority had to be identified by Spanish woolens.

In the meantime the arrival of luxury woolens from Europe never completely ceased. The high transportation costs between Spain and New Spain limited the number of Old World woolens that could be imported, but these costs did not limit demand. In fact, Old World clothing still arrived in New Spain, but in 1587, Viceroy Villamanrique complained that merchants charged outrageously exorbitant prices for these goods in high demand.[71] Spaniards still wished to dress like Spaniards in a New World, and that meant the wearing of woolens whenever possible. It also meant the relegation of cotton *mantas* to Indian bodies, and Indians largely produced their own clothing at home, with women continuing to weave by means of the pre-Columbian backstrap loom.[72] By the 1640s even moderately sized stores in the mining regions of northern Mexico were well stocked with woolens and items of Cordoban leather. Mexican leather shoes were distinguished clearly from the Cordoban in the inventories, and it was considered worthwhile to identify as little as two and one-half ounces of thread as being "fine Portuguese thread."[73] The homeland, the European continent, imposed value on goods, reassigning value to American wares.

The Spanish conquest of Mexico served as a transformation of ideas, values, and material culture. Not only were the gods and religious rituals of the native Americans attacked; in time, their clothing also was devalued by a new system of ranks that placed the wearers of Spanish dress at the top of a pyramid of social stratification. Early modern European sumptuary laws provided for the easy identification of rank by means of clothes. In 1529 Bishop Juan de Zumárraga clearly saw a hierarchical, as well as a moral, reason for the introduction of sumptuary laws to Mexico.[74] For proper order to be maintained in a society of ranks, people could not be allowed to live above their vocational station. Among other things, clothes had to be appropriately distributed according to rank. Clothes did not make the man, but clothes identified the man. What once had been valued by the Aztec elite as a luxury item, feathered cloaks, soon came to mean little in the values ascribed by the new Spanish elite. At its base, the language of exchange remained the same, but a few nuances were introduced with the introduction of a new elite at the top. The visible symbols of power were redefined. This was illustrated clearly by the fact that Amerindian caciques, the official male intermediaries between the *república de los españoles* and the *república de los indios*, petitioned for the right to wear Spanish noble dress and swords as natural lords of the land—a privilege granted them as loyal servants of the Crown.[75] The Spanish conquest meant an identification of Spanish clothes with wealth and power, a transformation by which the Indian *manta* and *sarape* became stigmas in a system of hierarchical symbols that placed the signs deemed Spanish at the very top—at least from the Spanish rulers' perspective. The quetzal feather, a symbol of power to the Aztecs, no longer had its immense value after the fall of Tenochtitlan.

Spanish *corregidores* were primarily responsible for the gathering of information in the *relaciones geográficas* at the end of the sixteenth century. Although they asked their questions of older Indians and the Indian nobility, the "progress" in clothing and civilization after the Spanish conquest must be seen as a sign of self-congratulatory flattery on the part of the Spanish mentality. Amerindian clothing before the conquest was often described as relatively poor when compared to Spanish clothing; at the same time, it was considered extremely hierarchical within its own confines. Unlike Cortés and Bernal Díaz, who compared the clothed Indians of Mexico to the "naked" Indians of the Caribbean, the *corregidores* of the 1580s were much harsher in their assessment of pre-Columbian dress. Time ensuing between the 1520s and the 1580s had clothed the surviving Amerindian populations of the Caribbean basin and New Spain in accordance with Spanish tastes. Therefore, common reports of the 1580s refer to pre-Columbian Mexican Indians as "*desnudos*," even though the men wore *maxtles* (loin cloths) and *mantas* and the women covered their breasts. Approximately five leagues from Tlaxcala, on October 29, 1581, Tetela issued a very standard report. The *corregidor* Jhoan Gonçales stated that prior to the conquest, the local inhabitants went about naked, with only some *mantas* to cover themselves.[76] In the Valley of Mexico, the *alcalde mayor* Alonso de

Contreras Figueroa reported that the Indians of the *cabecera* Ueipuchtla "went about naked with only some bandages worn in the manner of breeches, and *mantas* of cotton and maguey fiber, which is like Castilian *angero*."[77] When women's clothing is mentioned, as in the case of Atitalaquia and its subject towns, special note is made of feminine modesty: "In order to cover the breasts and the rest of the body, they made a dress which, among them, is called a *guipil*."[78]

Even descriptions that fail to use the word "*desnudo*" often speak volumes in their choice of words. In his *relaciones* for Yscateupa (Ichcateopan) and its *partido*, Captain Lucas Pinto, *corregidor*, reported that the men of Tzicaputzalco wore "only a *manta* on top and some *pañetes* with which they covered their shame."[79] He reported that the Indians of Alaustlan "formerly went about dressed with only a *manta*," and those of Quatepeque "went about naked in times of peace with only a short cloak bound at the shoulder and some *pañetes*."[80] In Tlacotepeque, also a subject town of Yscateupa, the male Indians wore *mantas* and *pañetes*, "without wearing anything else."[81] In these *relaciones* done under Pinto's direction from October 12 to December 1, 1579, it appears that "only" ("*sola*") and "without wearing anything else" ("*sin traer otra cosa*") are meant to bear the same connotation as "naked" ("*desnudo*"). Much had changed between Bernal Díaz's fundamental praise of Mexican Indian clothing practices at the time of the conquest and Pinto's selection of words some fifty years later.

By 1550 Amerindian use of the European fitted shirt was so common that "*camisa*" was one of the earliest and most prevalent of Spanish terms borrowed by Nahuatl speakers. By the early 1600s, trousers, jackets, doublets, hats, and shoes found their place in the attire of indigenous males, although the Mesoamerican cloak remained an item long retained by even the most affluent among Amerindians. Women's clothing remained more traditional, but the *huipilli* (*huipil*; *guipil*) bore a greater resemblance to European fashions than male dress.[82] By comparison, Mesoamerican male dress at the time of the conquest would have appeared tantamount to nudity. By Spanish standards, cloth *mantas* and *pañetes* were superior to Caribbean dress circa 1492, but Castilian dress, and attire closely resembling the Castilian, was definitely ascribed the hierarchical place of honor. By the 1580s the officials of the imperium expressed Spanish cultural superiority by noting that the indigenous populations of Mexico had taken to covering more of their bodies in the manner of Spaniards.

Ironically, even though the Spaniards themselves recognized a strict hierarchy in clothing (one often reinforced by sumptuary laws), Crown officials occasionally argued that the adoption of Spanish patterns in dress had helped to level distinctions within Amerindian communities. Reporting on the towns of Tequizistlan, Aculma, San Juan Teotihuacan, and Tepexa in the Valley of Mexico, the *corregidor* Francisco de Castañeda followed a simple formula in which he described the relative richness in the dress of *principales* vis-à-vis the simplicity of the commoners' clothing prior to the conquest:

In time of peace the *principales* commonly wore delicate *maxtles* and *mantas* of maguey fiber, but on feast days they dressed in decorated cotton *mantas*, and when they went outdoors, for protection from the sun, they each took a fan of feathers. All the *maceguales* wore only a rough *manta* of maguey fiber and a *maxtle*.[83]

Jhoan Gonçales, the same *corregidor* who reported on Tetela, wrote of pre-Columbian hierarchical distinctions between the *señores* and *maceguales* of Xonotla, describing the rich *mantas* and feathers of the *principales*.[84] For Castañeda and Gonçales, the male Indians' adoption of clothing for their legs and upper torsos represented a victory for Spanish culture and a leveling of Indian society: "And now everyone generally wears shirts, *mantas* and breeches of cotton."[85] In Oaxaca other *corregidores* noted this imperial victory, stating that the Indians continued to wear *mantas*, but that they were no longer naked.[86] In the 1580s Amerindians throughout New Spain wore "shirts like Spaniards," "Castilian shirts," and "Castilian clothes."[87] In *Textiles and Capitalism in Mexico*, Richard Salvucci notes that Spaniards lifted Aztec prohibitions on the wearing of cotton clothing by commoners, and *maceguales* seized the opportunity to abandon maguey fiber and dress like *principales* whenever they could.[88]

Despite a trend toward leveling in matters of clothing, distinctions persisted within an Amerindian community experiencing devastating flux. In Oaxacan Macuilsúchil, the *corregidor* Gaspar Asensio declared that only some Indians wore European-style dress, indicating that others may not have yet adopted vestments approved by the Spaniards.[89] The leveling function of "shirts and breeches" may have been limited to spots like Aculma, but in *The Aztecs under Spanish Rule*, Charles Gibson argues that by 1600 many among the native nobility lost tributary privileges granted them immediately following the conquest.[90] As Indian labor became a scarcer commodity as a result of the ravages of plague and pestilence, the demands of Amerindian noblemen were often sacrificed to satisfy Spanish labor demands. Thus a real leveling within the Indian population was occurring by the 1580s. Not all Indian noblemen may have been able to maintain distinctions in dress vis-à-vis the common *maceguales*.

The impoverishment of the Indian nobility was growing, but it was not universal.[91] In Tepuztlan, twelve leagues from Mexico City, Amerindians who possessed the means wore "cleverly painted *mantas*," "linen and cotton shirts," and "linen breeches."[92] Unsurprisingly, this financial capability was most often reserved for the remaining Indian nobility and new classes of Indian elite labor. In the Oaxacan *cabecera* of Chichicapa, the Amerindians wore "*camysas*" (shirts), "*çaraguelles*" (breeches), "*sayos*" (loose coats), "*capotes*" (short cloaks), and "*sombreros*" (hats), "especially the caciques, some of whom dress like Spaniards."[93] In Guaxilotitlan, "*jubones*" (doublets), "*sayos*," and "*jaquetas de algodon*" (cotton jackets) were primarily the clothing of *principales*. "Indians of little means" wore breeches, woolen jackets, and woolen *mantas*.[94] Likewise, the wives of the nobility were described as having "*huipiles*" (dresses) and "*naguas*" (shifts) that were more finely wrought and luxurious than those of the average Indian woman.[95] Finally, in relatively prosperous fishing, farming, and manufacturing communities like Tlacotalpan, Tustla, and Cotlastla (all approximately seventy leagues from Mexico City), many Indians seem to have adopted Spanish dress in its most formal sense. The *mantas, çaraguelles, camisas, jubones,* and *sombreros* of the male Indian peasant were superseded by *ropa de Castilla,* which Spaniards traded for fish, agrarian crops, and native textiles.[96] The implication is that the inhabitants of Tlacotalpan and its two subject towns of Tustla and Cotlastla did not want to wear the clothing Spaniards had deemed acceptable for the Indian peasantry, clothing that was like that of the Spaniards, but simple enough in its pajamalike appearance to differentiate finely dressed Spaniards from the Indian masses. More affluent Indians aspired to full-fledged "Spanishness" and all the privileges attached. This was also true of the Amerindian miners of Tasco, twenty-two leagues from Mexico City. Earning a decent wage for skilled labor, Indian miners, "who work among Spaniards in the mines," were dressed like Spaniards. Perhaps feeling the need to draw a distinction between Spaniards and Indians, the region's *alcalde mayor,* Pedro de Ledesma, wrote, "[the miners] dress like Spaniards, but imperfectly so."[97]

No matter what they did, Mexican Indians could never truly reach the pinnacle which Spaniards reserved for themselves. Their clothed bodies became more amenable to Spanish taste, but their bodies were meant to be stigmatized as vessels of an inferior sort, just as their understanding was so often identified as inferior: "By chance the more talented Indian will be like a Spanish boy, eight or ten years of age."[98] Everyday in the New World, Spaniards lived the Valladolid debate of las Casas and Sepúlveda. The Indians—their mental, physical, and spiritual status—confused the Spaniards and challenged their desire for dominance. The Spaniards generally responded by identifying those aspects of their worldview they would not abandon, learning to adapt and even discard nonessentials. Of course, individual Spaniards could differ on particulars within these confines. In matters of dressing the Amerindians "appropriately," perhaps no one spoke more succinctly than Juan de la Vega, the now forgotten *corregidor* of Ocopetlayuca (the present-day Tochimilco on the southern slope of Popocatepetl). In 1580 the Indians of this town wore clothing "in the style of *moriscos* of Granada."[99] In their dress, even after the conquest, de la Vega thus noted that Amerindians still combined the familiar and the alien, the acceptable and the unacceptable. They were like the somewhat exotic, somewhat threatening *moriscos* of familiar Spain. To resort to Claude Lévi-Strauss's terminology, they were "semi-cooked," which is to say, semicivilized by Spanish standards. In some ways this is where many Spaniards wished the Indians to remain: in constant need of Spanish supervision and dominance.

PUBLIC SPACE AND ARCHITECTURE

The transformation of visible symbols and material culture, the conquest of one set of values by another, was in no place more evident than in the reconstruction of public space. At the heart of the matter, the Spanish church and plaza replaced Indian pyramids, open public spaces, and ceremonial structures. Throughout the sixteenth century, from the construction of Villa Rica de la Vera Cruz in 1519 to the early seventeenth-century reports of town *cabildos*, numerous Spaniards in positions of authority focused on the importance of the plaza or town square. In the idealized layout of a sixteenth-century Spanish city, the main plaza was a central, open urban space from which the town's main streets radiated. It was encircled by the symbols of royal, ecclesiastical, and corporate authority: the cathedral, the general hospital, the jail, and any number of governmental buildings for audiencias and *cabildos* (depending on the size and importance of the town). Whereas many Old World towns continued to reflect the spontaneous growth and walled clutter of the Middle Ages, even lacking well-defined plazas, American towns were intended to be architectural embodiments of order and hierarchy mapped out by Italian Renaissance classicists.[100] Even more so than in the old Spain, towns and cities in the "new" Spain were meant to follow a "grid plan," with a central plaza surrounded by its church and its government buildings. The homes of the leading families were expected to be near the center of the town—power and social relations being defined by means of urban planning.[101]

In Juan Luis Vives's allegorical *Temple of the Laws* (1519), the Spanish humanist wrote of a city of justice, peace, and humanity in which the highest turret proved to be the "tower of divine justice," pointing its way to heaven.[102] Thus, every plaza had its cathedral or church to ensure urban adherence to divine rite and neighborly love. Since the idealized European society of the period was to be ruled by a sword of divine law and a sword of civil law, the Crown's officers also had buildings on the plaza. Finally, early modern Spaniards believed that a societal organism could "take ill," and they provided space for two sites of healing and purging: the hospital, of which more will be said later, and the jail. In 1525 Hernán Cortés wrote a letter that described what must be done for the "good treatment" of the Indians of Trujillo and La Natividad de Nuestra Señora. Among numerous suggestions to his lieutenant, all to provide the Indians with *policía*, he wrote the following:

Item: Begin immediately, with much diligence, to clean the site of this aforesaid town, which I left planned, and after the cleaning, following the plan which I left made, mark out the public places that are indicated on it, like the Plaza and Church, the Town Hall, prison, slaughterhouse, hospital [and] commerce house, [all] according to what I indicated.[103]

The plaza and its surrounding buildings were meant to define visually all aspects of Spanish authority to newly conquered Amerindians. As a result, it is not surprising that churches and cathedrals were constructed near the sites of old Indian places of worship, often with building stones that had been used in the temples' construction.[104] This was true of the Cathedral of Mexico City, which was built in part with the paving blocks from the Aztec temple precinct, and of the Franciscan church of Tlatelolco, which stands near the ruins of the great pyramid-temple described by Bernal Díaz.[105] Although cost effectiveness no doubt played a role in the cannibalization of used building materials, Spaniards deliberately transformed the Aztecs' centers of spiritual power in order to assert the superiority of their own spiritual power.

This message was not lost on the Mesoamerican Indians, who utilized public space and public architecture in highly effective ways and who recognized a conqueror's deities as deities demanding submission. Tenochtitlan, the Aztec capital, had its open space, strategically located before the Templo Mayor, where the human sacrifices that maintained the cosmos could be witnessed. Building on the work of Davíd Carrasco, Felipe Gorostiza identifies Tenochtitlan as "the symbol and the incarnation of the Aztec state."[106] The city was an ordered representation of the Aztec struggle for cosmic order and tributary empire. As such, the Spaniards could convert the preexisting notions concerning monumental architecture to their own ends. Value systems encrusted both the Aztec city and the Spanish city, and they were similar enough to allow for a mutual understanding of political power and display.

Hernán Cortés made much of Tenochtitlan's sense of order and beauty, describing it at length in his second letter to Charles V. Emphasizing that the inhabitants lived "almost like those in Spain," he also stressed the grandeur of Moctezuma's palace and the beauty of the large houses of the other Aztec lords. Marketplace activity was described as vigorous, with the plaza at Tlatelolco being praised as "twice as big as that of Salamanca." Cortés reported that sixty thousand people descended on it daily. Finally, he marveled at the architectural skill that constructed a city in the middle of Lake Texcoco.

The city itself is as big as Seville or Córdoba. The main streets are very wide and very straight; some of these are on the land, but the rest and all the smaller ones are half on land, half canals where they paddle their canoes. All the streets have openings in places so that the water may pass from one canal to another. Over all these openings, and some of them are very wide, there are bridges made of long and wide beams joined together very firmly and so well made that on some of them ten horsemen may ride abreast.[107]

Of course, as noted previously, Bernal Díaz found his first encounter with Tenochtitlan so otherworldly that he could compare it only to "the things of enchantment written about in the tale of Amadís."[108] He felt proud to report on the causeways as "things never heard of, seen or dreamed of before." The taking of Tenochtitlan by the Tlaxcalans, Spaniards and their allies was the supreme display, for the city "was so renowned throughout these parts" that the Tarascan lord of independent Michoacan sent ambassadors to Cortés when he learned about Tenochtitlan's fall. Cortés wrote, "It seemed to the lord of that province that, considering the great size and strength of the city, if it could not resist us then nothing could; thus, out of fear or because it pleased him, he sent some messengers to me."[109] The symbolism of violent display against the public manifestations of Aztec potency brought dividends, and while this was being accomplished, the Spaniards also dedicated time to constructing the physical manifestation of their own power.

To maintain control, the conquistadores immediately established manifestations of the punitive aspect of civil law. As early as the construction of Villa Rica de la Vera Cruz, Bernal Díaz noted the attention paid to constructing a pillory in the plaza and a gallows outside the town.[110] Audiencia and *cabildo* buildings, prisons, pillories, and gallows were the final expressions of civil power. If one ignored the confines of his or her station by theft, murder, and generally infringing upon the privileges and status of others, one could expect just punishment and retribution. European authorities deliberately made gallows and places of punishment extremely public, for as Michel Foucault has written:

In the ceremonies of public execution, the main character was the people, whose real and immediate presence was required for the performance. An execution that was known to be taking place, but which did so in secret, would scarcely have had any meaning. The aim was to make an example, not only by making people aware that the slightest offence was likely to be punished, but by arousing feelings of terror by the spectacle of power letting its anger fall upon the guilty person.[111]

During the actual conquest, Spaniards experienced the terror of watching their captured comrades and Indian allies sacrificed to Aztec gods.[112] After the conquest, they used terror to their own advantage by constructing permanent places of public punishment, execution, and dismemberment. The last Aztec emperor, or *tlatoani*, Cuauhtemoc himself, became a public example by means of his public execution for conspiracy during Cortés's march to Honduras. Countless others, both European and Amerindian, shared similar fates for the sake of maintaining public order, although the ruling Spaniards were quite willing to lessen the severity of punishment for a *república de los indios* not completely aware of the fine points of Spanish law and custom:

Recognizing the weakness of these *naturales* and the facility with which they have committed crimes, and that at present it has not been convenient to execute upon them the severity of the law, nor has it been to leave them unpunished, it appeared to us that the crimes deserving death be commuted to enslavement . . . but according to the new law, which prohibits their enslavement for whatever reason or crime, we have relinquished that manner of punishment until consulting with Your Majesty on whether to execute the severity of the law or condemn them to temporal service without branding their faces.[113]

Of course, forced labor benefited conquistadores and pobladores to no end, but it is difficult to prove that the act of commutation was not seen as an act of mercy at the same time that it satisfied economic needs.

Although motivated by ideals and ideas, the construction of a "Spanish"

Mexico City was shaped and influenced by local material realities and the ideals and ideas of New Spain's indigenous inhabitants. The *pipiltin* who commanded Nahua society had to be guaranteed roles as intermediaries, and the most immediate selection of forced labor was left to them. After the New Laws of the 1540s, encomienda tributary labor was phased out gradually, but it was replaced by *cuatequil* draft labor, a *repartimiento* in the hands of Spanish *jueces repartidores* and Indian nobles. Service was not to last longer than one week at a time and three to four weeks a year. Wages were paid, but skilled labor received the same *tomín* as the unskilled. Encomienda, *cuatequil*, and the wage labor that followed it by 1600 rebuilt what had been Tenochtitlan, and these Amerindian artisans were not automata. Already in 1948 George Kubler wrote that "the initial success of any colonial building campaign depends in part upon the state of building knowledge among the native peoples."[114] Building on racial and class biases, Spaniards assessed their situation and argued that although all Amerindians knew how to construct a wall and build a house, true artistry was lacking in the adobe houses of the common *maceguales*.[115] On the other hand, the houses of the lords and idols were majestic, though in the service of what were perceived as erroneous principles. The Anonymous Conqueror wrote that the lords' houses were full of large halls and rooms surrounding an open courtyard; that plazas were large, attractive, and open to frequent commerce; and that their tall temples were wretched places of human sacrifice.[116] Motolinía noted that "in all this land we found that in the best part of town they constructed a large square courtyard . . . enclosed by a wall, guarding its doors against the streets and principal roads."[117]

Surrounded by "demonic" pyramids and the practice of human sacrifice, this enclosed plaza was interpreted as the "courtyard of the Devil." Once again the Amerindians had demonstrated some *policía*, while falling short of the Spanish Christian ideal. In reality, Spaniards could not deny the mathematical precision and order of Amerindian construction. In this the Mesoamericans surpassed the geometric layout that Spaniards dreamed of from readings of Leone Battista Alberti and other Renaissance Italian architects, but all this was done to serve what were seen by Spaniards as illegitimate ends.[118] Motolinía observed that pre-Columbian Cholula attempted to construct a pyramid so large that it was a second Tower of Babel, and just as the Tower of Babel had been destroyed by God's displeasure, so too Cholula's grandiose design was abandoned because of divine intervention.[119] The Amerindians may have built plazas only dreamt of in Spain, and nobles' houses that resembled those of Spanish grandees, but they were still to learn from the self-justifying and rationalizing Spanish imperialist.[120] Motolinía wrote that after observing the work of stonecutters, Amerindians quickly learned to construct various arches, finely worked portals and windows, elegant churches, and houses for Spaniards.[121] They did all this, however, while contributing their sense of aesthetic and flare for geometrical complexity in decorative design. Amerindian artisans learned Spanish methods. They copied the vault. As early as 1524 or 1525, some among them had constructed a Spanish loom. They adopted European tools. Some Indians were even sent to Mexico City to learn from European masters, and in 1547 the Portuguese mason Diego Díaz of Lisbon even claimed to have taught all the Indian masons of New Spain their trade. More realistically, as early as the initial reconstruction of fallen Tenochtitlan in 1522, Amerindian artisans learned from European direction and actual practice. To this they brought their pre-Columbian experience, creating the wondrous architectural form known as *tequitqui*—a form in which the Judaeo-Christian Satan might readily be represented as a demonic owl man from Aztec religion.[122]

Obviously this cultural exchange came at a price. Motolinía wrote of ten plagues that struck New Spain for the sins of its Spanish and native inhabitants. The seventh plague was the building of Spanish Mexico City, an endeavor that in its first year involved "more people than in the building of the temple of Jerusalem in the time of Solomon."[123] Bringing materials on their backs, Indians were torn from their homes to fall from the skeletal structures of buildings under construction or to have buildings fall on top of them. Motolinía saw the Spanish Christians as enlightened by their faith, but the construction of their proud city "cast them into the dark." Amerindian labor was abused, and huge stands of timber in the Valley of Mexico were rapidly exhausted. Just as Castile had been deforested, New Spain would be deforested. Cortés used 6,906 "cedar" beams to build his own houses. The loss of mountainous trees, in turn, contributed to the silting of Tenochtitlan's Lake Texcoco.[124] The Spanish city would not be the same as the Aztec one.

By 1554 the professor of rhetoric at the newly created University of Mexico could describe an impressive "Spanish" city in his dialogues to train students in the fundamentals of Latin. Francisco Cervantes de Salazar, a humanist influenced by the works of Juan Luis Vives, unsurprisingly wrote his dialogue on "The Interior of the City of Mexico" to illustrate the layout of a well-ordered urban environment. Alfaro, a "second Ulysses," is taken down Tacuba Street to the Plaza Mayor. The houses of the city's wealthiest and noblest citizens resembled fortresses, guarding against an Indian uprising that never materialized, but they also impressed with their regular construction. Lintels and door frames were built of "large stones artistically arranged."[125] The chaos of the spontaneously developed cities of medieval Spain was notably absent. Roofs were uniformly flat with gutters of wood and tile, forcing Alfaro to admit that houses in Andalusia and both Castiles were not "roofed in the same way." Uniformity signified rationality and Renaissance planning from the dreambooks of Alberti and Filarete. In the words of Alfaro's interlocutor Zuazo:

For the same reason it was also proper not only for the streets to be wide and spacious, as you see, but also for the houses not to be too tall, as you well remarked, so that the city would be more healthful, with no very high buildings preventing the winds from blowing back and forth; for these along with the sun disperse and drive off the pestilential vapors which the neighboring swamp emits.[126]

According to Cervantes de Salazar, Mexico City rivaled European cities by more fully developing European urban ambitions. His character Alfaro noted that the main plaza could not be matched in either hemisphere for size and grandeur.[127] Utilizing the round, smooth columns of the ancient Roman architect Vitruvius, the plaza's royal palace contributed to the desired effect. At the plaza, memorials to Greco-Roman high culture vied with the activities of judges, lawyers, litigants, and merchants—the Audiencia of Mexico City sharing the same general space as merchants of "valuable merchandise" who came to sell at the plaza. Opposite the royal palace, the palace of Cortés amazed with its strong façade and construction of limestone and cedar. In fact, the only building that did not impress Alfaro was Mexico City's first cathedral, described as "deplorable in a city of such renown" and impoverished by its possession of small revenue.[128] In 1562 Cervantes de Salazar was no doubt relieved to see the construction of a second, grander cathedral to the west of the site occupied by the Templo Mayor of the Aztecs.

Truly, the most notable omission in the Alfaro dialogue is the absence of any reference to the impact of Aztec Tenochtitlan on the Spanish construction of Mexico City. A good classicist, Cervantes did write that Spanish names and customs were as outlandish to the Amerindians as their names and customs were to Spaniards, but he also noted, through Alfaro, that the Indian marketplace sold wares that were mostly "cheap and of very little worth." Nature was marvelous in providing the Amerindians with cacao beans to use as money, but Amerindian ingenuity was limited to devising huts so low and humble that they could not be properly observed from horseback! Amerindian agency was so denigrated by Cervantes de Salazar that he must be placed in the tradition of Juan Ginés de Sepúlveda. After all, cacao is clearly an article of nature, but the use of cacao as money is a development of human culture—in this case of Amerindian culture. Cervantes de Salazar's dialogue describes the workshops of Iberian artisans on a street perpendicular to Tacuba Street; the Indian artisans who participated in the construction of sixteenth-century Mexico City are forgotten, just as the Aztec open spaces, transformed into Spanish plazas, are forgotten.[129]

Although properly representing the flow of commerce in Mexico City, Cervantes de Salazar failed to focus on the importance of Amerindians in this arterial process. Just as cloth was channeled to Mexico City by means of Amerindian tribute, so too building materials arrived as Indian tribute. Dated 1531, the *Harkness Codex* of Huexotzinco (or Huejotzingo) demonstrates the Amerindian contribution to the construction of a "Spanish" Mexico. Among other things (including *mantas*), lime, adobe, building stones, and wood are items listed as tribute paid by the inhabitants of Huejotzingo.[130] Just as they contributed their aesthetic sense in the form of *tequitqui* art and architecture, Indian workmen moved stone and wood from the Mexican countryside to construct the cities of a "New Spain." In some places, like the Spanish city of Puebla de los Angeles, founded near Tlaxcala and Cholula in 1531, they were fortunate enough to move the materials from quarries that were only a "crossbow-shot" away.[131] At other sites they were not as fortunate. In any event,

despite the prejudices of Cervantes de Salazar, the architecture of New Spain
was fated to be a synthesis of European dreams and American influences,
Amerindians playing their significant roles as agents of change.

The Mexican Indians were judged by many Spaniards as knowing the general terms of *policía*, but those Spaniards in positions of authority grew quite
aware of subtle distinctions between Iberian and Mexican laws and customs.
The fundamental question was forever one of recognizing similarity and difference, and the primary mission was the definition and maintenance of *policía*.
In the 1530s and 1540s, before the cathedrals and churches could be completed, the early Franciscan open-air chapels aided in this mission by providing
public space for a public religion pressured by limited resources and a large
number of new converts.[132] By the 1580s, the *relaciones* seldom mentioned
open chapels, but the mission of urbanization and christianization continued to
be linked: "Spaniards who are granted Indians in encomienda are asked to
settle those Indians carefully in townships, and to build churches in them in
order to catechize them (the Indians) and teach them *policía*."[133]

Long before the hospital and the prison were to be applied as purgatives to a
diseased body politic, preventive measures were to be taken. Coastal places
were to be avoided where new townships were concerned, since they were not
considered healthful and since the inhabitants of ports "do not give themselves
to tilling and cultivating the land, nor to the establishment of good customs."[134]
Only a few evil but necessary ports were to be established in the Crown's
idealized vision of a "new world," but each town was to have a *plaza mayor* to
assist in its moral ordering. Dominated by "the sanctuaries of the Church," the
ideal plaza was also to be surrounded by the *Casa Real* (Crown offices) and
Casa de Concejo y Cabildo (Town Hall). Further, "the hospital for the poor
and uncontagious sick is to be placed near the church."[135] In 1573 the Crown
proceeded to decree what had already been enforced by Hernán Cortés, creating visible signs and symbols of Spanish majesty in order to introduce the
Amerindians to the meaning of Spanish culture and *policía*. An urban-agrarian
people who gathered in walled cities for defense against the Moors, Spaniards
literally identified civilization with city-dwelling. Their American mission included the settlement of nonsedentary Indians in *reducciones* and the maintenance of already existing Indian towns. By 1608 the existence of plazas and
clean, well-ordered streets, as well as churches, hospitals, and other public
buildings, proved this facet of the Spanish mission a success in places as far
north as the Nueva Viscayan Villa de Nombre de Dios.[136]

Following the precedent set by Ovando, the conde de Lemus, in 1604,
issued 355 questions on the condition of Spanish and Indian settlements in the
New World. Questions 12-18 specifically dealt with the physical layout of the
town and with the quality of its edifices.[137] Under the heading of "that which
concerns morality and politics," town *cabildos* and local officials reported on
the existence or nonexistence of governmental facilities and ecclesiastical structures, as well as on the condition of local housing. Certain Indian towns—like
Coatlan, near the Oaxacan town of Miaguatlan, and the Otomí pueblo of

Guauchinango—were described as having "very humble houses and edifices."[138] In Miaguatlan, "the Crown and municipal houses are low and humble, and there is not one [building] in that town that is not."[139] On the other hand, the Indians of Tanteyuc, in the province of Pánuco, were praised for having good, strong public buildings.[140] Civilization and city-dwelling were equated and defined in Spanish terms, and the *vecinos* of Pánuco and its environs were quick to identify themselves as hispanic, civilized, and urbanized:

The streets are ordinarily clear of grass, in such a way that one can easily walk in them. The royal edifices are enclosed with a wooden and mud fence: having their doors and windows, kitchen and stable: serving as quarters for the town council. There is also a hostelery for muleteers and a rectory enclosed with the same fence as the royal edifices. . . . Thus, the houses of the Spaniards, like those of the *naturales*, are made of clay and wood, erected on forked poles and posts, with wooden ceilings covered in straw: they are all low, and most of them have their door facing the sea, where the breeze is, in order to enjoy the coolness and protect against the heat of the town. Some houses have gardens.[141]

In general terms, Indian homes were of "stone and adobe" or "adobe and thatch," and distinctions in the elaborateness of the design were, of course, a function of wealth. By means of their wealth and power (still extant in the sixteenth century), caciques and *principales* were able to emulate the Spaniards, thus serving as "proper" intermediaries between Spanish lords and Indian tributaries. By means of outward signs, the Spaniards could prejudicially interpret the nobility as people of greater *policía* and *razón* than the common folk. Robert Haskett has demonstrated that in colonial Cuernavaca, the indigenous elite built Spanish-influenced houses in the immediate vicinity of that symbol of power and authority, the plaza.[142] Early *relaciones* from Coatepec in the Valley of Mexico and Xuchitepec in Oaxaca verify this pattern. In Coatepec, the *corregidor* Cristóbal de Salazar wrote:

The structure and framework of the houses that the *naturales* have are . . . [of] adobe walls: the ceilings are flat: some *principales* and caciques who have the means decorate and build them in the manner that Spaniards decorate them, because they have *curiosidad* [inquisitiveness].[143]

And in Xuchitepec, houses were "of straw and cane surfaces, very small after the fashion of pigsties in Spain . . . and other Indians, *ladinos*, make houses finished in adobe and wood and sealed with clay."[144]

Quite simply, "*yndios ladinos*," those adopting aspects of Spanish culture, seem to have been those nobles and other Indians who possessed the means, and who were therefore considered "inquisitive" by the Spaniards. The average *macegual* was derogatorily written about as living like a Spanish pig. Other Oaxacan *relaciones*, for the towns of Chichicapa and Guaxilotitlan, reveal even more Spanish prejudices where Indian homes were concerned. In both towns, adobe structures were described as short and of short duration; houses in Chichicapa lasting only fifteen to twenty years.[145] Elsewhere in Oaxaca, Cuicatlan suffered the indignity of having low houses that were also mostly constructed "of straw," as were the houses of Atlatlauca and Malinaltepec.[146] In eastern Oaxaca's Santiago de Nexapa, the houses were constructed of adobe walls and "covered with thatch." The *relación* reports that they could have been constructed of "lime and quarrystone and pine," but the poverty of the few Spaniards living there prevented such efforts. Spanish poverty also impeded the development of wheat agriculture among Indians, who were described as phlegmatic, dirty and drunken.[147] Far from being exceptional, descriptions similar to those given of Nexapa's houses were also given of the houses of Iztepexi, Tepeaca, Ahuatlan, Texaluca, Çoyatitlanapa, Coatzinco, Xonotla, Tetela and Chilapa in the diocese of Tlaxcala; and of Macuilsúchil and Tlacolula in the diocese of Antequera.[148] In the Tlaxcalan diocese the *alcalde mayor* of the *cabecera* Tepeaca, Jorge Çeron Carvajal, reported, "The form and structure of the houses of this province are commonly very small and low . . . made of adobe . . . and covered with light wood and thatch."[149] Wretched "*bohíos de paja*" (straw huts) were described as common domiciles in Çoyatitlanapa and Coatzinco.[150]

Amerindian houses were described similarly throughout New Spain. In the *cabecera* of Yscateupa (Ichcateopan) and the twelve towns of its *partido*, now in north central Guerrero, terms used to describe the homes of the indigenous population included: "*bajas*," "*de piedra y adobe*" and "*pequeñas*."[151] The small size and humble state of *macegual* dwellings were also crucial categories of identification for Spaniards reporting from Axocupan, Yetecomac, Chiconauhtla, Zayula, Mexicatzinco, Atitalaquia, the mines of Tasco, Tetela, Ueyapan, Tepepulco, and Cuauhquilpan: "The houses are low, of adobe and thatch, and very small, so that one enters them with difficulty for their being so narrow and low."[152] In describing the "*ruines edifiçios*" of the common Indians, Spanish officials revealed their own biases regarding social superiority and the necessity of hierarchy. They also described the decadence of a pre-Columbian class structure that had come to be determined by Spanish categories:

In structure and contrivance the houses of the common *maceguales* follow the fashion of their antiquity, and the *principales* who can build their houses according to our use, with stone and lime which are brought from outside this district [i.e., Tepepulco], and crafted wood, [do].[153]

Of course, the question remains to what extent Amerindian nobles actually abandoned older building practices in order to be "more like Spaniards" and to what extent their pre-Columbian practices resembled those of the Europeans. Likewise, the demographic chaos caused by the diseases, brutalities, and relocation after the Spanish arrival may very well have contributed to the poor construction methods the Spaniards so willingly perceived among the commoners. Using written Nahuatl sources, James Lockhart has come to the conclusion that "a general lack of information about structural details" makes it difficult to determine "when and to what extent Spanish influence affected Nahua house building."[154] In continuation of pre-Columbian building traditions, many Nahua households are referred to as building complexes, not single structures, and thus unlike European houses. In the complexes, interrelated members of an extended family often lived in separate buildings around a common patio, and attached structures provided storage space. Spaniards, influenced by Mediterranean and Moorish architectural traditions, were capable of building elaborate houses around open-air, inner gardens, but the rooms of such houses would be connected, unlike the separate, unconnected buildings of Nahua complexes described in the wills of the wealthy and noble.[155] What Spaniards might very well have done is emphasize the commonalities they perceived, while ignoring the cultural differences. That this was exercised where the nobles were concerned is unsurprising, since Spaniards interacted with those nobles to maintain rule in New Spain—they were allies, not demonized outside enemies. Likewise, Lockhart willingly admits that some evidence points to the possibility of single buildings unattached to any compound as having been the most common form of Nahua construction both before and after the conquest. All conclusions remain quite tentative, however, since the wills that provide so much of Lockhart's information were "restricted to high nobles" and, indeed, "Nahuatl writings about the preconquest period are vague about such matters as the layout of households."[156] Suffice it to say that the comfortable Nahua, like the comfortable Spaniard, maintained what the Spanish called a *casa poblada*, where extended family and servant familiars might gather in some common area. Spaniards could therefore recognize the shadow of the communal nest where primates of the same band can sleep together for comfort and protection. The fact that Amerindian nobles might have been the first indigenes who could have afforded adoption of new iron nails and the like would also have helped to set them apart from the poorer *macehualtin*. Proximity to the Spaniards in the hierarchy literally meant that the Spaniards would be more willing to seek the binding human universals. To be Spanish was to be urbanized in a hierarchical fashion. Although Spaniards never fully grasped the horizontal complexities of the pre-Columbian *altepetl* and its *calpolli* wards, they did respect the Aztecs' increased emphasis on hierarchy. The dream of the well-ordered Renaissance city was to be made a reality in the "New World."

As for the indigenous inhabitants of the Americas, some possessed characteristics needed to be deemed "like the Spanish" and "civilized," but Indians like those of sterile and cold Ocelotepec, in the moutains of south central Oaxaca, reflected the conditions of their natural environment:

In this town there are no streets, nor [is there] a plaza for [its] being situated in some hills, and thus the houses are separated from one another, because there is no more level ground after the site occupied by the Church.

In this town there are no royal buildings, nor a town hall, nor any edifice of moderate size: when justice comes to it, it lodges at the house of the curate.[157]

The Indians of Ocelotepec were not described as *desnudos* (nudity being foolhardy in their cold, mountainous environment), but they were considered "guilty" of speaking "a very coarse and corrupt Zapoteca."[158] They lived in such a remote area that they virtually lacked *policía* and served no one: "They do not know employment, nor do they occupy themselves in cultivating the land, nor do they raise livestock, because no one exerts himself in this town."[159] Interestingly enough, they were also given to revolt and to carrying on preconquest religious practices.[160] Appropriate housing, then, like appropriate clothing, served as a Spanish category of understanding and a basis for prejudicial assessment.

CONCLUSION

Frightened and intimidated by the unfamiliar and the alien, sixteenth-century conquistadores, pobladores, and royal bureaucrats were initially pleased to find the Amerindians of central Mexico relatively well housed and clad—which actually meant housed and clad in accordance with many of the Spaniards' cultural standards. These material circumstances provided an opportunity for mutual communication, including some understanding regarding the language of economic exchange. The production of clothing for sale was understood by Spaniards and Aztecs alike, just as the covering of genitals and female breasts was understood by both cultures—in pre-Columbian times the Aztecs ridiculing the Huaxtecans for their nakedness and perceived lasciviousness.[161] Likewise, the two cultures used clothing in a ritualistic fashion that went beyond the simple need to protect the body from natural forces. Cortés is reported to have deliberately dressed to impress Spaniards and Indians on a number of different occasions: "He wore a plume of feathers, with a medallion and a gold chain, and a velvet cloak trimmed with loops of gold. In fact he looked like a bold and gallant captain."[162] In this he resembled Moctezuma and the Nahua *pipiltin*, who wore their fine cotton, gold, and elaborate feathers to display and impress. Thus, the way in which a body was clad became a public expression of rank and purpose from the first moments of the conquest of Mexico to the adoption of Spanish clothes by Amerindian nobles. The manner in which a body was shielded from the natural elements became an expression of culture and the most basic manifestation of public space. It goes without saying that it also reflected, by means of culture, the innate human tendency to display dominance and hierarchy.

Dominance cannot be shared by all. As a result, often enough the struggle for dominance leads to great cruelty. Indeed, among the myriad manifestations of human behavior some of the cruelest appear to stem from efforts by the dominant to fend off challenges from their subordinates within the hierarchy. Ironically, it may be this competition for dominance that has lead to some of the most fabulous constructions of human culture—from the Egyptian pyramids and the Great Wall of China to the marvels of Tenochtitlan. Public space becomes the public displaying place of male dominance, and just as many

Amerindians died in the construction of the new Mexico City, many Chinese peasants died in the construction of the Great Wall. The beauty of the public display, like the beauty of a male peacock, may mask the violence that is implied, but the public display remains the great work of art of an elite that struggles to retain exclusive policing rights within a given culture. However, it must not be forgotten that such elites also create systems of conflict resolution and charity—law courts and hospitals—that minimize the violence that might otherwise transpire among subordinates. Self-consciously or not, subordinates are left reviewing their elites from the vantage point of cost-benefit analysis. Do the elites provide enough benefits to justify their exalted status and costly displays?

When all is said and done, the display, with its potential for violence and mercy, remains. It is not insignificant that Cortés should have replaced Huitzilopochtli and Tlaloc with the Virgin Mary and other saints at the Templo Mayor of Tenochtitlan.[163] This was behavior akin to any male animal's marking of territory, but it also encompassed a recognition of the importance of mercy and beneficence. The presence of the Virgin—the archetypical mother and parent—meant that paternalism and the hierarchical display of benevolence would not be forgotten. The next chapter will, in turn, make this apparent.

NOTES

1. W. C. McGrew, *Chimpanzee Material Culture* (Cambridge: Cambridge University Press, 1992), 171-72. Also 87.

2. Ibid., 79-80.

3. Ibid., 92.

4. Ibid., 96.

5. Ibid., 116.

6. Ibid., 117-18.

7. Ibid., 119.

8. Ibid., 82.

9. Ibid., 210; P. J. Baldwin, J. Sabater Pí, W. C. McGrew, and C. E. G. Tutin, "Comparisons of Nests Made by Different Populations of Chimpanzees (*Pan troglodytes*)," *Primates* 22:4 (October 1981): 474-86.

10. Edward O. Wilson, *Sociobiology: The New Synthesis* (Cambridge, MA: Belknap Press of Harvard University Press, 1975), 582.

11. Irenäus Eibl-Eibesfeldt, *Human Ethology* (New York: Aldine de Gruyter, 1989), 438.

12. Ibid., 63.

13. Ibid., 64.

14. Jane van Lawick-Goodall, *In the Shadow of Man* (Boston: Houghton Mifflin, 1971), 45-46, 66-67.

15. John Hemming, *Red Gold: The Conquest of the Brazilian Indians* (Cambridge, MA: Harvard University Press, 1978), 3-4.

16. "Memoria de las cosas y costa y indios de la Florida," *Colección de documentos inéditos relativos al descubrimiento, conquista y organización de las antiguas posesiones*

españolas de América y Oceanía, sacados de los archivos del reino, y muy especialmente del de Indias, ed. Joaquín F. Pacheco, Francisco de Cárdenas, and Luis Torres de Mendoza, 42 vols. (Madrid: Manuel G. Hernández, 1864-1884), 5:545. Henceforth *CDIR*.

17. "Testimonio dado en Méjico sobre el descubrimiento de doscientas leguas adelante, de las minas de Santa Bárbola, Gobernacion de Diego de Ibarra . . . . (1582-1583)," *CDIR* 15:81, 90.

18. Bartolomé de las Casas, *Brevisima Relación de la Destrucción de Indias*, ed. Manuel Ballesteros Gaibrois (Madrid: Fundación Universitaria Española, 1977), aiiii[b].

19. Bernal Díaz del Castillo, *Historia verdadera de la conquista de la Nueva España*, ed. Joaquín Ramírez Cabañas, 3 vols. (Mexico City: Editorial Pedro Robredo, 1944), 1:58. The above English translation is taken from Bernal Díaz del Castillo, *The Conquest of New Spain*, trans. J. M. Cohen (Harmondsworth: Penguin Books, 1963), 18.

20. Ibid., 1:57.

21. "Descubrimiento de las siete ciudades, por el P. Fr. Márcos de Niza (2 Setiembre, 1539)," *CDIR* 3:336, 343.

22. Hernán Cortés, "First Letter," in *Letters from Mexico*, trans. Anthony Pagden (New Haven, CT, and London: Yale University Press, 1986), 30.

23. Asunción Lavrin, "In Search of the Colonial Woman in Mexico: The Seventeenth and Eighteenth Centuries," in *Latin American Women: Historical Perspectives*, ed. Asunción Lavrin (Westport, CT, and London: Greenwood Press, 1978), 23-29, 36-38; Thomas Calvo, "The Warmth of the Hearth: Seventeenth-Century Guadalajara Families," in *Sexuality and Marriage in Colonial Latin America*, ed. Asunción Lavrin (Lincoln and London: University of Nebraska Press, 1989), 295; Patricia Seed, *To Love, Honor, and Obey in Colonial Mexico: Conflicts over Marriage Choice, 1574-1821* (Stanford, CA: Stanford University Press, 1988), 64-65.

24. On the harlot, see Bernardino de Sahagún, *Florentine Codex: General History of the Things of New Spain*, trans. Arthur J. O. Anderson and Charles E. Dibble, 13 vols. (Santa Fe and Salt Lake City: Monographs of the School of American Research/ University of Utah Press, 1950-1982), Bk. 10, chap. 15, pp. 55-56, and chap. 26, p. 94.

25. Cortés, "Second Letter," 112; Bernal Díaz, 1:343; Francisco López de Gómara, *Cortés: The Life of the Conqueror by His Secretary*, trans. Lesley Byrd Simpson (Berkeley and Los Angeles: University of California Press, 1964), 143.

26. Bernardino de Sahagún, *Historia general de las cosas de Nueva España*, ed. Angel María Garibay K., 4 vols. (Mexico City: Editorial Porrúa, 1969), Bk. 12, chap. 19.

27. In a 1529 letter to the Castilian Crown, Bishop Zumárraga argued the moral and hierarchical need for Mexican sumptuary laws. "Carta á su magestad del electo obispo de Méjico, D. Juan de Zumarraga, en que refiere la conquista que hizo de aquella tierra Hernán Cortés . . . (27 de Agosto de 1529)," *CDIR* 13: 170-71. Also see Jean Hippolyte Mariéjol, *The Spain of Ferdinand and Isabella*, trans. Benjamin Keen (New Brunswick, NJ: Rutgers University Press, 1961), 216-17.

28. Cortés, "First Letter," 35-36; and "Second Letter," 106, 146, 251.

29. Cortés, "First Letter," 30.

30. Bernal Díaz, 1:204, 278, 361. For the English citation, see Cohen, 123-24.

31. Cortés, "Second Letter," 72, 105.

32. Cortés, "First Letter," 35; "Second Letter," 105-6; and Bernal Díaz, 1:359-62.

33. Cortés, "Second Letter," 82.

34. Ibid., 107.

35. Bernal Díaz, 1:335, 346-50, 361.

36. Sahagún, *Historia*, 1:177, 181, 45, 69-70; Joseph de Acosta, *Historia natural y moral de las Indias*, ed. Edmundo O' Gorman (Mexico City: Fondo de Cultura Económica, 1940), 371.

37. Acosta, 404.

38. Sahagún, *Historia*, 1:187, 169.

39. Gerónimo de Mendieta, *Historia Eclesiástica Indiana* (Mexico City: Editorial Porrúa, 1971), 86-87.

40. Acosta, 403.

41. *Florentine Codex*, Bk. 12, chap. 20. On the Inquisition, see Sara T. Nalle, "Inquisitors, Priests, and the People during the Catholic Reformation in Spain," *The Sixteenth Century Journal* 18:4 (winter 1987): 557-83. For a dissenting view, see Henry Kamen, "Toleration and Dissent in Sixteenth-Century Spain: The Alternative Tradition," *The Sixteenth Century Journal* 19:1 (spring 1988): 3-23.

42. Mendieta, 421-29.

43. Ibid., 423.

44. Acosta, 447, 471-72; Sahagún, *Historia*, 1:27.

45. "Ordenanzas de Su Magestad hechas para los nuevos descubrimientos, conquistas y pacificaciones.—Julio de 1573," *CDIR* 16:142-87.

46. "Interrogatorio para todas las ciudades, villas y lugares . . . de las Indias Occidentales . . .," *CDIR* 9:59-60.

47. Ibid., 63, 66, 70.

48. Chloë Sayer, *Costumes of Mexico* (Austin: University of Texas Press, 1985), 65, 17-19.

49. Acosta, 290, 311.

50. Ibid., 290-91.

51. "Pleito contra el licenciado Juan Ortiz de Matiengo y Diego Delgadillo, para recuperar la renta del pueblo de Toluca que . . . habían dado a García del Pilar durante la ausencia de Cortés en España (año de 1531)," in *Tributos y servicios personales de indios para Hernán Cortés y su familia*, ed. Silvio Zavala (Mexico City: Archivo General de la Nación, 1984), 67-81; and "Precios de la ropa de Cuernavaca, 1535. . . . Comercio de productos del tributo en la ciudad de México," in *Tributos y servicios . . . para Hernán Cortés*, 115-19.

52. Sahagún, *Historia*, 3:134-35; Fray Toribio de Benavente o Motolinía, *Memoriales o libro de las cosas de la Nueva España y de los naturales de ella*, ed. Edmundo O'Gorman (Mexico City: Universidad Nacional Autónoma de México, 1971), 373.

53. For an assessment of just how the Spaniards replaced the Aztecs at the center of a trading and tributary hub, see Ross Hassig, *Trade, Tribute, and Transportation* (Norman: University of Oklahoma Press, 1985), 103-16, 142, 149-50, 237.

54. For more on the *cabildo*'s regulatory functions, see Hassig, 237.

55. *Tributos y servicios . . . para Hernán Cortés*, 115-16.

56. Ibid., 115-19. A *carga* might weigh from three to six bushels.

57. "Tasaciones de los pueblos de la provincia de Yucatán," in *Epistolario de Nueva España, 1505-1818*, ed. Francisco del Paso y Troncoso, 16 vols. (Mexico City: José Porrúa e hijos, 1939-1940), 6:91-92. Henceforth *ENE*.

58. Ibid., 5:119-21, 123-24, 126, 141.

59. Hassig, 240, 120.

60. *The Tlaxcalan Actas: A Compendium of the Records of the Cabildo of Tlaxcala (1545-1627)*, trans. James Lockhart, Frances Berdan, and Arthur J. O. Anderson (Salt

Lake City: University of Utah Press, 1986), 81.

61. Alonso de Zorita, *Life and Labor in Ancient Mexico: The Brief and Summary Relation of the Lords of New Spain*, trans. Benjamin Keen (New Brunswick, NJ: Rutgers University Press, 1963), 253.

62. Nigel Davies, *The Aztec Empire: The Toltec Resurgence* (Norman and London: University of Oklahoma Press, 1987), 135.

63. Diego Durán, *Historia de las Indias de Nueva España e islas de la tierra firme*, ed. Angel María Garibay K., 2 vols. (Mexico City: Editorial Porrúa, 1967), 2:205-10.

64. The term "cacique" was adopted by Spaniards in the Caribbean and universally applied to Amerindian nobles. It is derived from an Arawak word for one who keeps a house, "*kassiquan*."

65. Bernal Díaz, 1:352. See Cohen, 232, for the English.

66. Richard J. Salvucci, *Textiles and Capitalism in Mexico: An Economic History of the Obrajes, 1539-1840* (Princeton, NJ: Princeton University Press, 1987), 149, 3-9.

67. Colin MacLachlan and Jaime E. Rodríguez O., *The Forging of the Cosmic Race: A Reinterpretation of Colonial Mexico* (Berkeley, Los Angeles, London: University of California Press, 1980), 187-92.

68. Salvucci, 109, 125.

69. "Sobre las Cédulas del servicio personal de los indios (sin fecha)," *CDIR* 6:118.

70. MacLachlan and Rodríguez, 187-92.

71. "Al Rey de virrey Villamanrique (11 Hebrero 1587)," Archivo General de Indias, *Cartas y expedientes de los virreyes de Nueva España* (Seville: Centro Nacional de Microfilm, 1975), reel 4, number 1.

72. Salvucci, 19; Sayer, 17-19.

73. Peter Boyd-Bowman, "Two Country Stores in XVIIth Century Mexico," *The Americas* 28:3 (January 1972): 237-51.

74. "Carta á su magestad del electo obispo de Méjico, D. Juan de Zumarraga, en que refiere la conquista que hizo de aquella tierra Hernan Cortés . . . (27 Agosto 1529)," *CDIR* 13:170-71.

75. Examples may be found among the documents of the Mexican National Archives. Archivo General de la Nación, Fondo *Indios*, vol. 4, exp. 170-80, f. 55ª-56ª; vol. 6, 1ª parte, exp. 223-24 and 273, f. 57ª and 74ª⁻ᵇ. Also see Robert Haskett, *Indigenous Rulers: An Ethnohistory of Town Government in Colonial Cuernavaca* (Albuquerque: University of New Mexico Press, 1991), 161-62.

76. "Caueçera de Tetela," in *Papeles de Nueva España*, ed. Francisco del Paso y Troncoso, 7 vols. (Madrid: Sucesores de Rivadeneyra, 1905), 5:148. Henceforth *PNE*.

77. *Angero* was a coarse cloth that originated in Ajou, France. "Relación de Ueipuchtla y su partido (10 Octubre, 1579-24 Marzo, 1580)," *PNE* 6:16.

78. "Relación de Atitalaquia y su partido (22 Febrero, 1580)," *PNE* 6:206.

79. "Tzicaputzalco (12 Octubre, 1579-1 Diciembre, 1579)," *PNE* 6:96.

80. "Alaustlan," *PNE* 6:102; and "Quatepeque," *PNE* 6:119.

81. "Tlacotepeque," *PNE* 6:124.

82. James Lockhart, *The Nahuas after the Conquest: A Social and Cultural History of the Indians of Central Mexico, Sixteenth through Eighteenth Centuries* (Stanford, CA: Stanford University Press, 1992), 199-200.

83. "Aculma (22 Febrero, 1580-1 Marzo, 1580)," *PNE* 6:217. Also see *PNE* 6:224, 229, 235.

84. "Relación de Xonotla y Tetela (20 y 29 Octubre, 1581)," *PNE* 5:128.

85. "Aculma," *PNE* 6:217. Also "Xonotla," *PNE* 5:129.

86. "Relación de Papaloticpac y su partido (7-11 Diciembre, 1579)," *PNE* 4:90-91.

87. "Relación de Taliztaca (12 Septiembre, 1580)," *PNE* 4:179; "Relación de Macuilsúchil y su partido (9 Abrill, 1580)," *PNE* 4:106.

88. Salvucci, 29.

89. "Macuilsúchil," *PNE* 4:106.

90. Charles Gibson, *The Aztecs under Spanish Rule: A History of the Indians of the Valley of Mexico, 1519-1810* (Stanford, CA: Stanford University Press, 1964), 156-57.

91. As demonstrated by Robert Haskett in the *Marquesado* of Cuernavaca, indigenous nobles skillfully used cultural syncretism to retain some local autonomy and an intermediary role vis-à-vis the Spaniards. The adoption of Spanish dress, houses, furniture and other aspects of material culture aided and abetted this process. Haskett, 161-68.

92. "Relación de la Villa de Tepuztlan (19 Septiembre, 1580)," *PNE* 6:243.

93. "Relación de Chichicapa y su partido (15 Mayo, 1580)," *PNE* 4:118.

94. "Relación de Guaxilotitlan (10 Marzo, 1581)," *PNE* 4:200.

95. "Tepuztlan," *PNE* 6:243; "Coatepec y su partido (3 Diciembre, 1579)," *PNE* 6:56.

96. "Relación de Tlacotalpan y su partido (18-22 Febrero, 1580)," *PNE* 5:2-3.

97. "Relación de las minas de Tasco (1 Enero-6 Marzo, 1581)," *PNE* 6:278.

98. "Las minas de Tasco," *PNE* 6:265.

99. "Relación de Ocopetlayuca (6 Octubre, 1580)," *PNE* 6:258.

100. Felipe Gorostiza, "Space, Order and the Sign: The City in a New World," Unpublished paper, *The Sixteenth Century Studies Conference*, Philadelphia, October 17, 1991.

101. George M. Foster, *Culture and Conquest: America's Spanish Heritage* (Chicago: Quadrangle Books, 1960), 3, 38-49.

102. Juan Luis Vives, *Templo de los leyes*, in *Obras completas*, 2 vols., trans. Lorenzo Riber (Madrid: M. Aguilar, 1947-1948), 1:681-82.

103. "Carta de Hernando Cortés a Hernando de Saavedra (1525)," *CDIR* 40:191-92; Louise M. Burkhart, *The Slippery Earth: Nahua-Christian Moral Dialogue in Sixteenth-Century Mexico* (Tucson: University of Arizona Press, 1989), 86.

104. It must be emphasized that churches were not erected on the tops of pyramids themselves. See John McAndrew, *The Open-Air Churches of Sixteenth-Century Mexico: Atrios, Posas, Open Chapels, and Other Studies* (Cambridge, MA: Harvard University Press, 1965), 494.

105. George Kubler, *Mexican Architecture of the Sixteenth Century*, 2 vols. (New Haven, CT: Yale University Press, 1948), 1:163.

106. Gorostiza, 3; Davíd Carrasco, *Quetzalcoatl and the Irony of Empire: Myths and Prophecies in the Aztec Tradition* (Chicago and London: University of Chicago Press, 1982), 149-50, 160-70, 182-87.

107. Cortés, "Second Letter," 102-3. Also 104-11.

108. Bernal Díaz, 1:330.

109. Cortés, "Third Letter," 266.

110. Bernal Díaz, 1:176.

111. Michel Foucault, *Discipline and Punish: The Birth of the Prison*, trans. Alan Sheridan (New York: Vintage, 1979), 57-58.

112. Bernal Díaz, 2:97.

113. "Carta al rey, del presidente y oidores de la Audiencia de México, consultando ciertas dudas sobre el castigo de los indios, libertad de los esclavos (y otras cosas). . .

—De México, a 20 de febrero de 1548," *ENE* 5:87.

114. Kubler, 1:151, 142-45.

115. Motolinía, 242.

116. "El Conquistador Anónimo.—Relación de algunas cosas de la Nueva España y de la gran ciudad de Temestitán; escrita por un compañero de Hernán Cortés (Texto italiano y traducción.)," in *Colección de documentos para la historia de México*, ed. Joaquín García Icazbalceta, 2 vols. (Mexico, 1858-1866): 1:385, 392-96.

117. Motolinía, 82.

118. In actuality, only a few learned friars and laymen would have read Alberti, but the Italian's ideas were spread orally. By 1584 one Mexico City bookseller, Diego Navarro Maldonado, had at least four copies of Alberti and four copies of Vitruvius in his possession. See Kubler, 1:98-100, 104.

119. Motolinía, 84.

120. Kubler, 1:202.

121. Motolinía, 242.

122. Kubler, 1:155-59, 110; McAndrew, 196-98.

123. Motolinía, 27-28.

124. Kubler, 1:171-72.

125. Francisco Cervantes de Salazar, *Life in the Imperial and Loyal City of Mexico in New Spain and the Royal and Pontifical University of Mexico in the Dialogues for the Study of the Latin Language*, trans. Minnie Lee Barrett Shepard (Westport, CT: Greenwood Press, 1970), 38-39.

126. Ibid., 39.

127. Ibid., 41.

128. Ibid., 43, 47-48.

129. Ibid., 58-60, 63, 56, 40.

130. "Códice Harkness de Huejotzingo, 1531," in *Documentos Cortesianos*, ed. José Luis Martínez, 4 vols. (Mexico City: Universidad Nacional Autónoma de México/ Fondo de Cultura Económica, 1991), following 3:224.

131. Motolinía, 266.

132. McAndrew, 344-52, 295-300.

133. "Ordenanzas . . . hechas . . . Julio de 1573," *CDIR* 16:186.

134. "Lo que el Visorey é Gobernador de la Nueva Spaña y sus Provincias y Presidente de la Audiencia Real que rreside en la Ciudad de México, a de hazer en dicha Tierra, demas de lo contenido en los Poderes y Comisiones que lleva, por mandado de S.M. (Año de 1550)," *CDIR* 23:534-35.

135. "Ordenanzas . . . hechas . . . Julio de 1573," *CDIR* 16:175-76.

136. "Descripción de la Villa de Nombre de Dios . . . en Mayo de 1608," *CDIR* 9:231-47.

137. "Interrogatorio para todas las ciudades, villas y lugares . . . de las Indias Occidentales . . .," *CDIR* 9:59-60.

138. "Descripción del Pueblo de Guauchinango y otros pueblos de su jurisdicción (1609)," *CDIR* 9:122; "Descripción del Pueblo de Coatlan (1609)," *CDIR* 9:388.

139. "Descripción del partido de Miahuatlan (Febrero, 1609)," *PNE* 4:293.

140. "Descripción de los pueblos de la provincia de Pánuco (sin fecha)," *CDIR* 9:156.

141. "Descripción de la villa de Pánuco (sin fecha)," *CDIR* 9:138-39.

142. Haskett, 168.

143. "Coatepec," *PNE* 6:62-63.

144. "Relación de Xuchitepec (23-29 Agosto, 1579)," *PNE* 4:28.

145. "Chichicapa," *PNE* 4:119; "Guaxilotitlan," *PNE* 4:204.

146. "Relación de Cuicatlan (15 Septiembre, 1580)," *PNE* 4:188; "Relación de Atlatlauca y Malinaltepec (8 Septiembre, 1580)," *PNE* 4:175.

147. "Relación de Nexapa (12 Septiembre, 1579-20 Abril, 1580)," *PNE* 4:43, 31-32.

148. "Relación de Iztepexi (27-30 Agosto, 1579)," *PNE* 4:13; "Relación de Tepeaca y su partido (4-20 Febrero, 1580)," *PNE* 5:41; "Relación de Ahuatlan y su partido (19-24 Agosto, 1581)," *PNE* 5:84, 88, 93, 97; "Relación de Xonotla y Tetela (20-29 Octubre, 1581)," *PNE* 5:130, 150; "Relación de Chilapa (21 Febrero, 1582)," *PNE* 5:181; "Relación de Macuilsúchil y su partido (9 Abrill, 1580)," *PNE* 4:107; "Relación de Tlacolula y Mitla (12-23 Agosto, 1580)," *PNE* 4:150.

149. "Tepeaca," *PNE* 5:41.

150. "Ahuatlan y su partido," *PNE* 5:93, 97.

151. "Ichcateopan y su partido," *PNE* 5:92-93, 99, 105, 112-13, 121, 126, 131, 136, 143, 148, 151.

152. "Relación de Zayula (3 Febrero, 1580)," *PNE* 6:181. Also see "Relación de Ueipuchtla y su partido (10 Octubre, 1579-24 Marzo, 1580)," *PNE* 6:18-19, 23; "Relación de Chiconauhtla y su partido (21 Enero, 1580)," *PNE* 6:176; "Relación de Mexicatzinco (7 Febrero, 1580)," *PNE* 6:197; "Relación de Atitalaquia y su partido (22 Febrero, 1580)," *PNE* 6:207; "Relación de las minas de Tasco (1 Enero, 1581)," *PNE* 6:281; "Relación de Tetela y Ueyapan (20 Junio, 1581)," *PNE* 6:288; "Relación de Tepepulco (15 Abril, 1581)," *PNE* 6:301; "Relación de Cuauhquilpan (9 Octubre, 1581)," *PNE* 6:311.

153. "Relación de Tepepulco (15 Abril, 1581)," *PNE* 6:301. Also see "Tetela y Ueyapan," *PNE* 6:288; "las minas de Tasco," *PNE* 6:281.

154. Lockhart, 71.

155. Ibid., 64, 68.

156. Ibid., 62, 70.

157. "Relación del pueblo de Ocelotepeque (Marzo, 1609)," *CDIR* 9:226-27. Also *PNE* 4:304.

158. "Ocelotepeque," *CDIR* 9:226.

159. Ibid., *CDIR* 9:229.

160. Peter Gerhard, *A Guide to the Historical Geography of New Spain* (Cambridge: Cambridge University Press, 1972), 187-90.

161. Inga Clendinnen, *Aztecs: An Interpretation* (Cambridge: Cambridge University Press, 1991), 34-35.

162. The translation is J. M. Cohen's. See Bernal Díaz, *The Conquest of New Spain*, 47. Also see Bernal Díaz, 1:106.

163. Cortés, "Second Letter," 106.

6

Food: Dominance and Benevolence in Colonial New Spain

In the development of human culture, food and the rituals and prohibitions surrounding eating have always served as an important aspect of cultural self-definition.[1] Cooked food often is placed in juxtaposition to raw food as a sign of culture, learning, and civilization in contrast with crude nature.[2] Culture, in turn, sets humans apart from nature by focusing on the ways in which humans harvest, transform, and consume natural elements for their sustenance, thus emphasizing that people cook their food, whereas other animals eat theirs raw. Having developed different eating practices, individual human cultures have interpreted their own rituals of food preparation and eating as the only appropriate ones. When one cultural group has conquered another, these rituals have served as important tools in the process of imperialism, just as eating rituals are also used to establish hierarchy within a given society.[3] Out of cultural necessity, as conquerors of a new people and environment, sixteenth-century Spaniards used their learned food preferences and rituals to set themselves apart as an elite group and to manage their new material environment. In so doing they were imitating a European elite distinguished from the masses by their access to food.

However, human behavior is not monochromatic, nor is it solely given to exclusionist, hierarchical, and xenophobic tendencies. Food may deny access to a particular group, but it is primarily used to represent attainment of membership within a group. Through the use of comparative ethological methods, primatologists have postulated food-sharing as a fundamental means to community-building, with roots as deeply engrained as maternal relations with offspring. In addition, archaeological evidence points to the earliest of hominid base camps having been sites where food-sharing and food exchange no doubt took place. To the present day chimpanzee bases exhibit this very trait. Primates use food to establish bonds, and bonds are established by food. In this, the sixteenth-century Spaniards were no exception. Food was indeed used culturally to separate conquistadores and pobladores from Amerindian masses, but it was also used to bind those very same Amerindians, or at least select members of their group, to their Spanish conquerors on a number of different levels. The purpose of this chapter is to illustrate this binary tension and its fundamental relationship to natural primate tendencies. Whereas culture and the particular expression of hierarchy and altruism may be learned, human tendencies to use food to express dominance and benevolence are innate and important to understanding the conquest of Mexico.

As early as their experiences in the Caribbean, Spanish explorers and colonizers were struck by the foods found in the New World environment. Even men obsessed by "gold, glory, and God" needed sustenance, and an appropriate form of sustenance at that. They could depend completely on the produce of undirected Indian tributary labor, but this proved extremely difficult as Indian populations declined in the Caribbean and New Spain. It also irked Spanish sensibilities to eat only the food traditionally produced by the indigenous populations, even though some Spaniards seemingly acquired a gourmet's love of the unusual and praised the taste of maize and cassava bread.[4]

Others, like the Dominican priest las Casas, were so intent on defending Indian culture and the Americas that they deliberately praised New World foods like the peanut. Las Casas argued that the peanut was more delicious than any Spanish nut or dried fruit, but his praise was unusual and a reflection of his role as defender of the Indians. In fact, he was responding directly to Gonzalo Fernández de Oviedo, who described the peanut as not fit for Spanish consumption.[5] Likewise, the Franciscan Motolinía wrote favorably of the Aztec algae cake *tecuitlatl*: "To those of us who share Indian tastes it is very savory, having a salty flavor."[6] In some circles, a real debate existed, but for the most part American foods were subordinated to European foodstuffs. Affluent Europeans, of course, craved spices and other exotic fare, but they freely chose the novel items to be introduced into a diet still predominantly Eurocentric.[7]

The reception of Indian foods as tribute, without Spanish control or definition of those foods, satisfied hunger but diminished the Spaniards' sense of superiority and active agency. Eating Indian foods placed them on the level of the Indians, besides offending a Spanish palate accustomed to European grains, vegetables, fruits, and meats. Attempts were made to determine which New World foods were most like those of the Old World and therefore acceptable,[8] but from a very early date there was discussion of transplanting European foods to the Americas.

Cattle and wheat soon made their appearances in the Caribbean as a result.[9] Wheat, however, appeared only by means of transatlantic shipment, since European grains, grapes, and olives failed to take root in the hot Caribbean tropics.[10] As early as 1495 four caravels sailing for the Indies carried 180 *cahizes* (3,240 bushels) of wheat, 50 *cahizes* (900 bushels) of barley, 60 *toneles* (49.8 tons) of wine, 10 *toneles* (8.3 tons) of vinegar, 60 *toneles* (49.8 tons) of oil, 50 *quintales* (5,000 pounds) of figs, and ten to twelve peasant *labradores*.[11]

In one colonial *relación*, the Comunero Revolt of 1521 was denounced because it interfered with the shipment of wheat flour to the Indies.[12] Royal bureaucrats and clergymen discussed the need to introduce Castilian and Andalusian peasants to teach the Amerindians "appropriate" agricultural methods and serve as a civilizing force in the New World.[13] In the minds of these priests and lawyers, Old World agriculture and the Old World peasant (at his best) were the foundations of European civilization and the body politic, and ill-fated social experiments, such Puebla de los Angeles, were attempted to introduce the Indians to these fundamentals of European civilization.[14]

Although the Amerindians were seldom denied their humanity, even if labeled natural slaves, they were granted an inferior grade of humanity, and the Spaniards used their food and eating rituals to prove their bigoted case.[15] In terms of eating, the most obvious target was cannibalism, which was constantly referred to as a horrific and debauched sign of savagery. Although practiced in Europe during the most wretched famine conditions, cannibalism, except in its symbolic Eucharistic form, was denounced consistently as an unnatural and profane act.[16] In the Spanish frame of reference human sacrifice and cannibalism remained signs of a sick society and justified conquest, the just war being the most obvious means of civilizing this most barbarous element.[17] Indigenous eating practices other than cannibalism could be left to the Indians to distinguish them from Spaniards, and the Spanish documents make numerous references to the fact that Amerindians ate differently from Europeans; but perceived similarities could be used against the Indians also. Instead of complimenting Amerindian culture, Spaniards reinforced Spanish prejudices by identifying the praiseworthy in New World cultures as that most like European practices. In a 1575 *relación* to the Audiencia of Guadalajara, Juan de Miranda epitomized Spanish biases toward Indian eating practices by equating the peacefulness and civilization of *estancia* Indians with their cultivation of wheat and maize. He derogated the local Indians still free of Spanish rule by identifying them as "a barbaric people, inept and incapable, since they lack fields of maize and other produce, and sustain themselves with very vile and lowly staples."[18]

Significantly, foods and eating rituals, as well as forms of political organization and worship, were more commonly used to define the Amerindians as brothers or savages than was the color of their skin. In the service of conquest and colonization, European attention initially focused on political, religious, and culinary aspects of culture. Among the first conquerors and colonizers of New Spain, Cortés, Bernal Díaz, and others were not exceptional. Most of these early conquerors and colonizers of the mainland arrived after an initial period on the Caribbean islands. Cortés had raised European cattle for European consumption on the island of Cuba, and other members of his band had established similar agrarian and pastoral practices.[19] During the actual war with the Aztecs, Spaniards were provisioned with Indian maize and meats, but their preference, as evidenced by Bernal Díaz, was for European foods and eating habits:

What is more, we had hardly enough to eat. I do not speak of maize-cakes, for we had plenty of them, but of nourishing food for the wounded. The wretched stuff on which we existed was a vegetable that the Indians eat called quelites, supplemented by the local cherries, while they lasted, and afterwards by prickly pears, which then came into season.[20]

More than a matter of personal taste, food preference was an intrinsic part of the Spanish and Nahua concept of health and nutrition. Díaz del Castillo's complaint revealed a Spanish proclivity for high-protein foods, a preference that penetrated all levels of their society. When discussing Moctezuma's food, Bernal Díaz noted that he ate "maize-cakes kneaded with eggs and other nourishing ingredients."[21] Thus, the Aztecs obviously shared that proclivity as well, and the *Florentine Codex* identifies the foods of the lords as including a true sense of balance and a number of protein-rich foods. Turkey, rabbit, duck, rats, tadpoles, and fish were all embellished with chilis, tomatoes, and various sauces; squash, cactus fruit, avocado, and honeyed chocolate added to the diversity.[22] Bernal Díaz implied that maize-cakes and fruits alone were not enough for the wounded, and the Aztecs, of course, also recognized the human need for protein. In Spain the popular medical tracts of the day spoke of a need for a balance of meats, fish, fruit, and grains in the sick person's diet.[23] The physician Juan de Avinón, for example, suggested daily consumption of both meat and bread for his Sevillian patients: "Add a pound of bread and two of meat . . . half in the morning and half at night; and with this quantity, more or less, the health of the majority of Sevillian men can be maintained."[24]

Likewise, Aztec physicians prescribed turkey broth for an unsettled stomach, and a large fried or roasted lizard after a patient's purging had completed its course.[25] Primates require supplemental proteins in their diets—as evidenced by chimpanzee hunting and nut consumption—but a cultural truth, extrapolated from the animal tendency to hierarchy, is that the leading ranks of diverse cultures often enough have greater access to protein and food diversity. This was true of Spaniards and Aztecs, but with human tendencies to mutual aid also a truism, Spanish and Aztec elites provided opportunities for sharing within the ranks whenever possible. Greater accessibility to food remained the prerogative of the elite, but food-sharing in the midst of abundance was not out of the question. Among other things, it helped to provide a sense of social stability.

The Spanish definition of an appropriate diet necessarily included the meats and animal products to which a Castilian herding society had grown accustomed. In the early days of encomienda in any given region, Castilian chickens were one of the first items to make an appearance as common Indian tribute, chickens being the cheapest and least labor intensive European source of protein. By the 1580s, most Amerindian townships seem to have raised Castilian chickens and produced eggs.[26] Postconquest royal ordinances for the Hospital of San Lázaro in Mexico City reveal that the indigent were expected to receive protein-rich eggs as part of their diets.[27] Thus, outcasts and the poor also occasionally were included in the "Europeanization" of Mexico's nutritional regime. The preference for European eating habits was part of the imposition of a European order, since food was an intrinsic part of establishing boundaries and expectations in a hierarchical society.

From the moment he arrived in Mexico, Cortés took note of the foods produced and consumed by the Indians.[28] He also reported on the potential for conversion to Spanish methods of agriculture and husbandry:

From here to the coast I have seen no city so fit for Spaniards to live in [i.e., Churultecal—modern-day Cholula], for it has water and some common lands suitable for raising cattle, which none of those we saw previously had, for there are so many people living in these parts that not one foot of land is uncultivated, and yet in many places they suffer hardships for lack of bread.[29]

Although the foods they observed eaten were perceived as strange and even improper, the Spaniards nonetheless saw cultural similarities. One Aztec eating ritual in particular, Moctezuma's meals, struck Cortés as a strange amalgam of the proper and improper, thus emphasizing the ambiguity with which Europeans approached a "new world."[30]

Impressed by the opulence with which Moctezuma was served, Cortés reported in endless detail the manner in which the Aztec *tlatoani* ate, an observation repeated in the works of Bernal Díaz and López de Gómara (Cortés's secretary after he returned to Spain). The accounts vary in the number and types of dishes Moctezuma was served, as well as on the number of servitors, but thematic qualities remain constant.[31]

Each day at dawn there arrived at his house six hundred chiefs and principal persons . . . . When they brought food to Mutezuma [sic] they also provided for all those chiefs to each according to his rank; and their servants and followers were also given to eat . . . . Three or four hundred boys came bringing the dishes which, were without number, for each time he lunched or dined, he was brought every kind of food: meat, fish, fruit and vegetables. . . . They placed all these dishes together in a great room where he ate, which was almost always full. . . . One of the servants set down and removed the plates of food and called to others who were farther away for all that was required. Before and after the meal they gave him water for his hands and a towel which once used was never used again, and likewise with the plates and bowls, for when they brought more food they always used new ones, and the same with the braziers.[32]

Whatever the particulars given in the different accounts, two characteristics stand out. Moctezuma ate abundantly, and he shared this abundance with others according to their rank. To the Spaniards, this signified high culture. Just as population concentration was regarded as a mark of civilization, so the appropriateness of Moctezuma's rituals indicated cultural achievement in the Spanish system of values.

Food was shared, but always in terms of rank and hierarchy—López de Gómara uniquely noting that Moctezuma alone was served a full meal.[33] Nobles and their retinues were fed according to rank, while the *tlatoani* himself shared all he ate with some old men who sat apart from him.[34] In all accounts, it was observed that Moctezuma was served all sorts of food ("meat, fish, fruit and vegetables") in abundance, magically creating prosperity in a land that sometimes experienced dearth like that in sixteenth-century Spain.[35]

Although Cortés initially described Moctezuma's palace life as completely alien to Spanish experience, he went on to present its wonders according to the familiar frames of reference found in the classical and popular literature of the day.[36] Although he implicitly denounced the magnificence of Moctezuma's rituals as comparable to the ceremonies of sultans and infidel lords, these analogies were within the scope of Spanish experience.[37] The Aztecs were just as marvelous, civilized, and fascinating as the Moors of the Reconquista, but the absence of Christianity, according to the Spaniards, led to improper customs and some grievously abhorrent behavior. Both Cortés and Bernal Díaz noted that Moctezuma, like "some oriental potentate," ate behind a partition while simultaneously sharing his bounty with the nobles present.

Cortés's report of Moctezuma's eating was much more than a wonder tale. It revealed the presence of true hierarchy in Aztec society. Eating rituals surrounding Moctezuma identified his elite status, and those who ate in the palace were set apart as favored by their sharing of food with the *tlatoani*. Charles V, to whom the letter was addressed, was himself the subject of dominance display in his eating rituals. Although, as J. H. Elliott notes, the Spanish king dined alone in the seventeenth century—except for approximately twenty officials who waited on him—"Charles, with his peripatectic court, combined grandeur with a high degree of visibility."[38] In a letter written some twenty-nine years after the conquest of Mexico, Charles told his regents Maximilian and Mary how to govern Castile in his absence. In the midst of discussing dealings with the royal councils, frontier defense, and the raising of revenue, the emperor turned to the question of public ceremony. He ordered

that the aforesaid Prince and Princess continue to hear mass on Sundays and feast days, that they are seen to leave for the churches and monasteries where they will hear it, and that they eat publicly. That they hold court for some hours of the day in order to hear justly those with whom they wish to speak and receive the petitions and briefs which are given them.[39]

As the leader of a leadership elite and an entire society, the Spanish monarch was called to embody and illustrate appropriate behavior and custom. Fray Antonio de Guevara reported that Charles's wife Isabel always ate with and before others, except in the winter, when one sought the comfort of small heated rooms. Otherwise, prelates were present to bless her food and she was served in abundance with her courtiers.[40] For Isabel and Charles, eating with those who would execute their orders was a duty necessarily joined to other leadership responsibilities. Quite literally, they were bonding with their subordinates in the troop.

From an anthropological perspective, such linkage is quite natural, since the breaking of bread or food-sharing consistently serves as a fundamental rite of covenant-making and bonding. The Bantu as well as the Chinese traditionally establish covenants and contracts while eating, and the English word "companion" is itself formed from French and Latin words meaning "one who eats bread with another."[41] One need go no further in Western cultures than the Bible and Homer to find examples of the symbolic linkage between social bonding and food-sharing; and in sixteenth-century Catholic and Lutheran Christianity, communion, partaking in the body and blood of Christ, bound individuals to the mystical body of Christ, the Christian social organism found in 1 Corinthians 12.[42] To see the king or the representatives of his authority eat with others, like seeing them hear mass or petitions publicly, was to see them granting favor and status. In turn, they might receive loyalty and gratitude.

Across the boundaries seemingly established by particular customs and differences in transformational grammar, Cortés recognized a deep structure common to all primates. In his groundbreaking study of the captive chimpanzees of Arnhem, Frans de Waal noted that the dominant male Yeroen not only settled disputes among subordinate individuals but also shared "incidental, extra food" that came into his possession. Upon seeing a large pile of oak leaves on one occasion, Yeroen dashed to the pile, bluffing and displaying as he went. No other chimpanzee dared to challenge him, but upon acquiring firm possession of the pile he proceeded to distribute the leaves among the others. De Waal noted that whereas females were observed to share mainly with their children and close friends, quarreling with others in the band, "for the adult male, the amount that he himself possesses is not important. What matters is who does the distributing among the group."[43]

Far from being aberrant, such behavior is quite common among chimpanzees. One of Jane Goodall's first significant experiences in the wild was witnessing a chimpanzee named David Graybeard share a baby pig with a female actively engaged in begging by means of outstretched hands.[44] Since then, a number of studies at Gombe and other African sites have demonstrated that meat is commonly shared after a successful hunting expedition. Female chimpanzees in estrus appear to have some greater success in acquiring meat than other chimpanzees, but "eighty per cent of sharing involved adults of both sexes getting meat from males."[45] Where banana-sharing is concerned at Gombe, relatives are most definitely favored, but 14 percent of 457 transfers in one study were to non-kin. Aside from Jane Goodall's Gombe site, food-sharing has also been established at Kasoje and Taï. As with humans, most food-sharing among chimpanzees seems tied to reproductive strategies and kinship in some capacity or other, but this is not always the case. On Liberia's Bassa Islands, unrelated adult males have been seen sharing palm nuts. An individual who had gathered the nuts was seen giving them to another in possession of rocks used as a hammer and anvil to crack the nuts. Then they proceeded to share the protein-rich nuts once they were cracked.[46] The band to which a chimpanzee belongs serves as an extended family, a tribe of sorts, and sharing within its confines is not out of the question. It is only that more immediate relatives and potential or actual sexual partners are favored. Among the Spaniards and Mexica, there is no doubt that the majority of food-sharing was a matter of kinship, with Spaniards referring to the tables set for family members and servants, and the Mexica maintaining common food supplies for their clan units, or *calpolli*, in particularly difficult times. Although the mere fact that we share just a little below 99 percent of our DNA with chimpanzees should be enough to justify the pertinence of these pongid examples in suggesting humans' innate propensity to use food-sharing as a means of community-building, the evidence accumulated from archaeological sites and the behavior of human children is even more striking.[47]

Our living pongid cousins engage in all sorts of "tolerated scrounging," and early hominid sites at Koobi Fora and Olduvai, dating 2.5 to 1.5 million years ago, reveal base camps where tools were made and meat was collected, most likely for food-sharing activities. Since meat does not keep long in the African savannah, the sharing of one's successful hunt in the hope of receiving reciprocal treatment in the future would have been eminently logical.[48] In fact, Glynn Isaac readily sees food-sharing as the origin of home bases and as an encouragement to language and culture by creating the need to plan ahead and relate such plans to other individuals. Present-day human children, in fact, display just these tendencies. Children at ten to twelve months of age offer food to establish friendly contact. Young girls aged five to eight share in a fairly universal manner, and boys choose particular individuals and build coalitions through the sharing of candy and other objects. Most interestingly, dominant children tend to be the most active food-sharers. As with the dominant Yeroen, the Mexica *tlatoani*, and the Spanish king, engaging in benevolent behavior, as well as aggressive display, helps to define that dominance.[49]

In sixteenth-century Spain nobles were expected to maintain large households. Purpose and prestige, *hidalguía*, were demonstrated by a noble's, or colonial encomendero's, capacity to maintain a *casa poblada* and its table. Social status and prestige were demonstrated by feeding a host of relatives, guests, lackeys, and other dependents.[50] It was therefore quite easy for Cortés and any number of Spaniards to interpret significance in the way Moctezuma ate. Their culturally specific categories of understanding were bound to "hardwired," innate tendencies regarding human interaction—to a deeply structured human nature.

On a wider societal plane, food-sharing may also manifest itself in poor relief, and both Spain and Mexico provided ample opportunities for this particular manifestation. In Mexico drought and famine caused starvation and death from 1450 to 1455. In Castile poor agricultural techniques and the enclosure of arable lands for the sheep-herding activities of the Mesta generated insufficient harvests and an ever-growing population of beggars from 1502 to 1508.[51] European wheat production, from the fifteenth to the eighteenth century, was remarkable for its low yield: "For every grain sown, the harvest was usually no more than five and sometimes less." By contrast, maize grown in the dry zone of colonial Mexico yielded between seventy and eighty grains for every one sown, and was far easier to tend.[52] Sixteenth-century Spaniards came to the Americas to find raw abundance and fertility, but they accepted hunger and bread substitutes like chestnut flour as normal aspects of life confronting the common people.[53] As in Spain, poverty and famine were aspects of Aztec life and culture, and just as the Spanish elite chose to pursue its own economic interests while occasionally providing poor relief, the Aztec elite chose to hide misery behind its own prosperity. Humans are given to reciprocity and altruism, but such practices may be encouraged or discouraged by the learned process that is culture, and by the circumstances in any individual's environment. Both Spanish and Nahua cultures extolled the virtue of charity, had some system of poor relief, and recognized the role of charity in preventing rebellion and promoting social control.[54] However, the Anonymous Conqueror noted that only the Aztec lords had great variety in aliments and condiments, whereas the common people made do with little.[55] Cortés saw the presence of beggars as proof that the Nahuas were civilized: "And there are many poor people who beg from the rich in the streets as the poor do in Spain and in other civilized places."[56]

Public charity alone reaffirmed reciprocity and the rulership of elites during periods of dearth. In sixteenth-century Spain a saint's fiesta often was honored by vowing to hold a *caridad* on that day. This was the communal sharing of food, including the entire town or village and the poor of the region. Talavera, in New Castile, fed approximately two thousand poor at its annual *caridad*.[57] *Alhóndigas*, or public granaries, in both Europe and the Americas, provided the poor with a public dole in times of famine.[58] Public charity helped to build hegemony, and ordinances issued by Cortés after the conquest demonstrate the importance of the redistribution of bread to the community. Fixed weights and prices were to be maintained by a town board called the *"Fiel,"* and the poor were to be sustained:

Item: that bakeries selling bread sell it in the public plaza, and that the bread be of the weight ordained by the Council of the aforesaid town, and at the price assigned by it, and that it not be sold in any other manner; if any would sell it at less weight or higher price, they will lose [their earnings], and half will be applied to the aforementioned *Fiel*, and the other half to the poor of the Hospital.[59]

After the conquest of Mexico, the Spaniards maintained their interests in appropriate foods and bonding by means of sharing food. During the actual conquest they were forced to make do with maize, but once victorious they wanted to taste Castilian bread again and enjoy a prosperity defined in Castilian terms. The Jesuit Joseph de Acosta's *Historia natural y moral de las Indias* (1589) shows that the Castilian hierarchy of food was rooted firmly in a belief that God created plants principally for the sustenance of humanity:

Lastly, the Creator gave all lands their own form of "governance" [i.e., physical maintenance]; to this sphere [i.e., Europe] he granted wheat, which is the principal sustenance of men; to that of the Indies he granted maize, which after wheat holds the second place in the sustaining of men and animals.[60]

In "*fuerza y sustento*," maize was not considered inferior to wheat by Acosta, but to the European palate it was "hot and gross," causing skin irritation in those who ate it without care.[61] Maize was for Indian palates, a means of sustenance inferior to wheat simply because it was not of the Old World. Acosta believed that the introduction of Old World plants and animals to the Americas benefited the Indies far more than American flora and fauna benefited Europe. New World plants, he reported, failed to prosper in Spain, but wheat, barley, numerous vegetables, sheep, cattle, goats, horses, cats, and pigs did well when introduced to the Americas.[62]

Regardless of Acosta's claims, Spaniards had to struggle to control the new American environments and foster the growth of the European plants they preferred. Viceroys Mendoza and Velasco in their *relaciones* of 1550 and 1559 noted the production of more wheat as one of the chief goals of the growing Spanish colony.[63] Mendoza gave wheat production priority over the raising of livestock, arguing that Indians should learn wheat cultivation and practice it as commonly as they practiced the cultivation of maize.[64] Enrique Florescano, one of the early leading experts on colonial grain production and prices, noted that initial wheat production was a problem, but the mid-sixteenth century saw some 115 Spanish farmers growing as much as 400 *hanegas* of wheat around Mexico City itself, although the majority raised 30 to 60 *hanegas* on average.[65] By 1535 Mexico had already exported wheat to the Antilles and Tierra Firme, and by 1575 the Atlixco Valley alone produced 100,000 *hanegas* (150,000 bushels) of wheat a year.[66] Even though maize, grown in conjunction with beans and squash, might provide greater productivity and nutrition, the presence of wheat in Mexico became an important aspect of European ecological imperialism.[67] Once learned and culturally established, European identification of bread as the staff of life was not easily undone.

Wheat production was imperative because its consumption separated Spaniards from the mass of Indians, whereas acceptance of Spanish dietary patterns admitted the Amerindian elite to Spanish culture and the Spanish community. In this, the Spanish settlers replicated a European pattern by which the propertied elite was separated from the mass of the population by means of its more secure and regular access to wheat. As noted by Fernand Braudel, Piero Camporesi, and other scholars, many members of the European peasantry and urban working classes in the early modern period often enough had to substitute for wheat flour with such substances as chestnuts and acorns. Regular access to wheaten bread, especially white bread, was a symbol of power and, in the Mexican example, of conquest.[68]

After Cortés and other early inhabitants of New Spain introduced European grains, fruits, vegetables, and livestock, acculturated, affluent Amerindians began to produce and consume wheat, sheep, goats, and wine. Among acculturated Indians, Don Pedro Moctezuma described his possessions in Tula as "certain livestock *estancias* of sheep and goats, and fields of wheat and maize" —a mixture of European and American foodstuffs that can also be found in the tributary lists of the Indian governor of Coyoacan, Don Juan de Guzmán.[69] Listing the tribute owed him in the mid-sixteenth century, Don Juan ordered that "those who cultivate the fields of Cimatlan and Mixcoac are to reap wheat at Atepocaapan (for a week)."[70] He continued to receive most of his tributary foods in indigenous produce, but his reception of European crops demonstrates that they developed a market among powerful Indians who served as intermediaries with the Spaniards. The Amerindian elites were required to adopt certain aspects of Spanish material culture in order to assimilate properly with their superiors.

The Spaniards, for their part, demanded wheat, horse fodder, and European animals in the tribute ascribed to them, while still receiving the largest percentage of their tribute in maize and other native produce that could be sold and redistributed to Amerindian commoners. The tribute due Martín Cortés, the second Marqués del Valle (not to be confused with Hernán Cortés's other son of the same name by Doña Marina), from the towns of Coyoacan and Atlacubaya amounted to a yearly payment of 2,000 *hanegas* (3,000 bushels) of maize and 600 (900) of wheat.[71] Don Juan de Guzmán, the Indian *gobernador*, received 400 *hanegas* (600 bushels) of maize and 200 (300) of wheat in a 1553 accounting from the same towns.[72] In Toluca, Hernán Cortés tried a similar mixed tribute in maize and wheat but was foiled by frost's destruction of the wheat crop.[73]

Epidemic disease and the persistent decrease of the indigenous population made the direct organization of agricultural production for Europeans, by Europeans, imperative.[74] Nonetheless, Amerindians persisted in their own cultural hybridization with mixed results. Some European practices exacerbated the postconquest decline of the indigenous population. Indiscriminate pasturing of European cattle on Indian arable lands, for example, was partially responsible for decreases in the production of staple crops by the indigenes—and it created legal conflict between the Europeans and their subjects.[75] On the other hand, hungry for new sources of protein to supplement the native beans, algae cakes, domesticated fowl, fly eggs, turkey eggs, and table dogs, Amerindian communities engaged early on in sheep and cattle ranching. In 1547, for instance, Tlaxcala's *cabildo* reported the sale of 580 municipally owned muttons, and by 1580 some Spanish and Amerindian observers noted substantial consumption of European meats, especially chickens, by the Indians.[76] A Spanish description of Chichicapa and its subject towns reported that the *naturales* consumed large quantities of meat, and one of Tepevçila indicated Indian management of European livestock.[77] An abundance of European chickens was reported throughout the valleys of Mexico and Oaxaca, but sheep and goats were also reported in a number of Indian townships: from Tilantongo, Mitlantongo, Tamazola, Tetipac, Nochiztlan, and Mitla in the bishopric of Antequera to Totolapa, Yetecomac, Gueypuchtla, Tecpatepec, Chiconauhtla, and Zayula in the bishopric of Mexico City.[78] In recent work Elinor Melville has shown that around

Tula in the Valle del Mezquital, Amerindians received 78.9 percent of the grants made for sheepraising between 1560 and 1565, and they received license twice as often as Spaniards in the 1590s. If, as Melville argues, the raising of sheep beyond carrying capacity contributed to the desertification of the Valle del Mezquital, then Amerindian sheepherders played their part.[79] There were even Amerindian cattle raisers, and bovine livestock made an appearance in Spanish reports for Tamazola, Mitlantongo, and Tilantongo. And in the towns of Tetela and Ueyapan, south of Popocatepetl, the *corregidor* Cristóbal Godínez Maldonado emphasized that the Amerindians possessed quite a few head of cattle.[80]

Often enough, Spaniards saw this Amerindian interest in European livestock as an illegitimate encroachment by the mass of Amerindians on their control of European material culture. The fleece and meat of sheep were sold locally, but hides and tallow of cattle were in demand in larger Mexican and European markets, and Spanish cattlemen were quite unwilling to have Indian ranching increase and compete in their markets. As a result, slaughterhouses without viceregal consent were prohibited in Indian towns after 1560. At the same time, to the benefit of the Europeans, Spanish-owned cattle were allowed to destroy the base of indigenous sustenance, literally trampling countless maize fields.[81] In return, Indians may have benefited from the protein provided by cheap meat, but the extent to which Spanish regulations interfered with Indian meat consumption, and whether meat was distributed adequately throughout the Indian community, has not yet been determined.[82] Whether they did more to benefit Indian nutrition or to disrupt it, Spanish livestock were a vital element of the newly dominant culture. Conquest meant the Amerindians were affected by Spanish cattle as an aspect of Spanish cultural imperialism.

The late-sixteenth-century *relaciones geográficas* further demonstrate Spanish preoccupation with the production of European foodstuffs and the cultural integration of the American environment. In the early 1580s, among forty-three *relaciones* of the central region of New Spain that specifically mention wheat, twenty-seven report the successful raising of wheat in Indian townships. Five *relaciones*—those of Xalapa de la Veracruz, Yetecomac, the mines of Tasco, Coyatitlanapa, and Papaloticpac and its *partido*—specifically state that wheat could be grown if the Indians so desired, and eleven townships' *relaciones* report that it was impossible to engage in wheat agriculture because of inappropriate soil and climatic conditions.[83]

A major complaint of the Spanish *corregidores* and *alcaldes mayores* writing the reports was that the Amerindians could raise much more wheat and barley if they were so inclined. Cultural preferences for maize seem to have interfered with Spanish desires. Lines blurred between actual and potential wheat production when Chicoaloapa reported that some Indians grew a little wheat and barley whereas others idled; that more cereals could be produced but that little actually was.[84] In the *relaciones* of other towns, unrealized potential was emphasized as well. Thus, Papaloticpac and its *partido* reported that wheat could be raised there but was not because a Spanish population was lacking and the Indians failed to appreciate the benefits of wheat.[85] In Yetecomac, barley and wheat could be raised, but the *naturales* had not planted the cereals in forty years, ever since the death of their Spanish encomendero eliminated demand.[86] In Tetipac the Spanish observer wrote, "Wheat grows in this town and its subject villages . . . and it would grow in great quantity if the *naturales* devoted themselves to it," and in Tepepulco it was reported that wheat grew well but was grown and used sparingly.[87] Spanish demand and a pronounced Spanish presence were central to an Indian town's production of wheat: "Wheat and barley give very high yields. In this town [i.e., Coatepec] and its territory there are thirteen Spanish farmers, who have their farmlands dedicated to wheat and produce great quantities; and the Indians have begun to sow it."[88] Indeed,

This province of Tepeaca yields, in season, more than enough wheat. There is a valley named San Pablo where there are sixty Spanish farmers who sow, with oxen, two hundred to three hundred and four hundred *hanegas* of wheat; and they cultivate and harvest it with Indians. In this valley, every year they commonly harvest seventy to eighty thousand *hanegas* of wheat.[89]

At times, however, Spanish demand and coerced and cajoled Amerindian labor were not enough. In Iztepexi, priests made attempts to grow wheat, but these attempts failed for climatic reasons; in San Miguel Capulapa and San Francisco Çuçumbra, mountainous terrain interferred with wheat agriculture; and in the mining region of Zumpango, it was too hot for wheat production.[90]

Later *relaciones* for the northern and central regions of New Spain also reveal the extent to which Castilian agriculture prospered in the Mexican environment. In 1604 the conde de Lemus, then president of the Council of the Indies, revised the royal questionnaire to include 355 questions, numbers 170 and 171 specifically dealing with the cultivation of European grains and fruits.[91] To the northeast of Mexico City, Tampico and Pánuco disclosed that no wheat or Spanish fruit grew in their hot climates. Wheat flour had to be imported from the capital, Puebla de los Angeles, the port of Veracruz, and Campeche to satisfy Spanish consumers.[92] But still farther north in Nueva Viscaya, la Villa de Nombre de Dios was described as fertile land with a climate like that of Seville and the capacity to grow wheat and Castilian fruits, as well as maize and beans.[93]

In the densely populated and topographically elevated central and south central regions of New Spain, wheat agriculture had taken root at a fairly early date, thus explaining the ability of Mexico City and Puebla de los Angeles to export wheat to areas like Pánuco, which could not grow the grain. Wheat agriculture was proudly reported for Michoacan, and Motolinía even made a special point of praising Michoacan's ability to produce European plants:

Because of the fertility of this land and the mildness of its climate, many Spanish plants and trees have grown and multiplied—trees of cold as well as hot lands, and vineyards. Here there are many mulberry-trees, and already many of them begin to produce silk. . . . Wheat grows very well, and increases geometrically.[94]

On the other hand, in areas like Oaxaca, the common Indians adopted some Spanish ways but refused to produce many European foods on the lands they continued to hold. Thus, Spaniards were forced to take up farming with Amerindian labor to satisfy their own cultural needs.[95] Such a pattern was also observable in the Valley of Mexico. The Indian inhabitants of colonial Culhuacan cultivated European fruit trees, and the nobles of the Texcoco region engaged in this practice for sale and profit as early as twenty years after the conquest.[96] At the same time, the Texcocan Indians maintained their traditional dietary patterns to some extent. In the *relación* he wrote for Texcoco in 1582, the mestizo notable Juan Pomar wrote that "today's common people enjoy cattle and mutton, especially those who confer and converse more with Spaniards." However, Castilian bread was eaten as a "luxury" or "necessity." Pomar's *relación* spoke of a world in which maize remained the norm, for "the sustenance that they used previously is precisely that which they use today to maintain themselves, of which maize of different colors is the principal [item]."[97] This, in itself, reflected a method of cultural resistance following the Spanish conquest, but it was a resistance tempered by economic considerations. The higher price of wheat, and the fact that Indian wheat production was subject to tithing while maize was not, operated to make maize and other indigenous foods far more attractive to the Indians than European foods and the European tax obligations attached to them.[98] In the sixteenth century at the mines of Pachuca, now in the state of Hidalgo, wheat and flour from the Valley of Atrizo (Atlixco) sold at four pesos per *hanega*, maize at two to six pesos.[99] Enrique Florescano has shown that in Mexico City wheat and bread prices fell with consistency between 1529 and 1542, but they started to rise again in the 1560s. If anything, this only helped to exclude the Amerindian population from purchasing a grain reserved for European elites. Although an *hanega* of maize rose from five or six *reales* to more than twelve between 1565 and 1580, an *hanega* of wheat rose from ten, twelve, or fifteen *reales* to twenty or twenty-two in the same period.[100] The economical choice was obvious if one purchased one's grains and did not grow them directly. Likewise, the prestige of wheat was obvious. Maize agriculture remained the base agrarian economic activity throughout central Mexico, land of sedentary, urban Indians.[101]

Conversely, where Amerindians were not sedentary in preconquest times and were not abundantly present after the conquest, European foods came to dominate the geographical region. Thus, northern Mexico became "white Mexico." The great haciendas of the north produced cattle and wheat, and the extant records of the Zacatecas mines demonstrate that white miners and acculturated Indians consumed far more wheat than maize.[102] Even in the north, maize often sold at much lower prices than wheat. The Nueva Viscayan *cabildo* of la Villa de Nombre de Dios reported wheat prices at three or four pesos per *hanega*, while maize sold for literally half that price.[103]

The Spaniards destroyed the Aztec imperial rituals of human sacrifice and cannibalism but did not eliminate those aspects of Amerindian cultures that were not offensive to their moral and religious beliefs.[104] By eating differently from the Amerindians, the Spaniards felt superior. By eating differently from the Spaniards, the Amerindians felt they had retained a vital, basic aspect of their culture and world.[105] Whereas old pre-Columbian religious practices and spiritual values blended with the new Christian faith,[106] the most basic aspect of community and hearth, eating, remained in many ways relatively untouched for conquerors and conquered. Dietary syncretism occurred, but very slowly, unless pressured by need. In Spain itself only peasants of the most marginal agricultural regions experimented with maize. Thus, the seminomadic herdsmen of the northern province of Santander came to rely on maize as a staple crop as early as the seventeenth century. Nevertheless, even in that northern region, in the more fertile, more settled Valdemora, wheat remained the cereal of choice for bread.[107] In other areas of Spain and Europe, the spread of American crops was far from rapid, and both maize and the potato had widespread success only among the European poor in the seventeenth and eighteenth centuries.[108] In Mexico Amerindians craved European poultry and mutton, but they also continued to purchase dog meat, despite its high price in comparison with beef.[109]

Culture made visible the Spanish New World hierarchy of ethnic ranks, or *castas*, and food serves as a preeminent aspect of culture.[110] From the Spanish perspective consumers of Indian foods remained crude, whereas other Indians —the nobility, concubines, and the mestizo children of Spaniards and their mistresses—became part of Spanish civilization through spoken communication and the silent language of ritual. To help bind Spaniards, Spanish towns maintained their fiestas, in which eating represented a major portion of the ceremony and enjoyment, and their hospitals, which provided health care and food to the poor, thus binding them to the community and alleviating some social tension and discontent.[111] Likewise, traditional Amerindian fiestas persisted, and Amerindian communal lands and community chests cared for the indigenous poor in at least some areas.[112]

Imperialistic cultures of conquest must retain a sense of uniqueness in order to maintain a sense of superiority. Food bound Spaniards together and made Indians alien outsiders, members of the *república de los indios*. At their most prejudicial, Spaniards remarked that maize was fed to mules as well as to Indians.[113] It was the raw stuff of savage nature, but to Indians, it was the base of civilization.[114] In short, given human cultural divergence, maize signified both the savage and the civilized, the raw and the cooked. Although Moctezuma's eating rituals often paralleled Spanish custom, the Spanish never forgot that he ate what they deemed the wrong foods—from maize to human flesh. Convinced of their superiority, Europeans have consistently tried to alter nature to suit their ideals. For Spaniards in Mexico, this included the raising of cattle and the growing of wheat, grapes, and other crops alien to the environment.[115]

In the conquest and colonization of New Spain, the Spanish attitude toward food reveals a number of fundamental themes of the sixteenth-century Spanish mentality. Foremost among them is a sense of cultural superiority. Like the Aztec cosmology, the Spanish worldview was, in many ways, closed to anything outside its cultural experience. A sense of adhering to the one true culture bound Spaniards in the midst of an alien people, and it made them demand European foods. Human ethological studies demonstrate that the infantile fear of strangers is quite natural, and that infantile xenophobia crosses cultures from the Yanomami to the !Kung Bushmen. In fact, more than mere sight and sound may be at play, since "children blind from birth, even those born both blind and deaf, display fear of strangers."[116] In the wild, the innate infantile fear of strangers, perhaps even linked to the recognition of unknown scents, served as a vital survival mechanism. Since for most of human history people have lived in small groups—groups maintaining their distance from each other—this fear has evolved into the fear of strange customs and ways. Quite honestly, there is no natural benefit in incautiously trusting the unknown. Poison may thus be imbibed unknowingly, and an enemy might thus be allowed into one's home. In turn, novelty may interfere with the functioning of well-established hierarchies. The arrival of the Spaniards in Mesoamerica is in itself proof of this principle. Among Japanese macaques and other primates, dominant males demonstrate disinterest when a new object is introduced, thus avoiding loss of status through taking an unnecessary risk with the new and untried.[117] The system that has allowed one to climb hierarchically is usually favored and protected by the successful as a result. Natural human tendencies lead us to shy away from the unknown—to retreat into our own comfortable categories of understanding and customs—and the most successful within any given system may be the first to do this. Hence, it is not surprising that the conquistadores were not the grandees of Castile, and that once Spanish authority was established in a "New Spain," tried, true, and tired patterns of Spanish culture should emerge.

However, as in most instances, human populations exhibit complex and contradictory binaries, and humans are also creatures of curiosity. Once again, in diverse cultures, human children exhibit similar curiosity traits, primarily expressed through playful behavior. When given a stick, human infants will hit at objects and at people using downward strokes (much like chimpanzees in the wild) until they are told otherwise.[118] Learning may prevent the attack on others, but the natural tendency is to explore just how far one may go. Among other primates, females and young animals explore new areas, the most famous example being the two-year-old female Japanese macaque Imo. Imo literally invented a "preculture" by being the first in her band to wash the sand off sweet potatoes in salt water. This behavior was then learned most readily by male and female juveniles.[119] Curiosity, like xenophobia, is part of our nature, and we continue to pursue novelty into our old age through newspaper accounts and visits to museums.[120]

In the Spanish conquest of the Americas, the boldest individuals, those who acquired a love of cassava bread or who, like las Casas, defended the peanut, were few. So often in natural settings the bold risk danger and death as well as great reward. Most Spaniards and Amerindians were not willing to try new foods unless the reward was obvious. Therefore, Amerindian nobles and the more affluent among the indigenous population adopted Spanish foods to some extent, despite the financial and cultural cost, in order to interact more effectively with Spanish power. Serving as intermediaries in Spanish tributary systems and as local rulers, they thought this made eminently good sense. Likewise, poor Spaniards with little or no access to wheat were the first to adopt maize as a staple. Reward easily outweighed the risk in both cases. Where such cost-benefit analysis was less apparent, traditions proved victorious.

Although race, class, culture, and gender are useful categories of understanding to an extent, they fail to recognize the universal traits that cross such boundaries. Ironically, though not entirely aware of it themselves, Cortés and other sixteenth-century Spaniards recognized the humanity of the Nahuas by recognizing the human universalities of hierarchy and reciprocity in their food behavior. Food was used to reinforce cultural differences and to admit that "all mankind is one." In this, the Nahuas were no different, since the *Florentine Codex* readily states that Spanish food, though different, was "like human food."[121]

NOTES

1. Sidney W. Mintz, *Sweetness and Power: The Place of Sugar in Modern History* (New York and Harmondsworth: Penguin Books, 1986), 3-5; Peter Farb and George Armelagos, *Consuming Passions: The Anthropology of Eating* (Boston: Houghton Mifflin, 1980), 3-14.

2. Claude Lévi-Strauss, *The Raw and the Cooked*, trans. John and Doreen Weightman (New York: Harper & Row, 1969), 64-65, 169; Nur Yalman, "'The Raw: the Cooked:: Nature: Culture'—Observations on *Le Cru et le cuit*," in *The Structural Study of Myth and Totemism*, ed. Edmund Leach (London: Tavistock Publications, 1967), 71-73, 77, 85, 88.

3. For the way in which cannibalism is used in that vein, see Bernadette Bucher, *Icon and Conquest: A Structural Analysis of the Illustrations of de Bry's "Great Voyages"*, trans. Basia Miller Gulati (Chicago: University of Chicago Press, 1981), 61-64, 104-5.

4. Reay Tannahill, *Food in History* (New York: Stein and Day, 1973), 245-46; John Super, *Food, Conquest, and Colonization in Sixteenth-Century Spanish America* (Albuquerque: University of New Mexico Press, 1988), 25-26, 32.

5. Lewis Hanke, *All Mankind Is One: A Study of the Disputation between Bartolome de las Casas and Juan Ginés de Sepúlveda on the Religious and Intellectual Capacity of the American Indians* (De Kalb: Northern Illinois University Press, 1974), 39.

6. Fray Toribio de Benavente o Motolinía, *Memoriales o libro de las cosas de la Nueva España y de los naturales de ella*, ed. Edmundo O'Gorman (Mexico City: Universidad Nacional Autónoma de México, 1971), 373; Bernard R. Ortiz de Montellano, *Aztec Medicine, Health, and Nutrition* (New Brunswick, NJ: Rutgers University Press, 1990), 104.

7. The selection and control of herbs and plants was also the case in medicine, a field that was far more open to American uniqueness than the field of culinary custom. See Guenter B. Risse, "Medicine in New Spain," in *Medicine in the New World: New Spain, New France, and New England*, ed. Ronald L. Numbers (Knoxville: University of Tennessee Press, 1987), 12-63.

8. For example, in his "Relación del descubrimiento de las provincias de Antiocha (1540)," the *adelantado* Jorge Robledo wrote, "In this town of Quindio one finds a yellow fruit like grapes." *Colección de documentos inéditos relativos al descubrimiento, conquista y organización de las antiguas posesiones españolas de América y Oceanía, sacados de los archivos del reino, y muy especialmente del de Indias*, ed. Joaquín F. Pacheco, Francisco de Cárdenas, and Luis Torres de Mendoza, 42 vols. (Madrid: Manuel Hernández, 1864-1884), 2:304. Henceforth *CDIR*. Bernal Díaz also wrote of "local grapes," or granadillas, and "local cherries." Bernal Díaz del Castillo, *Historia verdadera de la conquista de la Nueva España*, ed. Joaquín Ramírez Cabañas, 3 vols. (Mexico City: Editorial Pedro Robredo, 1944), 1:229, 2:240.

9. Licenciado Çuaço described Hispaniola as extremely fertile and abundant in *"animales brutos,"* or raw nature, but the willingness and ability of Spaniards to transform this nature were constantly being criticized by royal officials. There were never enough husbandmen, and cattle were being consumed prodigally before reaching maturity. See "Al muy ilustre señor Monsieur de Xevres el licenciado Çuaço.—de Santo Domingo de la isla Española á 22 de enero de 1518," *CDIR* 1:305; "Relación de Gil González Dávila, contador del Rey, de la despoblación de la isla Española . . .," *CDIR* 1:341-42; "Relación de la isla Española enviada al Rey D. Felipe II por el licenciado Echagoian, oidor de la audiencia de Santo Domingo," *CDIR* 1:17; "Relación de Gil González Dávila . . . de la despoblación de la isla Española . . .," *CDIR* 10:114.

10. Alfred W. Crosby, Jr., *The Columbian Exchange: Biological and Cultural Consequences of 1492* (Westport, CT: Greenwood Press, 1972), 67-69.

11. "Memorial de las cosas que son menester proveer luego para despacho de cuatro caravelas que vaya para las Indias. Año de 1495," *CDIR* 24:15-17.

Modern approximations of the weights and measures listed above are as follows: 1 *quintal* = 100 pounds; 1 *tonel* = 0.83 ton; 1 *hanega* or *fanega* = 1.5 bushels; 1 *cahiz* = 12 *hanegas* or 18 bushels.

Of course, one must caution that these estimates are far from exact, and the *tonel* may represent a nautical measurement of displacement roughly equivalent to 5/6 ton, or merely a cask or barrel of a certain size. In addition, Spanish documents alternate between references to the Castilian *tonelada* (1.4 cubic meters) and the Viscayan *tonel macho* (1.683 cubic meters). Ten Viscayan *toneles* may have been equal to twelve Sevillian *toneladas*. In any event, the shipment described was feasible because the caravel was a vessel of 50 to 100 tons, early modern tonnage being measured in terms of the amount of cargo safely carried rather than the weight or displacement of the ship's hull. See Roger C. Smith, *Vanguard of Empire: Ships of Exploration in the Age of Columbus* (New York and Oxford: Oxford University Press, 1993), 34-46, 53, 142.

12. "Información de los servicios del adelantado Rodrigo de Bastidas, conquistador y pacificador de Santa Marta (22 de junio de 1521)," *CDIR* 2:375-76.

13. "Al Cardenal Ximénez de Cisneros, los priores de San Gerónimo, de Santo Domingo de la isla Española a 22 de junio de 1517," *CDIR* 1:287; "Capítulos de carta del licenciado Alonso de Çuaço al Emperador, su fecha en Santo Domingo de la isla Española á 22 de enero de 1518," *CDIR* 1:292; Lewis Hanke, *The Spanish Struggle for Justice in the Conquest of America* (Philadelphia: University of Pennsylvania Press,

1949), 46; and Lewis Hanke, *The First Social Experiments in America: A Study in the Development of Spanish Indian Policy in the Sixteenth Century* (Cambridge: Harvard University Press, 1935), 61-71.

14. Julia Hirschberg, "Social Experiment in New Spain: A Prosopographical Study of the Early Settlement at Puebla de los Angeles, 1531-1534," *Hispanic American Historical Review* 59:1 (1979): 1-33; and Henry Raup Wagner and Helen Rand Parish, *The Life and Writings of Bartolomé de las Casas* (Albuquerque: University of New Mexico Press, 1967), 35-45, 60-69, 83-93.

15. Even the portrayal of the Indians as "noble savages" degraded through its imposition of civilized nobility on a perceived savage state. It was the grafting of some admirable characteristics on the fundamentally disreputable. Hayden White, "The Noble Savage: Theme as Fetish," in *First Images of America: The Impact of the New World on the Old*, ed. Fredi Chiappelli et al., 2 vols. (Berkeley and Los Angeles: University of California Press, 1976), 1:129; and Bucher, 143-44.

16. Piero Camporesi, *Bread of Dreams: Food and Fantasy in Early Modern Europe*, trans. David Gentilcore (Chicago: University of Chicago Press, 1989), 40-55.

17. Bernal Díaz, 1:224, 235, 312; Hanke, *The Spanish Struggle for Justice*, 120; White, 1:126; Bucher, 61-64; "Información hecha por Rodrigo de Figueroa de la población india de las islas e costa de Tierra Firme . . . (1520)," *CDIR* 1:380; "Memorial que dió el bachiller Enciso de lo ejecutado por él en defensa de los Reales derechos, en la materia de los indios," *CDIR* 1:449.

18. "Relación hecha por Joan de Miranda, clerigo, al doctor Orozco, presidente de la Audiencia de Guadalajara; sobre la tierra y población que hay desde las minas de San Martín a las de Santa Barbara, que esto último entonces estaba poblada. Año de 1575," *CDIR* 16:566-67.

19. Bernal Díaz, 1:107, 197.

20. Ibid., 2:240, 242-43. The translation is taken from Bernal Díaz del Castillo, *The Conquest of New Spain*, trans. J. M. Cohen (Harmondsworth: Penguin Books, 1963), 365.

21. Bernal Díaz, 1:346. Also see the Cohen translation, 227.

22. Bernardino de Sahagún, *Florentine Codex: The General History of the Things of New Spain*, trans. Arthur J. O. Anderson and Charles E. Dibble, 13 vols. (Santa Fe and Salt Lake City: Monographs of the School of American Research/University of Utah Press, 1950-1982), Bk. 8, chap. 13, pp. 37-39.

23. Luys Alcanyis, *Regiment de la Pestilencia* (Valencia: Nicholaus Spindeler, ca. 1490), in Hispanic Culture Series, *Hispanic Books Printed before 1601*, Reel 33; henceforth to be refered to as *HCS*. Also see Juan de Cárdenas, *Primera Parte de los problemas y secretos marauillosos de las Indias* (Mexico City: Pedro Ocharte, 1591), 105-26, 175, *HCS* Reel 27; and Juan de Avinón, *Seuillana medicina*, ed. Nicolas Monardes (Seville: Andres de Burgos, 1545), xvi-xxii, *HCS* Reel 225. For the Arabic roots of the European notion of a balanced diet, see Tannahill, 178.

24. Avinón, xviii[b].

25. *Florentine Codex*, Bk. 10, chap. 28, pp. 141-42.

26. For the appearance of chickens in New World tax lists, see "Tasaciones de los pueblos de la provincia de Yucatán," in *Epistolario de Nueva España, 1505-1818*, ed. Francisco del Paso y Troncoso, 16 vols. (Mexico City: José Porrúa e hijos, 1939-1940), 5:103-81, 207-17; 6:73-112. Henceforth *ENE*. For a representative sampling of such townships in the valleys of Oaxaca and Mexico, see *Papeles de Nueva España*, ed. Francisco del Paso y Troncoso, 7 vols. (Madrid: Sucesores de Rivadeneyra, 1905), 4:9-

44, 58-68, 100-108, 163-82, 289-300, 308-13; 5:1-11, 55-65, 99-109, 124-82; 6:1-5, 12-19, 31-34, 87-152, 199-208, 291-305. In the *relaciones* of the 1580s, the response to question 27 deals with wild and domestic animals. Henceforth the *Papeles de Nueva España* will be referred to as *PNE*.

27. "Real cédula al virrey y audiencia de la Nueva España. . . . Valencia, 12 de abril de 1599," in *Ordenanzas de hospital de San Lázaro de México*, ed. France V. Scholes and Eleanor B. Adams (Mexico City: José Porrúa e hijos, 1956), 38.

28. Hernán Cortés, "First Letter," in *Hernán Cortés: Letters from Mexico*, trans. Anthony Pagden (New Haven, CT, and London: Yale University Press, 1986), 30.

29. Cortés, "Second Letter," 75.

30. Bucher, 153-54, 158-59.

31. Cortés, "Second Letter," 111-12; Bernal Díaz, 1:343-46; Francisco López de Gómara, *Cortés: The Life of the Conqueror by His Secretary*, trans. Lesley Byrd Simpson (Berkeley and Los Angeles: University of California Press, 1964), 143-44.

Other accounts include the derivative ones of Cervantes de Salazar and Torquemada. See Francisco Cervantes de Salazar, *Crónica de la Nueva España* (Madrid: Hispanic Society of America, 1914), 281-82; Fray Juan de Torquemada, *Monarquia indiana*, 3rd ed., 3 vols. (Mexico City: Editorial Salvador Chavez Hayhoe, 1943), 1:229.

32. Cortés, "Second Letter," 111-12.

33. López de Gómara, 143.

34. Cortés, "Second Letter," 111; Bernal Díaz, 1:344-45; López de Gómara, 143-44.

35. Woodrow Borah, *New Spain's Century of Depression* (Berkeley and Los Angeles: University of California Press, 1951), 2; George C. Vaillant, *Aztecs of Mexico: Origin, Rise, and Fall of the Aztec Nation* (Harmondsworth: Penguin Books, 1966), 135-48; and Nigel Davies, *The Aztecs: A History* (London: Macmillan, 1973), 92-94.

36. Cortés, "Second Letter," 109; Anthony Pagden, "Translator's Introduction," in Hernán Cortés, *Letters from Mexico*, xlviii.

37. Cortés, "Second Letter," 112.

38. J. H. Elliott, "The Court of the Spanish Habsburgs: A Peculiar Institution?" in *Spain and Its World, 1500-1700: Selected Essays* (New Haven, CT, and London: Yale University Press, 1989), 149. Also 145-46 and 154.

39. "Instrucciones de Carlos V a Maximiliano y María para el gobierno de Castilla" (Brussels, 29 September 1548), in *Corpus documental de Carlos V*, ed. Manuel Fernández Alvarez, 5 vols. (Salamanca: Consejo Superior de Investigaciones Científicas, 1973-1981), 3:33.

40. Antonio de Guevara, "Letra para el marqués de los Vélez, en cual se escribe algunas nuevas de corte" (Medina del Campo, 18 July 1532), in *Libro primero de las epístolas familiares de Fray Antonio de Guevara*, ed. José María de Cossío (Madrid: Academia Española, Biblioteca Selecta de Clásicos Españoles, 1950), 114-19.

By the time of Philip IV (1621-1665), the king and queen may have dined alone with greater frequency, but they still ate with courtiers and people of distinction at least once a week in an elaborate ceremony. As early as the 1560s, Cervantes de Salazar wrote that like many princes, Moctezuma ate alone, but Cervantes de Salazar then went on to report (no doubt borrowing from earlier accounts) that the *tlatoani* shared his meal with six elderly worthies. Regardless of variation from monarch to monarch, ceremonial, social dining did occur with some frequency. See Marcelin Defourneaux, *Daily Life in Spain in the Golden Age*, trans. Newton Branch (Stanford, CA: Stanford University Press, 1979), 50; Cervantes de Salazar, *Crónica*, 281.

41. Farb and Armelagos, 4.

FOOD

FOOD

[see below]

42. Maguelonne Toussaint-Samat, *A History of Food*, trans. Anthea Bell (Cambridge, MA, and Oxford: Blackwell Publishers, 1992), 230-31; David W. Sabean, *Power in the Blood: Popular Culture and Village Discourse in Early Modern Germany* (Cambridge: Cambridge University Press, 1984), 37-60; Robert Mandrou, *Introduction to Modern France, 1500-1640: An Essay in Historical Psychology*, trans. R. E. Hallmark (New York: Harper & Row, 1977), 14.

43. Frans de Waal, *Chimpanzee Politics: Power and Sex among the Apes* (New York: Harper & Row, 1982), 200.

44. Jane van Lawick-Goodall, *In the Shadow of Man* (Boston: Houghton Mifflin, 1971), 50-51.

45. W. C. McGrew, *Chimpanzee Material Culture: Implications for Human Evolution* (Cambridge: Cambridge University Press, 1992), 107.

46. Ibid., 111.

47. Jane Goodall, *Through a Window: My Thirty Years with the Chimpanzees of Gombe* (Boston: Houghton Mifflin, 1990), 206.

48. Glynn Isaac, "The Food-Sharing Behavior of Protohuman Hominids," in *Human Ancestors: Readings from Scientific American*, intro. by Glynn Isaac and Richard E. F. Leakey (San Francisco: W. H. Freeman, 1979), 114-21; McGrew, 114-15.

49. Irenäus Eibl-Eibesfeldt, *Human Ethology* (New York: Aldine de Gruyter, 1989), 341, 344.

50. Robert Himmerich y Valencia, *The Encomenderos of New Spain, 1521-1555* (Austin: University of Texas Press, 1991), 8-9; Defourneaux, 150-53; Colin MacLachlan and Jaime E. Rodríguez O., *The Forging of the Cosmic Race: A Reinterpretation of Colonial Mexico* (Berkeley, Los Angeles, London: University of California Press, 1980), 210, 224-25.

51. Jaime Vincens Vives, *An Economic History of Spain*, trans. Frances M. López-Morillas (Princeton, NJ: Princeton University Press, 1969), 302-4.

52. Fernand Braudel, *The Structures of Everyday Life: The Limits of the Possible*, Vol. 1: *Civilization and Capitalism, 15th-18th Century*, trans. Siân Reynolds (New York: Harper & Row, 1981), 120, 161, 152; Toussaint-Samat, 167-70; Ortiz de Montellano, 94-99.

53. In Castilian Extremadura, chestnut flour was used as a substitute for wheaten grains. See Braudel, 1:112; Toussaint-Samat, 711.
For the comparable impact of such conditions in early modern Italy, see Camporesi, 61-62, 120-21, 169-70.

54. Linda Martz, *Poverty and Welfare in Habsburg Spain: The Example of Toledo* (Cambridge: Cambridge University Press, 1983), 1-46; Abel Alves, "The Christian Social Organism and Social Welfare: The Case of Vives, Calvin and Loyola," *The Sixteenth Century Journal* 20:1 (spring 1989): 3-21; Bernardino de Sahagún, *Historia general de las cosas de Nueva España*, ed. Angel María Garibay K., 4 vols. (Mexico City: Editorial Porrúa, 1956), 2:321; Gerónimo de Mendieta, *Historia eclesiástica indiana* (Mexico City: Editorial Porrúa, 1971), 113; and Alonso de Zorita, "Breve y sumaria relación de los señores, y maneras y diferencias que habia de ellos en la Nueva España; y de la forma que han tenido y tienen en los tributos (sin fecha)," *CDIR* 2:20.

55. "El Conquistador Anónimo," in *Colección de documentos para la historia de México*, ed. Joaquín García Icazbalceta, 2 vols. (Mexico, 1858-1866), 1:379.

56. Cortés, "Second Letter," 75.

57. William A. Christian, Jr., *Local Religion in Sixteenth-Century Spain* (Princeton, NJ: Princeton University Press, 1981), 57.

58. Ross Hassig, *Trade, Tribute, and Transportation: The Sixteenth-Century Political Economy of the Valley of Mexico* (Norman: University of Oklahoma Press, 1985), 242-44; Jodi Bilinkoff, *The Avila of Saint Teresa: Religious Reform in a Sixteenth-Century City* (Ithaca, NY, and London: Cornell University Press, 1989), 16, 61-63, 76.

59. "Ordenanzas locales dadas por Hernando Cortés para que por ellas se rixan e gobiernen los vezinos, moradores, estantes e habitantes de las Villas pobladas e las demás que en adelante se poblaren," *CDIR* 40:179-80.

60. Joseph de Acosta, *Historia natural y moral de las Indias*, ed. Edmundo O'Gorman (Mexico City: Fondo de Cultura Económica, 1940), 267, 265-67.

61. Ibid., 265. Interestingly enough, Acosta may actually be referring to the condition of pellagra, which causes redness, peeling, and rashes on exposed areas of the skin. If Europeans ate maize as a basic complex carbohydrate without other foods rich in protein, niacin, and riboflavin, pellagra followed. The Aztecs always supplemented their maize with beans and vegetables. By the eighteenth century the "plague of corn" was well known in Spain as *mal de la rosa*. See Daphne A. Roe, *A Plague of Corn: The Social History of Pellagra* (Ithaca, NY, and London: Cornell University Press, 1973), 1-5, 13-17, 30-31; Toussaint-Samat, 172.

62. Acosta, 311-22.

63. François Chevalier, *Land and Society in Colonial Mexico: The Great Hacienda*, trans. Alvin Eustis, ed. Lesley Byrd Simpson (Berkeley and Los Angeles: University of California Press, 1970), 51-52; "Relación, apuntamientos y avisos, que por mandado de S. M. dió D. Antonio de Mendoza, virey de Nueva-España á D. Luís de Velasco," *CDIR* 6:492. Also see the following documents on the importance of introducing Old World plants and animals to the New World: "Carta a la reina, de fray Luís de Fuensalida, guardián del convento de religiosos franciscanos de México . . . pide que se mande ovejas merinas y olivos y que todas las naos de España traigan plantas . . . De México, a 22 de mayo de 1531," *ENE* 2:33-35; "Relación de los vecinos que había en la Ciudad de los Angeles el año de 1534. 20 de abril.—(Sigue una información de las plantaciones hechos por algunas de dichos vecinos, de viñas y árboles)," *ENE* 3:137-44.

64. "Lo que el Visorey e gobernador de la Nueva Spaña y sus provincias . . . a de hazer . . . de mas de lo contenido en los poderes y comisiones que lleva . . .," *CDIR* 23:530, 534.

65. Enrique Florescano, "El Abasto y la legislación de granos en el siglo XVI," *Historia Mexicana* 14:4 (April-June 1965): 574, 584.

66. Crosby, *The Columbian Exchange*, 70.

67. Ortiz de Montellano, 94-99, 113. An excellent study that deals with European ecological imperialism in broad terms is Alfred W. Crosby's *Ecological Imperialism: The Biological Expansion of Europe, 900-1900* (Cambridge: Cambridge University Press, 1986).

68. Braudel, 1:112; Camporesi, 61-62, 120-21, 169-70; Mintz, 94-95, 101, 121, 154.

69. Crosby, *The Columbian Exchange*, 127-34, 51-52; "Testamento y fundación de mayorazgo otorgado por D. Pedro Montezuma en 8 de setiembre de 1570," *CDIR* 6:85.

70. "Some perquisites of don Juan de Guzmán, governor of Coyoacan, mid-sixteenth century," in *Beyond the Codices: The Nahua View of Colonial Mexico*, trans. and ed. Arthur J. O. Anderson, Frances Berdan, and James Lockhart (Berkeley, Los Angeles, London: University of California Press, 1976), 154-55.

71. "Visitas a la villa de Coyoacán, del marqués del Valle, a mediados del siglo XVI, 1551, 1553, 1564," in *Tributos y servicios personales de indios para Hernán*

Cortés y su familia, ed. Silvio Zavala (Mexico City: Archivo General de la Nación, 1984), 250.

72. Ibid., 253. These references to Juan de Guzmán are to the same individual, a local *tlatoani* of the 1550s. Two other sixteenth-century *tlatoque* of the *altepetl* of Coyoacan bore the same name. See James Lockhart, "The Testimony of don Juan," in *Nahuas and Spaniards: Postconquest Central Mexican History and Philology* (Stanford, CA: Stanford University Press and UCLA Latin American Center Publications, 1991), 75-76.

73. "Pleito contra el licenciado Juan Ortiz de Matiengo y Diego Delgadillo, para recuperar la renta del pueblo de Toluca que . . . habían dado a García del Pilar durante la ausencia de Cortés en España (año de 1531)," *Tributos y servicios . . . para Hernán Cortés*, 70-74.

74. With no immunological resistance to European diseases such as smallpox and typhus, Indian populations decreased astronomically after the conquest. Woodrow Borah and Sherburne F. Cook estimated that in the Valley of Mexico alone a population of 25 million in 1519 was reduced to only 1.9 million Indians by 1580. See *The Cambridge History of Latin America*, Vol. 1: *Colonial Latin America*, ed. Leslie Bethell (Cambridge: Cambridge University Press, 1984), 212; Borah, *New Spain's Century of Depression*, 19, 25, 30; and Super, *Food, Conquest, and Colonization*, 27, 36.

75. Charles Gibson, *The Aztecs under Spanish Rule* (Stanford, CA: Stanford University Press, 1964), 280-82; "Pleito de Alonso Morcillo, vecino de Oaxaca, contra Hernán Cortés y los indios de Etla, para prohibir que los indios cultiven en la vecindad de la estancia de Morcillo (año de 1537)," *Tributos y servicios . . . para Hernán Cortés*, 121-40; Super, *Food, Conquest, and Colonization*, 55-56; and Crosby, *The Columbian Exchange*, 99.

76. "Municipal Council Records, Tlaxcala, 1547," in *Beyond the Codices*, 124-25; Hassig, *Trade, Tribute, and Transportation*, 222-23.

77. "Relación de Chichicapa y su partido (15 Mayo, 1580)," *PNE* 4:119; "Relación de Papaloticpac y su partido (7-11 Deciembre, 1579)," *PNE* 4:96.

78. "Relación de Tilantongo y su partido (1 Noviembre, 1579)," *PNE* 4:75; "Relación de Mitlantongo (12 Nobienbre, 1579)," *PNE* 4:79; "Relación de Tamazola (16 Nobienbre, 1579)," *PNE* 4:84; "Relación de Tetípac (15 Abril, 1580)," *PNE* 4:113; "Relación de Nochiztlan (9-11 Abril, 1581)," *PNE* 4:210; "Relación de Tlacolula y Mitla (12-23 Agosto, 1580)," *PNE* 4:150; "Relación de Totolapa y su partido (4 Septiembre, 1579)," *PNE* 6:10; "Descripción del pueblo de Yetecomac y su tierra (10 Octubre, 1579-24 Marzo, 1580)," *PNE* 6:23; "Descripción del pueblo de Gueypuchtla y su tierra (10 Octubre, 1579-24 Marzo, 1580)," *PNE* 6:30; "Descripción del pueblo de Tecpatepec y su tierra (10 Octubre, 1579-24 Marzo, 1580)," *PNE* 6:37; "Relación de Chiconauhtla y su partido (21 Enero, 1580)," *PNE* 6:175; "Relación de Zayula (3 Febrero, 1580)," *PNE* 6:181.

79. Elinor G. K. Melville, *A Plague of Sheep: Environmental Consequences of the Conquest of Mexico* (Cambridge and New York: Cambridge University Press, 1994), 137, 149, 114-15.

80. "Relación de Tetela y Ueyapan (20 junio, 1581)," *PNE* 6:288.

81. Vaillant, 140-42; Gibson, 346.

82. Super, *Food, Conquest, and Colonization*, 56-57; and Gibson, 566-67, chap. 12 n. 87.

83. The *relaciones* referred to all date from 1579 to 1582, with the exception of Villa Rica de Veracruz, which issued a *relaci'n* in 1571. All these *relaciones* can be

found in the *Papeles de Nueva España*. They are as follows.

Towns growing wheat: Tezcatepec, *PNE* 6:31-34; Gueypuchtla y su tierra, *PNE* 6:26-31; Tequizistlan, *PNE* 6:209-36; San Esteuan, *PNE* 5:151-57; Nochiztlan, *PNE* 4:206-12; Tetipac, *PNE* 4:109-14; Totolapa y su partido, *PNE* 6:6-11; Nexapa, *PNE* 4:29-44; Guaxilotitlan, *PNE* 4:196-205; Coatepec y su partido, *PNE* 6:39-65; Chicoaloapa, subjeto de Coatepec, *PNE* 6:79-86; Petlaltzingo, *PNE* 5:69-74; Taliztaca, *PNE* 4:177-82; Mitlantongo, *PNE* 4:77-82; Tilantongo, *PNE* 4:69-77; Texapa, *PNE* 4:53-57; Axocupan, *PNE* 6:13-19; Chiconauhtla y su partido, *PNE* 6:167-77; Tetela y Ueyapan, *PNE* 6:283-90; Tepepulco, *PNE* 6:291-305; Zayula, *PNE* 6:178-81; Tepeaca, *PNE* 5:12-45; Tetela, cauecera de obispado de Tlaxcala, *PNE* 5:143-50; Chilapa, *PNE* 5:174-82; Macuilsúchil, *PNE* 4:100-108; Ocopetlayuca, *PNE* 6:251-62; Ycxitlan, *PNE* 5:74-77.

Towns that could grow wheat: Xalapa de la Veracruz, *PNE* 5:99-105; Yetecomac, *PNE* 6:19-23; Las minas de Tasco, *PNE* 6:263-82; Çoyatitlanapa, *PNE* 5:89-93; Papaloticpac y su partido, *PNE* 4:88-99.

Towns incapable of growing wheat: Villa Rica de Veracruz, *PNE* 5:189-201; Tecpatepec, subjeto de Ueipuchtla, *PNE* 6:34-38; Texaluca, *PNE* 5:84-88; las minas de Zumpango, *PNE* 6:313-22; San Miguel Capulapa, subjeto de Tetela, *PNE* 5:157-63; San Francisco Çuçumbra, subjeto de Tetela, *PNE* 5:163-67; San Juan Tututla, subjeto de Tetela, *PNE* 5:167-73; Cuicatlan, *PNE* 4:183-89; Ucila, *PNE* 4:45-52; Iztepexi, *PNE* 4:9-23; Piastla, *PNE* 5:77-80.

84. "Chicoaloapa, subjeto de Coatepec," *PNE* 6:85.

85. "Relación de Papaloticpac y su partido (7-11 Diciembre, 1579)," *PNE* 4:92.

86. "Descripción del pueblo de Yetecomac y su tierra (10 Octubre, 1579-24 Marzo, 1580)," *PNE* 6:22.

87. "Relación de Tetípac (15 Abril, 1580)," *PNE* 4:112; "Relación de Tepepulco (15 Abril, 1581)," *PNE* 6:301.

88. "Relación de Coatepec y su partido (16 Noviembre, 1579)," *PNE* 6:61.

89. "Relación de Tepeaca y su partido (4-20 Febrero, 1580)," *PNE* 5:37-38.

90. "Relación de Iztepexi (27-30 Agosto, 1579)," *PNE* 4:20; "San Miguel Capulapa (20-29 Octubre, 1581)," *PNE* 5:162, 166-67; "Relación de las minas de Zumpango (10 Marzo, 1582)," *PNE* 6:314.

91. "Interrogatorio para todas las ciudades, villas y lugares . . . de las Indias Occidentales . . .," *CDIR* 9:68-69; and José Urbano Martínez Carreras, "Las 'Relaciones' de Indias," in *Relaciones Geográficas de Indias—Perú*, 3 vols., ed. Marcos Jiménez de la Espada (Madrid: Ediciones Atlas, 1965), 1:xlvii-lii.

92. "Descripción de la villa de Pánuco (sin fecha)," *CDIR* 9:134, 141; "Descripción de los pueblos de la provincia de Pánuco (sin fecha)," *CDIR* 9:153; "Descripción de la villa de Tampico (sin fecha)," *CDIR* 9:171; and Crosby, *The Columbian Exchange*, 65.

93. "Descripción de la Villa de Nombre de Dios . . . en Mayo de 1608," *CDIR* 9:232, 235, 243.

94. Motolinía, 280.

95. William B. Taylor, *Landlord and Peasant in Colonial Oaxaca* (Stanford, CA: Stanford University Press, 1972), 5.

96. S. L. Cline, *Colonial Culhuacan, 1580-1600: A Social History of an Aztec Town* (Albuquerque: University of New Mexico Press, 1986), 139.

97. "Relación de Tezcoco, por Juan Bautista Pomar (9 marzo 1582)," in *Nueva Colección de documentos para la historia de México*, ed. Joaquín García Icazbalceta, 5 vols. (Mexico, 1886-1892), 3:53.

98. Gibson, 322-23.

99. "Descripción de las minas de Pachuca (sin fecha)," *CDIR* 9:206.

100. Florescano, "El Abasto y la legislación," 597, 599.

101. James Lockhart, "Capital and Province, Spaniard and Indian: The Example of Late Sixteenth-Century Toluca," in *Provinces of Early Mexico: Variants of Spanish American Regional Evolution*, ed. Ida Altman and James Lockhart (Los Angeles: UCLA Latin American Center Publications, 1976), 114-15; Gibson, 311-12.

102. Chevalier, 59-114; P. J. Bakewell, *Silver Mining and Society in Colonial Mexico: Zacatecas, 1546-1700* (Cambridge: Cambridge University Press, 1971), 59-68.

103. "Descripción de la Villa de Nombre de Dios . . . en Mayo de 1608," *CDIR* 9:243.

104. Taylor, *Landlord and Peasant*, 35.

105. Crosby, *The Columbian Exchange*, 74.

106. Nancy M. Farriss, *Maya Society under Colonial Rule: The Collective Enterprise of Survival* (Princeton, NJ: Princeton University Press, 1984), 292-94; George M. Foster, *Culture and Conquest: America's Spanish Heritage* (Chicago: Quadrangle Books, 1960), 158-66; and S. L. Cline, 23, 25, 35, 41, 139.

107. Susan Tax Freeman, *The Pasiegos: Spaniards in No Man's Land* (Chicago and London: University of Chicago Press, 1979), 50-51; Susan Tax Freeman, *Neighbors: The Social Contract in a Castilian Hamlet* (Chicago and London: University of Chicago Press, 1970), 27.

108. Braudel, *Structures of Everyday Life*, 164-70; Crosby, *The Columbian Exchange*, 178, 183; Mintz, 122; Toussaint-Samat, 172-73, 717-20.

109. Gibson, 566-67, chap. 12 n. 87.

110. Lyle N. McAlister, "Social Structure and Social Change in New Spain," *The Hispanic American Historical Review* 43:3 (August 1963), 354-58. For a reduction of culture to economic status, see Woodrow Borah, "Race and Class in Mexico," *The Pacific Historical Review* 23:4 (November 1954), 332-34, 342.

111. On fiestas, see Foster, 167, 206, 218-19, 225; and Freeman, *Neighbors*, 90-93. Spaniards took great pride in their New World hospitals, seeing them as sure signs of a caring Christian community. See Motolinía, Pt. 1, chap. 51; "Carta al rey del arzobispo de México sobre el patronato y administración del Hospital Real de aquella ciudad.—México, 31 de marzo de 1566," *ENE* 10:130-31; "Descripción de Nuestra Señora de los Çacatecas (1608)," *CDIR* 9:191; and Risse, "Medicine in New Spain," in *Medicine in the New World*, 37-42.

112. Murdo J. MacLeod, "The Social and Economic Roles of Indian Cofradías in Colonial Chiapas," in *The Church and Society in Latin America*, ed. Jeffrey A. Cole (New Orleans: Tulane University Press, 1984), 73-96; Farriss, 266-70; Gibson, 132-33.

113. Bakewell, 63.

114. Lévi-Strauss, *The Raw and the Cooked*, 169; Vaillant, 133, 135.

115. "Ordenanzas de Su Magestad hechas para los nuevos descubrimientos, conquistas y pacificaciones.—Julio de 1573," *CDIR* 16:142-87. See especially 147-48.

116. Eibl-Eibesfeldt, *Human Ethology*, 174-75.

117. Edward O. Wilson, *Sociobiology: The New Synthesis* (Cambridge, MA: Belknap Press of Harvard University Press, 1975), 287.

118. Ibid., 583.

119. Hans Kummer, *Primate Societies: Group Techniques of Ecological Adaptation* (Arlington Heights: Harlan Davidson, 1971), 118.

120. Wilson, *Sociobiology*, 581.

121. "Human food" is the translation found in Miguel León-Portilla, ed., *The Broken Spears: The Aztec Account of the Conquest of Mexico*, trans. Angel María Garibay K. and Lysander Kemp (Boston: Beacon Press, 1962), 30-31. In the Anderson and Dibble translation of the *Florentine Codex*, "*auh in intlaqual iuhqujn tlacatlaqualli*" is translated "And their food was like lords' food." See *Florentine Codex*, Bk. 12, chap. 7, p. 19. Most recently, James Lockhart translates "*tlacatlaqualli*" as "fasting food," although he admits that the elements and construction of the word could also mean "people's food" or "human food." In either case, humans are implicitly or explicitly identified, for humans were assigned fasts as well as feasts. See Lockhart's translation of the twelfth book of the *Florentine Codex* in James Lockhart, ed. and trans., *We People Here: Nahuatl Accounts of the Conquest of Mexico* (Berkeley, Los Angeles, London: University of California Press, 1993), 80, 303 n. 41.

7

The Pursuit of Justice

Both in the wild and in captivity, one of the chief characteristics of a dominant male chimpanzee is his need to intervene in disputes between subordinates. Aggressive display, though necessary, is never sufficient to maintain
status in the complex world of "chimpanzee politics." At Gombe in Tanzania,
Jane Goodall early on took notice of a young male named Goblin: "He was
always determined to get his own way, he hated to be dominated, he was
intelligent and courageous, and he could not tolerate disputes among his subordinates."[1] By fourteen, Goblin could intimidate all the older males except
his patron, the alpha male Figan. However, he could intimidate them only on
an individual basis until the day he challenged the brothers Jomeo and Sherry
while they were together. The incident started with Goblin displaying while
the two brothers were grooming. They warned him off but were apparently
quite frustrated by his impertinence. Then an adult female, Miff, casually
wandered by, and the two angered brothers attacked her violently. When Sherry
stepped back from pommeling Miff for a moment, Goblin charged and eventually bit deeply into Sherry's neck, intimidating Jomeo, rescuing Miff, and
asserting his status in one brilliant maneuvre.[2] After a series of confrontations
with Figan himself, and after Figan's death, Goblin assumed alpha male status
in the early 1980s.

Throughout his rise to power and beyond, intervention behavior was demonstrated to Goblin's advantage, as well as to the advantage of his subordinates
and kin. When personal ties of blood were involved, his desire to intervene
even approached the extraordinary by chimpanzee standards. On one occasion
Goblin even charged 200 meters when he heard the screams of his mother,
Melissa, who was being attacked by another female.[3] Other chimpanzees will
commonly come to the aid of their mothers when they are in immediate
proximity, but they will not necessarily come from such a distance. Part of

Goblin's value as alpha male in his community at Gombe was his ability to keep the peace among his subordinates.

At the Arnhem Zoo in Holland in 1976-1977, Frans de Waal witnessed the fall of an old alpha male named Yeroen. A younger, stronger male, Luit, came to the fore after a series of confrontations with the old ruler. However, by October 1977, Yeroen had formed a coalition with a still younger male, his protégé Nikkie. Together they toppled Luit, and whereas Yeroen would greet Nikkie submissively, other chimpanzees in the community submitted with greater frequency to Yeroen: "The females and children 'greeted' him almost three times as often as Nikkie and five times as often as Luit."[4] De Waal is quick to suggest the reason:

The policing was done by Yeroen. Not counting the many times he and Nikkie intervened in each other's conflicts, Yeroen was a loser supporter 82 per cent of the time and Nikkie only 22 per cent of the time (measured in 1978-9). Nikkie was still, despite his position as the alpha male, a winner supporter.[5]

Yeroen had assumed the legendary position ascribed to men like Cardinal Richelieu of France, that of power behind the throne. In fact, de Waal is compelled to see Yeroen as a sort of Machiavellian archetype: the noble upon whose shoulders the young Nikkie ascended to the throne.[6] He did this through his capacity to form coalitions and make others dependent on him as the arbiter of disputes. In his *Sociobiology: The New Synthesis*, Edward O. Wilson was quick to establish that unlike bumblebees, paper wasps, and hornets, many primate societies—including those of rhesus monkeys and pig-tailed macaques as well as chimpanzees—are the farthest things from absolute despotisms. The dominant primates actually tend to rely on their subordinates' real willingness to submit, and the subordinates submit because of very real advantages: "Dominant animals . . . utilize their power to terminate fighting among subordinates."[7]

After the conquest of Mexico, the Spanish power elite did just that. Spanish authority justified its very existence by settling disputes where its Amerindian subordinates were concerned. In some instances, like Goblin's intervention on behalf of Miff, Spaniards were actually involved in creating the turmoil themselves. However, this was not always the case, and any dispute among Amerindians, or between Amerindians and Spaniards, allowed dominant Spanish officials to display their authority by providing what humans call justice. In an attempt to minimize strife and utilize the might of the Castilian Crown, Amerindians used the Spanish court system. By providing some justice to Amerindian communities, the Spanish Crown, in turn, gained some support from subordinates who found the system to their benefit. As with chimpanzees, human rulership is not just the story of aggressive display and actual violence.

Still, human rulership, in its capacity to provide justice, differs from primate intervention behavior on one very important count. When dominant humans intervene, it is through the multifaceted and multilayered creation that is human culture. Rites, rituals, and all sorts of learned behavior patterns are utilized. Machiavelli and Vico recognized that the gods and religious practices are used at the most primal level of culture to invoke fear and awe where the laws and justice are concerned. As a result, the laws of the ancient Israelites and the laws of the Romans were religious at their points of origin, *ius* being derived from *Ious* or Jove.[8] Over time, all sorts of legal precedent and ritualized court behavior came to be accumulated as law itself derived from custom, and custom itself was built on intervention behavior patterns found among dominant primates. Among the play groups of human children, older, more dominant children themselves reflect this primate pattern, intervening to settle disputes among their younger cohorts.[9] It is only in degree, not in kind, that humans are removed from other primates. Human culture is the source of that gap.

On January 21, 1592, Don Luis de Velasco, viceroy of New Spain, formally recognized that Spaniards demanded excessive tribute from their Indian vassals—in this case they wanted Castilian chickens. Addressing the *naturales* of Malinalco, he wrote that Indians suffered a great scarcity of chickens throughout the Valley of Mexico. Appealing to the abstract principle of justice, he proposed that the tributaries of Malinalco pay the Spaniards in *reales* rather than *ganado menor*, or lesser livestock.[10] This seemingly simple court decision was rooted in the complexity of sixteenth-century Spanish culture. Sensing that the chicken increased vitality and provided benefits far outweighing the costs of cultural transformation in this case, Amerindians demanded this European source of protein. Velasco, as representative of the king's justice, could not possibly deny the Crown's poor subjects the benefits of Castilian chickens. His solution provided for the exchange of symbols of value, rather than the actual exchange of goods produced by the primary economic sector. The use of money, a symbolic language of exchange, was to somehow save the indigenous population from want, need, and real suffering. How the *reales* were to be accumulated was never addressed.

A series of decisions were handed down in order to protect the Amerindians from the ravages of Spanish and Indian greed. On January 23, the *corregidor* Juan de Vallende was ordered by the viceroy to stop the devastation of Indian maize and vegetable fields by the mares, stallions, she-asses, and other livestock of the *estancias* of Juan Gutiérrez and the *regidor* Francisco Verarano. In defense of the indigenous population of Chichicapa, the *corregidor* was expected to keep a close watch of the *estancias* belonging to Verarano: San Miguel, Santiago, San Juan, and Santanna. The Indians were to continue their payment of tributary honey and silk to Spaniards, but the Spanish desire for luxury was not to interfere with the basic necessities of *maceguales*.[11] Similarly, the fields of common Indians in Toluca were not to be disturbed by the livestock of the Amerindian *principales* of Tlatelolco, and the livestock of *estancias* belonging to Francisco Péres were not to destroy the agricultural produce of the Indians of Guexoano.[12] In Tecama (eight leagues to the northeast of Mexico City), Spaniards were again making excessive tributary demands in wheat, maize, coin, and labor. Velasco decreed that Indians were to be freed from all duties as porters and were to be allowed to sell their wheat and maize in order to earn money to pay tribute exclusively in coin.[13]

Other cases demonstrate the Crown's practical definition of justice as the balancing of interests. In Tepozcolula, Spaniards causing disorder in the Amerindian township were banned from it. Velasco argued that the Crown had traditionally banned all wayward Spanish interlopers and freebooters from Indian townships in order to conserve "quietude and good police in the republic of the Indians."[14] In Coyoacan, the Indian *alcaldes mayores* were to retain their privileges to sell honey and other things, but in Tecama, the *principales naturales* were reminded that it was prohibited to use the lands of the *cajas de comunidad* for personal benefit.[15] In summation, these three decisions restated the all-important Spanish principles of hierarchy and reciprocity. Neither Spaniards nor Indian nobles were to abuse Indian commoners, who could expect their basic life sustenance to be provided them by the body politic, in times of need by *cajas de comunidad*. In turn, the rights and privileges of all natural and official lords, whether Spanish or Amerindian, were to be respected. This is what the Spaniards meant by *policía*, and its maintenance was reflected in apparel as well as in food.

On March 11, 1592, Viceroy Velasco granted two Indian caciques, Don Gerónimo de la Cruz of Ycpatepec and Don Pedro Ximénez of Tepeaca, the privilege of riding a horse and carrying a sword.[16] On April 14, Don Migo Hernández, cacique and *principal indio* of Teutitlan, was also granted this privilege.[17] In doing this, Velasco was providing these Indians with the signs of their ascension in the power structure and their role as intermediaries between the conquerors and the conquered *maceguales*. The number of Indian caciques granted these privileges was significant. Earlier, in July of 1589, Velasco had bestowed these honors on eleven *dons*—all on the very same day.[18] Whereas some other Amerindian lords may have lost wealth and status, these were at least wealthy enough to maintain a horse.[19]

However, the late-sixteenth-century decline in some Amerindian power may, in fact, be reflected by Velasco's decisions from January 21 to April 14 of 1592. One hundred years after the "discovery of a New World," the representatives of the Spanish Crown still found it necessary to protect Amerindian privileges and lands. This implies that the lands and privileges were constantly being violated. Unfortunately, although the decisions of viceroys and audiencias may have favored Amerindians on numerous occasions, there is very little substantial evidence of their actual enforcement.[20] In a political society that lived by the principle of "*obedezco pero no cumplo*," the compliance with and enforcement of a superior's orders were not always guaranteed. It is only by inference that we can determine the successful protection of Indian privilege— inference such as the continued Indian ownership of most of the lands in the Valley of Oaxaca well into the nineteenth century.[21] No doubt such a fact was also abetted by the general decrease in the colonial Indian population. Given a relative paucity of Spaniards (approximately 200,000 immigrants for all the

Americas in the sixteenth century) and the devastation of epidemic disease among the Amerindians, there was enough land to go around. Yet it is obvious that Indian possessions were challenged on occasion.[22] All in all, the enforcement of Viceroy Velasco's 1592 decisions was probably a story of mixed results, depending on the zeal, or lack thereof, of local Spanish *corregidores*. Theory seldom re-creates itself perfectly in the world of practical affairs, but it certainly does have its impact, whether beneficial or detrimental.

The development of legal protection of the Indians was slow. In 1551 the Audiencia of Mexico devoted one-half its time to suits involving Indians. By 1554 the Audiencia's *fiscal*, or Crown attorney, was entrusted with the task of defending Amerindians before the highest court in New Spain, but he was so preoccupied with cases involving the royal *hacienda* that this function was inadequately discharged. As a result, Viceroy Antonio de Mendoza (1535-1550) and his successor, the first Luis de Velasco (1550-1564), started the practice of hearing Amerindian complaints in a viceregal court. Not until the 1590s was the son of the first Viceroy Velasco, our Luis de Velasco (1590-1595; 1607-1611), able to establish a special bureaucracy within the viceregal administration to deal with Indian legal complaints. He created the General Indian Court of New Spain, with its salaried *defensor de los indios*, *letrado*, and *avogado*. Indians were free of the payment of fees, unless they were entire towns or caciques, but a general tax was levied on Indian townships to provide for the expenses of the court.

Procedurally, one of the most important issues dealt with by the Court was the question of *amparo*, which allowed appeal to a court of higher jurisdiction when traditional privileges had seemingly not been respected by a lower jurisdiction. The writ of *amparo* protected the possession of land or the exercise of some function as a traditional and hereditary privilege. To defend their land and the subsistence of their bodies from Spanish infringements and the infringements of other Amerindians, quite a few towns argued that *amparo* recognized their utilization of lands traditionally cultivated by their fathers and grandfathers. The cases dealing with the writ of *amparo* were numerous and have been explored by Woodrow Borah in *Justice by Insurance: The General Indian Court of Colonial Mexico and the Legal Aides of the Half-Real.*[23] In actuality, these cases reveal a recognition of territoriality as a basic primate trait. Although the innate territoriality of *Homo sapiens sapiens* and earlier hominids is hotly debated by anthropologists, it is interesting to note that

modern hunter-gatherer bands containing about 25 individuals commonly occupy between 1000 and 3000 square kilometers. This area is comparable to the home range of a wolf pack but as much as a hundred times greater than that of a troop of gorillas, which are exclusively vegetarian.[24]

Humans seemingly require space between groups to avoid detrimental competition and conflict.[25] This space may be achieved by means of outright aggression; or where culture has promoted peaceful resolution rather than violence (where a system of ritualized justice has arisen), laws and judges may be utilized. At its very best, human culture can clearly emphasize innate tendencies that restrain aggression and violence. Clearly, human beings are not solely creatures of peace or of violence. Both tendencies lie within our "hard-wiring," to a greater or lesser extent within particular individuals. It is the task of culture to promote or restrain violence through learning and exposure. Aggression may be encouraged or controlled, and it is quite clear that verbal duels minimize physical violence in human society.[26] On the other hand, children who are exposed to the aggressive mishandling of a doll, whether it be through direct exposure or media such as film and cartoons, "handled their doll more aggressively than control children who had not observed an aggressive model."[27] Humans are immensely susceptible creatures. Able to learn and draw on individual experience, humans can develop patterns of control or chaos through the medium of culture. Having been exposed to legal systems and legal judgment, Spanish and Nahua cultures used their prior imprinting to establish dialogue and counteract violence after the conquest of Mexico by Cortés.

The Spaniards obviously arrived in Mexico with a legal tradition built on Roman law, Canon law, and medieval Castilian customs codified in Alfonso the Wise's *Siete partidas*, yet the Nahuas of central Mexico also understood legal proceedings and judgments. Aztec law seems to have been most thoroughly developed in fifteenth-century Texcoco by Nezahualcoyotl. Here, Motolinía, Ixtlilxochitl, Pomar, and Torquemada stand as sources of our information. Of course, they wrote long after the events described, and they disagree on numerous details. Spanish terms and categories of understanding abound in describing the system imposed by Nezahualcoyotl, but according to Jerome Offner, an expert on Nahua law, some general, common trends are identifiable in all the sources. There was some sort of supreme legal council at Texcoco. It held a type of territorial jurisdiction, and its decisions could be appealed to at least two higher judges. A minimum of half the judges were from the nobility, and the ruler, or *tlatoani*, of Texcoco had final say in sentencing. Meetings of these judges were held regularly, and there were special chambers reserved for these occasions.[28]

Although, to the best of our knowledge, Tenochtitlan's legal tradition was not as sophisticated as Texcoco's, distinctions were still clearly made between proper and improper judicial proceeding. It is known that the principal merchants of Tenochtitlan retained independent jurisdiction over the regulation of the marketplace and their own personal activities, even to the point of exacting the death penalty.[29] More importantly, Sahagún's *Florentine Codex* reveals that Moctezuma the Great (1440-1468) established a tradition of observing proper legal proceeding at all costs. Meeting in assigned rooms, noble judges reviewed documents recorded in picture writing and heard witnesses as well as the people directly involved:

And the ruler, if he knew anything ill of these judges—perhaps that they needlessly delayed the case of common folk, that they deliberated two years or even four—[that]

they could not pronounce judgment because of either a bribe or kinship,—he then seized them and jailed them in wooden cages, exacted the penalty, and slew them, so that the judges might walk in dread.[30]

{Reprinted, by permission, from the *Florentine Codex: General History of the Things of New Spain* by Fray Bernardino de Sahagún. Book 8: Kings and Lords, p. 42. Translated by Arthur J. O. Anderson and Charles E. Dibble. Copyright 1981 by the School of American Research Press, Santa Fe.}

Although the evidence is not very detailed, there is some indication that learned culture among the Nahuas of Tenochtitlan and Texcoco was so powerful that it was actively interfering with the natural preferences for one's proximate gene pool as found in kinship. Many Nahuas had obviously learned enough about legal proceedings and the justice provided by the dominant that they could readily understand the Spanish system and adapt accordingly. The cultural stress in using a Spanish court would not have been significant given the evidence concerning pre-Columbian legal proceedings.

A case concerning Azcapotzalco and the Amerindian suburb of Spanish Mexico City, Santiago de Tlatelolco, clearly demonstrates this Amerindian familiarity with the use of judges, testimony, appeals, and numerous other elements of a legal discourse. Prior to the establishment of Velasco's General Indian Court, in 1561, the *principales* and *naturales* of Azcapotzalco brought suit before the Audiencia of Mexico City in a case of disputed water rights. Under the leadership of their Indian governor, Don Baltazar Hernández, the inhabitants of Azcapotzalco claimed hereditary right to the use of water found on *estancia* lands belonging to the Indians of Santiago de Tlatelolco.[31] Hoping to attain the privileged status of *miserables* in the eyes of the Crown,[32] the plaintiffs argued that they were so poor that they lacked a *caja de comunidad*. It was obviously hoped that royal officials, as defenders of the principle of reciprocity in theory and of the poor and downtrodden in practice, would thus lend a sympathetic ear. For two entire years the Audiencia heard evidence and testimony, while constantly being bombarded by pleas for justice presented by the Spanish lawyers representing Azcapotzalco and Santiago de Tlatelolco-Cristóbal de Pérez and Jhoan de Salazar respectively. Finally, on October 14, 1563, the *oidores* of Mexico City's Audiencia decided in favor of the governors and Indians of Santiago de Tlatelolco; the major factor in the decision was testimony from neighboring Indian townships that supported the *cabecera*'s case against the smaller Azcapotzalco. Of course, it should also be noted that this was the same, formerly dominant, Azcapotzalco that had been defeated by the Triple Alliance in 1425. The town's gambit to regain its former control of the Valley of Mexico's natural resources came to naught. The Indians of Azcapotzalco were ordered to desist from squatting on the *estancias* belonging to Tlatelolco and from using any water found on those *estancias*.[33] The *ganado mayor* of the Indian suburb of Mexico City had triumphed over the seemingly urgent water needs of another Indian group. One immediately wonders if

Santiago de Tlatelolco, as a *cabecera* (or town with administrative jurisdiction over a number of other Indian habitations), was able to sway the testimony of subordinate towns. Such matters can be left only to speculation, but the skill with which Amerindians employed the Spanish legal system stands as factual testimony to their resilience and understanding of law.

While clearly demonstrating the legal aptitude of Mesoamerican Indians, the Azcapotzalco case also illustrates that whereas many subordinate Amerindians maintained a traditional cultural preference for maize over wheat, the more affluent among them were just as enthusiastic as the Spaniards for the raising of cattle and sheep. Interestingly enough, whereas Spaniards were often ordered to remove their *ganado mayor* from occupied Indian lands, Santiago de Tlatelolco's livestock was protected at the expense of the water needs of Azcapotzalco.

Immediately following the Audiencia's decision, Tlatelolco sued Azcapotzalco for damages, and Cristóbal de Pérez emphasized Azcapotzalco's need yet again.[34] The Audiencia reaffirmed its decision, but the appeals continued, showing the willingness of Tlatelolco and Azcapotzalco to work within the legal system.[35] On July 24, 1565, the *fiscal*, Dr. Cespedes, issued an order that the *estancia* of Santa Anna was to be respected as land belonging to Santiago de Tlatelolco.[36] This was also the case with the *estancias* of San Juan and Santa Cruz.[37] Appeals still continued, and Dr. Cespedes had to reaffirm the decision against Azcapotzalco on April 11, 1567, with a final reaffirmation being issued by Mexico City's Audiencia on July 1, 1569![38] In the final reaffirmation, it was determined that justice was served by respecting Santiago de Tlatelolco's claim to the *estancias* of San Juan and Santa Cruz. In court, the *ganado mayor* of an Indian *cabecera* had won a final victory, but one wonders if squatters from Azcapotzalco continued to infringe upon the lands of Tlatelolco. William B. Taylor, in *Drinking, Homicide, and Rebellion in Colonial Mexican Villages*, noted that Indian townships sometimes settled their disputes with skirmishes and blows. The legal system was used, but it was not the only recourse, especially since official decisions and their enforcement were two separate matters entirely.[39] Still, just as the *relaciones geográficas* of the early 1600s marked a solidification of the Spanish conquest, so too the regular functioning of the General Indian Court marked a sort of normalization in the Spanish-Indian cultural exchange. Officials were kept on salary to ensure appropriate balance in the recognition of Spanish and Amerindian interests in the body politic.

One such official was a solicitor of the court named Joseph de Sali. In 1616, and throughout his long career, Sali experienced the actual process of Amerindian agency as it tried to maintain some autonomy within the confines of the Spanish imperium. On March 4, 1616, Sali presented the complaints of the Indian towns of Jecalpa, Huauchinantla, Mitepec, and Tamazula in the province of Teotlalco, now in southwestern Puebla. Having few water resources, this hot and dry country no doubt encouraged conflict over scarce resources.[40] On this occasion it seems that Spanish ranchers, in imitation of the noble sheepherders the Castilian Mesta, permitted their cattle to invade native lands, where they proceeded to eat fruit trees and crops. The Amerindians requested both payment for damages and the right to kill any invading cattle in the future. The viceroy not only granted this request; he ordered that any future offenders be fined for the expenses of the General Indian Court, and that the local *alcalde mayor* send testimony of compliance within twenty days.[41] This case was typical of the continued courtroom success experienced by Sali throughout his career.

On March 12 of the same year, Sali dealt with the delicate issue of clerical versus lay authority. Arguing on behalf of the Indians of San Juan Coscomatepec, who claimed to be poor and worn out by burdens, Sali asked for a viceregal decree forbidding their mistreatment by the local curate. The viceroy granted this decree, but he also stressed that proceedings for damages against the curate would have to continue in the episcopal court of Puebla, where they were already being heard.[42] On September 3 he merely acted as the agent of three Indians of Santa María Azompa in the Valley of Oaxaca. They had bought land from a *principal*, and the viceregal court approved the sale, since it was "among Indians."[43]

Throughout his career Sali dealt with issues of land ownership among the Amerindians. By extension he was dealing with issues concerning Indian sustenance and the maintenance of the *república de los indios*, with the practical application of *policía* and *justicia*. Official Spanish policy never denied the Indians food, but it did regulate the types of food they could produce and consume. Of course, this was blatantly apparent in the prohibitions enforced against cannibalism, but it was also present in the wheat tithes that may have made maize financially, as well as gastronomically, more acceptable to Indian palates. Restrictions on Indian slaughterhouses were also enacted, although it seems they failed to curtail Indian meat consumption in practice.[44]

In actual practice, the exchange and marketing of Indian foodstuffs became a matter of Spanish jurisprudence. This is unsurprising, since exchange and barter have been noted as fundamental human traits. It has even been speculated that the earliest form of barter may have arisen among hominids in "the exchange of meat captured by the males for plant food gathered by the females."[45] That the Spanish courts and Joseph de Sali should have entered into this was a function of dominance settling disputes among subordinates and, in the broadest sense possible, of human cultural creativity.

On March 24, 1616, Joseph de Sali represented San Nicolás Cuitlatetelco, subject town of Mezquique (also known as Mixquic or Amesquique). The Indians explained that custom provided that the town market be held every Saturday behind the church, but certain Spaniards and Indians were planning to move the market for their own benefit. Explicitly appealing to the writ of *amparo*, Sali successfully defended the rights of the town market against any interference.[46] In 1633 he dealt with similar issues when the local *alcalde mayor* of Atorpay and Chicuasontepec, in the province of Veracruz, was accused, together with other residents, of seizing Indian produce and paying lower than market price. The viceregal court ordered him to desist from this, and from forcing Indians to fish for him without pay.[47]

Joseph de Sali was also involved in disputes concerning that critical nexus of Iberian-Indian exchange and interchange: the manufacturing of cloth. On April 8, 1633, he represented Juan Miguel and his wife, Indians of the barrio of Santa Anna of Puebla, who complained that the *obrajero* Alonso Moreno had kept them prisoner for over two years to pay a debt accrued through the expenses of their marriage. They were forced to work day and night, as well as on feast days, in clear violation of restrictions imposed upon the forced labor of Amerindians in *obrajes*. Without delay, the viceregal court ordered the immediate release of these Indians, who had obviously already paid any debt accrued.[48] More than Sepúlveda's *Treatise on the Just Causes of War with the Indians*, the actions of men like Sali no doubt helped to ease a Spanish conscience racked by questions of the justice of conquest and imperialism.

The Spanish quest for justice in the Americas was quite real, but it was normally not a quest for utopia. There was room for the experiments of a Vasco de Quiroga, but most Spaniards took a far more cynical attitude, expecting sinful shortcomings on the part of both Spaniards and Amerindians. Whereas las Casas may have painted the Indians as too saintly and Sepúlveda as too demonic, Viceroy Antonio de Mendoza, as a practical man of affairs, steered a middle course accepted by many a Crown official. In the *relación* to his successor, he wrote:

Some will tell Your Lordship that the Indians are simple and humble people without malice, pride, or covetousness. Others will insist upon the opposite, and claim that they are very rich and lazy and do not wish to cultivate their lands. Do not believe one group or the other. Rather deal with the Indians as with any other people, without making special rules, and with caution for the devices of third parties.[49]

Unlike some cultural anthropologists, who argue that culture defines very real and fundamental distinctions in human beings, Mendoza looked for the universal and the innate. This set the tone for the establishment of some cross-cultural dialogue at the very top of the Spanish administration. The Spanish struggle for dominance in Mexico required that the symbols and uniforms of the conquerors be used in the public arena, but it also allowed for a certain level of communication with subordinates seeking assistance and redress.

Justice in the Americas was to be the balancing act that it already was in Spain, with hierarchy and reciprocity serving as the antipodes, and privileges granted by *amparo* serving as weights and counterweights. Thus, on February 20, 1590, the second Viceroy Velasco did both in the pursuit of the common good, just as any monarch would. He granted Don Joseph Sánchez, a *principal* of Guatinchan (in the *partido* of Puebla de los Angeles), the privileges and responsibilities of maintaining "*haciendas y grangerías*," of living wheresoever he wished, and of paying tribute to maintain *doctrineros* to instruct the local Indian population in the faith. Velasco also forbade the governors and *principales* of Guatinchan from the forced sale of meat to local *maceguales*.[50] In doing this, he was merely following a tradition established by Mendoza and carried on by future viceroys.

Still, for the system to operate, subordinates were often enough required to take the initiative. As has been demonstrated, *cofradías* were used by Amerindians to regulate and control festivals and the redistribution of wealth in their own local communities.[51] Far from being illicit and a form of rebellion, these lay brotherhoods, though deplored by many local curates, were officially sanctioned by viceroys. As late as February 4, 1619, Don Diego Fernández de Córdoba gave license to the Indians of Tehuacan (in the southeast of the present-day state of Puebla) to form the Cofradía de la Limpia Concepción.[52] The Habsburg tradition of "absolutism" allowed for compromise, leeway, and some initiative from below, hence the famous *"obedezco pero no cumplo."* Neither a society of the free nor the enslaved, New Spain was a society of the privileged. Only the centralizing Bourbon reforms of the late eighteenth century and the laissez-faire liberal principles of La Reforma later disrupted this, with the culminating blow being the late nineteenth century's disintegration of communally held *ejido* lands and privileges.

The dramatic transformation from Amerindian-held lands to ever-growing latifundia was most drastic after New Spain had become the independent state of Mexico. The Ley Lerdo of 1856, with its opposition to corporately held Church lands, including those lands held by *cofradías* for charitable purposes, paved the way for the demise of the communally held Indian *ejido*, vital to both husbandry and agriculture. Although the Ley Lerdo exempted *ejidos* as necessary to the maintenance of Indian villages, in actual practice, parts of the *ejidos* began to be sold. Finally, the Porfiriato's land laws and railroad development aided disentailment at the expense of free village peasant agriculture. It has been estimated that, at independence, about 40 percent of all agriculturally productive land in central and southern Mexico was owned communally by peasant villages. By 1910 only 5 percent was held in this fashion. The Mexican Indians' devastating loss of lands in the nineteenth century is well recorded by such historians as Jan Bazant and John H. Coatsworth, and there is no need to review this history here.[53] But there is a need to recognize how the Spanish monarchy's acceptance of communally held land blended nicely with already extant Indian views on the subject, and how the introduction of laissez-faire principles in the nineteenth century may have been far more devastating to the native population than any colonial economic measures. Such things are extremely difficult to determine, especially when the enforcement of decisions arrived at in colonial courts cannot be fully known, but the known instances of decline in Indian landownership after La Reforma may be evidence enough. The pre-Columbian and colonial quest for justice was recast in liberal terms by nineteenth-century leaders. Corporate privileges became individual rights, and a greater cultural gap was thereby created between many whites and Indians—individuals like Benito Juárez excepted.

The case of Atlatlauhca stands as a prime example of the Spanish social organism's functioning in New Spain, and of its eventual demise. On December 10, 1538, the *licenciado* Jhoan de Salazar, on behalf of the cacique Don Diego de Gusmán, demanded justice of Viceroy Antonio de Mendoza for the Indians of San Matheo Atlatlauhca. He stated that for many years the Indians had held land in common as the heirs of their forefathers. This *ejido* land was being violated by Spaniards and their livestock, causing incredible damage to fields cultivated by the Amerindians for their sustenance, the sustenance of their livestock, and the payment of their tribute. Salazar demanded a *merced*, or privileged favor, of Viceroy Mendoza, granting this land in perpetuity to the township of Atlatlauhca.[54] In January 1539 Mendoza granted just title to the Indians, forbidding the forced alienation or sale of the traditional lands of Atlatlauhca: "And, at present, in the name of His Majesty, we grant the said lands as a *merced* so that you can raise your livestock and cultivate your fields on them without impediment."[55]

The *merced* had been granted, and what followed shows the difficulty with which Crown officials enforced such grants, but it also demonstrates the serious efforts made by the Crown. On January 15, 1544, Mendoza forbade the Spaniard Tomás de Rijoles from establishing an *estancia* on land granted Atlatlauhca in perpetuity.[56] On two other occasions, sixteenth-century viceregal courts defended the Amerindians of Atlatlauhca from Spanish livestock. In 1714 a similar defense of Atlatlauhca's *merced* was yet again reiterated.[57] The Spaniards of New Spain were not living in a perfect world, and as a result their laws and edicts were broken, just as ours are today. These legal ideals were nonetheless recorded, and in the case of Atlatlauhca, it appears that viceroys were willing to respect these principles for nearly two hundred years. Perhaps even more importantly, the Amerindians of Atlatlauhca trusted in the enforcement of Spanish law as a defense over this same period of time. On September 3, 1853 (three years before the Ley Lerdo went into effect), the *principales* of Atlatlauhca made a final pathetic plea to have the ancient privileges of their *ejido* recognized by the government of independent Mexico.[58] The response of the government is not recorded, and neither is any indication of government interest in the case. By 1853 a new economic and political discourse called liberalism was changing some of the terms of engagement where elites and subordinates were concerned. Such a cultural shift would require time to be taught and accepted, and in so many ways the course of twentieth-century Mexican history, since the Revolution of 1910, has been an attempt to bridge the cultural gap between the world of the *ejido* and that of free markets and private property held by individuals. Today, while a Mexican government struggles to privatize and liberalize a mixed economy, Zapatista rebels in the highlands of Chiapas can still cry out in defense of the *ejido*. The conquest and colonialism are far from forgotten.

In colonial times the customary Amerindian claims to communal lands were "legalized" by the dominant Spaniards' cultural recognition of such practices. Mexican Indians, who had adhered to similar laws and customs before the conquest, actively participated in the construction of a synthetic legal tradition.

Indian land was stolen and abused by Spaniards, but the Spanish Crown made innumerable efforts to curb the complete victimization of the Amerindians. At the same time, Amerindians learned to use Spanish methods to defend themselves. Like other primates, the humans of sixteenth-century Mexico learned to use the dominant among them to curtail violence and disputes among subordinates. Through the mutual agreement of Spaniards, Nahuas, and other Amerindians, verbal duels replaced physical conflict in many cases. Cultural imperialism obviously took place, but not without resistance and complicity on the part of the Spaniards' conquered subjects.

NOTES

1. Jane Goodall, *Through a Window: My Thirty Years with the Chimpanzees of Gombe* (Boston: Houghton Mifflin, 1990), 138.

2. Ibid., 142-43.

3. Jane Goodall, *The Chimpanzees of Gombe: Patterns of Behavior* (Cambridge, MA, and London: Belknap Press of Harvard University Press, 1986), 376.

4. Frans de Waal, *Chimpanzee Politics: Power and Sex among the Apes* (New York: Harper & Row, 1982), 151.

5. Ibid., 150.

6. Ibid., 153.

7. Edward O. Wilson, *Sociobiology: The New Synthesis* (Cambridge, MA: Belknap Press of Harvard University Press, 1975), 287.

8. Niccolò Machiavelli, *Discourses on the First Ten Books of Titus Livius*, trans. Christian E. Detmold, in *The Prince and the Discourses* (New York: Modern Library, 1950), Bk. 1, chap. 11, pp. 146-47; Giambattista Vico, *The New Science of Giambattista Vico*, trans. Thomas Goddard Bergin and Max Harold Fisch (Ithaca, NY, and London: Cornell University Press, 1984), Bk. 2, sec. 1, chap. 2, para. 398, p. 125. Also see Bk. 2., sec. 2, chap. 4, para. 433, p. 141.

9. Irenäus Eibl-Eibesfeldt, *Human Ethology* (New York: Aldine de Gruyter, 1989), 600-602.

10. Archivo General de la Nación, Fondo *Indios*, vol. 6, 1ª parte, exp. 41, f. 10ª. Henceforth *AGN*.

11. *AGN*, Fondo *Indios*, vol. 6, 1ª parte, exp. 56, f. 13ª.

12. Decisions rendered in February 1592. *AGN*, Fondo *Indios*, vol. 6, 1ª parte, exp. 118, f. 28ª and exp. 172, f. 44ª.

13. A decision rendered in February 1592. *AGN*, Fondo *Indios*, vol. 6, 1ª parte, exp. 222, f. 57ª.

14. March 10, 1592. *AGN*, Fondo *Indios*, vol. 6, 1ª parte, exp. 220, f. 56ᵇ.

15. January 23, 1592. *AGN*, Fondo *Indios*, vol. 6, 1ª parte, exp. 52, f. 12ª.

16. *AGN*, Fondo *Indios*, vol. 6, 1ª parte, exp. 223-24, 57ª.

17. *AGN*, Fondo *Indios*, vol. 6, 1ª parte, exp. 273, f. 74ᵃ⁻ᵇ.

18. *AGN*, Fondo *Indios*, vol. 4, exp. 170-80, f. 55ª-56ª.

Subjected to Francisco Tello de Sandoval's *visita* in the mid-1540s, Don Antonio de Mendoza was questioned about nine Amerindian notables to whom he granted the privilege of carrying a sword. One, Luis de León, interpreter to the Audiencia, lost the privilege by becoming a drunkard. "Fragmento de la Visita hecha á D. Antonio de Mendoza.—Interrogatorio por el cual han de ser examinados los testigos que presente por su parte D. Antonio de Mendoza (8 enero 1547)," in *Colección de documentos para la historia de México*, ed. Joaquín García Icazbalceta, 2 vols. (Mexico, 1858-1866), 2:87-88.

19. Charles Gibson, *The Aztecs under Spanish Rule* (Stanford, CA: Stanford University Press, 1964), 194-217.

20. Woodrow Borah, *Justice by Insurance: The General Indian Court of Colonial Mexico and the Legal Aides of the Half-Real* (Berkeley and Los Angeles: University of California Press, 1983), 139, 156.

21. "At most, Spanish estates accounted for one-third of the land in Oaxaca, and the largest holdings were suited only to grazing." William B. Taylor, *Landlord and Peasant in Colonial Oaxaca* (Stanford, CA: Stanford University Press, 1972), 163. Also see 43, 67, 82-84, 107-8, 199.

22. Nicolás Sánchez-Albornoz, "The Population of Colonial Spanish America," in *The Cambridge History of Latin America*, ed. Leslie Bethell, Vol. 2: *Colonial Latin America* (Cambridge: Cambridge University Press, 1984), 15-16.

23. Borah, *Justice by Insurance*, 25, 52-55, 63-78, 91-94, 104-5, 144-74.

24. Wilson, 565.

25. Ibid.

26. Eibl-Eibesfeldt, 375.

27. Ibid., 366.

28. Jerome A. Offner, *Law and Politics in Aztec Texcoco* (Cambridge: Cambridge University Press, 1983), 55-59, 83-85, 157, 243-55.

29. Bernardino de Sahagún, *Florentine Codex: General History of the Things of New Spain*, trans. Arthur J. O. Anderson and Charles E. Dibble, 13 vols. (Santa Fe and Salt Lake City: Monographs of the School of American Research/University of Utah Press, 1950-1982), Bk. 9, chap. 5, pp. 23-24.

30. Ibid., Bk. 8, chap. 14, pp. 41-43; Offner, 82-85.

31. *AGN*, Fondo *Tierras*, vol. 1, 1ª parte, exp. 17, f. 22[a-b].

32. A legal term referring to the poor in need of the Crown's protection and assistance.

33. *AGN*, Fondo *Tierras*, vol. 1, 1ª parte, exp. 160, f. 165[a]-82[a].

34. *AGN*, Fondo *Tierras*, vol. 1, 1ª parte, exp. 167-68, f. 189[a]-90[b].

35. *AGN*, Fondo *Tierras*, vol. 1, 1ª parte, exp. 174-76, f. 196[a]-98[a].

36. *AGN*, Fondo *Tierras*, vol. 1, 2ª parte, exp. 248, f. 5[a].

37. *AGN*, Fondo *Tierras*, vol. 1, 2ª parte, exp. 267, f. 14[a]-15[a].

38. *AGN*, Fondo *Tierras*, vol. 1, 2ª parte, exp. 284, f. 32[a], and exp. 462, f. 204[a].

39. William B. Taylor, *Drinking, Homicide, and Rebellion in Colonial Mexican Villages* (Stanford, CA: Stanford University Press, 1979), 145.

40. Peter Gerhard, *A Guide to the Historical Geography of New Spain* (Cambridge: Cambridge University Press, 1972), 310.

41. *AGN*, Fondo *Indios*, vol. 7, exp. 30, f. 14[a-b]. The idea to review the cases of Joseph de Sali came from his constant appearance in Woodrow Borah's *Justice by Insurance*, 121-226.

42. *AGN*, Fondo *Indios*, vol. 7, exp. 31, f. 15[a].

43. *AGN*, Fondo *Indios*, vol. 7, exp. 104, f. 51[a-b].

44. Gibson, 346.

45. Wilson, 553.

46. *AGN*, Fondo *Indios*, vol. 7, exp. 36, f. 17[a-b].

47. September 6, 1633. *AGN*, Fondo *Indios*, vol. 7, exp. 142-48, f. 77[b]-82[b].

48. *AGN*, Fondo *Indios*, vol. 10, exp. 149, f. 83[a-b].

49. Quoted in Borah, *Justice by Insurance*, 67.

50. *AGN*, Fondo *Indios*, vol. 4, exp. 276-77, f. 83[b]-84[a].

51. Murdo J. MacLeod, "The Social and Economic Roles of Indian Cofradías in Colonial Chiapas," in *The Church and Society in Colonial Latin America*, ed. Jeffrey A. Cole (New Orleans: Tulane University Press, 1984), 73-96.

52. *AGN*, Fondo *Indios*, vol. 7, exp. 351, f. 170[a].

53. Jan Bazant, "Mexico from Independence to 1867," in *The Cambridge History of Latin America*, ed. Leslie Bethell, Vol. 3: *From Independence to c. 1870* (Cambridge: Cambridge University Press, 1985), 455-56; John H. Coatsworth, *Growth against Development* (DeKalb: Northern Illinois University Press, 1981); Friedrich Katz, "Mexico: Restored Republic and Porfiriato, 1867-1910," in *The Cambridge History of Latin America*, ed. Leslie Bethell, Vol. 5: *c. 1870 to 1930* (Cambridge: Cambridge University Press, 1986), 48.

54. *AGN*, Fondo *Tierras*, vol. 11, 1[a] parte, exp. 2, f. 24[a]-36[b].

55. *AGN*, Fondo *Tierras*, vol. 11, 1[a] parte, exp. 2, f. 27[a-b].

56. *AGN*, Fondo *Tierras*, vol. 11, 1[a] parte, exp. 2, f. 32[a]. Also *AGN*, Fondo *Mercedes*, vol. 2, f. 246 vuelta.

57. *AGN*, Fondo *Tierras*, vol. 11, 1[a] parte, exp. 2, f. 32[a]-33[a]; *AGN*, Fondo *Mercedes*, vol. 7, f. 359 vuelta; *AGN*, Fondo *Tierras*, vol. 11, 1[a] parte, exp. 2, f. 33[a]-35[a]; *AGN*, Fondo *Mercedes*, vol. 21, f. 323 vuelta; and *AGN*, Fondo *Mercedes*, vol. 61, f. 243 vuelta.

58. *AGN*, Fondo *Tierras*, vol. 11, 1[a] parte, exp. 2, f. 36[a-b].

8

The Hospital: The Right to Distribute Favor

In the evolution of primate behavior, the distribution of resources is quite crucial. Among other things, adequate resources assure the survival of the individual and the continuation of that individual's genes through reproduction. Chimpanzee females enhance their survival chances, and those of their offspring, by usually foraging alone. However, females are the resource imperative to ensuring male reproduction, and males must develop strategies to acquire mating opportunities. Whereas male gorillas, like baboons, use pronounced sexual dimorphism to acquire and dominate harems, male chimpanzees use other methods. Above all else, male chimpanzees have learned to share food with non-kin. Although they will share meat from a kill with other males, males rarely beg from each other. However, females almost exclusively beg from males, and the protein they acquire enhances the survival chances of their offspring. Chimpanzee males have learned to build cohesiveness with females, and sometimes with other males, by sharing food, and the male who provides meat for his pregnant or lactating mate is literally enhancing the chances of his genes' survival.[1]

Of course, food-sharing and benevolent behavior are first learned from the mother who nurtures and associates with a hunting male. Glynn Isaac and others have made much of the development of human culture as a result of food-sharing, and they believe that the fact that chimpanzee and hominid males have developed a variation on the mother's task is crucial to understanding male behavior.[2] Whereas females continue to share with their offspring, male food-sharing increases male dominance. It is quite literally the birth of paternalism—in which males will deny themselves some resources in order to promote cohesiveness and their own dominance by nonviolent means. Nineteenth-century human individualism and Social Darwinism defined a struggle for existence that pitted individuals and races against each other, but primate behavior is never so simplistic. In actuality, to cite W. C. McGrew, "evolution should favor those individuals capable of balancing competition and cooperation with peers by calculating the appropriate trade-offs of costs and benefits in particular contexts."[3] Primate males have learned this, and they have also learned that generosity gains prestige and respect. It is therefore only natural that the cultural manifestation of the sixteenth-century European hospital should represent both benevolence and dominance. It is also only natural that Spanish males should want the hospital defined by their own vision of the world—excluding Amerindian methods and women as much as possible. A source of male prestige, the public distribution of nurturing resources was jealously guarded, with women being confined to a motherly role at home and a subordinate role in public.

Within the confines of culture, the sixteenth-century hospital was a most public and communal entity. In the words of a 1582 *real cédula* confirming the 1572 establishment of the second leprosarium of San Lázaro in Mexico City: "It is a most laudable custom in all well-ordered republics to avoid carefully all things which can be harmful to corporal as well as spiritual health."[4] In both Spain and New Spain, the Crown envisioned the hospital as a place where spiritual and bodily ills that threatened the entire social organism could be arrested, elimi-nated, isolated, and perhaps even cured. At the founding of any particular hospital, the medical and material mission was linked necessarily to and imbued with spiritual and moral values. Christian values of brotherly love demanded the care of the unfortunate and impoverished. Public health concerns demanded the isolation of the diseased.[5]

Unfortunately for those who wished to maintain a static ontology in the face of change, the European "discovery" of a New World and its indigenous medicinal practices and plants helped to open medical discourse to a collection of new cures and solutions. The Hippocratic and Galenic traditions were challenged by Amerindian medical practices never witnessed by the Greeks and Romans. European medical men adopted some new practices to increase their curative powers and social prestige, at the same time trying to fit the new and unfamiliar into their old categories of understanding. By extension, they began to interpret the hospital's prime function as being a place of material healing, never fully forgetting its mission of Christian charity, but sometimes relegating the spiritual mission to the background. Richard Greenleaf noted that "medical men . . . often found themselves at odds with the religious establishment." A kindred spirit to Paracelsus, the self-trained physician Pedro de la Torre claimed that God and nature were one, bringing him before the Inquisition in the 1550s, and in the 1570s rumors spread that Dr. Pedro López was a heretic or judaizer.[6] Just as the Copernican revolution led to an increase in the number of confrontations be-tween speculative theology and theoretical science, this new applied medicine challenged the previously undisputed primacy of charity and applied religion.

Traditionally, the curative and material role of hospitals was less important than their spiritual end, the provision of Christian charity. If anything, this followed naturally from the inadequacies of European medicine at the time. In Pedro de Alcocer's history of Toledo, six chapters described the city's hospitals, "where they perform works of great service to Our Lord, curing, sustaining, clothing and housing the poor and the sick, and marrying female orphans in need."[7] Therefore, spiritual and material goals were linked in Toledo, the center of hospital reform in Old World Spain. The Toledan hospital of Santiago, specializing in the treatment of syphilis, was placed carefully on the outskirts of the city, as was typical of other urban areas. In this manner, attempts were made to protect the material well-being of the community by preventing the spread of a disease recognized as contagious. Likewise, spiritual goals were fostered, and Alcocer was quick to point out that penance and indulgences could be earned by dying in a hospital or by visiting the sick and performing works of charity there.[8] In sixteenth-century Catholic fashion, poor relief and social welfare practices merged with medical pursuits at the Toledan Hospital del Nuncio:

And in addition to the great service it does Our Lord by curing the sick, this Hospital also does another very great one, clothing and sustaining in it 12 poor old men who have fallen into need, giving them a home and their necessities before they die, when others will enter in their place.[9]

In Toledo urban and royal officials, private donors, clerical administrators, and lay doctors joined in the founding and maintenance of hospitals, and such efforts were duplicated elsewhere. By the middle of the sixteenth century Avila had twelve hospitals for the poor, including Doña María de Herrera's Nuestra Señora de la Anunciación, which cared for "up to twenty poor and elderly but respectable citizens of Avila."[10] Hospitals were the homes of outcasts, from the leper, the syphilitic, and the madman to the impoverished old man. They incorporated the marginal who belonged to no recognized order, class, or estate with its own particular vocation to be fulfilled for the common good of all estates.[11] In the words of the 1582 *cédula* that recognized the founding of Mexico City's San Lázaro, hospitals were meant to be places where the poor, even lepers, were to learn the value of Christian virtues and communal life.

In Mexico City's San Lázaro, founded in the 1570s by Dr. Pedro López, the social function of the poor lepers was made clear,[12] and they were actually granted an estate, or rank, vital to the maintenance of the body politic. The *real cédula* of June 11, 1582 recognized them as Christ's poor, the least of his brethren spoken of with fondness in the gospels. Thus, the lepers were the objects of the good works of the Christian community, as well as exemplars of Christian poverty and communalism. They were expected to pray, to work if sufficiently able-bodied, and to live chastely if unmarried.[13] Chapter seven of the *cédula* also decreed that they live communally, sharing all goods and owning no private property.[14] In return for fulfilling these duties, like all other estates, the lepers of the San Lázaro received privileges. They were provided with such necessities as clothing and two meals a day. The doctor assigned to the San Lázaro was to care for the lepers with diligence, thinking of their honored position as Christ's beloved poor and placing their interests before his own honor and position as a physician.[15] For as stated in the *cédula*, if the Mosaic law merely isolated lepers to protect the community from contagion, the New Testament's ordinances decreed that the powerful and prosperous should provide for the weak.[16] In the preface to the edict, the Crown explicitly stated its mission to provide for the physical well-being of the spiritually weak Amerindians so they might better serve their creator and the divinely ordained terrestrial order.

Attempting to construct community under the most adverse conditions, the hospital was the preferred fortress from which to combat social disintegration. Alleviating the dissatisfaction of the poor with material relief was a safety valve against rebellion. In New Spain, Indians who lost the comfort of traditional community through the devastation of epidemics or the demands of encomenderos could flee to the hospitals as a refuge readily provided by some of their Spanish lords. According to Vasco de Quiroga, the Mexican pueblo-hospitals he founded were meant to use all their lands, rents, and endowments to benefit these impoverished Amerindians:

for the maintenance and indoctrination of spiritual as well as civic morality and the good *policía* of poor Indians and miserable persons—wards, widows, orphans and mestizos whom their mothers would have killed for not being able to raise them in their great poverty and misery.[17]

The establishment of New World hospitals was part of the Spanish attempt to correct disliked custom and behavior—even caring for the mestizo bastards of the conquistadores. On this point, the eighteenth-century biographer of Vasco de Quiroga, founder of two Mexican pueblo-hospitals, was quite clear. Don Vasco found his Indians in utter misery, "scattered, naked and so hungry," and he used his hospitals to teach them Christian doctrine, "civilizing them with social morality."[18] In the words of Don Vasco himself, the Indians required good police: "Everything transpired among them as among barbarous and ignorant people, scattered and without law, without having the order of good *policía*, which is all that I decree, and without which nothing, no human intercourse, can be well-ordered and without corruption."[19]

Hospitals provided some of the order requisite for such human social activities as economic production and exchange. During the *cocoliztle* epidemic of 1576, Viceroy Martín Enríquez (1568-1580) not only noted its devastation among the laboring population in general, and the mining population in particular; he linked discussion of the effects of epidemics to the discussion of commercial and agricultural matters, thus revealing the status of Indians, blacks, mestizos, and mulatos as economic units of production. The Crown necessarily had to support charitable hospitals in an attempt to combat the decimation of economic activity in the Indies. The Crown's Christian mission and economic interest were not mutually exclusive.[20]

THE ESTABLISHMENT OF HOSPITALS

The first attempt to subordinate Amerindians to these European institutions of *policía* was on the island of Hispaniola. In 1502 Isabella of Castile instructed Governor Nicolás de Ovando "to build hospitals where the poor can be housed and cured, whether Christians or Indians." By 1503 the governor had erected the Hospital of San Nicolás, soon to be followed by San Andrés in 1512.[21] Therefore, when Hernán Cortés founded the first general hospital in New Spain sometime before 1524, he had ample precedent. In accordance with the wishes of Queen Isabella, this Mexico City hospital, named Hospital de la Limpia y Pura Concepción de Nuestra Señora y Jesús Nazareno, was designed to care for both Spaniards and Indians. The common medical knowledge of the day was considered, and diseases thought to be contagious or dangerous, like "leprosy" and syphilis, were excluded from treatment at this general hospital.[22] Such a practice followed not only Toledo but also the pattern set in Seville, the port of departure for Cortés and so many conquistadores. There, one hospital was maintained for contagious diseases and another for noncontagious ones.

Cortés financed the first hospital in Mexico City out of his own personal wealth as a pious act of penance and charity. He provided for the hospital's initial endowment by donating a thousand ducats, and his will made elaborate arrangements for a permanent endowment, detailing which of his estates were to sustain the hospital and the type of staff that the hospital was to maintain.[23] In this task he was joined by a number of his fellow conquistadores, and together they established a *cofradía* to supervise the management of the hospital's estates and rents. Private charity was the chief source of hospital support, but individual donors like Cortés were complemented by royal support. Portions of church revenues and tithes granted the Crown through the *patronato real* were often channeled to the support of hospitals, along with subsidies derived from Indian tribute and profits from royal pharmacies and monopolies.[24] However, support from an indebted Crown could often be hesitant, and sometimes nonexistent.

As early as the 1530s Fray Gerónimo de Mendieta noted that the Crown authorized the construction of the Hospital Real de San José de los Naturales (to be staffed by Mexico City's Franciscan friars)—its expressed purpose to care for Indians.[25] Due to lack of initial royal support, its doors were soon closed, even though the Crown continued to support the founding of hospitals in royal discourse. On October 7, 1541, Charles V ordered "that Hospitals be founded in all the Cities of Spaniards and Indians . . . where the sick poor will be cured and Christian charity will be exercised."[26] Responding to this and to the persistent complaints of viceroys, bishops and audiencias, Philip II issued a 1556 *cédula* that expanded and rebuilt the Hospital Real de San José.[27] The royal coffers provided an initial sum of two thousand pesos and an additional annual rent of four hundred pesos.[28] With eight wards, the establishment accomodated more than two hundred poor and destitute Amerindians. Five chaplains, two physicians, two surgeons, and various apprentices served as staff. In 1587 an order of Viceroy Villamanrique expanded the institution's support by having each Indian town of New Spain provide the

Hospital Real with one *hanega* of maize out of every one hundred tributary *hanegas* collected.[29] This was the *medio real de hospital*, allowing the monarchy to care for the "Crown's poor" with the poor's own resources. It eventually became a standard clause in the instructions of provincial governors.

Elsewhere, Franciscans and Augustinians ran other hospitals exclusively for Indians, and the Tlaxcalan Hospital de la Encarnación was joined by the Michoacan hospitals of Tiripetio (1537), Uruapan (1561), Taximaroa (1580), San Martín Turundero (1595), Cuitzeo (1550), Periban (1541), and Tarecuato (1541). All were supported by the contributions of Indian *cofradías* and community chests.[30]

Hospitals proliferated in the sixteenth-century Hispanic world, and by the beginning of the seventeenth century there were approximately 128 hospitals in New Spain, strategically located in the *cabeceras* and most densely populated areas.[31] There were 12 hospitals in the area surrounding Mexico City, 72 in Michoacan, and 9 in Colima in the far west. Royal questionnaires on the progress of the New World possessions asked about the existence and status of hospitals for Europeans and Indians. In 1604 the Council of the Indies, for example, requested information from New World *cabildos* on the number and types of hospitals in any given area, their origin and income, and the salaries of the permanent staff. The Crown was also interested in the number of patients the American hospitals could accomodate and whether their capacity to perform good works had grown or diminished since their particular founding dates.[32]

In response, New World *cabildos* provided more or less detailed information, even if it was to report the absence of hospitals, as in the case of towns under the jurisdiction of Pánuco, ten leagues from Tampico.[33] *Cabildos* in towns like Nuestra Señora de los Çacatecas and Nombre de Dios related their prosperity and charity by describing their hospitals. Çacatecas readily identified itself as a healthful city with little need for a hospital, but it still possessed two: the Spanish hospital of Veracruz and the Indian institution of San Francisco. Founded by a Spaniard named Diego Hernández de Silva, Veracruz had no lands, rents, or incomes other than charitable donations. The Indian hospital was administered by Franciscans and only four years old, but Veracruz was a full thirty years old.[34] In Nueva Viscaya, Nombre de Dios reported one desegregated Hospital de la Caridad with an income derived from landed rents and annuities, but without any patients.[35]

For better or worse, many hospitals functioned without physicians, since there were few licensed professionals in New Spain. In 1545 there was one fully licensed physician in Mexico City, but between 1607 and 1643 six different physicians, six surgeons, three bonesetters, and eight druggists were paid to serve the public by the capital's *cabildo*. The paucity of physicians remained chronic: "Between 1607 and 1738 the University of Mexico conferred 438 bachelors' degrees in medicine, an average of 3.35 a year."[36] Mexican hospitals were to be charitable institutions occasionally visited by a physician. Proliferating rapidly, with variable financing, they often proved to be social and medical experiments of questionable success.

As the sixteenth century progressed in New Spain, hospital segregation came to mirror the segregation of the republics of Spaniards and Indians both inside and outside the Valley of Mexico.[37] Hospitals became a testing ground of the degree to which Spanish and Amerindian cultures would integrate. San José de los Naturales was reserved for Amerindians, whereas other hospitals like the Hospital de San Juan de Dios, founded in the 1530s and also known as the Hospital of the Love of God, cared only for Spaniards suffering from syphilis. A 1572 *cédula* approved the establishment of a hospital to care specifically for mulatos.[38] Whereas some institutions chose to treat only one of the races, or *castas*, others continued to be established in accordance with Isabella's demands that they fully serve both whites and Indians. As late as 1580, a few hospitals, like that of Xalapa de la Veracruz, halfway between the port of Veracruz and Mexico City, treated "Spanish passengers who come from Spain with the flotillas" as well as "the Indians who sicken in their service as porters and drivers."[39] More typically, Amerindians resorted to their own hospitals and *curanderos*, who were far more available than physicians and surgeons certified in Spanish medicine. In this they paralleled the large *morisco* subculture present in sixteenth-century Valencia and Aragon.[40] Indeed, not all Spanish physicians would treat Indians, and during the smallpox epidemic of the 1540s only Pedro de la Torre, a self-trained Spanish healer, dared to treat sick Indians and blacks in Mexico City.[41] Indian communities learned to care for their own poor and sick by means of the charity of lay brotherhoods called *cofradías* and the produce of communal lands managed by town *cabildos*. For times of hardship, the magistrates of the *cabildo* kept communal funds in designated *cajas de comunidad*. The brotherhoods, or *cofradías*, venerated the cult of a particular patron saint, while retaining a portion of communal produce to be used for good works, and Amerindian communities retained a degree of affiliation that aided them to survive the devastations of conquest and pestilence.

Rather than depending on irregular donations and endowments from prosperous Spaniards, Amerindian communities retained their own autonomy through the local management of poor relief and hospital funds, a communitarian mission with antecedents in pre-Columbian times.[42] Ironically, Spaniards saw Amerindian enthusiasm for hospitals as a sign of the sincerity of their conversion. The maintenance of a hospital was a work by which the faith of a *cofradía* was known, and the Crown's Council of the Indies was actively interested in the existence of *cajas de comunidad*, requesting information on their activities in the *relaciones* of local *cabildos*.[43] Action in the material world revealed spiritual motivation:

And as God grants them new grace each day, and as they come to learn God's law, and this same God being charity and love, they who once sacrificed men now in many places build hospitals where they console and cure the sick and poor. In spite of giving so little, of many small donations, constantly given, a large sum is amassed in such a way that the hospitals are well-provided, and they who know how to serve so well that it appears they were born for this lack nothing, and now and then go in search of the sick throughout the province.[44]

Motolinía, the author of the above passage, went on to describe the maintenance of an Indian hospital, the Hospital de la Encarnación, founded in the city of Tlaxcala in 1536. In this hospital, 130 of the indigent sick were treated and maintained by the generous gifts of their fellow Indians. On Easter Sunday of that year, the Tlaxcalans donated maize, beans, turkeys, and European sheep and pigs. The offerings were so steady that seven months later the hospital's endowment was already worth a thousand pesos in land and livestock.[45]

Despite their proliferation, the actual medical benefits of the hospitals to Amerindian populations is debatable. Racked by European diseases such as smallpox in 1520 and measles in 1530, Mexican Indian populations decreased as European and indigenous medicine proved impotent in the face of mass epidemics. If the estimates of Borah and Cook are accurate, epidemic and pandemic disease reduced the population of central Mexico from approximately 25 million on the eve of the conquest to 16.8 million in 1523.[46] European hospitals, upon which the New World hospitals were patterned, tried to isolate diseases thought to be contagious from noncontagious patients, but the most basic elements of modern hygiene were ignored. Visiting Spanish physicians and surgeons failed to wash hands and implements as they traveled from patient to patient, firmly believing that bad air, not actual contact, transmitted disease. In the Toledan Hospital of Tavera between 1559 and 1649, the average percentage of mortality was 16.4, but years of epidemic sickness and grain shortage witnessed much higher rates: 26.7 in 1595, 30.2 in 1598, and 28.7 in 1600. The Toledan hospitals were well organized enough to respond to the periodic subsistence crises that struck the city, but they could not hold famine and disease at bay indefinitely.[47] In the Americas,

whether removing the sick to hospitals decreased the spread of disease among the remaining population remains unclear. Nevertheless, the comfort, rest, and nourishment given to those hospitalized probably saved many lives by improving their nutrition and resistance to disease. Above all, hospital care for the Indians bolstered morale in times of hunger and despair, abuse and pain.[48]

Hospitals for the Indians occasionally even became the sites of social experimentation, places where society's sins and ills would be cured once and for all. Thus, Vasco de Quiroga (1477?-1565), a judge of the second Mexican Audiencia, hoped to ameliorate the abuses suffered by the Indians at the hands of their Spanish encomenderos. Influenced by Thomas More's *Utopia*, he advocated the reconstitution and purification of society, using the Amerindians as virgin raw material. To the benefit of their bodies and souls, the Amerindians were to learn Christian doctrine and productive labor.[49] His plans called for the creation of isolated Indian pueblos consisting of six thousand extended families of ten to sixteen married couples of the same lineage.[50] Christian morality would be supervised by the friars and lay Spaniards in charge of the facilities, while the biological epidemics so devastating to the Indian community would be combated at a hospital for contagious diseases. The hospital was to be administered by a superintendent or *mayordomo*, a *dispensero* or full-time dispenser of first aid, a physician, a surgeon, and an apothecary.[51] Having gained royal approval, Quiroga actually started a crusade to construct these utopias with the founding, near the capital, of the Hospital de Santa Fe de México in 1531. In 1534 the founding of a more celebrated pueblo, the Hospital de Santa Fe de la Laguna, near Lake Pátzcuaro, followed. Both settlements were populated with young, acculturated Indians who had been raised in Spanish monasteries, and with poor, orphaned, dislocated and sick Amerindians who had suffered from epidemics and the exploitation of encomenderos. Quiroga's work attracted both royal and private support, and he was rewarded in 1536 by being appointed bishop of the new diocese of Michoacan. In short, his public display of benevolence was duly rewarded by his rise in the hierarchy.

In 1580, some fifteen years after his death, his pueblo hospitals still existed, although the total number of inhabitants had declined steadily. At about that time Santa Fe de México reported approximately 120 families, while Santa Fe de la Laguna reported 100. Still, the experiments were successful enough to attract rich endowments and the envy of powerful authorities. In 1572 the urban magistrates of Mexico City tried to take over the administration of Santa Fe de México on the grounds that Quiroga's will was not being followed and that the hospital had cared for only a handful of sick inhabitants and a few nonresidents in the preceding months of that year. The Council of the Indies rejected this argument, but it is clear that Quiroga's hospitals were far more successful at converting and educating the Indians to the fine points of artisanal crafts and social police in Christendom than they were at the provision of health care, necessarily limited as they were by the knowledge of that time.[52]

Despite the inadequacies of health care, it must be reiterated that many powerful Spaniards continued to see the hospital's mission as social, religious, and medical. In his ordinances of 1573 Juan de Ovando, president of the Council of the Indies, reconfirmed royal policy by decreeing that general hospitals for noncontagious diseases were to be located near the central plaza, whereas hospitals specializing in contagious illnesses were to be placed on the outskirts of town, "in a place where no hurtful wind passing it can injure the remaining population."[53] Prompted by the Hippocratic notion that miasma, or bad airs, caused disease, the *Ordenanzas Ovandinas* stressed that health factors be taken into account when sites were selected for towns or other habitations. Above all else, disease-bringing winds were to be avoided.[54]

The hospital for the poor and noncontagious sick is to be placed near the Church, and set apart from it; for the contagious sick, build a hospital in a place where no hurtful wind passing it can injure the remaining population; and if you were to construct it in an elevated place, it would be better.[55]

Finally, the marqués de Villamanrique, viceroy of New Spain from 1585 to 1590, reasserted that hospitals were to provide physical care and spiritual comfort to poor Amerindians and Spaniards alike. Like Charles earlier in the century, he cited the Crown's special role as combating those selfish interests which would defraud hospitals of their endowments, and in a series of ordinances for the convalescent hospitals of Mexico City, he specifically demanded the maintenance of clear and precise account books to eliminate the opportunity for fraud. He also emphasized that hospitals were called to provide the blessed sacrament to the dying and isolate contagious patients from other sufferers. Therefore, as late as 1587 Philip II and his royal deputies attempted to respect the words and works of Isabella and Charles V before them.[56]

In fact, if anything, the hospital proved to be a matrix of binaries, reflecting the complexities of innate human tendencies and the learned cultural interface with those tendencies. Despite its very real claims to being a cultural expression of innate human tendencies toward altruism, the hospital was also an expression of tendencies toward hierarchy and the need for reciprocity in human relationships. It was a place where the indigent were cared for in a charitable fashion, but it was also another means by which the wealthy and powerful could display their preeminence and hierarchical status in a very public fashion. To the present, hospital wings will indeed often bear the names of their benefactors, honoring the memory of those who have served their community in this fashion. It should not surprise us that in an era when the hospital was associated with religion and poor relief as well as health care, Hernán Cortés founded one on the site where he first met Moctezuma. The Hospital de Jesús Nazareno spoke to the benevolent and religious intentions he wished his own Spanish culture to see in his conquest of the Mexica and their empire. As on so many other occasions, Cortés was displaying. Just like Yeroen at the Arnhem Zoo, the fact that he distributed benefits was intrisically important, whether those benefits be measured in oak leaves for chimpanzee subordinates or bread for poor humans. A hospital displayed just who was on top and why subordinates should bear to tolerate the existence of hierarchy. More importantly, hospitals also reinforced what humans call ethical behavior by providing very public rewards to their founders and benefactors.

According to the groundbreaking work of Jean Piaget, it is through a series of social interactions that the child abandons initial egocentricity. At first the child cannot take the viewpoints and interests of others into account. The world is virtually equated with the child's interests, consciousness, and ego. Through repeated social interactions, the child learns that there are other wills extant in the universe and that they cannot be controlled by the child's desires. In short, the child must take other actors into account when making decisions. Herein lies the origin of human ethics, rooted in certain innate ways of seeing the world that construct the human intellect.[57] The Piagetian Lawrence Kohlberg has delineated six sequential stages of ethical reasoning, from dependence on external sanctions and controls to the internalization of ethical standards. At the very start of ethical development, the avoidance of punishment and the desire for reward stand foremost. Throughout the centuries this tendency has been replicated again and again by that form of religious, moral behavior that relies entirely on ethical choices made to attain heaven and avoid eternal damnation. Out of this may arise implicit conformity and dutifulness, based on an internalized sense of guilt. Eventually, contracts and laws may be recognized as arbitrary but necessary to the maintenance of the common good. A final stage is attained when positive law may be recognized as harmful, all this being judged by a completely internalized process called conscience.[58]

Before conscience asserts a role, culture reinforces whatever innate tendencies humans may have toward kindness and reciprocity. At the heart of the matter, kindness seems to be most naturally displayed toward kin. Thus, primate mothers normally care for their offspring with great affection and interest. At Gombe, Jane Goodall has noted a tendency toward adoption among siblings, with young males serving as efficient caretakers upon the death of a mother. Thus, Prof cared for his four-year-old brother Pax when their mother Passion died.[59] To go beyond these immediate ties is unusual among primates, and it appears that human culture has taught "other-orientation" by various means of approval and disapproval. Being recognized as "good" by the cultural standards of one's society or religion has no doubt reinforced the construction of hospitals and the granting of justice and charity by elites. Still, it goes without saying that some unique individuals may consistently let their consciences serve as guides. Only this could explain some of the actions taken by individuals like Vasco de Quiroga and Bartolomé de las Casas.

In fact, this last stage, the development of conscience, is extremely difficult, if not impossible, to gauge from surface actions alone. Suffice it to say that

the historical development of tribes and states has shown, however, that man's ability to identify sympathetically with other members of the ingroup on the basis of an extended family ethos preadapts him to identify with members of an anonymous society, provided that these are characterized by many features in common.[60]

Of course, such behavior is easiest among small groups like those maintained by the !Kung Bushmen. Still, it is noted by anthropologists that sanctions to maintain appropriate reciprocity are continuously enforced and reinforced. On a larger scale, relatedness has to be maintained by shared ideologies or cosmic visions. Thus, Amerindians used the European hospital to coalesce in the midst of devastation. At their best, religion and the secular ideologies of the Enlightenment tradition do this when they speak of universal brotherhood. At their worst, religion and secular ideologies can exacerbate "tribal" tensions by arguing for the necessity of eliminating dangerous outsiders—love and hate perhaps being the most basic of all human binaries.

The hospital was to be one place where Spaniards and Amerindians were to learn just how closely they were related in the Spanish scheme of things superimposed through conquest. The hospital was yet another place to express Spanish hierarchy, but it was also a place of reciprocity, altruism, and fraternity in the midst of human suffering. Tendencies toward segregation and desegregation were equally expressed.

MEDICINE IN THE HOSPITALS

Created to fulfill the social welfare obligations of Christians and to display benevolence, hospitals became sites where medical technique received the attention necessary to foster the improvement of humane conditions for the indigent sick.[61] As such, they often served as empirical counterweights to a theoretical medicine steeped in the Hippocratic and Galenic corpus. In the New World, the adoption of Amerindian medical practices and medicinal plants assisted in the general sixteenth- and seventeenth-century undermining of traditional scientific discourse.

The medicine taught at early modern universities was based primarily upon the Hippocratic corpus, the works of Galen, Aristotelian science, and Arabic commentaries on these ancient sources. The individual human body was seen as a microcosmic reproduction of a greater cosmos composed of the traditional elements of earth, air, fire, and water. The qualities of heat, wetness, cold, and dryness found in the four elements were also found in the composite humors, or vital fluids, of the human body. Blood, intrinsically hot and wet, had qualities analogous to the element air; yellow bile, hot and dry, was comparable to fire; black bile was perceived as dry and cold like earth; and phlegm was compared to water in being wet and cold. Bodily health was a balance of the four humors, and the healthy diet was a balance of hot, cold, wet, and dry foods—of meat, grains, vegetables, milk products, and fruits. Illness was caused by the ascendancy of one humor at the expense of the others.[62] In political and social organization, God had decreed that the estates of man were to work together for the common good. In medicine, the humors were perceived as working in unison for the common good of the organism. Science, as well as political and social organization, was thus shaped by religious metaphor.[63]

This obviously interfered with the individual's ability to pursue questions and inquiries regardless of the consequences to religious belief, yet it is itself an understandable cultural development. Religion counterbalances the dissolving power of high individual intelligence according to Edward O. Wilson, as extrapolated from the work of Henri Bergson and others. Religion certifies something as beyond question in such a way that the individual, impressed by the rituals, power, and traditions of religion, "is ready to reassert allegiance to his tribe and family, perform charities, consecrate his life, leave for the hunt, join the battle, die for God and country."[64] Many humans seek paradigms and indoctrination by which to guide their behavior. Religion provides these things. In the context of the sixteenth-century Spanish hospital, this meant that charities would be performed for the "least of Christ's brethren," but it also meant that medicine was confined by religious parameters.

The writings of sixteenth-century European medicine traditionally paid homage to man's place within the divine cosmic plan. Often it was argued that the best way and time to heal individuals could be read in the stars, some physicians and astrologers writing that God's created harmony was so detailed that the celestial order and individual humans experienced empathetic and predictable patterns of development.[65] The universe was so ordered that if God had created a poison or venomous animal, he also surely provided an antidote in the immediate vicinity of that threat. Sixteenth-century Spaniards thus saw themselves as part of their environment. They understood that environment to include wheat and cattle for the body's nourishment, and Christianity and police for the soul's sustenance. They also preferred it to resemble the wide open plains and plateaus of Castile and the Valley of Mexico. Tropical and humid regions, and those regions with salty soil, were to be avoided for a number of reasons: Wheat did not grow in such areas; cattle died; and Hippocratic medicine taught, on the basis of its experience, that diseases flourished. The Hippocratic corpus itself argued that colonies were to be avoided in these places, since hot and wet climates produced "bad air" or miasma. Such climates could cause all sorts of fevers and imbalances in the humors, and endemic and epidemic disease could lead to social instability.[66] The *cabildo* of San Estéban de Pánuco confirmed this view by reporting a normally hot climate in which north winds brought colds, fevers, coughs, and all sorts of pulmonary ailments.[67]

Always small in number, the first licensed Spanish doctors in the New World were well versed in the traditional texts and quite unprepared to face the challenge of medical practices and medicinal plants that did not fit into Old World categories. Their first reaction, like that of the conquistadores and royal bureaucrats, was to defend their worldview and the paradigmatic procedures in which they were trained. For many of them, "in spite of the adoption of native remedies, the medical system brought over from Europe remained intact."[68]

In this sense, it was quite fitting that the first medical work published in New Spain was an erudite, Latin recapitulation of classical and Islamic medicine. Francisco Bravo's *Opera Medicinalia* (1570) served the function of introducing the accepted medical canon to Mexico. Although interested in the nature and properties of New World flora like sarsaparilla, Bravo focused on such topics as the Hippocratic doctrines of critical days and on miasmatic exhalations as the cause of disease in the Valley of Mexico.[69]

Just as epicycles were used by astronomers to explain the retrograde motion of the planets relative to a stationary earth in the Ptolemaic system, so too doctors tried to understand New World medicinal practices and plants by means of older categories and paradigms.[70] Fairly early on, however, medical writers began to argue that some New World plants and practices were far more efficacious than those of Europe. In their desire to heal by means of the case study, the ultimate aim of the entire Hippocratic corpus, doctors, and those nonprofessionals interested in medicine were sometimes more willing to accept novelty than other Europeans. They began to admit that some things in the Americas could not be made to fit into the Hippocratic and Galenic discourses and that some Amerindian practices were far superior to European ones. Likewise, Ortiz de Montellano and other anthropologists have shown how indigenous *curanderos* borrowed from European traditions without abandoning their Mesoamerican roots. Cultural syncretism flourished.[71] Without being fully conscious of it, European and Amerindian healers were undermining the traditional Judaeo-Christian and Greco-Roman cosmos.

Just as Cortés admired Mexican architecture and certain aspects of Amerindian social development, so too he was more than willing to use indigenous medicine when it seemed effective and no European alternatives were at hand.[72] However, as soon as the time came for settling his New Spain, he turned to Spanish methods of organizing health care, the hospital being the primary case in point. Aztec medicine nonetheless found its advocates, and friars like Motolinía and Sahagún were among the first to praise its benefits in print:

They have their physicians, experienced *naturales* who know how to apply many herbs and medicines, which suffice for them; and there are some among them of such experience that many ancient and grave illnesses, which have caused Spaniards to suffer without cure for countless years, are cured by them.[73]

Using the same basic principles as the Hippocratic appeal to medicine based on experience, Motolinía judged Aztec medicine superior to European medicine in certain areas. In fact, the Aztecs had some very real skill where the setting of bones and the treatment of wounds were concerned. They used both traction and countertraction in bonesetting, while salves of maguey sap, rather than cauterization, were used to heal wounds.[74] Given tales of Aztec success, the empirical underpinnings of the Hippocratic and Galenic methods would lead Spanish physicians and surgeons to strain at the boundaries of their traditional cosmology and its practices.

By the 1570s, only fifty years after the conquest of Mexico, the Crown was quite ready to foster empirical research in medicine. The years 1565-1574 saw the publication of the three volumes of Nicolás Monardes's *Historia medicinal*. These books presented detailed descriptions of the medical value of various New World plants and herbs, as well as the healing qualities of snow and the bezoar stones produced in the bladders of American animals. Monardes used the general structure of a Galenic catalogue of medicinal plants to discuss plants Galen had never known. His own knowledge of the plants came from his thirty-year use of them as a practicing physician in Seville, the port of entry for American goods. In an introductory statement by King Philip II, his original two volumes were granted a six-year monopoly on the "sale" of information regarding the medicinal value of plants and animals in the Indies. Thus, royal approval was given for this work, which went on to popularize the curative powers of guaiacum, tobacco, and sarsaparilla.

Monardes began his first book with a description of the Western Indies as incredibly rich, yielding new lands, new precious stones and metals, and new medical cures for Spain and the whole world.[75] He perceived the New World as new, but the ancient philosopher Aristotle made it possible for him to accept the possibility of completely new regions with flora never before seen by Europeans: "As the Philosopher says, all lands do not have the same plants and fruits, and one region or land bears certain trees, plants and fruits which another does not bear."[76] Among these plants peculiar to the Americas were guaiacum, sarsaparilla, and tobacco. Both guaiacum and sarsaparilla were praised by Monardes for their efficacy in treating syphilis (las bubas). Like Motolinía and Sahagún, the Sevillan physician not only lionized New World medicinal plants; he also praised the effectiveness of Amerindian medical practice, writing, "Since a Spaniard suffered great pain from syphilis given to him by an Indian, the Indian who was of the physicians of that land gave him Guayacan water (i.e., guaiacum), which not only stopped the pain which he suffered, but cured him of the evil."[77]

Monardes accepted the scientific assumptions of his day. If God had created such a deadly disease as syphilis among the Amerindians, he also necessarily must have provided those same Indians with the cure. A benevolent God was not expected to abandon the human race to utter misery, and Amerindians were definitely fully human in Monardes's estimation, although he wavered between viewing them as equals and interpreting their cultures as barbaric. At times he described their doctors as knowledgeable fellow practitioners of the medical arts, yet on occasion he referred to Amerindians in general as "these barbarous peoples."[78]

The Indians especially were praised for their use of tobacco to treat head ailments, asthma, and fatigue. Monardes compared the sot weed to opium in its ability to relax its users euphorically after a hard day's work. As a result, he prescribed the drug for both encomienda Indians and African slaves, thereby blurring the distinctions between the practice of public health and that of social control.[79] Of course, twentieth-century science has proven tobacco to be a poison, not a panacea, and has refuted the efficacy of guaiacum and sarsaparilla in curing syphilis. Still, Monardes stood at the cutting edge of scientific investigation in his day by presenting a series of case histories and experimental results to argue for the benefits of new drugs not found in the Hippocratic-Galenic canon. In this fashion he stepped outside the accepted circle of definition and interpretation, even though his conclusions were often erroneous and the organizational structure of his Historia medicinal was patterned on the traditional medieval catalogue of medicinal plants and herbs. Monardes had new, tangible drugs with which to experiment, not fabulous tales from Pliny. He may have described all new American drugs in terms of the Galenic qualities of dryness, wetness, heat, and cold, but above all else he claimed the primacy of the empirical evidence in case studies. He knew that sarsaparilla was an effective treatment for syphilis and other diseases because he had used it effectively in sixteen years of medical practice.[80] His perception and his claim were his reality, and together with Paracelsus, Old World surgeons and other early moderns, he helped to discard old medieval paradigms by bringing new remedies and techniques into the old hegemonic discourse. New wine eventually would rupture the old wine skins. A New World demanded new interpretation.[81]

Always searching for practical results and opportunities to extend its power, the sixteenth-century Spanish Crown and its American officials took part in promoting the broadening of medical knowledge, just as they actively supported the reform of poor relief, that other facet of the hospital. Medicine was perceived as a "social science," since it involved the health of the public. For the Crown, regulation of the common good necessarily included regulation of medical practice. Thus, the *Ordenanzas Ovandinas* (1570-1573) and the 1604 questionnaire sent out by the conde de Lemus asked for a description of the most common illnesses in the Americas and of the local herbs, roots, and minerals by which they could be cured.[82] A few *corregidores* and *cabildos* were happy to comply with this request. Pánuco, for example, mentioned the Indian use of chili, hot honey, and sarsaparilla to cure pulmonary illnesses, but other *cabildos* remained silent on this specialized matter, and some individuals, like Xonotla's *corregidor*, Jhoan Gonçales, admitted their ignorance.[83] Of Indian herbal cures, Gonçales wrote, "And they cure themselves with many herbs that they raise in the mountains and crags; of the names, I can not recall since they are very different from the herbs of Spain."[84]

For Gonçales, a man of no medical training, New World herbs and cures may have been hopelessly different from those of Spain, but for trained physicians and surgeons the New World was formulated carefully within the confines of Old World constructs. This was true of the mental categories by which physicians and surgeons first came to understand the New World, but it was also true of their institutional and professional organization. Aztec healers found their professional preeminence displaced as medical practice in New Spain was organized along lines similar to those established in Castile, the New World yet again being perceived as a *tabula rasa* waiting to have a perfected vision of Spain inscribed upon it.

To the chagrin of the most prejudicial among Spaniards, Mexico had its own healing tradition before the conquest. The role of the Nahua *ticitl*, or healer, offended many Spanish perceptions concerning religion and gender roles.[85] As in Spain, healing involved prayer—in this case, to the Aztec gods. There were also both male and female healers. If Spaniards were to express their dominance as the distributors of benevolence from their hospitals, they would have to eliminate Nahua elements that challenged their own prejudicial cultural assumptions. Prayers to Aztec deities associated with healing and healing by women were direct affronts to a Spanish elite vision of something called "New Spain." However, the real lack of a prevalent Spanish medical presence in the countryside would allow for the continuance of pre-Columbian healing traditions among men and women whom Spaniards called *curanderos* and *curanderas*.

Within the social hierarchy described by the *Florentine Codex*, the *ticitl*, or physician, may be a woman skilled in herbs, roots, trees, and stones: "[She is] one who has [the result of] examinations; she is a woman of experience, of trust, of professional skill: a counselor."[86] A real medical professional who took observation into account, the female physician set bones and cut growths from the eyes. The codex contrasts her to her evil counterpart, a witch who "kills people with medications" and has "a friction-loving vulva."[87] One cannot be absolutely certain to what extent Sahagún's Nahuatl interlocutors were influenced by the characteristics commonly ascribed witches by European clerics—characteristics that included lasciviousness and the use of poisons. These stereotypes were central to the definition of witches in the *Malleus maleficarum*, the fifteenth-century work so often reissued as a guide to witch hunters.[88] After the Spanish invasion, Nahua women who persisted in trying to maintain the tradition of female healers would be attacked as superstitious *curanderas* and witches by male Spanish "shamans." Cultural transmission by women would not always be easy in the midst of Spanish biases, and Nahua women who healed were prime targets for prejudicial priests.

To the prejudicial parish priest of Atenango in the early seventeenth century, Hernando Ruiz de Alarcón, it became the task of those well versed in secular and ecclesiastical law to seek out "fraud" and "corruption" hiding behind a Christian façade. In a treatise he wrote to this effect, he made much of female healers.[89] His targets included Isabel María of Temimiltzinco, who "cured" with spells and needle prickings; Magdalena Juana of Tepequaquilco, who treated urinary ailments; and Ysabel Luisa of the Mazatec nation, who tended fevers.[90] Like female healers among the *moriscos* in Spain, these women readily crossed the boundaries between the natural and the supernatural, taking up roles assigned to male medical men and priests by Spanish authority.[91] In the village of Iguala, the *ticitl* Mariana reported that she learned to heal from her sister, who in turn claimed to have learned magical healing from an angel while under the influence of the hallucinogenic *ololiuhqui*.[92] During her mystical experiences, the sister was subjected to astral crucifixion, and Ruiz de Alarcón denounced the claim as a diabolical perversion of the "true" faith. Surprisingly, he failed to note that the mystical crucifixion smacked of Nahua traditions of autosacrifice. He also failed to mention that supernatural visitations abounded in European popular mysticism and in the ecclesiastically approved visions of St. Teresa of Avila.[93] Truly, Mariana's world of magic paralleled Ruiz de Alarcón's world of sacraments, but it did so without his sanction or that of other male clerics and elites. Even in Spain, this lack of patriarchal clerical approval was often the major determinant in distinguishing between a female heretic and a female saint.[94]

Male authorities of the church, university, and educated bureaucracy retained the privilege of distinguishing categories of legitimacy and illegitimacy. Ruiz de Alarcón, in fact, felt a clear obligation to identify the *curandera* with illicit magic. Although magic and religion played their roles in both Spanish and Nahua healing, practical experience and practical cures persisted among *curanderas* and *curanderos* alike. Even after the Spanish conquest, the Nahua *ticitl* continued to use splints for bone fractures and effective, nerve-numbing copal to deaden the pain of toothache.[95] Of 118 different medical applications for various plants in Nahua healing, approximately 60 percent show some form of desired biochemical or physical activity according to the anthropologist Ortiz de Montellano.[96] Given European medicine's bleeding cures and phantasmagoric belief in miasmas, or bad airs, as the cause of contagion, Nahua healers were not so much superstitious savages as they were proponents of a rival cosmology. In the end, the hospital was still a place of prayer, and the *ticitl* was a cultural, religious, and political opponent. Spanish medicine men took from the Nahuas where they deemed fit, and Spanish hospitals would also set the pace for the all-important distribution of aid and comfort to the poor and sick. The issue of control stood foremost in any struggle that existed between Spanish authority and Nahua tradition, and despite the Amerindians' official exemption from the jurisdiction of the Holy Office of the Inquisition in 1571, Noemí Quezada has identified thirteen Amerindians among the Inquisition's proceedings against seventy-one healers from 1613 to 1806.[97] In the Americas, Nahua healers were more typically placed under the jurisdiction of the provisor (i.e., vicar general) of each diocese or archdiocese.[98] Although harrassed by Spanish officials and punished with beatings and other forms of discipline falling short of the stake, most native healers probably went about their business with little interference, given the lack of a Spanish presence in much of the Indian countryside. Today, anthropologists like López Austin and Ortiz de Montellano find distinct remnants of Nahua healing traditions in Mexican folk medicine as a result.[99]

In 1525 the municipal magistrates of Mexico City appointed the barber-surgeon Francisco de Soto the first *protomédico* of New Spain. His task, similar to that of Castilian *protomédicos*, was to regulate medical practice, to grant licenses to practitioners, and to maintain and improve public health. However, it was limited in application and scope to those who sought out Spanish medicine—to Spaniards for the most part. Interestingly enough, it is known that mestizos, mulatos, blacks, and Spaniards, in addition to Amerindians, sought out indigenous physicians. The recognized offices of Spanish healing were increasingly given the honors attached to dominance, but they did not necessarily dominate in the practical, applied art of healing. The challenge to a closed worldview was obvious, but the lines of Spanish authority persisted.

In 1527 the *licenciado* Pero López assumed the position of *protomédico*, and with its inception the Audiencia of Mexico assumed control of the *protomedicato*.[100] The sponsor of an alchemical laboratory in his own palace, Philip II placed the capstone on royal supervision of medicine in New Spain in 1571 by appointing one of his own court physicians, Francisco Hernández (1517-1587), as a special *protomédico* with powers to study all plants of medicinal value in the colony. Hernández was also to direct medical examinations and issue licenses, but only with the approval of Mexico City's Audiencia. Soon learning that the Audiencia was quite unwilling to allow him to issue licenses in lieu of the *protomédicos* it had appointed, he turned all his attention to the experimental and exploratory aspects of his mission.[101]

Around 1574 Hernández visited the Hospital de Santa Cruz, established in 1569 at Huaxtepec by Bernardino Alvarez. The physicians at the hospital used native plants to treat a variety of diseases, including syphilis, and Hernández used his experience there to write his *Nova Plantarvm, Animalivm Mexicanorvm Historia*. Like Monardes, he explained Aztec medicine in terms of humoral pathology and was openly critical of the indigenous healers' inability to use European medical discourse. Hernández found great value in the American flora and fauna, but value was determined in European terms for European benefit.[102] Born near Toledo, commissioned by the Spanish Crown, and representative of Spanish culture, Hernández had great difficulty in accepting Indian medicinal practice on its own terms. Like Monardes, he could accept innovation only within the terms of his training and categories of understanding.[103]

Physicians and surgeons with a lifetime of experience in New Spain were more capable of combining Spanish and Amerindian knowledge. Martín de la Cruz, an Indian physician who was a teacher at the Imperial College of Santa Cruz of Tlaltelolco, composed an Aztec herbal in 1552. This herbal has come to be known as the Vatican Library's Badianus Manuscript, its pages preserving Aztec herbal pharmaceutical treatments in the original Nahuatl and in Juan Badiano's Latin translation.[104] In turn, the work of another longtime resident of New Spain and recipient of a Mexican doctorate, the Spanish physician-turned-friar Agustín Farfán recommended native plants as substitutes for scarce European pharmaceuticals. In his *Tractado brebe de anathomia y chirurgia* (1579) and its revision, *Tractado brebe de medicina* (1592), Farfán prescribed approximately sixty indigenous drugs, including pulverized avocado pits as an antidiarrheic; chili, vanilla, and rhubarb as purgatives; hot chocolate as a laxative; copal as an astringent resin; and sarsaparilla as a diaphoretic. He was actively interested in devising effective daily cures. For those with weak stomachs he prescribed a diet of light meats such as chicken and goat, fresh eggs and warm cinnamon-flavored water in place of wine. Of course, guaiacum appeared as the cure for syphilis.[105]

Farfán's willingness to explore and experiment was rooted firmly in the case study method of Hippocratic medicine, but his enthusiasm for the new could also lead to the gradual deterioration of the accepted norms of ancient European biology and medicine, as new observations challenged the conclusions reached by the original Greco-Roman empiricism.

In two other works published in sixteenth-century Mexico City, the experience of the clinic began to challenge accepted theories. These were the barber-surgeon Alonso López de Hinojosos's *Suma y recopilación de cirugía* (1578) and the physician Juan de Cárdenas's *Primera parte de los problemas y secretos marauillosos de las Indias* (1591). With López de Hinojosos and Cárdenas, Mexican medical books began to reflect the process and growth of the clinical experience in medicine. This included the observation of case studies, the performance of autopsies and detailed diagnoses, and the experimental use of new drugs. It was medical empiricism based on sensory observation and the interpretation of that observation.

Employed as a barber-surgeon and phlebotomist at both the Hospital Real de los Naturales and the Hospital de la Concepción de Nuestra Señora, López de Hinojosos based his surgical treatise in large part on the medieval works of Guy de Chauliac, but he deplored the use of medieval medical jargon. He wrote in simple Spanish so that his work would be of use to those who lived in isolated areas, and he engaged in a number of autopsies under the direction of Francisco Hernández to determine the cause of the *cocoliztle* epidemic of 1576. In addition to a European theriac containing opiates, alcohol, and some fifty other compounds, López prescribed such Indian remedies as *coanenepilli*, a root with antispasmodic and antimalarial properties. Joining the Jesuits as a brother in 1585, López's 1578 treatise strikes the contemporary reader with the religiosity of some of its language. When discussing the *cocoliztle* of 1576, for example, López casually noted that the Archbishop of Mexico City cared more for the salvation of the Indians than for their bodily health. Medicine definitely played a secondary and subordinate role here.[106]

Still, some in Spanish medical practice cautiously took the new into account, despite the overall reliance on dogma. Disease-ridden airs, the traditional miasma, still appeared as the cause of both endemic diseases and epidemics in Juan de Cárdenas's work.[107] The good doctor took time to explore the medicinal benefits of new plants such as cacao and chili peppers, but he did so within the confines of humoral pathology.[108] Like Monardes, he argued for the benefits of tobacco, extending the argument to coca in a chapter entitled "Why Coca and Tobacco, When Taken Orally, Give Strength and Sustenance to the Body."[109] More importantly however, Cárdenas was exceptional in posing a direct challenge to miasmatic causality—one of which he was not fully aware, given his general acceptance of that theory.

In discussing baldness among Indians and Spaniards in the New World, Cárdenas cited several diseases traceable to miasmas as causes, but he also listed other environmental factors and causes not linked to bad airs. Among Spaniards, hair loss could result from "the contagious evil of syphilis," which was recognized as a result of sexual intercourse.[110] Among Amerindians, however, a lack of abundant facial hair was linked to "seminal reasons" found in the engendering male parent:

Turning to the second question on the problem of the cause of beardlessness, or the sparseness of beards among Indians, I respond that the growth of a beard is an accident like color that follows the semblance to one's parents, that is to say, that just as a black father naturally generates a black son, and a white a white son, likewise is the growth of a beard, that if the father is smooth-skinned and without a beard, like the Indian is, so too is the son . . . and they will be so in any province of the world where they should live, and this is because they are, since birth, without a beard.[111]

According to Cárdenas, then, Indians are born "beardless" as a result of a property or accident intrinsically linked to their nature as Indians. A change of environment would not change the Indian's beardlessness. Cárdenas's observations led him to approach the veil behind which the principles of genetics were hidden. While Paracelsus used occult language to try to capture the newness of his medical hypotheses, Cárdenas resorted to old Aristotelian terms like "accident" to describe dependent characteristics.

As illustrated by Luis Alcañiz's *Regiment de la pestilencia* (ca. 1490), a proper diet was accepted readily as an appropriate means to combat disease. Cárdenas took this commonly held notion and boldly dared to expand its impact in the realm of public health. Not only did he see poor diet as contributing to baldness among Spaniards;[112] he saw it as an important contributing factor to the shorter life expectancy of Spaniards in the Americas. After acknowledging that violence, disease, and the hot, humid climates of the Indies were major factors in the early deaths of Spaniards, Cárdenas went on to attack the nutritional value of American foodstuffs, arguing that Europeans could only grow weak on a diet of American foods. Unfortunately, Cárdenas failed to list the foods to which he was referring, and the reader is left to wonder if he wrote of native American foods like maize or of all foodstuffs, including European plants and cattle, raised in a New World environment.[113] The conquistadores and friars craved European grains and proteins. Cárdenas believed that a European diet would maintain the health of Europeans. Along with the ideals of religion and politics, the Spaniards were determined to maintain the roots of their sustaining material culture. Over the centuries, they had created their cultural values, and by the sixteenth century, they were products of this culture. Their very bodies, individual and social, were crafted by their cultural norms in sickness and in health.

CONCLUSION

Learning can be both an aid and a detriment in the evolution of the human animal. Benevolence can be inculcated and learned through the prism of religion, yet paradigmatic dogmas can interfere with human acceptance of reality. Learning occurs through symbols and models that pattern themselves on physical nature, but sometimes those signs and paradigms are accepted as reality itself. As a result of this, sixteenth-century Spanish medical men were confined by biblical and Greco-Roman paradigms. They were also confined by the dominant male's desire to retain control over the public distribution of benefits, and here they were joined by Spanish priests who were concerned with the Nahuas' use of a pre-Columbian cosmology in their healing practices. Spaniards on all sides wished to control charitable and medical discourse. They saw it as a right granted them by their dominance.

However, it must always be remembered that alpha males among the chimpanzees do not control all situations.[114] Likewise, the tale of politics at the top is not the whole story in human history. Although Spaniards established their rulership in numerous ways, they could never hope to control every action undertaken by subordinated Amerindians. Thus, Amerindians, finding what was similar to their own practices in Spanish culture, adopted the hospital, *cofradía*, and *caja de comunidad* to protect themselves. Given a lack of Spanish physicians and a desire to salvage as much of their culture as possible, they continued their own healing traditions in the face of Spanish prejudice. Not only were their practices quite capable by sixteenth-century standards; they also allowed for female physicians, when such healers in Europe were being deemed witches by the elite. In having female physicians, the Nahuas were actually much closer to a natural pattern where "mother" means comfort and care in times of need. Spaniards, on the other hand, had culturally adapted the hospital and the healing profession to serve as a form of male display by means of benevolence. Still, such a display is not to be taken lightly, since males do not necessarily seek to display first and perform benevolence only as an afterthought. The two are intrinsically intertwined in such a way that doctors are judged and ranked according to their care and concern, as well as their knowledge. Thus, a self-trained physician, an accepted male *curandero*, like Pedro de la Torre could build a reputation by his actions—actions that included caring for Amerindians and Africans when no one else would. By 1568 he was a *protomédico*, despite his lack of a truly verifiable diploma.[115] Rather than being a handicap, like his lack of formal training, his care and concern proved to be a benefit accrued by a willingness to display benevolence among contagious individuals who were deemed inferior in Spanish hierarchical thought. Other Spaniards praised him for this, for his practical medical skill, and for treating the poor for free.[116] Likewise, Vasco de Quiroga did not know that he would become Bishop of Michoacan as a result of his hospital-building activities. Male benevolence can be quite real, but it is often jealously guarded by a male elite. Whereas women like Doña María de Herrera, the founder of an important hospital in Avila, can learn to play the male game, men often enough wish to control a set of complex rules. Any male elite in possession of the power both to make the rules and then play by the rules they have made is in possession of an undue advantage. Even when those rules express a degree of paternalistic benevolence—as in those set by the Spanish law code explored in chapter 7—it can never be forgotten that subordinates are usually not allowed to participate in the rule making. When subordinates are not heard in rule making, then there is no "ideal speech situation." Even the most benevolent of paternalists assumes his subordinate to be a child. Adult Nahuas seeking medical assistance and poor relief were not children, and Spaniards could have learned a great deal more than they did from Nahua physicians, including *curanderas*, had they not listened so selectively through the filter of their own models and paradigms.

NOTES

1. W. C. McGrew, *Chimpanzee Material Culture: Implications for Human Evolution* (Cambridge: Cambridge University Press, 1992), 114. Also see 106-15 in the same

volume; and J. Patrick Gray, *Primate Sociobiology* (New Haven, CT: HRAF Press, 1985), 53-65.

2. Glynn Isaac, "The Food-Sharing Behavior of Protohuman Hominids," in *Human Ancestors: Readings from Scientific American*, intro. by Glynn Isaac and Richard E. F. Leakey (San Francisco: W. H. Freeman, 1979), 110-23.

3. McGrew, 115.

4. "Real cédula para que . . . sean bien curados y gobernados los pobres al Hospital de San Lázaro de México de la Nueva España. Lisboa, 11 de junio de 1582," *Ordenanzas del Hospital de San Lázaro de México*, ed. France V. Scholes and Eleanor B. Adams (Mexico City: José Porrúa e hijos, 1956), 15. Also Archivo General de Indias, *Cartas y expedientes de los virreyes de Nueva España* (Seville: Centro Nacional de Microfilm, 1975), reel 2, number 31-A. Henceforth *AGI*. All translations, except where indicated, are my own.

The first San Lázaro was founded between 1521 and 1524 by Hernán Cortés and was defunct by the 1530s. See Josefina Muriel, *Hospitales de la Nueva España*, 2 vols. (Mexico City: Editorial Jus, 1956-1960), 1:49-50.

5. Thus, "The Cortes of Valladolid of 1538, just three years after Spanish medical law had been extended to America, enjoined the doctor to keep in mind the cure of the soul, for even the cure of the body sometimes required it." John Tate Lanning, *The Royal Protomedicato: The Regulation of the Medical Professions in the Spanish Empire*, ed. John Jay TePaske (Durham, NC: Duke University Press, 1985), 201.

For a discussion of the hospital's use in the acculturation of the Indians of New Spain, see Cecilia Barba, "Un acercamiento a la metología de colonización: la primitiva obra hospitalaria de los franciscanos en la Nueva España," in *The Church and Society in Latin America*, ed. Jeffrey A. Cole (New Orleans: Tulane University Press, 1984), 53-71.

6. De la Torre was fined a hundred pesos, whereas López was never interrogated. Richard E. Greenleaf, *The Mexican Inquisition of the Sixteenth Century* (Albuquerque: University of New Mexico Press, 1969), 103-7.

Ironically, the nonuniversity-trained de la Torre appeared once again in the records of New Spain, replacing Agustín Farfán as *protomédico* after the latter had become a friar in 1568. John Tate Lanning, *Pedro de la Torre: Doctor to Conquerors* (Baton Rouge: Louisiana State University Press, 1974), 100-101.

7. Pedro de Alcocer, *Hystoria, o descripcion de la imperial cibdad de Toledo* (Toledo: Juan Ferrer, 1554), 118[b], in Hispanic Culture Series, *Hispanic Books Printed before 1601*, Reel 33. Henceforth *HCS*.

8. Ibid., 119[a].

9. Ibid., 120[b].

10. Jodi Bilinkoff, *The Avila of Saint Teresa: Religious Reform in a Sixteenth-Century City* (Ithaca, NY, and London: Cornell University Press, 1989), 43, 60.

11. Linda Martz, *Poverty and Welfare in Habsburg Spain: The Example of Toledo* (Cambridge: Cambridge University Press, 1983), 19-21, 32-34, 70-72, 64.

12. Here the term "leper" is being used in its sixteenth-century sense to signify anyone with a skin disease thought to be leprosy and contagious. This could include syphilis.

13. "Real cédula . . ., 11 de junio de 1582," *Ordenanzas del Hospital de San Lázaro*, 21-22, 27-28.

14. Ibid., 23-24, 37-39.

15. Ibid., 25.

16. Ibid., 16-17.

17. Vasco de Quiroga, *Información en derecho del lic. Quiroga sobre algunas provisiones del Real Consejo de Indias*, in *Don Vasco de Quiroga: Documentos*, ed. Rafael Aguayo Spencer (Mexico City: Editorial Polis, 1939), 276.

18. Juan José Moreno, *Fragmentos de la vida y virtudes del v. ilmo. y rmo. Sr. Dr. D. Vasco de Quiroga*, in *Quiroga: Documentos*, 29-30. Also see Quiroga, *Información*, in *Quiroga: Documentos*, 389-90.

19. Quiroga, *Información*, in *Quiroga: Documentos*, 343.

20. "Carta al rey de Martín Enríquez, virrey de Nueva España, 6 de diciembre de 1580," *AGI*, reel 2, number 30.

21. Muriel, 1:34.

22. Ibid., 1:37-48.

23. "Descripción. Hospitales de la Ciudad de México (16 Henero 1570)," in *Papeles de Nueva España*, ed. Francisco del Paso y Troncoso, 7 vols. (Madrid: Sucesores de Rivadeneyra, 1905), 3:23. Henceforth *PNE*. Also Gordon Schendel et al., *Medicine in Mexico: From Aztec Herbs to Betatrons* (Austin and London: University of Texas Press, 1968), 90; Muriel, 1:40-43.

24. Guenter B. Risse, "Medicine in New Spain," in *Medicine in the New World: New Spain, New France, and New England*, ed. Ronald L. Numbers (Knoxville: University of Tennessee Press, 1987), 37-38; Aristides A. Moll, *Aesculapius in Latin America* (Philadelphia and London: W. B. Saunders, 1944), 139; Martz, 81.

25. Gerónimo de Mendieta, *Historia eclesiástica indiana* (Mexico City: Editorial Porrúa, 1971), Bk. 4, chap. 30.

26. Cited in Schendel, 95.

27. Muriel, 1:115-30; "Carta al rey del arzobispo de México, sobre el patronato y administración del Hospital Real de aquella ciudad.—México, 31 de marzo de 1566," in *Epistolario de Nueva España, 1505-1818*, ed. Francisco del Paso y Troncoso, 16 vols. (Mexico City: José Porrúa e hijos, 1939-1940), 10:130-31.

28. "Descripción. Hospitales de la ciudad de Mexico," *PNE* 3:25.

29. 1 *hanega* = 1.5 bushels. "Carta al rey del Marqués de Villamanrique, 28 de abril de 1587," *AGI*, reel 3, numbers 11, 11-D.

30. Risse, 38-40; Woodrow Borah, "Social Welfare and Social Obligation in New Spain: A Tentative Argument," *University of California Center for Latin American Studies Reprint No. 282* (Berkeley, 1966), 54.

31. Risse, 41-42.

32. "Interrogatorio para todas las ciudades, villas y lugares . . . de las Indias Occidentales . . .," *Colección de documentos inéditos relativos al desubrimiento, conquista y organización de las antiguas posesiones españolas de América y Oceanía, sacados de los archivos del reino, y muy especialmente del de Indias*, ed. Joaquín F. Pacheco, Francisco de Cárdenas, and Luis Torres de Mendoza, 42 vols. (Madrid: Manuel Hernández, 1864-1884), 9:77. Henceforth *CDIR*.

33. "Descripción de los pueblos de la provincia de Pánuco (sin fecha)," *CDIR* 9:154. For some quick references to the existence or nonexistence of hospitals and their endowments, see *CDIR* 9:106-7, 125, 154, 191, 246, 346, 385, 451.

34. "Descripción de Nuestra Señora de los Çacatecas (1608)," *CDIR* 9:191.

35. "Descripción de la Villa de Nombre de Dios . . . en Mayo de 1608," *CDIR* 9:246-47; Muriel, 1:269-70.

36. Lanning, *Protomedicato*, 139, 32-33.

37. Schendel, 88-94.

38. "Descripción. Hospitales de la ciudad de México," *PNE* 3:23-25; "Real cédula de 23 de abril de 1572," *AGI*, reel 1, number 82.

39. "Relación de Xalapa de la Veracruz (20 Octubre, 1580)," *PNE* 5:105.

40. Risse, 51; Luis Garcia Ballester, *Historia social de la medicina en la España de los siglos XIII al XVI*, Vol. 1: *La minoría musulmana y morisca* (Madrid: Akal Editor, 1976), 74-75, 133, 182.

41. Greenleaf, 103-5; Lanning, *Pedro de la Torre*, 14-18.

42. Borah, "Social Welfare," 53; and Murdo J. MacLeod, "The Social and Economic Roles of Indian Cofradías in Colonial Chiapas," in *The Church and Society in Colonial Latin America*, 73-96.

43. "Interrogatorio para todas las ciudades, villas y lugares . . . de las Indias Occidentales," *CDIR* 9:62.

44. Fray Toribio de Benavente o Motolinía, *Memoriales o libro de las cosas de la Nueva España y de los naturales de ella*, ed. Edmundo O'Gorman (Mexico City: Universidad Nacional Autónoma de México, 1971), 159-60.

45. Ibid., 160.

46. Woodrow Borah and Sherburne F. Cook, "New Demographic Research on the Sixteenth Century in Mexico," in *Latin American History: Essays on Its Study and Teaching, 1898-1965*, ed. Howard F. Cline (Austin: University of Texas Press, 1967), 2:717-22.

Of course, these figures are hotly contested, although a sharp decline in the indigenous population is not. Estimates of the pre-Columbian population of the Western Hemisphere range from 8.4 million to 100 million, with Angel Rosenblat estimating a population of only 4 million for central Mexico on the eve of the conquest. See Angel Rosenblat, "The Population of Hispaniola at the Time of Columbus," in *The Native Population of the Americas in 1492*, ed. William M. Denevan (Madison: University of Wisconsin Press, 1976), 45. Also see Woodrow Borah's "Estimating the Unknown," 30 (in the same collection).

47. Martz, 219-22; Schendel, 96.

48. Risse, 42.

49. Quiroga, "Reglas y ordenanzas para el gobierno de los hospitales de Santa Fe de México y Michoacán," in *Quiroga: Documentos*, 250-52.

50. Ibid., 258-59.

51. Ibid., 262-63.

52. Ibid., 40-41; Fintan B. Warren, *Vasco de Quiroga and His Pueblo-Hospitals of Santa Fe* (Washington, DC: Academy of American Franciscan History, 1963); and Silvio Zavala, *La "Utopia" Tomás Moro en la Nueva España* (Mexico City: El Colegio Nacional, 1950).

53. "Ordenanzas de Su Magestad hechas para los nuevos descubrimientos, conquistas y pacificaciones. Julio de 1573," *CDIR*, 16:176.

54. Ibid., 153, 155.

55. Ibid., 176; Risse, 38; Schendel, 95.

56. "Carta al rey del Marqués de Villamanrique, 28 de abril de 1587," *AGI*, reel 3, numbers 11, 11-D. For more on Philip's support of hospital ventures, see David C. Goodman, *Power and Penury: Government, Technology and Science in Philip II's Spain* (Cambridge: Cambridge University Press, 1988), 209-15.

57. John L. Phillips, Jr., *The Origins of Intellect: Piaget's Theory*, 2nd ed. (San Francisco: W. H. Freeman, 1975), 73-74.

58. Edward O. Wilson, *Sociobiology: The New Synthesis* (Cambridge, MA: Belknap Press of Harvard University Press, 1975), 562-63; Lawrence Kohlberg, "Stage and Sequence: The Cognitive-Developmental Approach to Socialization," in *Handbook of Socialization Theory and Research*, ed. D. A. Goslin (Chicago: Rand McNally, 1969), 347-480; Anne Colby and Lawrence Kohlberg et al., *The Measurement of Moral Judgment*, Vol. 1: *Theoretical Foundations and Research Validation* (Cambridge: Cambridge University Press, 1987).

59. Jane Goodall, *Through a Window: My Thirty Years with the Chimpanzees of Gombe* (Boston: Houghton Mifflin, 1990), 197-99.

60. Irenäus Eibl-Eibesfeldt, *Human Ethology* (New York: Aldine de Gruyter, 1989), 713.

61. Risse, 42; Schendel, 87-88.

62. Juan de Cárdenas, *Primera Parte de los problemas y secretos marauillosos de las Indias* (Mexico City: Pedro Ocharte, 1591), 105-26, 175, in *HCS* Reel 27; Luys Alcanyis, *Regiment de la pestilencia* (Valencia: Nicholaus Spindeler, ca. 1490), HCS Reel 33; Juan de Avinón, *Seuillana medicina*, ed. Nicolás Monardes (Seville: Andrés de Burgos, 1545), xvi-xxii, *HCS* Reel 225; and Charles Singer and E. Ashworth Underwood, *A Short History of Medicine* (Oxford: Oxford University Press, 1962), 27-47.

63. Andrés Velásquez, *Libro de lo melancholia, en el qval se trata de la natvraleza desta enfermedad, assi llamada melancholia, y de sus causas y simptomas* (Seville: Hernando Díaz, 1585), 19ᵃ, *HCS* Reel 74.

64. Wilson, 561-62.

65. As late as 1607, this view was prevalent enough in Mexico City to warrant publication of Juan de Barrios's attack on the astrological notion of critical days for the healing of patients. Following a standard argument of the time, Barrios stated that the stars, planets, and airs might have some impact on human bodies, just as the moon influenced tides. However, such general astral and climatic influence could not be particularized in judicial astrology or the casting of individual horoscopes. See Juan de Barrios, *De la Verdadera Medicina, astrologia, y cirvgia* (Mexico City, 1607), 43ᵇ-52ᵃ, *HCS* Reel 333.

66. George Rosen, *A History of Public Health* (New York: MD Publications, 1958), 33-34, 70, 103-4.

67. "Descripción de la villa de Pánuco," *CDIR* 9:133, 136.

68. Risse, 52. For a detailed study of the manner in which theoretical paradigms determine experimentation in science, see Thomas S. Kuhn, *The Structure of Scientific Revolutions*, 2nd ed. (Chicago: University of Chicago Press, 1970).

69. Risse, 45.

70. Any system, like the Ptolemaic, with the earth as the center of the universe, runs into grave difficulties explaining the fact that a number of planets seemingly reverse their orbits around the earth. In fact, they are orbiting around the sun at a much slower rate than the earth, and our planet catches them and proceeds to pass them in their orbits. Epicycles literally had the planets going around in circles that were tangential to their orbit around the earth. This all proved to be a very complicated attempt to salvage an unworkable system, one that finally was surpassed by Copernican heliocentricism. See Marie Boas, *The Scientific Renaissance, 1450-1630* (New York: Harper & Brothers, 1962), 39-49.

71. Bernard Ortiz de Montellano, *Aztec Medicine, Health, and Nutrition* (New Brunswick, NJ, and London: Rutgers University Press, 1990), 193-94, 235.

72. Hernán Cortés, "Second Letter," in *The Letters from Mexico*, trans. Anthony Pagden (New Haven, CT, and London: Yale University Press, 1986), 142-44.

73. Motolinía, 160. Also see Bernardino de Sahagún, *Historia general de las cosas de Nueva España*, ed. Angel María Garibay K., 4 vols. (Mexico City: Editorial Porrúa, 1956), Libro Décimo, Cap. XIV. "Mujeres de baja condición," 3:129; Libro Decimo, Cap. XXVIII. "Enfermedades del cuerpo humano," 3:168-83.

74. The European practice of bleeding was avoided by the Aztecs, but they were nonetheless criticized for combining their empirical cures with "inappropriate" prayers to "demons." See Ortiz de Montellano, 172-74, 181-82; Bernardino de Sahagún, *Florentine Codex: General History of the Things of New Spain*, trans. Arthur J. O. Anderson and Charles E. Dibble, 13 vols. (Santa Fe and Salt Lake City: Monographs of the School of American Research/University of Utah Press, 1950-1982), Bk. 10, chap. 28, pp. 153, 161-62.

75. Nicolás Monardes, *Dos Libros, el vno que trata de todas las cosas que traen de nuestras Indias Occidentales, que siruen al uso de la medicina, y el otro que trata de la piedra bezaar, y de la yerua escuerçonera* (Seville: Hernando Díaz, 1569), Av[a], *HCS* Reel 225.

76. Ibid., Av[b].

77. Ibid., Dii[a].

78. Nicolás Monardes, *Segunda Parte del libro de las cosas que se traen de nuestras Indias Occidentales, que siruen al uso de medicina* (Seville: Alonso Escriuano, 1571), 23, *HCS* Reel 225.

79. Ibid., 7-23.

80. Monardes, *Dos Libros*, Fi[b].

81. Alfred W. Crosby, *The Columbian Exchange: Biological and Cultural Consequences of 1492* (Westport, CT: Greenwood Press, 1972), 9. For a discussion of how the boundaries of medical debate were also being questioned in the Old World, see Miriam Usher Chrisman, *Lay Culture, Learned Culture: Books and Social Change in Strasbourg, 1480-1599* (New Haven, CT, and London: Yale University Press, 1982), 170-81.

82. "Interrogatorio para todas las ciudades, villas y lugares . . . de las Indias Occidentales . . .," *CDIR* 9:67.

83. "Descripción de la villa de Pánuco (sin fecha)," *CDIR* 9:136. Also see "Relación de Cuzcatlan (26 Octubre, 1580)," *PNE* 5:52; "Relación de Ahuatlan y su partido (19-24 Agosto, 1581)," *PNE* 5:96; "Caueçera de Tetela, obispado de Tlaxcala (20-29 Octubre, 1581)," *PNE* 5:149; "Relación de Tetela y Ueyapan, obispado de México (20 junio, 1581)," *PNE* 6:288.

84. "Relación de Xonotla y Tetela (20-29 Octubre, 1581)," *PNE* 5:141.

85. Even in his Spanish summary of the *Florentine Codex*, Sahagún wrote of "*médicas*" who knew the healing properties of herbs, roots, trees, and stones. See Sahagún, *Historia general*, 3: 129.

86. *Florentine Codex*, Bk. 10, chap. 14, p. 53.

87. Ibid.

88. Julio Caro Baroja, "Witchcraft and Catholic Theology," in *Early Modern European Witchcraft: Centres and Peripheries*, ed. Bengt Ankarloo and Gustav Henningsen (Oxford: Clarendon Press of Oxford University Press, 1990), 30-31.

89. "Prologo," in Hernando Ruiz de Alarcón, *Tratado de las supersticiones y costumbres gentilicas que oy viuen entre los indios naturales desta Nueva España*, in *Tratado de las idolatrías, supersticiones, dioses, ritos, hechicerías y otras costumbres*

gentilicas de las razas aborígenes de México, ed. Francisco del Paso y Troncoso (Mexico City: Librería Navarro, 1953), 21-22. Also see Hernando Ruiz de Alarcón, *Treatise on the Heathen Superstitions That Today Live among the Indians Native to This New Spain, 1629*, trans. and ed. J. Richard Andrews and Ross Hassig (Norman: University of Oklahoma Press, 1984), 41; and the edition translated and edited by Michael D. Coe and Gordon Whittaker as *Aztec Sorcerors in Seventeenth Century Mexico: The Treatise on Superstitions by Hernando Ruiz de Alarcón* (Albany: Institute for Mesoamerican Studies, State University of New York at Albany, 1982), 61. Henceforth "P y T" will be used to identify the Spanish edition, "A-H" will identify the Andrews and Hassig edition, and "C-W" the Coe and Whittaker version.

90. "Tratado sexto, capítulos xxiv, xxviii y xxix." P y T, 166, 171, 172; A-H, 192-93, 198, 199; C-W, 273, 283, 285. Coe and Whittaker identify the passages differently: "Seventh Tract, chapters 21, 25 and 26."

91. Luis García Ballester, *Los Moriscos y la medicina: un capítulo de la medicina y la ciencia marginadas en la España del siglo XVI* (Barcelona: Editorial Labor, 1984); Mercedes García-Arenal, *Inquisición y moriscos: los procesos del tribunal de Cuenca* (Madrid: Siglo XXI de España Editores, 1983).

92. First Treatise, chap. 7. P y T, 52; A-H, 66-7; C-W, 94-95. *Ololiuhqui* is cactus-derived peyote of the *datura* family in potion form.

An old male *curandero*, Domingo Hernández of Tlaltiçapan (deemed a saint by Amerindians throughout Cuernavaca), also claimed to have received his healing gifts from a supernatural visitation—in this case the Virgin Mary, St. Veronica, and another woman. Ruiz de Alarcón, Sixth treatise, chap. 19. P y T, 157-58; A-H, 184-85. In the Coe and Whittaker edition, this tale is found in chapter 16 of the seventh tract, 259-60.

93. On Nahua autosacrifice, see Alfredo López Austin, *Cuerpo humano e ideología: las concepciones de los antiguos nahuas*, 2 vols. (Mexico City: Universidad Nacional Autónoma de México, 1980), 1:438-39. For Teresa's strategic compromises with male authority, see Alison Weber, *Teresa of Avila and the Rhetoric of Femininity* (Princeton, NJ: Princeton University Press, 1990), 40, 70-71, 121, 136-48.

94. Jodi Bilinkoff, "A Spanish Prophetess and Her Patrons: The Case of María de Santo Domingo," *The Sixteenth Century Journal* 23:1 (spring 1992): 21-34; Richard L. Kagan, "Politics, Prophecy, and the Inquisition in Late Sixteenth-Century Spain," in *Cultural Encounters: The Impact of the Inquisition in Spain and the New World*, ed. Mary Elizabeth Perry and Ann J. Cruz (Berkeley, Los Angeles, Oxford: University of California Press, 1991), 105-24.

95. Actually, *copalli* was a name applied to a variety of resins used in incense and for healing. Ruiz de Alarcón, Sixth treatise, chaps. 8 and 22. P y T, 147, 162-65; A-H, 172-73, 189-92. For the modern use of copalite sealant in dentistry today, see the "Editors' Introduction" in the Andrews and Hassig edition, 34. Also see their "Glossary of Nahuatlisms and Hispanisms," 310.

96. Ortiz de Montellano, 190-91.

97. Noemí Quezada, "The Inquisition's Repression of *Curanderos*," in *Cultural Encounters*, ed. Perry and Cruz, 39, 41-45.

98. Richard E. Greenleaf, "Historiography of the Mexican Inquisition: Evolution of Interpretations and Methodologies," in *Cultural Encounters*, 261-62.

99. López Austin, 1:33-34, 296-318; Ortiz de Montellano, 214-35.

100. This *licenciado* Pero López should not be confused with a second Dr. Pedro López who arrived in New Spain after 1548 and founded the hospitals of San Lázaro and Los Desamparados in the 1570s. Lanning, *Pedro de la Torre*, 18 n. 35.

101. Lanning, *Protomedicato*, 58-62.

102. Francisco Hernández, *Nova Plantarvm, Animalivm et Mineralivm Mexicanorvm Historia* (Rome: Sumptibus Blasij Deuersini, & Zanobij Masotti Bibliopolarum, 1651), 228, 247, *HCS* Reel 469. Also see Ortiz de Montellano, 25-29.

103. Risse, 29-31, 40, 44; Goodman, 234-38.

104. Schendel, 46.

105. Agustín Farfán, *Tractado brebe de medicina, y de todas las enfermedades* (Mexico City: Pedro Ocharte, 1592), 3^b-4^a, 87^a-89^b, 90^a-93^a, 161^a; Risse, 48-49.

106. Risse, 46-48.

107. Juan de Cárdenas, *Primera parte de los problemas y secretos marauillosos de las Indias* (Mexico City: Casa de Pedro Ocharte, 1591), 57-58, *HCS*, 27.

108. Ibid., 105-13, 124-26.

109. Ibid., 132-38.

110. Ibid., 185^b.

111. Ibid., 187^b-88^a.

112. Ibid., 185^b.

113. Ibid., 174^b-75^b.

114. Jane Goodall, *The Chimpanzees of Gombe: Patterns of Behavior* (Cambridge, MA: Belknap Press of Harvard University Press, 1986), 424.

115. Lanning, *Pedro de la Torre*, 100-101.

116. Ibid., 16-17.

9

Gender and the Creation of Mexico

Although the hospital in New Spain provided elite males in particular with a means of displaying benevolence, assuming leadership, and promoting cultural inculcation, these characteristics are necessarily more human than they are exclusively male. As a result, women in New Spain also demonstrated the universal human capacity for cultural construction by means of leadership and inculcation. They did this when the very public sixteenth-century male hierarchy ignored their functions and when male leaders were absent. During periodic breakdowns in male hierarchical and patriarchal behavior, women came to the fore, and when patriarchy banned women from the public arena, they worked in the shadows. Throughout all this, they spoke in a "voice" different from the hierarchical male voice already explored, but they also used available opportunities to adopt roles males tried to retain exclusively for themselves. Women are also quite capable of participating in hierarchical struggles involving males, yet there seem to be general observable tendencies toward female leadership in the midst of male hierarchical breakdown—toward female mediation in particularly difficult periods. Without a hierarchical system of justice, many men fall apart. Women's system of ethical decision making is still effective in the midst of cultural disarray.

Since the appearance of *In a Different Voice* in 1982, Carol Gilligan and her collaborators have emphasized the observable difference between the linguistic responses of males and females to moral issues.[1] Although Gilligan does not see the two different voices as necessarily biological in origin, she has argued that as they develop, boys and girls define morality in terms of hierarchical justice and empathetic care respectively. Whereas boys rank goods and evils, concentrating on what are perceived as duties, girls identify with the hurt, loneliness, and feelings of others found in difficult situations. Although initially her subjects were mostly middle-class New England children and adolescents, her more recent work has demonstrated nearly the same trends among lower-class, multiracial inner-city youth. Putting moral attitudes and tendencies into effect may be altered by environmental circumstances, but "universal moral constructs" are still evident to youths of low socioeconomic status. Likewise, "The hypothesis of a different voice, defined by a focus on care concerns and associated empirically with women, is born out across a variety of circumstances and settings."[2] Women in colonial Mexico empirically embodied Gilligan's "different voice," just as men in the public sphere spoke a language of hierarchical justice already observed in the previous pages.

The hierarchy of the Spanish conqueror was more concerned with destroying the hierarchy of the conquered Aztec than it was in interfering in domestic elements that could be used to set the Nahuas apart. Much of Amerindian culture was overlooked when it was not a threat to the power structure. Particularly the domain of women was overlooked, and they became a vehicle for Amerindian cultural survival. Amerindian female cultural resistance in the private sphere coexisted with the occasional public leadership of women, and La Malinche became an archetypal mediator of Spanish and Nahua cultures in the public arena. However, when a woman entered the public sphere as a mediator, she had to contend with Spanish male clerics, a special category of "neutered" male who attempted to reserve cultural mediation as an expression of their power and privilege. They, in turn, were in competition with their spiritual rivals: Amerindian female healers. Male, female, and neutral elements in both culture groupings thus all played their indispensable roles in redesigning a viable society. The intent of conquistadores may have been to create a "New Spain," but the Spanish Empire found an equal adversary; not in brute strength, since disease brought down the Aztec warrior, but in the permanence of universal social structures. In the end, Mexico became a wholly original cultural synthesis, different in customary particulars from either of the brutal empires that spawned it.

In the midst of brutality, sixteenth-century Mexico was fortunate to have some creative and stabilizing forces. They included Spanish members of the hierarchy like Antonio de Mendoza and the two Velasco viceroys, but they also included the *pipiltin* who learned to salvage Amerindian communalism by means of the *cofradía*, *cabildo*, *ejido*, and hospital. They included Cuauhtemoc, who through a resistance that would eventually cost him his life, gave Amerindian males a hero to turn to in their darkest moments. They included the rulers of Tlaxcala and Texcoco as well, for their choice to side with the Spaniards provided yet another means to Amerindian survival within a dominant Spanish culture. However, the cultural innovators also included the friars and priests who spoke of brotherhood and the women who effectively salvaged some of the most long-lasting of Mesoamerican cultural traditions. Cultural influence is not necessarily the domain of political or social leadership alone, but the response of leadership can give weight to either innovation or the status quo.

The work of Bartolomé de las Casas and other "defenders of the Indians" had made the achievements of Indian cultures and the shortcomings of Spanish culture quite apparent, but their tracts were not the only reality checks present by the end of the sixteenth century. The Castilian Crown itself, in its role as arbiter of societal disputes, had researched the condition of New Spain and other New World territories with exceptional thoroughness. From the first *relaciones* and viceregal reports to the *Ordenanzas Ovandinas* and their written responses, the Spanish monarchy had learned to accept New Spain and its other American possessions as subject to the same problems of corruption and dissension as Castile and Aragon. However, the Crown had also learned of cultural and customary differences between Spaniards and Amerindians, and of the way those differences could be used to create a system of checks and balances between overly ambitious conquerors and the conquered. If common Indians wished to continue to eat foods to which they were accustomed, this modicum of comfort could be allowed them. If their caciques wished to dress and eat like their conquerors, this could be allowed them as intermediaries between Spanish tributary demands and Indian execution of those demands. If local Amerindian communities wished to use *cofradías* and other Spanish methods of poor relief and religious observance to bolster Amerindian communalism, this too was permissible. Likewise, European demands for wheat and meat, churches and clothes, were met. The Crown learned to satisfy and dominate a hybrid culture by adapting its institutions and laws to it, but in its desire to dominate, the Crown could easily find room to rationalize and defend some of the most abhorrent practices. Spaniards were to use institutions like encomienda forced labor to teach the Indians to avoid "evil custom":

If, according to the quality, conditions and ability of the said Indians, the aforesaid religious or priests determine that it best serves God and the good of the said Indians that they be granted in encomienda to the Christians, then we order it so that they abandon their vices, especially homosexuality and the eating of human flesh, in order to be instructed and taught good customs and our Faith and Christian doctrine, in order to live in *policía*.[3]

As a conquering agent, building on the previous experience of the Reconquista, the Crown used its Christian worldview, a cultural creation, to explain brutal institutions of dominance like encomienda and even the Inquisition. In reality, the affiliative and tribal nature of religion typically leads to the creation of ingroups and outgroups. The Spanish Crown hoped to "let" Amerindians into Spanish society in a distinctly subordinate capacity, so it could then make Amerindians dependent on a paternalistic Crown for protection and use them as a distinct counterbalance to Spanish conquistadores and encomenderos. Given the confines of their culture, Spanish kings could also truly believe they were doing Amerindians a service at the same time. Such distinctions created division and justified the Crown's existence as the final arbiter of disputes and the most dominant of alpha males.

However, the Crown did not graft culturally determined definitions of jus-

tice onto hierarchical displays without a great deal of assistance from subordinate leaders, nor did it do so without taking economic and political circumstances into account. Appointed official "Defender of the Indians" at Charles
V's court, Bartolomé de las Casas, who had firsthand experience of New
World Spanish atrocities, consistently presented a case against encomienda
and its cruelties.[4] Rejecting the "just war" matrix as an excuse for enslaving
the Amerindians, the Crown's New Laws of 1542 were partially the result of
las Casas's direct influence on Charles V. His far-reaching defense of Indian
culture and customs led to the Crown's "problem-specific response," a gradu-
alist attempt to eliminate encomienda, which prospered as Amerindian populations declined and service and tributary allotments from forced labor lost their
value.[5] By the early seventeenth century, encomienda would be eliminated
from central Mexico, but this was directly related to the profitability of employing day-laborers for a fixed, minimal time. The Crown's moral attempt to
end forced labor was assisted by environmental conditions. Where conquests
persisted, as in New Mexico, encomienda in fact continued to be introduced in
the early stages of Spanish settlement.

While Spaniards at the pinnacle of the hierarchy were working to create
moral principles and regulations that would be applied according to rank,
Amerindian women were struggling to maintain reciprocity and benevolence at
the lower levels. In 1583 Amerindian officials of Tocuillan's *cabildo* granted a
woman named Ana, her husband, and her son the right to measure land for a
house site in this town under the jurisdiction of Texcoco. The archival document in which the tale is found is one of the many that James Lockhart
copiously gathered and analyzed for his groundbreaking *The Nahuas after the
Conquest*, and it is one that tells us much about a Nahua woman after the
Spanish ascendancy in Mexico. Like other Nahua women recorded in Spanish
documentation, it is Ana of Tocuillan who serves as spokesperson for her
family. Some Spanish officials saw this as an indication of inappropriateness in
Nahua culture, with women taking an active rather than a passive role, but
Lockhart is quick to point out that this "social convention" perhaps reflects on
the fact that it would have been a loss of honor for men "to ask for something."
Great respect is accorded Ana, and it must be noted that her older brother was
one of the *regidores* (i.e., magistrates) of the *cabildo*, but she is also quite
subordinate throughout the document, as noted by Lockhart: "Ana promises
obedience to her older brother as long as she is under his roof, and when the
elders come, Ana leaves the room while they eat the meal she has prepared for
them."[6] She weeps in gratitude when the men of the *cabildo* decide to grant her
the land she requests.

The case study of Ana is one of a woman acting within the cultural confines
of gender as ascribed by patriarchal male dominance. Ana must show subordination to gain her boon, providing food and serving the men who will make
the important decision. What Lockhart fails to recognize is that her request and
the means used to attain it reflect upon inherent ethological patterns and the
cultural exaggeration of those patterns. Providing food to her potential bene-

factors, Ana also begs in the tradition of innumerable chimpanzee females who beg meat of the males after a successful hunt. She accepts a submissive discourse and gender role, but she does so to gain benefits for her husband and her little son Juan. Ana begs to sustain her family and her home, using the means approved by a patriarchal regime. Whereas her husband may not have been willing to suffer a loss of prestige by begging, she altruistically subordinated herself to her family's needs as well as to her brother's *cabildo*. In doing this, Ana reflected the different voice of empathetic concern, a voice that places the needs of the other (in this case, her husband and son) before selfish pride. In the conquest of Mexico and the creation of New Spain, it was women who struggled to maintain the integrity of Nahua culture in the confines of the home. Ana, like so many other Amerindian women, made the tortillas and other indigenous foods that would survive the conquest. Nahua women made clothes with ancestry dating to pre-Columbian times, and they joined some of their menfolk as the healers and shamans who would salvage medicinal customs and religious practices dating to the years before the coming of Cortés.

Before efficient birth control women had very little choice in matters of maternity. That may help to explain the subordinate role generally played by women in the sixteenth century, for young children do demand a great deal of care and concern. However, it must also be noted that men dedicated a great deal of time to devising gender-biased rhetoric and institutions. As such, many women were confined to the domestic sphere, but this did not neutralize their influence as inculcators of culture. Mexican women alleviated some of the shock and disruption that followed the vying of two male coalitions for hierarchical supremacy. They preserved as well as innovated in matters of culture. On occasion, they even came to the fore to provide a type of cultural leadership in the public sphere.

It was in the domestic sphere, however, that Mesoamerican cultural practices in food and clothing would survive and even go on to influence and infiltrate Spanish customs in Mexico. Not only did women continue to use Mesoamerican metates (*metl* in Nahuatl) to make the maize tortillas used to identify people of Amerindian cultures; women continued to use the backstrap loom to weave cloth in a Mesoamerican fashion that persists to the present day. Much of the most successful cultural resistance discussed in previous chapters was spearheaded in the domestic sphere maintained by Ana and her fellow Amerindian women. This is not to say that men did not struggle for the maintenance of customs dear to them. To the present day, entire families have maintained the *temazcalli*, or sweathouse, of pre-Columbian Mesoamerica. But women made the *huipilli*, the upper garment that when combined with a skirt failed to offend Spanish modesty, while simultaneously continuing customs abandoned by men who by the late sixteenth century were increasingly adopting Spanish breeches and shirts. In the words of James Lockhart, "Women's clothing, as often in such situations in world history, was more conservative than men's . . . [and] given the frequency of reference to shirts, it is hard to agree with the remark of the late-sixteenth-century official and writer Gonzalo

Gómez de Cervantes that Indian men except for noblemen went naked save for 'a bandage' . . . and a cloak."[7]

At home women sustained cultural practices taught them by their mothers— the domestic sphere retaining some independence from Spanish influence. Pressure to conform to social divisions was applied, and wheat was more heavily taxed than maize, thereby making maize economically more attractive to Amerindians. However, it was also the case that Amerindians after the conquest described wheaten bread as sweet, but as also tasting like "the pith of a cornstalk." The tortilla was a traditional source of comfort in a public cultural sphere undergoing vast changes. It cannot be doubted that many Amerindians enjoyed their tortillas and traditional condiments, just as they sought effective new sources of protein in sheep and pigs. Interestingly, the *Florentine Codex* reports that pre-Columbian men sold meat and fish, whereas women sold hot maize, bean, fruit, or chili *atole* in the marketplace. Although there is some confusion of gender in the written texts, the illustrations show women as the sellers of *tamales* and tortillas; in contrast, postconquest Castilian wheat and meat sellers are clearly illustrated as males. In Oaxacan marketplaces of the 1960s, men continued to sell prestigious meat and wheaten bread, and women sold the maize and beans that have always been staples in Mexico.[8] In short, cultural compromise was to be effected in aspects of material culture, and here women played a major role and served as a type of control.

However, some women also entered the public sphere as leaders, and here they faced many of the same problems faced by Amerindian men. Women of property now had to adopt the Spanish will, and in the *cabildos* that appeared in Amerindian towns, female elders and nobles served as *cihuatepixque*, or officials who had some vaguely described jurisdiction over women and their activities.[9] Women appeared in courts and worked in the fields. In 1570-1573 Tula's *cofradía* of the Most Holy Sacrament even listed 264 female members and only 166 males.[10] In the public sphere, leading Amerindian women had to adapt to many Spanish customs, just as Amerindian noblemen raised wheat and drank wine; but interestingly, the public functions explored by such historians as S. L. Cline, James Lockhart, and Robert Haskett point to a real division of labor between the sexes. Cline finds that as in the *Florentine Codex*, documentation for colonial Culhuacan identifies a women's tools as those used in food preparation and cloth making. In Culhuacan, Simón Moxixicoa gave a hoe, an axe, and a metal-tipped digging stick to his son "'because he is male.'" A woman named María Salomé gave a substantial amount of land to her daughter in her will but then pondered, "'Because she is a female, how is she going to work it?'"[11] Women certainly helped in the fields, and Spaniards definitely confined men in the textile *obrajes*, but the fields were still seen as a man's provenance, whereas "food preparation was a woman's main job, literally a daily grind of preparing corn for cooking."[12] S. L. Cline writes, "In essence, biology was destiny, an aspect of Aztec culture not disturbed by the Spanish conquest."[13]

If women played a major role in the charitable works of Tula's *cofradía* of the Most Holy Sacrament, this was not far removed from the work demanded of them as mothers. Like Nahua women, Spanish women held land, and Isabella of Castile even reigned and ruled, but both Nahua and Spanish women alike received cultural roles that extrapolated on the earliest divisions of labor in communities of *Homo sapiens* hunters and gatherers. The *Florentine Codex* even notes that in pre-Columbian times, baby girls received the "equipment of women" during their naming ceremony: "the spinning whorl, the batten, the reed basket, the spinning tool, the skeins, the shuttle, her little skirt, her little shift."[14] Little boys received a little bow, arrows, and parched maize kernels, among other things. Girls were exhorted in life to "seize the broom" and to "look well to the drink, to the food."[15]

William Taylor has even argued in his *Drinking, Homicide, and Rebellion in Colonial Mexico* that Amerindian women were deemed liminal, or marginal, from the perspective of the male maintenance of public hierarchy and public order. As a result of this, some of their most public functions came during rebellions and in the sale of the intoxicating beverage *pulque*. Women appeared publicly in the midst of disorder, at least from a patriarchal perspective. In fact, Taylor notes that in the seventeenth and eighteenth centuries— centuries for which documentation survives—at least one fourth of the rebellions in central Mexico and Mixteca Alta involved Amerindian women as leaders or as visibly more aggressive than men.[16] This corresponds to comparable evidence concerning the involvement of French and Dutch women in bread and commons riots.[17] On the other hand, they were also much more frequently the victims of murder than they were ever murderers in colonial Mexico.[18] Without a doubt, colonial Mexican women were quite capable of acting publicly, but numerous factors (not least among them violent male behavior) prevented them from entering the public arena. If women were liminal, such status parallels observable patterns of behavior among our pongid cousins.

In a natural setting, chimpanzee females fail to form strong coalitions or pronounced hierarchies. They take advantage of their peripheral status to move from community to community, avoiding the intense hierarchical politics of more stationary males. This changes when chimpanzees are forced to adapt to a confined captive environment. Under such conditions, females groom each other, form coalitions, and in the absence of males, form true hierarchies with pronounced displays by the dominant female. Before the arrival of males at Frans de Waal's Arnhem colony, a female named Mama "performed charging displays as spectacular as those of any male. Dethroned by newly introduced males, Mama reconciled herself with her new position only after Moniek was born."[19] Motherhood provided consolation for Mama, but it is interesting to note that she continued to maintain strong ties with her dyadic partner "Gorilla." When males became too unruly during the period of de Waal's study, Mama and other females would still unite to control the male displays. Closer female-female relations seemingly develop in captivity, even giving rise to Amazon behavior in the absence of males. It is important to note that whereas political behavior in the wild tends to be dominated almost entirely by males, in the Taï Forest of the Ivory Coast females do support each other in coalitions and develop special friendship alliances.[20]

Chimpanzee females generally ignore chimpanzee politics in the wild, but they more readily engage in politics when confined. They learn and adapt, playing the male game when they cannot run away. Indeed, the all-consuming altruistic tasks of a mother may divert chimpanzee females from political activity, yet in the absence of pregnancy and childrearing, females perform with the males. At de Waal's Arnhem colony, a lesbian female named Puist spent much more time with the males than with other females. De Waal took special note of her mounting other females, while avoiding intercourse with males. She has successfully set males on other females, demonstrating a level influence in the male hierarchy. De Waal writes, "She is even compared to a witch."[21] At Gombe, the sterile female Gigi was noted for her sexual popularity with males (until irregularity developed in her periods) and for her persistent participation in male patrols: "Gigi's behavior is very like that of a male. She is large and strong for a female, and often aggressive. Her display rate is high. . . . She is assertive in her interactions with other community members, even on occasion standing up to attacks by adult males."[22]

Like women, chimpanzee females can readily engage in hierarchical activities, but on many occasions they wander at the peripheries of troops, avoiding the intensity of male hierarchical competition and coalition construction. Many chimpanzee females influence through the teaching role of the mother, but others have also come to the fore as leaders and even as mediators between troops. Here, biological sex plays its role, whereas among humans, the intertwining complexities of sex and culturally constructed gender must be taken into account.

On the shores of Lake Tanganyika, Jane Goodall has noted that the precise number of females in any one troop of chimpanzees is difficult to determine, writing in 1986 that "even today we seldom know the precise number of adolescent and adult females in our community in any given year. Some vanish for months at a time, only to reappear later."[23] This is because female chimpanzees travel between troops, emigrate to other troops, and sometimes establish themselves on the periphery of one troop. When females are in estrus and experiencing a sexual swelling in the genital region, neighboring males from another troop will be stimulated to sexual behavior, rather than aggressive territorial behavior. The swelling in fact serves as a signal to "*intercommunity* interactions," and Goodall writes, "We have observed no instances of brutal attacks on stranger *swollen* females at Gombe."[24] Likewise, although males will force sex on females, and force some into unwanted exclusive consortships for a time, sexually experienced, mature females have shown skill in controlling mating. In fact, among chimpanzees, high-ranking alpha males are never entirely successful at preventing females from copulating with lower ranking males and strangers. Although much research remains to be done in the area of chimpanzee sexual behavior, it is clear that through their interaction with many males, females help to promote the health of the genetic pool. They even mate with members of rival communities. At the Arnhem Zoo, captive chimpanzee females were also observed to form successful female coalitions in order to control aggressive male behavior. The captive females' coalitions do not seem to occur normally among females in a natural state, however; yet at the most basic of levels, chimpanzee females play a role in moderating male behavior and at maintaining intergroup and intragroup relations.[25]

During the actual conquest of Mexico, attempts at coalition building often included the granting of Amerindian women to Spanish strangers. Likewise, other human cultures offer strangers access to women of their own group as a sign of hospitality. Thus, sexual relations involving strangers has always served as a source of intercommunal bond building. Of course, this has often, if not usually, involved women who are forced into relations. In reality, they are raped, just as Romulus raped the Sabine women. Most horrifically, the rape may have been the idea of fathers acting as true patriarchs. It is quite true that female chimpanzees are sometimes forced into sexual relations against their will, but their sexual travels between communities are often at no male's behest. Human culture and learning, as in so many other areas, may in fact have exaggerated male dominance in ways well beyond the wiles of our own chimpanzee cousins. Yet with humans, as with chimpanzees, sex makes females the mediators between communities.

Although there can be no doubt that official interracial marriages were not common in colonial Latin America, they were not an impossibility. In reality, royal decrees that officeholders and encomenderos must be married only helped to encourage the interracial marriages that did occur in the earliest years of conquest and colonization. This was especially the case in that in the Indies, as late as 1560-1579 only 28.5 percent of the registered emigrants from Seville were Spanish women.[26] Unsurprisingly, in 1514, of the 146 married *vecinos* of Santo Domingo, 54 were married to Amerindian wives, and nearly all the founders of Santa Fe de Bogotá took Chibcha brides. Of course, as time went on and "more suitable" Spanish brides could be found, interracial marriage on the part of white males of the elite became virtually nonexistent, especially since "men could maintain illicit relations with women of lower socioethnic groups and avoid legal commitment." Nonetheless, sixteenth-century marriages between whites and women of Amerindian, African, or mixed ancestry have been estimated to fall between 10 and 15 percent.[27] In addition to this, illicit unions, from concubinage to rape, also added to the number of mestizos in the Americas and in New Spain. Mediation of the cultures and races occurred, and one means to this was sex, which involved women as both willing and violated participants. Implicit in patriarchy is the perception of a woman's body as something passive to be dressed and undressed, possessed and conquered, and in this capacity, where Mexican history is concerned, the prime example must be Malintzin, mistress to Cortés and wife to the Spaniard Juan Jaramillo.

Praised for her valor and intelligence by Bernal Díaz del Castillo, Malintzin has come to be seen as a traitor by many modern Mexicans. In fact, from the very start her life has served as a literary device, and Bernal Díaz himself hid the real woman behind the conventions of chivalric romance. When she meets the family that sold her into slavery among the Maya, she grants forgiveness for past wrongs in a manner akin to that of the biblical Joseph and the literary Amadís. Still, throughout the literary usage of her person, she is established as the translator who greatly facilitated the Spanish conquest. Disinherited by her family and her culture, Malintzin became Doña Marina, and in the words of Sandra Messinger Cypess:

For Bernal Díaz and Bernal Díaz's Marina, however, the end result is the important thing, that is, the assimilation by Marina of Spanish culture. Bernal Díaz presents her initiation into Spanish culture and its results all in one chapter as the appropriate context within which his readers may then place the subsequent deeds of Doña Marina as related in the following chapters.[28]

Ironically, although the name Malintzin may stand for the honored Malinalli, it may also be little more than a Nahuatl variant of her Spanish name Marina, especially since the Spanish *r* is often replaced by *l* in Nahuatl.[29] To those around her, both Spanish and Nahua, Malintzin was the cypher of cultural interaction and exchange on multiple levels. Whereas many present-day Chicana authors focus on what her enslavement and being used might have felt to her, others focus on her revealing the Cholulan plan to slaughter the Spaniards— even after she was promised a noble Cholulan husband to silence her. Cypess writes:

Her renunciation of the Amerindian male is perhaps the most serious of the charges that cling to her image; it becomes a metaphoric act signifying the repudiation of the native in favor of the foreign. Her role as mistress to Cortes and her marriage to Juan Jaramillo provide further substantiation of the paradigmatic behavior called *malinchismo* today.[30]

From the perspective of this study, Malintzin's renunciation of the Amerindian male was simply because all the cultural trappings associated with that male were quite meaningless to her. Amerindian and Spanish males had treated her as chattel. To Amerindian males, she was another Amerindian woman. To the Spaniards, she was a unique and valued translator and cultural mediator—a woman finally ascribed a position of importance in the public world of male hierarchies. In the hierarchical world of competition and coalition, Malintzin served as a bridge. Through her ability to communicate in Nahuatl, Maya, and Spanish, she was the source of the earliest intercommunal interaction in Mexico. Through the birth of her son, Martín, the officially recognized child of Hernán Cortés, she was mother of mestizos. Later, in 1526, she would have a daughter, Doña María Jaramillo, about one year before her premature death. Frances Karttunen puts it best, writing, "She had no people and nowhere to flee. Her best hope of survival was to accept whatever situation was assigned to her and to try to make herself useful and agreeable."[31] At the start of affairs leading to the destruction of the Aztec Empire, she was just another Amerindian woman given to the Spaniards by Amerindian men. By the end of the tale, Bernal Díaz described her as one of the men and brave like a man. A mediator between cultures in the midst of violence, Malintzin also demonstrated that women, of course, can play a role in the world of competition and hierarchy. However, that role may be somewhat different, and "the different voice" of Malintzin cries forth through the record of her forgiving the relatives who sold her into slavery. She dealt with the Spaniards because they presented her with opportunities never offered her before, and she could see very little real difference between the Spaniards and Amerindian men.

There is evidence that aside from aiding Cortés, Malintzin taught others to translate and also translated for the first friars to arrive in New Spain.[32] By engaging in the latter activity, she had direct contact with a group of Spanish men who wished to serve as bridges between the Spanish and Amerindian cultures of New Spain. On one level, many of these men were willing to seek out cultural similarities and human universals, but they were also tied to some very culturally specific "truths" that they were unwilling to abandon. To them, Christian revelation was the only true spirituality, although they often admitted that they could see the universal human quest for spirituality in the "false beliefs" of the Amerindians. A desire to interact and mediate would constantly exist in tension with a desire for spiritual conquest among the priests and brothers of New Spain. What many of the early priests and brothers brought, however, was a desire to ameliorate some aspects of male violence. Violence was more than permitted by these males to uphold the hierarchy of the Church, but it was to be divorced from its associations with sex.

Sixteenth-century Spanish clerics tried to sublimate and repress male desires for sex and power. Whereas Nahua lords had been honored with tribute and concubines, and Spanish conquistadores had taken Amerindian women, Spanish priests, at their best, tried to demonstrate that human males can be more than lascivious creatures of violence, desperately trying to perpetuate their genes through brutal competition. If Doña Marina could "become a man," Spanish priests aimed at adopting characteristics and tendencies that were generally ascribed to the female realm by their culture—characteristics and tendencies that world history and Carol Gilligan also demonstrate to be female tendencies. Spanish priests often spoke a language of care and concern, which grew out of the maternal images embedded in the New Testament Jesus—the suffering servant and sacrificial lamb of God who would suffer the little children to come unto him. The problematic twist was that male Spanish priests would never entirely lose a certain dedication to martial tendencies—to the violent, competitive, hierarchical tendencies found among male primates.

Perhaps the prime example here would be the founding of Ignatius of Loyola's *Compañía de Jesus* in 1540. Ignatius had been a warrior given to chivalric romances, and his *compañía* (as in military company) was a clear attempt to control his violent passions. The Jesuits were to report to captains and a Father General, yet they were to serve lepers, the poor, and young students. Setting the example himself by studying at the University of Paris as a mature man, Ignatius was to abandon the sword for the pen, and to leave the ladies of chivalric romance for the Virgin Mary.[33] But the Jesuits were to be "freebooting" males, with no subsidiary order of nuns, even though the sister of Philip II of Spain was allowed to become a Jesuit secretly referred to by a male codename. Likewise, violence was always looming in the background of Jesuit activity, and Ignatius himself made use of battlefield imagery in his *Spiritual Exercises*.[34] If anything, the Jesuits epitomized the "male-female" tension in Spanish priests, but it is exactly that tension that was important. If other Spanish males fully embraced the gore and violence of chivalry, of hierarchy and coalition construction, priests were somewhat ambivalent. The Inquisition was always there, but so too was Gilligan's language of empathetic care and concern, as found in Motolinía, Vasco de Quiroga, and Bartolomé de las Casas. It is that voice, functioning within the Spanish hierarchy, that ameliorated some aspects of conquest brutality, and that ability to seek the human and humane across cultural differences was initiated by Dona Marina's acts of translation, just as it would be continued by the priest Molina's Nahuatl dictionary as an aid to conversion.

Therein lies the tension. Many Spanish priests desired some cultural exchange, but they wished to control that exchange on their own terms. The sixteenth century was not an age of ecumenism, and if Sahagún could recognize a body politic among the Aztecs, it was still a "sick" body politic. In fact, many of the signs of health were directly related to hierarchy. Spanish priests jealously guarded their place as official mediators in the public hierarchy. As such, they opposed any attempts by Amerindian women to take their roles as mediators out of the home and into the public arena. As a result Spanish priests went to war with female *curanderas* as well as male *curanderos*.

Never published in his lifetime, Hernando Ruiz de Alarcón's *Tratado de las supersticiones desta Nueva España* was completed by 1629.[35] It aimed at bolstering a prejudicial and rationalized Christian theological order against the religious syncretism employed by Nahuas of central Mexico in an attempt to salvage aspects of their pre-Columbian culture. Nahua deities were interpreted as demons and any surviving religious customs were seen as the work of the Devil. Not all Spanish clerics were as harsh, but as early as 1614 Hernando had held illegal *autos de fe* in his parish of Atenango. Reports reached the offices of the Inquisition in Mexico City, and Ruiz de Alarcón himself was called into question, since inquisitorial practices like the full-fledged *auto de fe* were officially reserved for non-Amerindians. Ruiz de Alarcón's actions were beyond the bounds of the acceptable, but the Inquisition determined that he acted out of ignorance rather than malice. To channel his zeal, he was appointed an investigatory ecclesiastical judge in 1617: his explicit commission, to report instances of idolatry and syncretism to bishops and other noninquisitorial superiors with Amerindian jurisdiction. He took the task to heart, and his treatise for Archbishop Francisco Manso y Cúñiga resulted some twelve years later.[36]

To Ruiz de Alarcón, it became the task of those well versed in secular and ecclesiastical law to seek out "fraud" and "corruption" hiding behind a Christian façade.[37] As a result, his focus became oral tradition spells and healing practices. His targets included female healers, or *curanderas*, like Isabel María of Temimiltzinco, Magdalena Juana of Tepequaquilco, and Ysabel Luisa of the Mazatec nation.[38] Like popular healers in Europe, these women combined natural and magical practices, and they challenged this biased Spanish priest's claim to exclusive control of the religious realm. Like other abusive males, Ruiz de Alarcón had a control problem; the *curanderas*, for their part, were trying to salvage aspects of their own cultural traditions. A sixteenth-century culture war ensued, and Ruiz de Alarcón stopped at nothing to identify female healers and local wise women with the Devil. In discussing mythic claims to the supernatural death of a "*nahualli* witch," who according to Spanish sources used a cayman familiar to "do evil," Ruiz de Alarcón writes:

With this, everyone of the settlement said that the said woman had always been considered a *nahualli* witch. In view of what had taken place, what was always believed of her proved to be true, that the Devil had payed her in his own coin with the last of his evils, testing on her body the fire which he had prepared for her soul forever in Hell.[39]

Thus, Hernando Ruiz de Alarcón is not hesitant to cast his rival, the *curandera*, as the Devil's own. He is equally as harsh with male *curanderos*, but the important point is that here were Nahua women actively engaged in the semipublic defense of aspects of their pre-Columbian culture. As the hierarchical male religion of bloody conquest and sacrifice necessarily fell before the Spanish conquest, quieter and more durable aspects of the Mesoamerican cosmic vision were maintained by humble men and women at the village level. Human sacrifice at Tenochtitlan's Templo Mayor was an eminently public event associated with Aztec potency, but the healing arts could be maintained in the privacy of homes, representing a side of the deities and nature that reflected care and concern. Nahua women easily entered into this facet of Mesoamerican life, and as Spanish priests struggled to eliminate it by making it the public object of shame, they faced very successful *curandera* resistance. For although the old healing practices were syncretically blended with aspects of Christianity, they were never entirely eliminated, existing to this day in Mexico and Central America. In this, their survival parallels Irene Silverblatt's findings for the Andes, where indigenous women struggled to maintain the aspects of pre-Columbian religion not so directly associated with Inca imperialism and hierarchical structures.[40] As men who had been near the top of the pre-Columbian hierarchy tried to associate what they could with the new Spanish hierarchical game, women of the lower orders continued to heal and care, make tortillas and clothing, in adherence with traditional cultural patterns. And this has proven to be a substantial and long-lasting form of cultural resistance in the less violent realm that Fernand Braudel and other structuralist-inspired *Annaliste* historians have identified as the sphere of the *longue durée*—a sphere not as subject to the vicissitudes and disruptions of the more openly public and political aspects of culture.[41]

Like their rivals, the Spanish priests, *curanderas* provided an ethos of care and concern, a "different voice" in the midst of violence and conquest. This is not to say that they never cursed or practiced maleficient magic, but the priests were also quite capable of approving of torture, the whip, and the stake. At their best, however, both parties alleviated some of the harshness and brutality inherent in their world. This demonstrates that male tendencies to hierarchy and competition and female tendencies to care and concern need not be the exclusive property of males and females respectively. Although this study has primarily been concerned with males acting violently and reciprocally in the public sphere that is the arena of conquest, it also argues that much more work has to be done on what has historically eased the pain of conquest situations, for certainly the Amerindians of Mesoamerica have proven to be great survivors. On one front, this survival has been an aspect of the search for compromise and human universals that was enacted by both conquered and conquerors. On another, it has been the result of altruistic and mediating influences represented archetypically and biologically by the mother. From the perspective of human ethology, it cannot be forgotten that food-sharing, reciprocity, and altruism are skills eminently present in most mothers and taught by mothers. From the perspective of Mexican history, it cannot be forgotten that the patroness of Mexico, the veritable goddess of Mexico, is the dark-skinned Tonantzin, the Virgin of Guadalupe. In this imagery the work of those uncomfortable allies, the priests and *curanderas*, paradoxically met.

Among the higher primates, care and concern are most closely identified with the mother-child bond. Altruism, or behavior that benefits another with some cost to the altruist, is most commonly found in instances of offspring coming to the aid of mothers, and mothers coming to the aid of offspring. Jane Goodall has observed:

At Gombe a mother will risk severe punishment by attacking an adult male who is harming her child (during a charging display, for instance). Melissa even leaped at alpha male Mike as he dragged her infant during excitement; he let go of the infant and attacked Melissa. Another time, when the high-ranking and unusually aggressive adult male Humphrey attacked the adolescent Little Bee, her mother and younger sister both hurled themselves at the aggressor—who fled! There are many occasions when an infant or juvenile tries to help his or her mother when she is being attacked.[42]

Goodall adds, "In the higher primates affiliative bonding in early life is of crucial importance for the developing youngster."[43] Chimpanzees removed from their mothers during the first year of development have proven to be less able to concentrate on problem-solving tasks, and humans deprived of maternal affection are more likely to show stress during crises in adulthood.[44] The kiss itself, the premiere human sign of affection, has derived from primate maternal kiss-feeding. Across human cultures, mothers kiss-feed their infants, as do the anthropoid apes. Likewise, "chimpanzee friends embrace and kiss-feed or greet each other in fleeting mouth-to-mouth contact."[45] Without a doubt, "the invention of parental care is the starting point for the development of higher differentiated social systems." Irenäus Eibl-Eibesfeldt writes, "Mutual feeding (trophallaxis), a behavior derived from parental care, is the most important group-cementing element in insect societies."[46] By extension, humans and the higher primates engage in food-sharing, an activity to which they would have first been exposed by their mothers. Comparative ethology clearly points to the mother-offspring bond as the birth of sociability. It is thereby unsurprising that in the exaggerated world built by human culture, using biological building blocks, women appear as defenders of the most basic communal bonds and mediators to conflict. The "different voice" of care and concern is expressed in Ana begging for her son; in Malintzin's forgiveness and endurance; and in the *curanderas'* traditional healing arts. While men jockeyed for hierarchical position, women sustained. In the long run, the metate and the tortilla became the most successful of acts where cultural resistance was concerned. Food and clothing were thereby essential to conquest and cultural survival in sixteenth-century Mexico.

By the seventeenth century, Spaniards like Hernando Ruiz de Alarcón were quite aware that Amerindians were not a *tabula rasa*. They would adopt certain aspects of Spanish culture, but they would also struggle to maintain aspects of their own, primarily succeeding away from the top tiers of the hierarchical pyramid. Still, at the very top, existing as an organic symbol of care for all of Mexico, stood the Virgin of Guadalupe.[47] Although her cult was written about primarily by Mexican-born Spaniards, the *criollos* of the seventeenth century, she is one symbol that can unite white, Amerindian, and mestizo on her feast day in December. In myth, her appearance in 1531 was to a Nahua named Juan Diego: This dark lady appeared replete with the trappings of a Nahua goddess—in the midst of flowers and cacti. Called "our honored mother," or *Tonantzin*, she bears the trappings of Nahua mother goddesses, even though she is named for a Spanish Mary. Early-sixteenth-century Francsicans made note of how Nahuas honored the Virgin of Guadalupe on Mexico City's adjacent Tepeyac Hill in such a manner that old ways of honoring the Aztec Mother of the Gods were preserved. They disapproved of this, but they failed at stopping the development of a syncretic Amerindian spirituality.[48] That the patroness of Mexico should be the Virgin of Guadalupe is the final revelation of the human tensions that manifested themselves in Mexico. Even in the midst of male display and hierarchical struggle, a language of care, concern, and reciprocity—embodied in a mother's altruism—was never entirely lost. Humans, like other primates, manifest both brutal and generous tendencies.

Since the best ethological evidence today points to our being capable of vast brutalities and vast kindnesses, the importance of what is learned, of culture, cannot be underestimated. Although this study has been primarily about male actors playing male hierarchical games, it is worthy to note that reciprocity, through real food-sharing and other means, played its real role in sixteenth-century Mexico. When all is said and done, the leaders of New Spain, who gave birth to the "cosmic race" that is the Mexican people, included many more individuals than could be found at the pinnacle of the male hierarchy. They included countless, anonymous women who taught reciprocity, altruism, food-sharing, and human bonding at that most basic level that is motherhood. If in Oaxacan marketplaces of the 1960s, men sell prestigious meat and wheaten bread, women continue to sell the maize and beans that have always been staples in Mexico. Likewise, women continue to wear the *huipilli*, and they continue to comfort (and sometimes curse) as *curanderas*. In colonial times, they rioted; more recently they have been the *soldaderas* of the Mexican Revolution of 1910. The leadership of Mexican women has gone far beyond that of the great feminists Sor Juana Inés de la Cruz and Rosario Castellanos. It is a willingness to participate in society as counterpoint to all the ridiculous display associated with machismo. Rather than being a traitor, Malintzin was a diplomat and mediator in a cockfight.

This has been a study of male competition, reciprocity, and display. However, male infants and female infants alike first experience sharing with their mothers. A study of Mexican motherhood and female leadership from an ethological perspective has yet to be done. In studying men, this work merely wishes to recognize that women are a substantial and moderating influence where men are concerned. If in 1810 Father Miguel de Hidalgo y Costilla cried for the liberation of Mexico and the death of New Spain and Spaniards, he did so under the banner of the Virgin of Guadalupe. A source of gentle comfort, the primate mother, it must also be remembered, often attacks an alpha male when her young are threatened. As human beings, Mexicans, like their honored mother—like all human beings and human images—are creatures of violence and concern.

NOTES

1. Carol Gilligan, *In a Different Voice: Psychological Theory and Women's Development* (Cambridge, MA, and London: Harvard University Press, 1982).

2. *Mapping the Moral Domain: A Contribution of Women's Thinking to Psychological Theory and Education*, ed. Carol Gilligan, Janie Victoria Ward, and Jill McLean Taylor, with Betty Bardige (Cambridge: Center for the Study of Gender, Education and Human Development, Distributed by Harvard University Press, 1988), 170-73, 289.

3. "Capitulación que se tomó con Francisco de Montejo para la conquista de Yucatan (1526)," *Colección de documentos inéditos relativos al descubrimiento, conquista y organización de las antiguas posesiones españolas de América y Oceanía, sacados de los archivos del reino, y muy especialmente del de Indias*, ed. Joaquín F. Pacheco, Francisco de Cárdenas, and Luis Torres de Mendoza, 42 vols. (Madrid: Manuel G. Hernández, 1864-1884), 22:220. Henceforth *CDIR*. Also see "Capitulación que se tomó con Pánfilo de Narvaez, para la conquista del Rio de las Palmas (1526)," *CDIR* 22:239-

41; "Capitulación que se tomó con Pedro de Alvarado, sobre el descubrimiento de las Islas del Mar de Sur (1532)," *CDIR* 22:317; "Idem que se tomó con Diego Gutiérrez sobre la conquista de Veragua (1540)," *CDIR* 23:85, 93; and "Lo que Licenciado Rodrigo de Figueroa, Juez de Residencia en la Isla Spañola, a de saber, para la informacion que toca a la materia de los indios, y lo que a de hacer en este camino, por mandado de S.M. (1518)," *CDIR* 23:333.

4. Lewis Hanke, *All Mankind Is One* (DeKalb: Northern Illinois University Press, 1974); Colin M. MacLachlan, *Spain's Empire in the New World: The Role of Ideas in Institutional and Social Change* (Berkeley, Los Angeles, London: University of California Press, 1988), 52-65.

5. MacLachlan, 58-61.

6. James Lockhart, "And Ana Wept: Grant of a Site for a House, San Miguel Tocuillan, 1583," in *Nahuas and Spaniards: Postconquest Central Mexican History and Philology* (Stanford, CA: Stanford University Press and the UCLA Latin American Center Publications, 1991), 69. Also see Lockhart's *The Nahuas after the Conquest: A Social and Cultural History of the Indians of Central Mexico, Sixteenth through Eighteenth Centuries* (Stanford, CA: Stanford University Press, 1992), 85-87, 455-59.

7. Lockhart, *Nahuas after the Conquest*, 199-200.

8. Bernardino de Sahagún, *Florentine Codex: General History of the Things of New Spain*, trans. Arthur J. O. Anderson and Charles E. Dibble, 13 vols. (Santa Fe and Salt Lake City: Monographs of the School of American Research/University of Utah Press, 1950-1982), Bk. 10, chap. 22, p. 80; chap. 26, p. 93; chap. 19, pp. 69-71. Also see illustrations 125, 127, 128, 133, and 134 in the same volume after p. 62.

In the marketplaces the hierarchical value placed on European foodstuffs is reflected by the traditional society's division of labor. In the maketplace of San Antoinio Castillo Velasco, thirty kilometers south of Oaxaca City, all the sellers of tortillas, tortilla dough, *atole*, and ground beans in the late 1960s were women. In juxtaposition, there were twenty-two male bread sellers and only one woman; all the retailers of beef were men; and the pork vendors included six men and one woman.

See Ronald Waterbury and Carole Turkenik, "The Market place Traders of San Antonio: A Quantitative Analysis," in *Markets in Oaxaca*, ed. Scott Cook and Martin Diskin (Austin and London: University of Texas Press, 1976), 213; Scott Cook and Martin Diskin, "The Peasant Market Economy of the Valley of Oaxaca in Analysis and History," in *Markets in Oaxaca*, 21.

9. Lockhart, *Nahuas after the Conquest*, 44; S. L. Cline, *Colonial Culhuacan, 1580-1600: A Social History of an Aztec Town* (Albuquerque: University of New Mexico Press, 1986), 54.

10. Lockhart, *Nahuas after the Conquest*, 226.

11. Cline, 112-13.

12. Ibid., 112, 140.

13. Ibid.

14. *Florentine Codex*, Bk. 6, chap. 37, p. 201.

15. Ibid., chap. 18, p. 95.

16. William B. Taylor, *Drinking, Homicide, and Rebellion in Colonial Mexican Villages* (Stanford, CA: Stanford University Press, 1979), 53, 116.

17. George Rudé, *The Crowd in the French Revolution* (Oxford: Oxford University Press, 1959), 69; Merry E. Wiesner, *Women and Gender in Early Modern Europe* (Cambridge: Cambridge University Press, 1993), 246.

18. Taylor, 84.

19. Frans B. M. de Waal, "Chimpanzee's Adaptive Potential: A Comparison of Social Life under Captive and Wild Conditions," in *Chimpanzee Cultures*, ed. Richard W. Wrangham, W. C. McGrew, Frans B. M. de Waal, and Paul G. Heltne (Cambridge, MA: Harvard University Press, 1994), 254, 257.

20. Ibid., 255.

21. Frans de Waal, *Chimpanzee Politics: Power and Sex among Apes* (New York: Harper & Row, 1982), 66, 64.

22. Jane Goodall, *The Chimpanzees of Gombe: Patterns of Behavior* (Cambridge, MA, and London: Belknap Press of Harvard University Press, 1986), 66-67.

23. Ibid., 86. Also see 86-92.

24. Ibid., 483.

25. Ibid., 477-87; de Waal, *Chimpanzee Politics*, 56-57.

26. Lyle N. McAlister, *Spain and Portugal in the New World, 1492-1700* (Minneapolis: University of Minnesota Press, 1984), 115, 126.

27. Asunción Lavrin, "In Search of the Colonial Woman in Mexico: the Seventeenth and Eighteenth Centuries," in *Latin American Women: Historical Perspectives*, ed. Asunción Lavrin (Westport, CT: Greenwood Press, 1978), 33. Also see 31 and Patricia Seed, *To Love, Honor, and Obey in Colonial Mexico: Conflicts over Marriage Choice, 1574-1821* (Stanford, CA: Stanford University Press, 1988), 17. For the estimation of 10-15 percent, see Daisy Rípodas Ardanaz, *El Matrimonio en Indias: Realidad social y regulación jurídica* (Buenos Aires: Fundación para la Educación, la Ciencia y la Cultura, 1977), 10.

28. Sandra Messinger Cypess, *La Malinche in Mexican Literature: From History to Myth* (Austin: University of Texas Press, 1991), 31. Also see 30.

29. Ibid., 33.

30. Ibid., 35.

31. Frances Karttunen, *Between Worlds: Interpreters, Guides, and Survivors* (New Brunswick, NJ: Rutgers University Press, 1994), 22.

32. Ibid.

33. *St. Ignatius' Own Story as Told to Luis González de Cámara*, trans. William J. Young, S.J. (Chicago: Loyola University Press, 1980), 9-11.

34. Ignatius of Loyola, *The Spiritual Exercises of St. Ignatius*, trans. Louis J. Puhl, S.J. (Chicago: Loyola University Press, 1951), 60-63.

35. Michael D. Coe and Gordon Whittaker, "Introduction," in *Aztec Sorcerors in Seventeenth Century Mexico: The Treatise on Superstitions by Hernando Ruiz de Alarcón*, trans. Michael D. Coe and Gordon Whittaker (Albany: Institute for Mesoamerican Studies, State University of New York at Albany, 1982), 19.

36. J. Richard Andrews and Ross Hassig, "Editors' Introduction," in Hernando Ruiz de Alarcón, *Treatise on the Heathen Superstitions That Today Live among the Indians Native to This New Spain, 1629*, trans. J. Richard Andrews and Ross Hassig (Norman: University of Oklahoma Press, 1984), 6-7.

37. "siendolo tanto la embriaguez, que ella misma se publica, y aun prueba, y da a manosear que es y a sido la total causa de acabarse los indios."

Hernando Ruiz de Alarcón, *Tratado de las supersticiones de los naturales de esta Nueva España*, in *Tratado de las idolatrias, supersticiones, dioses, ritos, hechicerías y otras costumbres gentilicas de las razas aborigenes de México*, ed. Francisco del Paso y Troncoso (Mexico City: Librería Navarro, 1948-1952/ reprint of 1892 Museo Nacional edition), 17-18. Also see the following English translations: *Treatise on the Heathen Superstitions That Today Live among the Indians Native to This New Spain, 1629*, trans. J. Richard Andrews and Ross Hassig (Norman: University of Oklahoma Press, 1984), 39; *Aztec Sorcerors in Seventeenth Century Mexico: The Treatise on Superstitions by Hernando Ruiz de Alarcón*, trans. Michael D. Coe and Gordon Whittaker (Albany: Institute for Mesoamerican Studies, State University of New York at Albany, 1982), 59. Henceforth, the Spanish edition will be referred to as "P y T," the English editions as "A-H" and "C-W."

38. "Tratado sexto, capítulos xxiv, xxviii y xxix." P y T, 166, 171, 172; A-H, 192-93, 198, 199; C-W, 273, 283, 285. Coe and Whittaker once again identify the passages differently: "Seventh Tract, chapters 21, 25 and 26."

39. C-W, 65.

40. Irene Silverblatt, *Moon, Sun, and Witches: Gender Ideologies and Class in Inca and Colonial Peru* (Princeton, NJ: Princeton University Press, 1987), especially 159-96.

41. See Stuart Clark, "The *Annales* Historians," in *The Return of Grand Theory to the Human Sciences*, ed. Quentin Skinner (Cambridge: Cambridge University Press, 1985), 179-98. Also Colin M. MacLachlan and Jaime E. Rodríguez O., *The Forging of the Cosmic Race: A Reinterpretation of Colonial Mexico* (Berkeley: University of California Press, 1980), 198, 230.

42. Goodall, 376.

43. Ibid., 379.

44. A. M. D. Brodkin et al., "Retrospective Reports of Mothers' Work Patterns and Psychological Distress in First-Year Medical Students," *Journal of the American Academy of Child Psychology* (1984) 4:479-85.

45. Irenäus Eibl-Eibesfeldt, *Human Ethology*, (New York: Aldine de Gruyter, 1989),138. Also 138-47.

46. Ibid., 169.

47. The classic study is still Jacques Lafaye, *Quetzalcóatl and Guadalupe: The Formation of Mexican National Consciousness 1531-1813*, trans. Benjamin Keen (Chicago: University of Chicago Press, 1976).

Recently, Louise M. Burkhart has emphasized the *criollo* use of the cult of the Virgin of Guadalupe to incorporate Amerindians into such movements as the independence movement of 1810. By allowing for Amerindian perspectives on Mary, *criollos* provide Amerindians with a place under the banner of Guadalupe, which was first raised as a rallying totem for Mexicans by *criollo* authors in the seventeenth century. See Burkhart's "The Cult of the Virgin of Guadalupe in Mexico," in *South and Meso-American Native Spirituality: From the Cult of the Feathered Serpent to the Theology of Liberation*, ed. Gary H. Gossen and Miguel León-Portilla. Vol. 4 in *An Encyclopedic History of the Religious Quest*, gen. ed. Ewert Cousins (New York: Crossroad, 1993).

48. For a brief account, see MacLachlan and Rodríguez, 131.

10

A Question of Methodology

At this point, the reader may still wonder why an ethological approach was adopted to study sixteenth-century Mexico, and why food, clothing, and shelter became particular foci of investigation.

In response to the first enquiry, it should be recalled that Mesoamerican and European populations were isolated from each other for millenia, yet parallel developments are quite discernible in their diverse cultures. So often the ploy of science fiction authors, parallel cultural development inherently serves as evidence of commonality. Those who would emphasize the innate foreignness of alien cultures should constantly remind themselves of the most basic biological realities. Nothing biological stops the different races of humanity from interbreeding, and by extension, it should be noted that cultural traditions can be syncretized. Mexico provides a superb example through the continued existence of such syncretic developments as the worship of Christ-Kukulcan in the Yucatan; the worship of the Virgin of Guadalupe throughout Mexico; and the continued recognition of the cycles of life and death through the celebration of the Day of the Dead, during which candied skulls replace the human sacrifices and skull racks of Aztec times. That a Maya god can be identified with Christ, and the power of Nahua female divinity with Mary, is strong evidence of the interchange that is possible between cultures. Cultures are not untranslatable, though translation and exchange are not easy. Likewise, Mexico presents us with a "cosmic race," evolved and developed from Amerindian, European, African, and even some Asian ancestors. The mestizo was not always the child of legitimate and loving marriage; but the mestizo, the majority of the Mexican population, exists as evidence to our common humanity.

In response to the second enquiry regarding food and protection from the elements as major foci in this monograph, it should be apparent that these are the basic human necessities as defined by biology and described by material culture. Just as contemporary primatologists use developments in chimpanzee cultures to deal with the thorny issue that is the nature-nurture debate, I adopted a focus on these areas to deal with human biological needs that can give rise to different cultural expressions. Food and protection from the elements provided a heuristic device to understand differences and similarities in cultures as well as such species-specific behavior as hierarchy, reciprocity, benevolence, altruism, violence, food-sharing, xenophobia, tribalism, and curiosity.

Of course, throughout all this, the importance of the reciprocal interaction between individuals and groups should not be underestimated. There is a necessary place in ethological history for biography and social history—two subdisciplines that have often enough been uneasy with each other, although some indications of rapprochement have arisen since the publication of Carlo Ginzburg's *The Cheese and the Worms*.[1] Individuals, like the potato-washing Japanese macaque Imo, do have influence. It is ridiculous to underplay the significant choices that were made by Moctezuma and Cortés as they searched for allies in central Mexico. One can speculate on Moctezuma's ability to raise an army during the harvest, but he did ultimately choose to have Cortés advance within a context made up of a number of environmental circumstances. Likewise, Cortés sank his means of escape and played a duplicitous game with Mexica representatives to further his own advance. The Spaniards acted with Cortés as their leader, just as Xicotencatl the Elder and his fellow rulers of Tlaxcala chose to cast their lot with these new Spanish allies.

However, all innovative individuals involved did not act in a vacuum. They responded to very real material circumstances around them and took the masses into account. In turn, the masses of social history had their impact. It must not be forgotten that the sufferings of dying Amerindian populations led Spanish viceroys to be concerned with Mexico's demographic crisis. Even if this was primarily because of a substantial loss of labor power, Amerindian suffering led to a humanitarian outpouring by royal bureaucrats and priests who wished to see benevolence as well as dominance expressed vis-à-vis the masses. But the devastation of disease also led to mass donations by Amerindians in places like Tlaxcala, where they constructed and managed their own hospitals under the guidance of their own responsive leaders.

The individual must return to history, but the individual must be studied in a broad behavioral and cultural context. Amerindian religious syncretism occurred because of women like Mariana of Iguala and other individual *curanderas* who struggled with the prejudices of a foreign priest like Hernando Ruiz de Alarcón. The "masses" also have individuals, although the extent to which common general patterns of behavior will be followed has also been noted. Thus, Xicotencatl the Younger opposed his father's pro-Spanish policy, fearing the worst from these strangers. He died for this, as did David's son Absalom in the Bible. Gombe's Goblin proved far more fortunate in using his alpha male mentor Figan to acquire that status himself after challenging his "father figure." By pointing out common patterns of behavior across cultures, myths point to our common biological heritage as human beings and primates. Younger males do challenge older males within hierarchies. In Mexico, Xicotencatl the Elder and Xicotencatl the Younger played out a very old script indeed. If official archival documents omit a great deal through their formulae, foci and official "spins," myths are also guilty of not telling the whole truth, but they do reveal something about human universals, as well recognized by Sigmund Freud, Carl Jung, and Claude Lévi-Strauss.

For decades now historians have shied away from the application of psychology to history. Although a few embraced what was called "psychohistory" after the publication of Erik Erikson's *Young Man Luther,* many more were rightfully distrustful of the Freudian underpinnings inherent in the endeavor.[2] Sigmund Freud himself actually engaged in psychoanalyzing a historical figure like Leonardo da Vinci, but in applying his psychoanalysis, he applied a metaphysical system that assumed far too much. He invented a tripartite division of the personality that certainly went beyond the bounds of materialism with its references to the existence of physically unobservable entities like the ego, superego, and id. The injection of Freudianism into history was a deserved failure, although some individuals persist in practicing it. However, this does not mean that history benefits from ignoring psychological studies of human beings—especially those done in accordance with scientific procedure. Human ethology and comparative ethology have much to contribute to history, the humanities, and the social sciences. Biologically based, they can help to show us fundamental human characteristics beneath the trappings of culture.

If culture alone is studied and emphasized, as it has been done recently in the social sciences and humanities, a primary focus on "uniqueness" or "difference" is often quite tempting. Not only has the individual always been there in the midst of general cultural traits; the unique traits of different cultures often enough only disguise human universals. It may be the great irony of postmodernism that in its pursuit of multiple selves and roles within the same individual, postmodernism undermines its own ability to make sense of any phenomena. It takes us back to a precultural inability to recognize, order, use, and alter patterns. It would actually deny the primate nature we share with chimpanzees, for what have deconstructionists constructed, while chimpanzees adopt and adapt tools? Ironically, in the postmodern world of will, where all systems of knowledge vie for power without privilege, there is nothing but a struggle for existence without self-awareness. It is time to step beyond the tribal struggles and see why all humans engage in them without favoring Western imperialists and without falsely accusing human logic and science of being Western logic and science—the tools of imperialism and only the tools of imperialism. The Chinese, the Aztecs, and the Zulus also had empires and committed atrocities. Unfortunately, empire and atrocity, like logic and the pursuit of knowledge, are human cultural developments that cross cultures.

Late-twentieth-century historians often feel so overwhelmed by the accumulated details regarding early modern European towns and regions that they fail to generalize or hypothesize regarding Europe, let alone the world or diverse sections of it. Blessed and cursed with a certain naïveté arising from their cultural experience and learning, sixteenth-century Spaniards considered it quite natural to make gross generalizations—to compare and contrast with their cultural tradition, which they mistakenly took for a universal truth. In so doing, however, their sources, from the letters of Cortés and early works of Franciscan friars to the *relaciones geográficas*, present much worthwhile ethnographic and ethological data to be sorted by the present-day scholar. Whereas the sixteenth-century Spaniard wrote comparisons and contrasts to praise or condemn Amerindians from the narrow perspective of his own culture, the contemporary scholar can actually gain perspective from the gift of hindsight. And whereas the Eurocentric feel compelled to defend the Spaniards, and the multicultural rush to defend the Aztecs, from a broader perspective, which includes our living chimpanzee cousins, there is much in the behavior of both Spaniards and Aztecs that reflects upon humanity's common animal nature. Cultures may teach different variations, but some common themes remain the same. When other animals are taken into account, the genetic base of aggression and benevolence, hierarchy and reciprocity, xenophobia and curiosity can even be hypothesized as genetic mapping is further developed. History and the social sciences must see themselves as debates rather than dogmatic bodies of knowledge, but even debates allow for overarching regulations and structures that are agreed to in common. Unlike sixteenth-century Spaniards, we need not defend "our" Spanish imperium or "our" common Christianity. As a result, we come closer to Jürgen Habermas's "ideal speech situation" by leaving a little more cultural baggage at the door than they could.

The conquest of Mexico was selected as a case study, and as such it demonstrates the tensions inherent in the human animal. Where some might see Cortés's ability to feed starving Mexica while destroying Tenochtitlan as evidence for the existence of multiple selves, it is a demonstration of the extent to which human nature is constructed from binary, even contradictory, traits. Here, no doubt, recognition is demonstrated by the cultural and religious tradition of yin and yang in Daoism. But religion, like other culturally developed traditions, can emphasize, extrapolate, and mask. The Christian mass and Aztec human sacrifice were not the same, but both spoke of sacrifice and suffering in a world besieged by the Four Horsemen of the Apocalypse. To both the Spaniards and the Aztecs, Famine, Pestilence, War, and Death were biological realities not metaphysical entities. Is it any wonder that their religions should have developed and extrapolated on common themes related to the brutality and punishment inherent in life. To make amends for wrongdoing before their gods, some Spaniards whipped themselves, whereas the Mexica *tlatoani* and priests pierced their ears, tongues, and penises. The practices, as taught by culture, were different, but the underlying motivation was the same.

As a creation of human culture, this study hopes to extrapolate upon the learning factor and adaptive potential inherent in culture by trying to make us aware of our animal nature so that we might adapt our cultural traditions to promote the benevolent rather than the violent and agonistic. In the early sixteenth century, the *auto de fe* and human sacrifice inculcated visions of tribalism, dominance, violence, brutality, and xenophobia. In our century, Adolf Hitler and the Nazi movement demonstrated how hate can be nurtured to a fever pitch. By studying our animal traits, we can also learn to encourage love. However, humans must be well aware that even in the midst of teaching love, Christianity and other world religions have found ample room to hate—and even Hitler taught one to love one's fellow Aryan. Humans constantly develop ingroups and outgroups, but the great *reductio ad absurdum* of tribalism is that all human cultures demonstrate it. Just as the Spaniards and the Aztecs had brutal religions that also taught charity, they had prejudices where the outsider was concerned. Whereas Spaniards demonstrated their prejudices vis-à-vis Moriscos, Jews, and Amerindians, the Aztecs spoke of "stupid" Otomí and "lascivious" Huaxtecans. Unfortunately, the common proclivity toward the prejudgment of individuals based on perceived differences in groups is yet another proof of our common humanity. But so too is the presence of a certain level of self-criticism in Spanish and Nahua cultures. Both Spaniards and Nahuas invented noble savages who lived purer lives than they. Alonso de Zorita, Motolinía, Mendieta, and las Casas perceived a humility they aspired to in suffering Amerindians, while pre-Columbian Aztecs dreamed of the land of the caves, fabled Aztlan, where their abandoned ancestors lived much longer and holier lives than they. Spaniards and Aztecs alike recognized with pride the achievements of human culture, but many among them also recognized culture's ability to distort our natures and desires. Just as some Spaniards and Nahuas demonstrated a degree of self-consciousness and self-criticism which Hernando Ruiz de Alarcón obviously did not, we too might learn self-awareness while looking for commonalities.

NOTES

1. Carlo Ginzburg, *The Cheese and the Worms: The Cosmos of a Sixteenth-Century Miller*, trans. John and Anne Tedeschi (Baltimore: Johns Hopkins University Press, 1980).

2. Erik H. Erikson, *Young Man Luther: A Study in Psychoanalysis and History* (New York: Norton, 1958).

Bibliographical Essay

Having attempted to extend the trajectory of the twentieth-century dialogue between natural history and human history, this work is indebted to those historians who have recognized the impact of the natural environment on human history and the concomitant impact of humans on the environment. Taking into account such fundamental human issues as climate and caloric intake, Fernand Braudel's work has served as an overarching inspiration in the historiographical realm: especially his *Civilization & Capitalism: 15th-18th Century*, trans. Siân Reynolds, 3 vols. (New York: Harper & Row, 1981-1984). In a more direct fashion, the pioneering work of Alfred W. Crosby and Enrique Florescano has served as a starting point for the study of food in this volume. Florescano's "El Abasto y la legislación de granos en el siglo XVI," *Historia Mexicana* 14:4 (April-June 1965): 567-630 remains an important introduction to the discussion of maize and wheat in colonial Mexico. Crosby's *The Columbian Exchange: Biological and Cultural Consequences of 1492* (Westport, CT: Greenwood Press, 1972) and his *Ecological Imperialism: The Biological Expansion of Europe, 900-1900* (Cambridge: Cambridge University Press, 1986) are classics that head the list of an ever-growing field that now includes such works as Elinor G. K. Melville, *A Plague of Sheep: Environmental Consequences of the Conquest of Mexico* (Cambridge: Cambridge University Press, 1994); Bernard R. Ortiz de Montellano, *Aztec Medicine, Health, and Nutrition* (New Brunswick, NJ: Rutgers University Press, 1990); and John Super, *Food, Conquest, and Colonization in Sixteenth-Century Spanish America* (Albuquerque: University of New Mexico Press, 1988). Without a doubt, biological matters have entered into the study of colonial Mexican history, but not in terms of approaching human behavior as a natural phenomenon.

In recent years, the term "psychohistory" has been haunted by its association with the metaphysical system known as Freudianism. While psychologists, ethologists, and biologists have interpreted behavior in ways akin to the methods employed by historians, historians themselves continue to identify psychology with the speculations of Sigmund Freud and Michel Foucault. This study attempts to integrate history with contemporary advancements in the behavioral sciences. For a general overview of the field of contemporary ethology one can do no better than Irenäus Eibl-Eibesfeldt, *Human Ethology* (New York: Aldine de Gruyter, 1989).

Just as historians debate their interpretations of documents (which are themselves human interpretations of events), ethologists struggle for the best possible interpretations of behavior patterns. In so many ways, the two fields are ready for dialogue, and the call for a dialogue between the natural and social sciences actually has been initiated by the natural scientists. See Jane Goodall's *In the Shadow of Man* (Boston: Houghton Mifflin, 1971) and *The Chimpanzees of Gombe: Patterns of Behavior* (Cambridge, MA, and London: Belknap Press of Harvard University Press, 1986). Overviews of chimpanzee behavior patterns can be found in Frans de Waal, *Chimpanzee Politics: Power and Sex among Apes* (New York: Harper & Row, 1982); W. C. McGrew, *Chimpanzee Material Culture: Implications for Human Evolution* (Cambridge: Cambridge University Press, 1992); and *Chimpanzee Cultures*, ed. Richard W. Wrangham et al. (Cambridge, MA: Harvard University Press, 1994). For more parallels between pongids and hominids and for the importance and evolution of human culture, see Richard E. Leakey and Roger Lewin, *Origins* (New York: E. P. Dutton, 1977) and *Origins Reconsidered: In Search of What Makes Us Human* (New York: Doubleday, 1992).

Although this work employs ethological methods, it remains a study in colonial Mexican history. As such, it has deliberately chosen well-trodden and accessible sources to facilitate the testing of the hypothesis recorded herein. Among other primary sources, central ones have included *Colección de documentos inéditos relativos al descubrimiento, conquista y organización de las antiguas posesiones españolas de América y Oceanía, sacados de los archivos del reino, y muy especialmente del de Indias*, ed. Joaquín F. Pacheco, Francisco de Cárdenas, and Luis Torres de Mendoza, 42 vols. (Madrid: Manuel G. Hernández, 1864-1884); Francisco del Paso y Troncoso, ed., *Epistolario de Nueva España, 1505-1818*, 16 vols. (Mexico City: José Porrúa e hijos, 1939-1940); and Francisco del Paso y Troncoso, ed., *Papeles de Nueva España*, 7 vols. (Madrid: Sucesores de Rivadeneyra, 1905). Among the chronicles of the conquest era, see Bernardino de Sahagún, *Florentine Codex: General History of the Things of New Spain*, trans. Arthur J. O. Anderson and Charles E. Dibble, 13 vols. (Santa Fe and Salt Lake City: Monographs of the School of American Research/University of Utah Press, 1950-1982); Bernal Díaz del Castillo, *Historia verdadera de la conquista de la Nueva España*, ed. Joaquín Ramírez Cabañas, 3 vols. (Mexico City: Editorial Pedro Robredo, 1944); Hernán Cortés, *Hernán Cortés: Letters from Mexico*, trans. Anthony Pagden (New Haven, CT, and London: Yale University Press, 1986); Fray Toribio de Benavente o Motolinía, *Memoriales o libro de las cosas de la Nueva España y de los naturales de ella*, ed. Edmundo O'Gorman (Mexico City: Universidad Nacional Autónoma de México, 1971); Heinrich Berlin and Robert H. Barlow, ed. and trans., *Anales de Tlatelolco: Unos Anales historicos de la nación mexicana y Codice de Tlatelolco* (Mexico City: Antigua Librería Robredo, de José Porrúa e hijos, 1948); Alonso de Zorita, *Life and Labor in Ancient Mexico: The Brief and Summary Relation of the Lords of New Spain*, trans. Benjamin Keen (New Brunswick, NJ: Rutgers University Press, 1963); and Diego Durán, *Historia de las Indias de Nueva España e islas de la tierra firme*, ed. Angel María Garibay K., 2 vols. (Mexico City: Editorial Porrúa, 1967). Archival sources have included documents from the *Fondos* "Indios" and "Tierras" in the Archivo General de la Nación in Mexico City; and microfilm copies, housed at the University of Massachusetts at Amherst, of viceregal documentation from Seville's Archivo General de Indias.

Aside from primary documentation, a number of secondary sources on sixteenth-century Mexico have been particularly helpful in binding heretofore unrelated historical strands concerning food, clothing, and shelter; the redistribution of resources; and the healing of societal disputes and physical ailments in a body politic. Questions concerning clothing and redistribution are covered in Ross Hassig, *Trade, Tribute, and Transportation* (Norman: University of Oklahoma Press, 1985); Richard J. Salvucci, *Textiles and Capitalism in Mexico: An Economic History of the Obrajes, 1539-1840* (Princeton, NJ: Princeton University Press, 1987); and Chloë Sayer, *Costumes of Mexico* (Austin: University of Texas Press, 1985). General architectural themes are discussed in Pedro Carrasco and Johanna Broda, ed., *The Great Temple of Tenochtitlan: Center and Periphery in the Aztec World* (Berkeley: University of California Press, 1987); and George Kubler's classic *Mexican Architecture of the Sixteenth Century*, 2 vols. (New Haven, CT: Yale University Press, 1948). When normal redistribution methods and social intercourse failed, the Spanish court system provided an avenue of redress that could even integrate with pre-Columbian legal traditions. See Woodrow Borah, *Justice by Insurance: The General Indian Court of Colonial Mexico and the Legal Aides of the Half-Real* (Berkeley: University of California Press, 1983); and Jerome A. Offner, *Law and Politics in Aztec Texcoco* (Cambridge: Cambridge University Press, 1983). For a summary overview of Spanish hospitals, one can still profit from Josefina Muriel's *Hospitales de la Nueva España*, 2 vols. (Mexico City: Editorial Jus, 1956-1960). A more recent survey of Spanish medicine in the Americas is found in Guenter B. Risse's chapter in *Medicine in the New World: New Spain, New France, and New England*, ed. Ronald L. Numbers (Knoxville: University of Tennessee Press, 1987). Aside from the work by Ortiz de Montellano already cited, excellent background information on Nahua medicine can be found in the introduction to the Andrews and Hassig edition of the treatise of Hernando Ruiz de Alarcón: Hernando Ruiz de Alarcón, *Treatise on the Heathen Superstitions That Today Live among the Indians Native to This New Spain, 1629*, trans. and ed. J. Richard Andrews and Ross Hassig (Norman: University of Oklahoma Press, 1984). For background information on the Nahuas and their social theory and practice, both before and after Spanish rule, see Geoffrey W. Conrad and Arthur A. Demarest, *Religion and Empire: The Dynamics of Aztec and Inca Expansionism* (Cambridge: Cambridge University Press, 1984); and James Lockhart, *The Nahuas after the Conquest: A Social and Cultural History of the Indians of Central Mexico, Sixteenth through Eighteenth Centuries* (Stanford, CA: Stanford University Press, 1992).

Finally, this work's suggestions for a more detailed study of gender, from the perspective of cultural and intellectual history, are derived from Carol Gilligan, *In a Different Voice: Psychological Theory and Women's Development* (Cambridge: Harvard University Press, 1982). Excellent first steps in this direction have been taken in two recent volumes: Patricia Seed, *To Love, Honor, and Obey in Colonial Mexico: Conflicts over Marriage Choice, 1574-1821* (Stanford, CA: Stanford University Press, 1988); and Asunción Lavrin, ed., *Sexuality and Marriage in Colonial Latin America* (Lincoln: University of Nebraska Press, 1989). Also see the overview found in *El Matrimonio en Indias: Realidad social y regulación jurídica* by Daisy Rípodas Ardanaz (Buenos Aires: Fundación para la Educación, la Ciencia y la Cultura, 1977). Colonial Mexicanists eagerly await the day when a summary view of women, in all aspects of their lives, is written. Obviously, this has not been that work.

In many ways *Brutality and Benevolence* has been yet another endeavor, albeit a different one, in the genre of intellectual and cultural history. In that field, a major inspiration has been *The Forging of the Cosmic Race: A Reinterpretation of Colonial*

Mexico by Colin M. MacLachlan and Jaime E. Rodríguez O. (Berkeley: University of California Press, 1980). Although pioneered by Lewis Hanke in such works as *Aristotle and the American Indians: A Study in Race and Prejudice in the Modern World* (Bloomington: Indiana University Press, 1959), the genre of colonial Latin American intellectual history has recently been continued and nuanced by literary scholars like Rolena Adorno in her *Guaman Poma: Writing and Resistance in Colonial Peru* (Austin: University of Texas Press, 1986). The field is now once again blossoming. A recent work of interest is Fernando Cervantes's *The Devil in the New World: The Impact of Diabolism in New Spain* (New Haven, CT: Yale University Press, 1994). Whereas these works are influenced by the best of contemporary literary theory, *Brutality and Benevolence* borrows from the natural sciences. Rather than being a final statement on the conquest of Mexico, this work hopes to introduce new elements and a new hypothesis into a scholarly debate that touches upon the origins of modern European imperialism in all its varied forms.

Index

About the Author

ABEL A. ALVES is an Assistant Professor of History at Ball State University. His earlier writings have appeared in *The Sixteenth Century Journal*, *CLIO*, and in the book *Coded Encounters*.